STATE OF ISRAEL
ITS FRIENDS AND ENEMIES
PROPHETIC FUTURE

STATE OF ISRAEL
ITS FRIENDS AND ENEMIES
PROPHETIC FUTURE

ALEXANDER ZEPHYR

iUniverse, Inc.
Bloomington

State of Israel. Its friends and enemies. Prophetic future

iUniverse books may be ordered through booksellers or by contacting:

iUniverse
1663 Liberty Drive
Bloomington, IN 47403
www.iuniverse.com
1-800-Authors (1-800-288-4677)

ISBN: 978-1-4759-5133-2 (sc)
ISBN: 978-1-4759-5134-9 (ebk)

Printed in the United States of America

iUniverse rev. date: 01/08/2013

CONTENTS

PROLOGUE

There is a river which rests on Saturdays. It is named Sambation. The Ten Tribes of Israel were exiled by the Assyrian king Shalmanezer V (727-722b.c.) to the other side of this river (Midrash Breishet Rabba 73:6). Nobody knows the exact location of this mysterious river. Some researchers point to India, others to China. An Israelite traveler of the 900's Eldad from the Tribe of Dan said that this river is located in Africa between Sudan and Ethiopia. Rabbi Samuel of Tzangoli said it is in Egypt.

Nachmanides said that it was the Biblical River Gozan in Media. Pliny the Elder thought it was to be found in the land of Judaea. Josephus Flavius placed this 'Sabbatical River' in Antiochia. Yet others replaced it by the river Euphrates. According to Midrashic sources, concerning the exile of the Ten Tribes of Israel, 'beyond Damascus' has the same meaning as 'beyond the Sambatyon River' (Yalkut Shimoni, Shir HaShirim 985). This may imply that Damascus and its surroundings is nearby the Sambatyon itself.

But everyone is in agreement that the River Sambation is a barrier, preventing the Ten Tribes from returning to the Promised Land. The legend says that the Sambation carrying huge stones flows for six days and nights with a ravaging storm-like thundering and deafening noise. On Friday night, when the Sabbath starts, the vehemence of the river subsides, and it stays quiet and still. Even on the Sabbath Israelites cannot pass over this river because it is covered by thick clouds and a devouring fire that nobody within three miles can approach.

Will the Ten Tribes ever be able to overcome the Sambation River's barrier and return to the Promised Land? God says that they will!

"Yet the number of the children of Israel shall be as the sand of the sea, which cannot be measured nor numbered; and it shall come to pass, that in the place where it was said unto them, 'You are not my people, there it shall be said unto them, You are the sons of the living God" (Hosea 1:10).

INTRODUCTION

A Quick Skim through Human History and Politics

What is going on in our chaotic world? One crisis comes after another. Calamities follow calamities. Humans desperately fight each other. Dictatorships, nationalism, religious fanaticism, communism, terrorism,—everything serves to cause hate and divisions amongst the nations. The wars, man-made disasters, and disease epidemics continually surround the days of our live. Violent death and suffering have never stopped since the dawn of civilization, and on top of it—the wrath of nature. Mother Nature has erupted with increasingly powerful earthquakes, deadly tsunamis, hurricanes, mud slides, floods. Death tolls have numbered in the hundreds of millions. And we see no end to it. The people of the World have been distressed. Rumors and agonizing feelings of imminent wars and disasters have penetrated human societies. Too many nations have possessed nuclear arsenals and other weapons of mass destruction. It is only a matter of time as to when these weapons will be in the hands of terrorists and be used by accident or design. Are we inevitably doomed to nuclear holocaust that will annihilate our planet?

There have been many prophets who have tried to show us what will come in 'latter years'.

"The fanaticism of Islamic nations will ignite World War III,"—said Nostradamus (1503-1566). The way things are going, this is not far from the truth.

Others have said that an apocalyptic nuclear war will speed up the destruction of the Earth's ecological balance and cause the extinction of all life on Earth.

Mayans seemed to believe that on December 22, 2012, the world, as we know it, will dramatically end.

Proponents of 'The End of the World' theories have gone even farther, attributing it to a special Galactic Alignment of the planets in the Milky Way.

Some predict that Earth will be destroyed by huge meteorites. Others invented a theory of the mysterious Planet 'X'—Nibiru, or Nemesis (retribution), or Marduk. This giant planet has a highly elliptical orbit and passes by Earth on closest distance every 3,600 years. This monstrous planet will have a massive gravitational effect on all the planets of the Solar system causing them significantly change the orbits and the magnetic poles. The planet Earth, they explain, will undergo enormous destruction and calamities because of a Geomagnetic Reversal, due to weakening of the planet's magnetic field, triggered by a massive Solar flare, which will cause a shifting of the North and South magnetic poles, resulting in a huge tectonic catastrophe equal to the release energy of billions of atomic bombs.

The NASA astronomers say that this theory is nothing else but a hoax and have nothing to do with planetary science. There is no Nibiru or Planet X coming to destroy Earth in December 22, 2012.

New Agers have advocated a theory of Global transformation of consciousness, when the old Astrological Age of Pisces will be replaced by a New Astrological Age of Aquarius—everything being tied to the date of winter solstice—December 22, 2012.

Twentieth Century saw many significant historical events. Two World wars resulted in more than 65 million killed. The Armenian genocide (1915) committed by the Republic of Turkey, successor of the Ottoman Empire, eliminated between one to one and a half million Armenians.

The Russian Great October Revolution in 1917 led to the creation of Communist Soviet Union under the leadership of Vladimir Lenin and his successor Joseph Stalin, who became one of the bloodiest dictators in modern history.

In 1932-1933 alone an artificially organized by Stalin and his NKVD famine in Ukraine killed around seven million people, including three million children. During the years1927-1938 Stalin through 'The Great Terror' exterminated more than ten million of his own people.

We witnessed in 1991 the collapse of the 'evil Communist Empire'—the Soviet Union. A shocking series of events between 1989 and 1991 had led to the fall of communist regimes in Eastern Europe, collapse of the Berlin Wall and reunification of East and West Germany.

Despotic leaders brought genocide on their people. Pol Pot of Cambodia (1975-1979) annihilated one million seven hundred thousand. Kim II Sang of North Korea—one million six hundred (1948-1994). Jean Kambanda of Rwanda (1994)—eight hundred thousand. Chairman Mao of China (1958-1969 and Tibet 1949-1950)—from fifty to seventy eight million. Saddam Hussein of Iraq (1987-1990)—six hundred thousand. Mullah Omar of Afghanistan (1986-2001, Taliban)—four hundred thousand. Adolf Hitler of Germany (1939-1945, concentration camps and civilians WWII)—twelve million. This list can go on and on.

The Great British Empire was the largest Global Empire in human history. It acquires one quarter of the Earth's total land area. This expanse was 150 times the size of itself, and consisted of one quoter of the world population at the time (1922). Remember 'Britannia rules the seas', 'The sun never sets on the British Empire'? So, what happened to this mighty Empire? With the last major colony Hong Kong, given away to China in 1997, Great Britain met an End of Empire. Just, 'Gone with the wind.'

In our days we have seen the resurrection of a new Holy Roman Empire—a European Union with the leadership of Germany. This revived ancient Empire will be unified and cemented together by the Roman Catholic Church—the Vatican. This superpower will play an important role in the 'latter years'. Recent Balkan Peninsula wars (1991) have clearly shown who is in control of the former countries of Yugoslavia and the Mediterranean Sea. Germany used USA military power and NATO forces under the EU umbrella in order to achieve its Imperial goals.

The way geopolitics goes, and the Middle East in particular, it seems that Germany will push America out of the peace process between Israel and the Palestinians, and assume the dominant role on this diplomatic front. We might see soon European Union international peacekeeping forces surrounding Jerusalem. It would not be surprising to see all nuclear weapons, stationed on USA and NATO bases in Europe, changing hands overnight, suddenly making the EU a nuclear superpower. Iran, Iraq and the rest of the regional powers will be dealt swiftly by the EU 'fourth beast' (Daniel 7:23), and with an iron hand. All the Middle East will be under the full control of this European Superpower.

The 'Lost' Ten Tribes Found and Indentified!

America's fate will be the same that of her sister, England. Actually, to say it more correctly, these two countries are brothers: Manasseh and Ephraim respectively, sons of Joseph, of the tribes of Israel. There are a few people in the world, Christians and Jews alike, who have devoted their lives to find and rightly identify the so called "Ten Lost Tribes" of Israel. They have done tremendous research in human history, Scriptures, migration of the nations, cultures, languages, art effects and archeology. Now they have furiously been working towards the happy end—reunification of all tribes of Israel in their historical God given Holy Land to fulfill the prophecy: "Therefore, behold, the days come, saith the Lord, that they shall no more say, The Lord lives, which brought up the children of Israel out of the land of Egypt; But, the Lord lives, who brought up and which led the seed of the house of Israel out of the north country, and from all countries whither I had driven them: and they shall dwell in their own land" (Jeremiah 23:7-8).

These people are Herbert W. Armstrong (died in 1986), his follower, editor-in-chief of the Philadelphia Trumpet Gerald Flurry, the founder of Brit-Am Yair Davidiy, the Kol Ha Tor organization, the esteemed Bible scholar and theologian writer Steven M. Collins and many others.

There is a book more than three thousand years old, called the Bible (Deuteronomy 17:18). The Hebrew Bible. The rise and fall of empires, economic and military upheavals, nations alliances, threats of nuclear war, terrorism, disease epidemics,—everything has been prophesied up to this day with Divine precision. People cannot solve all the problems of the world—God will! He has shown us the future events of 'Latter Years' up to the 'End Time.' Yes, there will be great tribulations, especially for the house of Jacob (what is new?), wars, famines, incurable diseases, and death. At the appointed time God will surely intervene. Nations at last will be at Peace. Planet Earth will be cleansed and the land rested. We will usher in the Messianic Age.

For what can be done against Force, without Force?

Let us briefly come back to America, the most single powerful nation in the world (Genesis 48:19). Sorry, not any more, used to be. The fraud and corruption, financial and economic crises, policies of appeasement and political correctness, astonishing national debt, indulging in materialism, devaluation of moral and family values—America is sick at heart. For a long time there have not been the great, God fearing, wise leaders of the caliber of Abraham Lincoln or Winston Churchill. America lacks the will-power to deal with countries like North Korea, Iran, and China.

Obama's government prefers compromises and appeasement. They have abounded their friends such as Poland, the Serbs, Czechs, Ukraine. Tiny Israel, USA's most reliable ally in the Middle East, was betrayed by her "Big Brother" in hopes of boosting its image in the eyes of the Muslim world. Taiwan is the next—to please China. America has wasted its enormous military strength in vain. All efforts that have been made in the Iraqi War in the terms of death sacrifices and money spent ultimately will be nullified, because radical Islamists of Shiite Iran will take over to rule "Democratic" Shiite Iraq. The same end will repeat itself in Afghanistan. America's war against terrorism is far away from a conclusion. Islamic terrorism is blooming around the world.

Communist North Korea, despite all peace initiatives, economic sanctions, intimidations and threats of military assault, has produced atomic weapons and joined other countries in the "nuclear club". Soon the same scenario might repeat of itself with the radical state-sponsoring of terrorism Muslim Republic of Iran. President Ahmadinejad has announced publicly on a few occasions the intention to "wipe Israel of the map". The USA has to revaluate its policy on the Middle East and face reality. Appeasement, political correctness and indecision cannot help in the case of Iran. The aggressiveness and defiance of this rogue nation can be stopped only by a superior force. "For what can be done against force, without force?" rhetorically asked Roman statesman Cicero.

America cannot decisively deal with Iran but effectively prevents Israel from acting forcibly in self-defense against the nuclear threat of the Islamic Republic.

Violent push of the King of the South

There is another prophetic possibility described in the book of Daniel 11:40-43. As far as geopolitics is concerned, Iran will take over control of most of the oil-producing countries of the Middle East and will become the leader of the Arab-Muslim world. The Bible calls this leader the 'King of the South'. There will come a time when Iran, in order to pursue their nuclear ambitions, will use the 'Petroleum weapon' (Oil productions, artificial ups and downs of the prices) against the industrialized countries of the Common Market of Europe (EU). The Bible calls the EU group of nations the 'King of the North'. That is how the Bible describes the Iranian 'push':

"And at the time of the end shall the king of the south push at him: and the king of the north shall come against him like a whirlwind, with chariots, and with horsemen, and with many ships; and he shall enter into the countries, and shall overflow and pass over" (Daniel 11:40).

The United Europe under the undisputed leadership of Germany will attack Iran and Co. in a blitzkrieg manner and take over all the Middle East. Egypt, Libya and Ethiopia 'shall not escape' (11:43).

With this possible scenario, it might not be the Israelis or Americans who stop the aggressiveness of Iran and prevent its final development of nuclear weapons. For us it is very clear that heavy industrialized Europe, which cannot survive without oil, will not quietly sit and wait for a positive outcome of Iran's oil political games and let this evil radical regime intimidate western continents and choke their economies. It would seem that the Daniel prophecies will come alive in our days. Geopolitical events around the globe are good indicators of it. Apparently, America under this President has chosen a different path. In the end she will be abandoned and betrayed by her 'lovers' in a similar way to what she did to her friends. Allies ('lovers') will turn against and destroy her, unless America repents and turn to God.

State of Israel

In 1948 a new state was born in Palestine, the Jewish state of Israel, which is the main subject of this work. All above mentioned events, including creation of the state of Israel, were exactly prophesied by the Bible, on which account we will present Scriptural proofs in the following chapters. The readers will see all the evidence for it and will judge for themselves.

As Rabbi Ephraim Sprecher noted in his article, 'Is the Jewish state of 1948 prophesied in the Torah?' the year of 1948 corresponds to the Hebrew year 5708. The Kabbalah teaches that every historical event written in the Bible is reflected in the verses of the Torah. Thus, the Hebrew year of 5708 points to Deuteronomy 30:3, "That then the LORD your God will turn your captivity, and have compassion on you, and will return and gather you from all the nations, where the LORD your God has scattered you."

This means that the creation of the State of Israel in 1948 was predicted exactly by verses of the Hebrew Bible!

Naming the Jewish state "Israel" has caused too much confusion among the nations. The majority of people have thought that it is the same Israel as that of kings David and Solomon. But, in fact, it is not the case. According to Scripture and secular history, this state should bear the name Judea, not Israel. Of course, the Promised Land is rightfully called the Land of Israel. The Jews are representatives of the Tribes of Judah, Benjamin and of Levi. Ever since the division of the United Monarchy of Israel in circa 930b.c, there had existed the two independent, often antagonistic, kingdoms of Judea and Israel. The northern kingdom of Israel was defeated by Assyrians and taken into captivity in a few stages: from 741b.c.to 722b.c. The Bible states that these Israelite tribes disappeared and nobody knows their whereabouts. But at all times they have been guided by God, because He has a prophetic Plan for them to fulfill in the End Times. Meanwhile, until they meet their future destiny, "Ephraim, he hath mixed himself among the nations . . . Israel is a swallowed up: now shall they be among the Gentiles as a vessel wherein is no pleasure" (Hosea 7:8; 8:8). Nevertheless, even thou, the God of Israel foretold His People "That which comes into your mind shall not be at all, that you say, We will be as the Gentiles, as the families of the countries, to serve wood and stone" (Ezekiel 20:32).

As we mentioned before, these so-called "Ten Lost Tribes of Israel" are found and thoroughly identified as the modern countries of Great

Britain, the USA, Canada, Australia, New Zealand, South Africa, and about a dozen countries of Europe. They are multitudinous in numbers, hundreds of millions, precisely as prophesied.

"Yet the number of the children of Israel shall be as the sand of the sea, which cannot be measured nor numbered" (Hosea 1: 10).

Many Bible prophecies of the 'latter days' speak of Israel as a significant participant in the eschatological future. The problem with Israelite's nations—is that they have lost their national identity, their Israelite's origin. The light of the Torah has no more shined on them. Although they have forgotten the God of their fathers, the Almighty has not forgotten them. "Israel is my son, my firstborn" (Exodus 4:22).

The time will come, when they repent and turn to the God of Israel. They still have remained God's chosen people, the same way as the Jews are! Is it not exiting?! A beautiful, glorious future has been prepared for them by the Almighty.

Definition of 'Jew' and 'Israel' (the Ten Tribes)

The divine Torah was revealed to Moses circa 1313b.c. at Mount Sinai. There were no Jews at that time. A People, led by Moses out of Egypt, called themselves Israelites or Hebrews. They all were descendants of Shem. The Bible states that they should be recognized by the name 'Hebrews' because "Shem was the ancestor of all the sons of Eber" (Genesis 10:21), indicating that this progenitor was so important, that all his descendants should have been named after him. So, it was not surprising that one of the 'sons of Eber', Abraham, was named by his name, which cannot be revised and replaced by the word 'Jew' because it has nothing in common with it. In the Hebrew language the world 'ha-ivri' translated as 'the Hebrew', may be understood as 'outsider', 'stranger', or 'one who crossed over' from another place. As it says in Genesis Rabbah, 'Abram separated himself from a world steeped in idolatry and polytheism by crossing over to worship one God, the Creator of all things'. Rashi commented the same way, and never translated 'ha-ivri' as 'Jew'. Most commentators of the Bible agree that it is correct to consider Eber as the eponymous ancestor of the Hebrews.

Isaac also was neither an Israelite nor a Jew because the name 'Israel' was given by the Almighty to his son Jacob (Genesis 35:10). Even then, when God changed the name of Jacob to Israel, Jacob could not have been called 'Jew' because the Jews originated much later and were named after one of his twelve sons who was called Judah.

Judah is the only nation of all the Israelite nations, who has not abounded the Torah and the Law for thousands of years, despite of persecutions and unparalleled sufferings.

The Jews are those, who historically belong to the state of Judaea, the physical descendants of Judah, Benjamin and the tribe of Levy, collectively known as the modern day Jews, where the tribe of Judah always has been dominant. Naturally, to be a Jew, one has to be born of a Jewish mother, or have some Jewish ancestral background, or be properly converted to Judaism.

The Jews are part of Israel, just two [and a half] tribes among twelve. By no means is it correct to substitute them for the Ten Tribes of Israel. Today the two terms are not synonymous. Likewise, the Israelites are not the Jews. It is safe to say that all Jews technically can be called "Israelites', whereas not all Israelites can be called Jews.

When God speaks of Israel in Scriptures, generally He means the Ten Tribes of Israel, who are also called 'Ephraim' or 'Manasseh' (Genesis 48:16, 19). Exception could be, when it is specifically mentioning 'all families of Israel,' or the 'house of Jacob', it depends on the context of the verse. When God speaks of Judah, He means the Jews only, which in Scriptures are also called 'Zion', 'Jerusalem' or 'the House of Judah'. Again, there are some exceptions, when the term 'Israel' may indicate the Jewish People alone (Ezra 2:2, 59-70; 3:1; Ezekiel 3:5; 8:10-12; 14:1). Therefore, Judah and Israel are not synonyms. They are completely different nations, living in different countries on the face of the earth and having different histories, cultures, traditions, and religions. God's prophets have always carefully distinguished the terms 'Judah' and 'Israel'. They have never stated that the Jewish People are the same as the Israelite People, the way they were at the time of Moses. They have always spoken of them as two separate entities. Whoever does not understand or rejects this plain Biblical truth, goes against God's Word. Basically, to see that what we are saying is true, just take a look at the two chapters of Genesis 48 and 49 plus the famous 'two sticks' prophecy of Ezekiel 37: 16-28. This should be satisfactory enough for any skeptical reader.

Countries of Israelite Origin

America, England and Israel are the three most prominent countries of Israelite origin in the modern world. Their respective biblical ancestor's names are: Manasseh, Ephraim and Judah (Israelis). Most European countries with population of the Hebrew descent have small (but sometime large) groups of people: Scotland, Ireland, Belgium, France, Switzerland, Denmark, Sweden, Finland, and Norway. Their descendants are also found in Canada, New Zealand, Australia, and South Africa.

The USA and Great Britain have enjoyed a special brotherly relationship for many decades. They (especially the American People) also have helped the young Jewish state in times of need on many occasions. At the present time this brotherly special relationship among these countries has severely deteriorated. Even this trend was prophesied in details by the Bible: ". . . they shall eat every man the flesh of his own arm: Manasseh, Ephraim; and Ephraim, Manasseh; and they together shall be against Judah." (Isaiah 9:21).

In Zechariah 11:14 God said: "Then I cut asunder mine other staff, even Bands, that I might break the brotherhood between Judah and Israel." Wow! This is exactly what is happening in front of our own eyes: America and England are becoming increasingly hostile towards Judah, the State of Israel, and each other.

The Middle East and the Peace Process

The Middle East peace process between the Israelis and the Palestinians is a bone of contention. It happens that little Israel is in the middle of the clash between Christian and Muslim civilizations. No one side really cares about Israel. Arabs hate her openly, Christians—hypocritically, secretly. Oil rich Arab countries have very much interest in keeping the region in a state of bloody conflict and constant tension in order to gain huge profits. The Faith of the Palestinians is not what interests them. There is no Palestinian problem for them at all. Indeed, if they really cared, King Hussein of Jordan would not have given an order to his army in 1970, in the month known as 'Black September', to squash them with tanks. They kicked their brother Palestinians out of the Jordanian kingdom. This resulted in tens of thousands dead. Neither Egypt, nor Jordan, when they were in possession of Gaza and the West Bank, had even considered to helping the Palestinians establish an autonomy or independent state.

Obviously, there is a Jewish problem. The single Jewish state is alongside twenty-two Arab nations in the neighborhood. Out of necessity, the Jews have fought and miraculously won many wars. The Arabs do not want Jews around. As Benjamin Netanyahu said," Our enemies do not want an Arab state next to Israel. They want an Arab state instead of Israel".

'The True Torah Jews against Zionism'. Neturei Karta

If the positions were reversed, with the Palestinians powerful and the Jews defenseless, (God forbid!), there would not now be a single Jew left alive. This includes the Orthodox Torah Jews against Zionism, called Neturei Karta, many elite intellectuals from the Universities and the press, international 'activists,' and leftist peace loving demagogues who are united in their efforts along with the Arabs and anti-Semite elements around the world to delegitimize and destroy the Jewish state. They want to live under the Democratic Palestinian Authority. No less, nor more. There is no such a thing! Arabs prefer dictatorship to democratic principles. Just look at Hamas who rule Gaza and the Palestinian Authority of the West Bank. They are enemies. There is no unity, no peace and no democracy. More Palestinians have been killed by Hamas and Fatah, for spying and collaborating with Israel or for voicing of dissent, than by the IDF. Hitler had massacred all Jews, regardless as to whether they were religious, secular, communist, democrat, liberal, German patriots or elite intellectuals.

Approximately one million Arabs live in the State of Israel, officially enjoying equal citizenship with the Jews, democratic rights and freedoms, serving in army, voting, and representation in Parliament. Of course, there are some tensions and imperfections in relationship with Government and the majority Jewish population but such a situation is common for countries and societies with minority groups. The fact is that the Israeli Arabs like to live in Israel under Israeli Government and strongly object the any offer to resettle them in a future independent Arab State on the West Bank or Gaza and to make them join the majority of Arabs.

Can you imagine Jews living in Gaza or in the West Bank unprotected? Everybody knows the answer: Arabs do not want Jews living among them. There are many instances of the killing and lynching of Jews caught in Gaza and the West Bank.

The Two States Solution

The President Obama administration, pressurized by oil producing Arab regimes and the international pro-Palestinian community, has continued a one sided policy of arm-bending, imposing its will on the Israeli Government. America has helped Israel to survive on many occasions. It was a consistent ally and true friend. But now her policy has been changed, and she has acted as an enemy of the Jewish people, forcing them to act against their own security and survival.

If the USA President "commits to Israel's security and wants to put an end to the Israeli-Palestinian conflict", as he pronounced recently, why does he then send the wrong messages to the Arabs? No wonder, they have stopped negotiating and started violent riots from Jerusalem to Jaffa, including rocket attacks from Gaza. The Palestinians see that America is distancing itself from Israel and clearly taking their side.

The lessons of the past have been ignored. Instead of peace through withdrawals, prisoner releases and 'land for peace' concessions, Israel has got thousand of rockets, destruction and bloody wars,—A heavy price for the peace treaties of Oslo, South Lebanon and Gaza!

How can you make peace and establish two independent states out of the two nations, if one is the sworn enemy and committed to destruction of the other? The Palestinian leadership does not want live in peace with the Jews. They have denied the rights of the Jews to settle in the Holy Land. They have denied the right of the Jewish State to exist from the first day it was born. On the next day after the United Nations partition resolution in 1947, the Mufti of Jerusalem declared: "What the UN wrote in black ink, we will write in red blood." All they have dreamed of is to throw the Jews into the sea, all of them. The Prime Minister of Israel B. Netanyahu proudly challenges them," Our existence does not depend on the willingness of the Palestinians to make peace with us. Our existence is secured by our right to live in this land and our capacity to defend that right. The state of Israel will never be finished!"

One of the greatest obstacles to a permanent peace solution is the status of Jerusalem. Both parties cannot compromise on it. Certainly, not Israel, who proclaimed that Jerusalem will remain its undivided capital.

From the Scriptural point of view peace in the Middle East is impossible, until God's intervention, resulting in the Final Redemption of the House of Israel and House of Judah, with the advent of Messiah, son of David. **Sharing the Holy Land with Israel's enemy is an anti-Torah solution.**

Siege of the Nations against Jerusalem

The prophet Zechariah in chapters 12 and 14 has told us in detail what is going to transpire in Jerusalem in the latter years. Today's international geopolitical events are inevitably leading the Nations to war against Jerusalem and the State of Israel. The same motive is expressed in Micah 4:11-13: "Now also many nations are gathered against thee . . . Arise and thresh, O daughter of Zion, for I will make thine horn iron, and I will make thy hoofs brass: and thou shalt beat in pieces many people; and I will consecrate their gain unto the Lord, and their substance unto the Lord of the whole earth."

The outcome of this siege of nations against Judah and Jerusalem is very obvious. Zechariah's prophecy is a huge blow to Neturei Karta and all of their theological camp. They deny the Scriptural legitimacy of the State of Israel based, in large part, on exegetical analysis of the Three Oaths of the Song of Songs.

According to their position, it is forbidden by Torah for the Jewish people to end the Exile and establish an independent State in the Holy Land, until God sends the Messiah. Is it really so? Of course, not! No wonder, they are so silent about this prophecy [of Micah 4:11-13 or Zephaniah 2:7], and many, many others, with which we will be dealing in the following chapters. Seems, they do not even understand or ignore the differences between Judah and Israel, the people of Israel and people of Judah. Meanwhile, may we ask what nation will be at the epicenter of international military attacks against Jerusalem in the latter days? The answer is Judah, the Jews, living now in the state of Israel, the Israelis. Not the house of Israel: The timing of Zechariah's prophecies is still before the redemption and advent of the Messiah. If God, according to Neturei Karta, had prohibited the Jewish people to emigrate to the Promised Land and establish there an independent state, how is it possible, that the same God, in His Holy Word, plainly and clear tells us that the House of Judah will already have been living in the land of Israel, in order to meet the requirements of Zechariah 12 and 14? God obviously predicted, allowed and blessed the Jewish State! He is in full control of human history. These prophecies are certain. They represent the Divine Plan of the Almighty. He will make Jerusalem 'a cup of trembling unto all people round about, a burdensome stone.'

God loves and will protect Judah. All they "that burden themselves with Jerusalem, shall be cut in pieces" (Zechariah 12:2-3; Micah 4:13). The **Nations better heed and obey God's message, before it is too late!**

Christianity and Judaism

The Christian religion is the second largest in the world, after Islam, with a population of over two billion. It is widely understood that Christianity has accepted the Torah and Tanakh, the Hebrew Bible, as a sacred canonical book, inspired by God. The inerrancy of the Bible also has not been disputed. Judaism has given to Christianity the knowledge of One God, the written Scriptures, the Patriarchs, the Prophets, and the Apostles. Their Son of God and Savior, Jesus, was born into the Jewish family of Mary and Joseph. He never denied his Jewishness. He was proud of it. On the eight day his parents circumcised him in the Temple in Jerusalem, and he had his Bar Mitzvah on his thirteenth birthday. He kept the Laws of Moses. Every move, act or word of Jesus in the New Testament traditionally has found confirmation and the approval by the Christian fundamentalists in the Old Testament: "Thus said the Lord", or "Thus said the Prophet."

Instead of eternal gratitude to Jewish people, Christianity has become their cruel prosecutors. Forceful conversions, Crusaders, expulsions, burning alive, pogroms, anti-Semitism, anti-Zionism, the Holocaust,—all these show their attitude towards the Jews for two thousand years of recorded history. In order to prove their theological dogmas, they have rewritten Holy Scriptures, taking verses out of context, manipulating texts to prove points, and applying misleading translations. All of these actions have been taken just to prove that the

New Testament is superior to the Old one; that God rejected Israel, and that Christians became a new spiritual Israel in place of the Jews.

They ought to be reminded that before Christianity had been established as a new religion, the Hebrews had been worshipping the God of the Universe, their Creator, for two thousand years, ever since the Patriarch Abraham, the Hebrew, accepted monotheism. The Scriptures were written in the Hebrew language and for them, so the Israelites and their brilliant Sages have known how to translate and read them. Nobody could have taught them how to worship God of Israel better than the wise men of Israel: Moses, David and Solomon, the Prophets, R. Hillel, R. Akiva, Rambam, Ramban, Rashi, and countless more. God has always remembered His people: "For a small moment have I forsaken thee; but with great mercies will I gather thee" (Isaiah 54:7).

In contrast, there are growing numbers of Christians, especially among Evangelicals and Protestants, who have interpreted the Bible literally as a mandate for unconditional support of Israel as the Chosen People of God. They have rejected the "Replacement Theology" that presents Christians as being spiritual Israel, as a direct contradiction to the Bible's teaching. One of the most significant figures of this movement is Pastor John Hagee. His uncompromising position of solidarity and love for Israel for many years has earned him the deep appreciation and respect of Jewish People around the world, alongside controversy and rejection among by Christian clergy, who often call him a heretic.

Pastor John Hagee and Others.
'Biblical advocates' for the Jewish People

It is not a secret that the Bible has shown Almighty to be protector and defender of His people Israel. "I am a father to Israel, and Ephraim is my firstborn" (Jeremiah 31:9). Moreover, the Bible states in Zechariah 2:8 that the Jewish people are "the apple of God's eye". In Genesis 12:3

God said to Abraham that He would "bless those who bless you, and curse him who curses you".

Well known to Christian world Global Evangelist Pastor John Hagee's response to these passages is that it is unscriptural to go against Israel, because by doing so, one, in effect, pocking God in the eye! This is not very wise thing to do! On Genesis 12:3 he commented: "I want to be blessed, not cursed, by God". In his words, it is not possible to say, "I am a Christian" and not love the Jewish people. What a man!

Now millions of Christians from all denominations have started a movement of returning to the Hebraic roots of the original faith. They have realized that the House of Israel is still the Covenant people chosen by God; that the return of the Jews to the Promised Land and establishment of the State of Israel in 1948 and recapturing Jerusalem in 1967, which again become their undivided capital, is in fulfillment of Bible prophecies. It is the first stage of the final restoration of all families of Israel. Awakening pro-Israeli Christians are supporting Judah across the world. They believe that they are from the ancient non-Jewish house of Joseph, from the Ten Lost Tribes of Israel.

The third international Christian Zionist Congress, held in Jerusalem in February 1996, proclaimed:

"God the Father, Almighty, chose the ancient nation and people of Israel, the descendants of Abraham, Isaac and Jacob, to reveal His plan of redemption for the world. They remain the elect of God, and without the Jewish nation (we should correct: 'and without the **Israel** nation') His redemptive purposes for the world will not be completed."

The most prominent Christian Zionist leaders are Billy Graham, Pat Robertson and Jerry Farwell. They are "Biblical advocates" for the Jewish People and the State of Israel. Jerry Farwell's position is very similar to that of John Hagee:

"**To stand against Israel is to stand against God.** We believe that history and Scripture prove that God deals with nations in relation to how they deal with Israel". Indeed, it could not be said better! God himself confirms it:

"No weapon that is formed against thee shall prosper; and every tongue that shall raise against thee in judgment thou shell condemn" (Isaiah 54:17).

We hope that the nations of the world are listening to these warning messages of Almighty God.

The Greatest Exodus Ever

The greatest prophecy of the Bible is the prediction of the final ingathering and redemption of the nations of Israel and Judah in the latter years with the advent of Messiah son of David. This 'Great Exodus' of all 12 tribes of Israel will be much greater that the miraculous return of the Jews in 1948, even greater than the Exodus from Egypt in circa 1300 b.c. under Moses. All families of the House of Israel finally will be reunited under the leadership of the King of Israel, their Messiah son of David in one sinless, redeemed, God-obedient nation on the Mountains of Israel. They will truly become a Holy nation of priests, the light to the World. God's knowledge will cover the Earth. All nations will serve the God of Israel. Justice and Peace at last will prevail. People will usher in the Golden Age of Humanity—the Messianic Era, and altogether will strive to merit life in the wonderful, spiritual, everlasting Heavenly Kingdom of God—the World-To-Come, the ultimate purpose of Creation. With the redemption of the whole World and establishing of the Kingdom of God, the mission of Israel on the planet Earth will have been successfully completed.

CHAPTER I:
ZIONISTS AND THEIR GOALS

By the waters of Babylon . . .

Zionism. What is it? When did it start? Many researchers pointed out that Zionism officially begun in 1897 at the First Zionist Congress in Basel, Switzerland. In fact, Zionism had started much earlier. When king Nebuchadnezzar of the mighty Babylonian Empire conquered the Jewish kingdom of Judaea, destroyed Solomon's temple and exiled all the Jews to Babylon in 597b.c. and 586b.c. they cried and prayed to God:

"By the waters of Babylon there we sat and wept when we remembered Zion. We hanged our harps upon the willows . . . How shall we sing the Lord's song in a strange land? If I forget thee, O Jerusalem, let my right hand forgets her cunning. If I do not remember thee, let my tongue cleave to the roof of my mouth" (Psalm 137).

Babylonian captivity was God's punishment of the sinful nation of Judah for their idolatry and disobedience. The exile and the dispersion of the Jewish People to the lands of their enemies was not only a sign of their temporary punishment, but rather a prerequisite for their future repentance and redemption. God had not rejected them. He has always been a faithful husband unto them, "For thy Maker is thine husband" (Isaiah 54:5).

All He wanted is to correct and purify them.

"When Israel merits it, the majority of them will be in the land of Israel and a minority in Babylonia, but when they are unworthy of it, the majority will be in Babylonia and the minority in Ereẓ Israel" (Gen. R. 98:9). As evidence show, today the majority of Israel (the

Ten Tribes) still remains in exile and a minority (half of the Jewish population) lives in the Land of Israel.

When in captivity, deprived of the Holy Land, the First Temple and freedom, the Jews, in their longing for Zion, repented and turned to their God. This was the earliest time. This was when Zionism was born.

After seventy years in captivity, as prophesied by Jeremiah 29:10, the Jews were heard and forgiven by the God of Israel. His anointed one, the Persian King Cyrus the Great, issued the Royal Decree, letting the captives go back to their Promised Land in 538 b.c. to build Jerusalem and the Temple. It is interesting to note, that not all Judeans came back. The majority had chosen to stay in the Diaspora. The same thing happened in the Third Return of the Jews in 1948 (the First Return we count as the Exodus from Egypt). Up until today, more Jews live in the Diaspora than in the State of Israel.

The huge difference between the Exoduses is that the Jewish people in the Return from Babylon, at least those who physically came to the Promised Land, were spiritually uplifted in belief to God and His Torah. The Third Return of the Jews to the newly created State of Israel (the first stage of return) was, in large part, in unbelief, because most of the people were not religious, Torah obedient Jews. This includes the Zionist's leadership. It does not mean that the unseen mighty hand of Providence had protected only those of the previous Returns. We have more than enough Scriptural evidences proving that the God of Israel has also blessed the Jewish people of the Third Return. The Zionists and their newly born State of Israel, manifestly have been abundantly blessed by the God of Israel, as part of the First Stage of the Final Redemption of all the House of Israel, as Divine Plan for Humanity outlined in the Holy Bible.

Many books have stereotypically been written about the Zionists and their ideologies. Who were these people? What motivated them? What were their goals? Why so many controversies, accusations and justifications?

Portraits and Teachings of the Famous Zionists

Hess, Moses (1812-1875).

Moses Hess was born in Bonn, Germany. He studied philosophy before becoming a correspondent for the Paris' daily socialist newspaper the "Rheinische Zeitung". Hess' most famous book, "Rome and Jerusalem", was published in 1862. He was the first to recognize Karl Marx, and was greatly influenced by Marxism. In his twenties, he felt himself thoroughly German, and believed in Jewish assimilation. After personally suffering from anti-Semitism, he re-evaluated his position and became a classic of Zionism.

His ideas are: The Jews will always remain strangers among the European people; the Jewish type is indestructible, and Jewish national feelings cannot be uprooted.

The only solution for the Jewish people is to move to Palestine and establish their own State.

Leon Pinsker (1821-1891).

He was born in Poland. From his father, a Hebrew language writer and teacher, Leon inherited a strong sense of Jewish identity. He was admitted to Odessa University to study the law. After realizing that, being a Jew, he had no chance of becoming a lawyer, he chose the career of a physician. In his early years, Pinsker favored the assimilation of the Jewish people. When he experienced a wave of anti-Jewish hostilities, the Odessa pogrom of 1871, then his views radically changed. He no longer believed that humanism and emancipation would defeat anti-Semitism. In his pamphlet "Auto-Emancipation", published in 1882, Pinsker called for establishment of a Jewish National Homeland in the Land of Israel. The root of Jewish hatred is that they are foreigners everywhere, except in their original homeland.

Theodor Herzl (1860-1904).

Herzl was born in Hungary. His parents were German-speaking, assimilated Jews. In his early years, Theodor developed a passion to be a journalist. Religions and Judaism were not his interest. He grew up as a 'thoroughly emancipated, and traditional, secular, would-be German boy'. Herzl studied law in Vienna, but devoted his career to journalism. He worked as a correspondent for the newspaper 'Neue Freie Presse' in Paris, London, and Constantinople.

The Alfred Dreyfus Affair deeply affected Herzl's views. Dreyfus was a Jewish officer in the French army. In 1894 he was found guilty of treason and sentenced to life imprisonment. After a lengthy campaign, he was exonerated as wrongly convicted. The Dreyfus trial, anti-Semitic in nature, was politically motivated. France was deeply divided. Herzl witnessed mass rallies in Paris, where many chanted "Death to the Jews!"

"In Paris, above all, I recognized the emptiness and futility of trying to combat anti-Semitism." He grew to believe that the only way to avoid anti-Semitism is the establishment of a politically independent Jewish state. His main work "The Jewish State" was published in 1896. After the First Zionist Congress in 1897, Herzl proudly wrote in his Diaries: "If I were to sum up the Basel Congress in a single phrase, which I would not dare to make public, I would say: in Basel I created the Jewish State." His last words, before he died, were: "I wish to be buried in the vault beside my father, and to lie there till the Jewish people shall take my remains to Palestine. Greet Palestine for me. I gave my heart's blood for my people."

Chaim Weizmann (1874-1952).

He was born in Belarus in the Russian Pale of Settlement. He was one of fifteen children of a Jewish timber merchant. In 1899, he was awarded a doctorate with honors at the University of Freiburg,

Switzerland. He worked as a lecturer at the Universities of Geneva and Manchester. His first Zionists steps began at an early age. Weizmann became the most prominent figure in the Zionist Movement. In 1910, he got British citizenship. During World War I, he was director of the British Admiralty laboratories from 1916 until 1919.

His first visit to Jerusalem was in 1907. He had been involved with the Balfour Declaration, the Paris Peace Conference, the Peel Commission, and the British Mandate for Palestine. He had served as president of the World Zionist Organization twice in 1920-1931 and in 1935-1946. After the establishment of the State of Israel, Weizmann became its first President in 1949.

His views: "A state cannot be created by decree, but by the forces of a people and in the course of generations. Even if all the governments of the world gave us a country, it would only be a gift of words. But if the Jewish people will go build Palestine, the Jewish state will become reality—a fact."

"We have never based the Zionists movement on Jewish suffering in Russia or in any other land. These suffering have never been the mainspring of Zionism. The foundation of Zionism was, and continues to be to this day, the yearning of the Jewish people for its homeland, for a national center and a national life."

Chaim Weizmann was buried at the Weizmann estate, which is located on the grounds of Israel's science research institute.

Vladimir Jabotinsky (1880-1940).

Jabotinsky was born in Odessa, Russia. He was raised in a Jewish middle-class home. His upbringing was divorced from the Jewish faith and tradition. At an early age he developed talents as a writer, translator, orator, and polemicist for the Zionist cause. After the Kishinev pogrom of 1903, Jabotinsky joined the Zionist movement, where he soon became a powerful speaker and an influential leader. During the pogroms, he organized self-defense units in Jewish communities across Russia. He worked as a journalist in Rome and Vienna. After Herzl's death in 1904, he became the leader of the right-wing Zionists. In 1925 he established the Revisionist Party as a protest against the exclusion of Transjordan from the British Mandate of Palestine. He also set up the party's youth movement, Betar. He was an exceptionally talented and versatile man, an original thinker and ideologue, and a powerful political leader. His followers worshiped him, while his enemies detested him with equal passion.

Jabotinsky ideas are: "The Arabs loved their country as much as the Jews did. Instinctively, they understood Zionist aspiration very well, and their decision to resist them was only natural . . . No Agreement was possible with the Palestinian Arabs; they would accept Zionism only when they found themselves up against an "iron wall", when they realize they had no alternative but to accept Jewish settlement."

He was the first to warn the Zionist Movement of the inevitable clash between Jewish and Palestinian nationalisms, which should not be ignored. He advocated the "Iron Wall" doctrine. "I devoted my life to the rebirth of the Jewish State, with a Jewish majority, on both sides of the Jordan."

Ze'ev Jabotinsky was buried together with his wife in Jerusalem at Mount Herzl Cemetery. In Israel, there are more streets, parks and squares named after Jabotinsky than any other figure in Jewish or Israeli history.

David Ben Gurion (1886-1973).

Ben Gurion was born in Poland. He studied in a Hebrew school, established by his father, an ardent Zionist. In his mid-teens, led a Zionist youth group "Ezra", whose members spoke only Hebrew among themselves. At the age of 18 Ben Gurion became a teacher in a Warsaw Jewish school and joined the Socialist-Zionist group "Workers of Zion." He arrived in Palestine in 1906. During the WWI, he was a member of the Ottoman Turkish Army, but later (in 1918) joined the Jewish Legion in the British army. In the early 1920's he founded the "Histadrut", the trade union parent organization. In 1935 was elected chairman of the World Zionist Organization and Jewish Agency. Ben Gurion's passion for Zionism culminated in his instrumental role in the founding of the state of Israel. He led Israel to victory in the 1948 Arab-Israeli War.

He served as Prime Minister and Defense Minister in Israeli governments. Ben Gurion became the chief statesman and political leader of the modern state of Israel. He is still revered as the "Father of the Nation." On May14, 1948 with trembling voice he read: "We, the members of the National Council, representing the Jewish people in the Land of Israel and the Zionist Movement . . . do hereby proclaim the establishment of a Jewish State in the Land of Israel."

Ben Gurion thoughts:

"The state of Israel will prove itself not by material wealth, neither by military might, nor by technical achievement but by its moral character and human values."

"Without moral and intellectual independence, there is no anchor for national independence."

"We offer peace and neighborliness to all the neighboring states and their people, and invite them to cooperate with the independent Hebrew nation for the common good of all."

Numerous streets throughout Israel, as well as the Ben Gurion International Airport, the Ben Gurion University of the Negev, and a desert research center (Midreshet Ben-Gurion) were named in his honor.

Abraham Isaac Kook (1865-1935).

Rav Kook was born in Latvia, the oldest of eight children in the family of Rabbi Shlomo Zalman Ha-Cohen Kook. He studied in Volozhin Yeshiva for about 18 hours a day. In 1887 he was given the first rabbinical position as a rabbi of Zaumel, Lithuania. In 1904 he moved to Palestine, where he received the rabbinical post of Jaffa. After WWI, Rav Kook was appointed in 1921 as Ashkenazi Chief Rabbi of Palestine.

Rav Kook was a master of Halakha, and at the same time he possessed an unusual openness to new ideas. He loved the Jewish people regardless, as to whether they were secular Zionists, religious Zionists, or traditional non-Zionist Orthodox Jews. He became the main ideologue of modern religious Zionism. Carefully, with love and patience, he built bridges of communication and political alliances between the various Jewish groups. He believed that the end of 2000 years of exile and establishment of a Jewish state of Israel in the land of Israel had profound theological significance, approved by the Almighty. All Jews taking part in this process were agents of a grand Divine Plan to bring about the Messianic Era, the final spiritual redemption of all Israel. Unlike other Zionist leaders, Rav Kook's motivations were based solely on Jewish Law, Biblical prophecy and Judaism.

Rav Kook's thoughts:

"Secular Zionists may think they do it for political or social reasons, but in fact—the actual reason for them coming to resettle in Israel is a religious Jewish spark in their soul, planted by God. Without their knowledge, they are contributing to the divine scheme and actually committing a great Mitzvah.

The role of religious Zionists is to help them to establish a Jewish State and turn the religious spark in them into a great light. They should teach them Torah with love and kindness. This would show the Zionists that the real source of Zionism and the lodging for Zion is Judaism. In the end, they will understand that the Laws of Torah are the key to true harmony and a socialist state that will be a light for the nations and bring salvation to the world."

Speaking of Religious Zionism, it is worth mentioning, in addition to Rav Kook, two outstanding personalities, earlier forerunners of Zionism: Rabbi Yehuda Solomon Alkalai (1798-1878), founder of political Zionism; and Rabbi Zvi Hirsch Kalischer (1795-1874), who was considered a founder of modern Religious Zionism. The list of Zionists Leaders would not be complete without mentioning the names of Max Nordau, Dov Ber Borochov, Nahum Sokolow, Moshe Sharett, Menachem Begin, Abba Eban, Aaron David Gordon, Uri Zvi Greenberg, Ahad Ha'am, Golda Meir and many, many more.

What had motivated all these people, religious and secular, to be actively involved in the Zionism Movement? They were highly educated in various fields: philosophers, lawyers, journalists, scientists, writers, rabbis. They had lived in an era of Enlightenment and Emancipation, when the new ideas and revolutionary movements originated. The France Revolution (1789-1799) promoted principles of citizenship and inalienable rights, Freedom, Equality, and Brotherhood. The Industrial Revolution also had an influence. So too, there was the Birth of Communism in Europe under Karl Marx and Frederick Engels with its written "Manifesto" in 1848. The philosophers Rousseau (1712-1778) and Voltaire (1694-1778) had formed the ideas of Socialism, civil liberties, and freedom of religion. At the same time, they had witnessed arousing national liberation movements and wars for independence around the world.

In 1832, after a long struggle, independence was finally granted to Greece; in 1878 to Romania, Bulgaria, Montenegro and Serbia; in 1912 to Albania, in 1917 to Finland, in 1918 to three Baltic States of Estonia, Latvia and Lithuania. Czechoslovakia, Yugoslavia and Poland became independent in 1918. The Republic of Turkey under Mustafa Kemal won independence in 1923. Only the Jews had remained the same, with no homeland, no national recognition, no rights,—foreigners in the countries of exile. Not welcome anywhere. Even when they assimilated, they were no equal to the indigenous population, and often reminded of it. Their fabulous past, the United kingdom of Israel, its victories and glory, kings David and Solomon, the epoch of the first and second Temples, independence and freedom of worshipping the God of Israel,—these memories were still alive amongst the residents of Ghettos and Shtetles (mestechkis). The last time the Jewish people secured their independence, was in 167-160b.c. during the heroic Maccabean War of national liberation, when the Jewish Hasmonean kingdom was established, so that they could freely worship their God and live by the Torah. But Judaea did not last long. In 63b.c. the Roman general Pompey conquered Syria, and Judaea became a Roman province. Two attempts were made by Jewish freedom fighters to regain independence for Judea in the first Jewish-Roman War (66-73b.c.) and the Bar Kokhba revolt of 132-135 b.c. Both efforts to free the Jewish people and liberate the homeland failed.

Darkness had descended on the Jewish nation. Since the destruction of the Temple in 70 a.c. and defeat in 135 a.c., hundreds of thousands Jews had been murdered, sold into slavery and dispersed throughout the Roman Empire. The Emperor Hadrian made an attempt to root out Judaism. He executed Judaic scholars, prohibited the Torah laws and burned the sacred scrolls. The names of Judea and Israel were wiped off the map and replaced with "Palestine." Jerusalem was replaced as the Roman pagan polis of "Aelia Capitolina." Ages of hatred and persecution had begun.

The Zionist leaders, being all of Jewish descent, knew Jewish history very well. Their hearts were bleeding because of injustices and sufferings that befell their people. Europe was full of anti-Semitism. Pogroms, synagogues burning and mob attacks had intensified in Russia and Poland. The entire world was indifferent and cold blooded to the faith of the Jews. What has to be done? There were two opinions: Patiently wait and pray, until the time, when God would decide to end the exile and send the Messiah to bring the House of Jacob to the Promised Land and redeem them; Or themselves actively seek redemption and freedom with self-determination in the land of their fathers, as other nations had done. They choose the second way, establishing a political international movement among the Jews, which held that the Jews were a nation entitled to a national homeland in Palestine. One of the priorities of this movement was to establish a politically independent State of Israel, support its development and defense, and to encourage Jews to immigrate and settle there.

Many critics, especially the Satmar group, the Torah Jews against Zionism, and the fanatical Orthodox sect called Neturei Karta, have blamed the Zionists for creating what they saw as an atheistic State, in which Torah and Judaism have no part, and whose government is not theocratic. They claimed that the Zionists had acted against the will of God, therefore the State of Israel should cease to exist, the Jews have no rights to their homeland without permission from God, and the Holy Land has to be given back to the Palestinians. But the point is that these objectives never have been the goals of the Zionists and they had not even pretended that it was otherwise. We are speaking here, mainly, of political, not religious, Zionism. Secular, no Torah—observant Jews, they still heard the cry of their brothers and sisters. They felt their pain. They had witnessed pogroms and murders of their people. They could not sit and wait any longer for special permission from God to end the exile, while the Jews over dully suffering from oppression and death all over the world. It was clear for them that this situation would never change, unless the Jewish people, as a nation, had their own politically independent homeland in Palestine, where they could live safely and free. Being secular, does not mean that they did not know the Bible, the millennia—old lodging for Zion, the dreams and aspirations of the Jewish people for the Redemption and the Messianic Age.

As Rav Kook said, the Zionists might think that they had done everything for political or social reasons, but in fact—the actual reason for them is a religious Jewish spark in their soul, planted by God. Without their knowledge, they contributed to the divine scheme and actually carried out a great Mitzvah. These people have been the best visionaries, gutsy idealists and romantics, the Jewish nation could offer. The real patriots, heroes of the Jewish nation, they had devoted their energy, money, health and even life to fulfill their goals—to liberate and gather the Jews from all over the world and bring them to the Promised Land, to the magnificent country, they have organized and built, sacrificed their life for it, the Jewish State of Israel, the only democracy in the Middle East. This is the country, where the Jews from four corners of the Earth have found a safe heaven, happiness, and freedom.

Modern State of Israel and the Holy Land

Before creation of the State of Israel in 1948, Jews really had no choice as to remain citizens of their countries of exile. Now they have a choice to live in their own country; the country, where the rights of its citizens protected and guaranteed, where Jews once again live uplifted and proud. An ancient dream has become a reality. The country, where all religions are free: Christians, Muslims and Jews worship the way they chose. Just in Jerusalem, there are 1240 synagogues, 230 Churches, and 73 Mosques. Judaism is blossoming, and Torah observant Jews feel at home. Their everyday prayer to God, "Bring us in peace from the four corners of the earth and lead us upright to our land," has finally been realized in the beautiful Land of Israel.

The land of the Prophets, who brought to the world knowledge of the Creator of the Universe, the God of Israel, and His Torah with the highest values of human dignity, morality, justice, and law. The land with a greater level of Holiness from all other lands. "You shall posses it, and dwell therein," said the Lord (Deut. 11:31). God is the First Zionist before anybody. As our Sages said, "Dwelling in the land of Israel is equal to all Commandments of the Torah", or "Said the Almighty: a small assembly in the Land of Israel is dearer to me than a full Sanhedrin outside the Land" (Palestinian Talmud, Sanhedrin 6:5).

Ramban (Nahmanides, 1194-1270 A.C.), our great Sage, encouraged the Jewish people to settle in the Holy Land as a positive

Commandment: "It is a mitzvah to take possession of Israel and live in it. We are commanded to conquest the Land in every generation."

The People of Israel can fulfill their destiny, as a Kingdom of Priests and a Holy Nation, only in the Promised Land. Here they will complete their mission and bring God's Redemption to the World. After two thousand years of exile, these Zionists have finally managed to restore the Jewish people, the lawful owners, to the Land of Israel.

The action of spiritual sanctification that is effected in the Land of Israel is constantly at work. As Rabbi Yehudah Ha Levi said: "The People of Israel can realize themselves only in the Land of Israel. It is impossible for their particular national talent to reach its Divine realization without being in the Land of Israel."

"The air of the Holy Land makes wise" (Baba Batra 158b). Only in the Land of Israel the phenomenon of prophecy appears. The Zionists have revived pride in the label 'Jew'; they restore Hebrew as the national language. Jewish culture is flourishing. Judaism is encouraged in the schools.

In their 2004 program, WZO declared:

"Israel—a Jewish, Zionist and Democratic State with a unique moral and spiritual character, with mutual respect for the multifaceted Jewish People, rooted in the vision of the Prophets, striving for peace and the betterment of the world."

Through their successful struggle for national liberation and self-determination, the Zionists have achieved both political and spiritual goals. Jews of all persuasions, religious and secular, from left and right, have joined the Zionist movement in order to fulfill the common goal of Freedom and a Jewish State in the Land of Israel. To call them heretics and rebels against God, are baseless accusations. Such an attitude is in contradiction to Scriptures and Judaism. There is no justification for it.

13

Rabbi Kook strongly rejected these accusations and developed theological base against anti-Zionists:

Zionism was not merely a political movement by secular Jews. It was actually a tool of God to promote His divine scheme and to initiate the return of the Jews to their homeland—the land He promised to Abraham, Isaac and Jacob. God wants the children of Israel to return to their home in order to establish a Jewish sovereign state in which Jews could live according to the laws of Torah and Halakha and fulfill the Mitzvoth of Eretz Israel (these are religious commandments which can be performed only in the land of Israel). Moreover, to cultivate the land of Israel was a Mitzvah by itself and it should be carried out. Therefore, the settling of Israel is an obligation of the religious Jew and helping Zionism is actually following God's will.

Moses, Nebuchadnezzar, Cyrus, Herzl—all servants of God

It is not the first time in history of Israel that God has used men of flesh and blood, not necessarily the righteous ones, to carry out His prophetic Plans. Moses was chosen to liberate the Israelites from Egypt (Exodus 3:10). He did not know the religion of Abraham, Isaac and Jacob. He grew up, worshipping the idols of Egypt. He was a sinful man. Despite this, God used him as an instrument to accomplish His Plan to free Israel from the bondage of Egypt, and gave him on the Mount Sinai the Divine Torah, which has became the heart and soul of Israel. Moses became the greater Prophet Israel ever had, 'Father of all Prophets', the only one God had spoken with 'mouth to mouth' or 'face to face'. Moshe Rabbeinu, our Leader and Teacher, who excellently accomplished the God given mission!

King Nebuchadnezzar of the mighty Babylonian Empire also acted as God's instrument to carry out His plan of retribution against Judah, which tragically ended with destruction of the First Temple and Babylonian captivity. These actions forced Judah to repent by making them realize that only in God lay their salvation. Any person who fulfills the will of God, consciously or without even aware of it, is a servant of God:

"My servant Nebuchadnezzar" (Jeremiah 25:9).

Another example of the same nature is the gentile Persian king Cyrus the Great. He was anointed by God for the purpose of liberating the Jewish people from Babylonian captivity.

The prophet Isaiah wrote 150 years before Cyrus issued his famous decree in 539 b.c. allowing the Judeans to return to their land and rebuild Jerusalem and the Temple.

God said of Cyrus: "He is My shepherd; he will certainly do as I say. He will command, "Rebuild Jerusalem"; he will say, "Restore the Temple" (Isaiah 44:28).

What a Zionist he was, this Gentile anointed ruler of the world, King Cyrus the Great! He also accomplished perfectly God's mission!

The Bible knows many accounts of similar stories. If God had used men for His purposes in the past, who can say that He could not use Theodor Herzl or David Ben Gurion later? The Scriptures tell us that God definitely, in order to fulfill His Heavenly Prophetic Plan, will use men in the future, Messiah ben Joseph and Messiah ben David, for instance.

Rabbis of Neturei Karta and the Satmar group have been using against Zionists the same theological arguments of the Three Oaths of the Song of Songs over and over again during the last century. They could not come up with anything else. We will deal with the Three Oaths and their other 'proofs' in details in the appropriate chapters.

CHAPTER II:
STAGES OF REDEMPTION.
SCRIPTURAL PROOFS OF
THE BIBLICAL LEGITIMACY OF
THE STATE OF ISRAEL

The First Stage of Redemption

It is worth mentioning here again, that the partial return of the Jews to their homeland and establishing the State of Israel in 1948 was in accordance with the Divine Plan, on which account we have many Scriptural proofs. The return was partial because not all of Israel was involved and not all the Land of Israel taken. Anyone, who denies or undermines this return of the Jews to the Holy Land as a will of God, will be accountable for it before the Almighty.

In the first stage of redemption, represented by the Jewish people in the modern Israel, God does not require all of them to repent and 'know their God'. The first physical regathering of the Jews to the Land had happened in unbelief. They had certain tasks to carry on: First of all, they had to save their lives by escaping from hostile countries and bloody persecutions; then to settle and cultivate the wasted and desolate land, that "the wilderness will be a fruitful field" (Isaiah 32:15); to build defense forces and establish a secure environment; to create a western type economy, communications and infrastructure; to prepare the way for multitudes of their brothers and sisters of the House of Israel, who will join them soon in the final stage of the redemption.

"But ye, O mountains of Israel, ye shall shoot forth branches and yield your fruit to My people Israel; for they are at hand to come" (Ezekiel 38:8).

Rashi translated this verse literally as it reads: When the Land of Israel, its fields and trees, will produce crops and fruits abundantly, then it is time for the ingathering and redemption of God's People Israel. This is the one of many realistic signs given in the Scripture of the approaching reunification of the whole House of Jacob and the Messianic Age.

"And they shall say, this land that was desolate is become like the garden of Eden; and the waste and desolate and ruined cities are become fenced, and are inhabited" (Ezekiel 36:35).

The Israelis will have accomplished all of it!

The presence of the Jewish People in the Land of Israel and in Jerusalem is A Mandatory Requirement of the Hebrew Bible!

"The Lord God which gathered the outcasts of Israel saith, yet will I gather others to him, beside those that are gathered unto him" (Isaiah 56:8).

The message is very clear here. First, God will cause some remnants of Jews to immigrate to the Promised Land right in the aftermath of WWII and the Holocaust to create the State of Israel with the ratification of the United Nations. Then they will encourage more Aliyah; organize the defense forces for their security; build up the economy, cities and towns, infrastructure, communications, and agriculture. They will do everything possible to accommodate needs of those hundreds of millions of their brothers of the Ten Tribes of Israel whose imminent coming to the Promised Land is 'at hand'.

"Lift up thine eyes round about, and see; all they gather themselves together, they come to thee; thy sons shall come from far, and thy daughters shall be nursed at thy side" (Isaiah 60:4).

What joy and cheerfulness will overflow the hearts of the Jewish People when they see the mass Exodus of their brothers and sisters of the 'Lost' Ten Tribes of Israel coming to the Holy Land to join them. For many years the Jews have struggled with countless numbers of enemies for their survival and the right to live in the God-given Land of their fathers. Their endless lonely battle against an unjust and corrupt World will have exhausted and wearied them. The God of Israel will have heard them and answered their prayers. When they see the multitude of Israelites coming to them with all their military might and power, the Jews will understand that the time of Redemption and Freedom finally has come. Their hearts 'will be thrilled and exult with joy and their eyes will shine'.

God revealed to Isaiah that the Israelites will come home to the Promised Land by planes and ships with all of their wealthy possessions of silver and gold (Isaiah 60:8-9).

"Who are these that fly along like clouds, like doves to their nests? Surely the coastlands shall wait for me, and the ships of Tarshish first, to bring your sons from afar, their silver and their gold with them, unto the name of the LORD your God, and to the Holy One of Israel, because he has glorified you".

This last Exodus will be a grandiose spectacle of huge magnitude such as the world has never experienced. The Nation of Judah will be shocked to see the immense multitudes of their lost brothers of the House of Israel, who will come to the Land of Israel for final reunification in the 'Days of Mashiach'.

"Then shalt thou say in thine heart, who hath begotten me these, seeing I have lost my children, and am desolate, a captive, and removing to and fro? And who hath brought up these? Behold, I was left alone; these, where had they been" (Isaiah 49:21)?

What a precise description of this touching moment! These words beautifully described travails and history of the Jewish People. They were forcefully (by sword) exiled from the Holy Land to the lands of their enemies. For twenty six hundred years they will have been harshly persecuted, banished from one country to another, their population immensely reduced by murders and plagues. They were never accepted by the nations, hated without reason, and targeted as the Biblical sacrificial escape-goat for all woes, misfortunes, and shortcomings. They lost contacts with the rest of their brothers and sisters of the Ten Tribes. The Second WWII and Holocaust significantly reduced them in numbers. But nothing could have destroyed their faith in the God of Israel. They were the only people of the Twelve Tribes of Israel who upheld the Laws of God and lived by His Torah. As a result of their faithfulness and unparallel misery and humiliation, their God will restore them (first) to the Promised Land. He will reunite the long-suffering Jewish People with the rest of the Tribes, and redeem the whole House of Israel. That is what the Prophet Isaiah was writing about in Chapter 49, verse 21.

Another significant proof of the restoration of the Jewish People to the Promised Land is the Book of Zephaniah, who lived in the time of Josiah, king of Judah (640-609b.c). His prophecies aimed for "the great Day of the Lord," in the latter years.

"And the sea cost shall be for the remnants of Judah; . . . for the Lord their God shall visit them, and turn away their captivity" (Zephaniah 2:7). This prophecy refers to the Jewish people only, not the Israelites. God will have mercy on them and settle their remnants (what a precise definition!), in the aftermath of the Holocaust and WWII, (these were the marks of the end of the Exile for Judah), on the sea cost of Canaan, exactly the part of territory the UN allotted to the Jews in its decision in 1947 to partition Palestine. On May 14, 1948, the prophecy of Zephaniah became a reality with the creation of the state of Israel in one day.

The Prophet Hosea in 1:7 confirms: "But I will have mercy upon the house of Judah, and will save them by the Lord their God, and will not save them by bow, nor by sword, nor by battle, by horses, nor by horsemen."

In Joel 3:1, 2 God continues to explain that before the final redemption and reunification of the two houses of Jacob, first He will return the captivity of Judah: "For, behold, in those days, and in that time, when I shall bring again the captivity of Judah and Jerusalem"(Verse 1).

On quite a few occasions Scripture has indicated that Judah would be the first among the house of Jacob to immigrate to the Promise Land, because they have a task to perform—to prepare the Land for a massive return of hundreds of millions of Israelites, their brothers and sisters from the 'Lost' Ten Tribes of Israel. They have to organize the State; to cultivate the land to produce enough bread, vegetables and fruits; they have to create a Western style economy; build communications and infrastructure; hospitals schools, universities; they have to maintain an Army to protect their freedom and security—the Jewish people have to do everything possible to accommodate the return of the rest of the House of Israel.

This is a monumental task God has imposed on Judah and Israelis together with the Jews of Diaspora and the awakening Ten Tribes of Israel will act exactly the way God has outlined it in His prophetic Word.

"Also, O Judah, He hath set a harvest for thee, when I return the captivity of My people" (Hosea 6:11).

He will punish the nations for all evil they brought upon "My people and My heritage Israel" (verse 2). And again and again God speaks of Judah only, not Israel: "The children also of Judah and the children of Jerusalem have ye sold unto the Grecians, that ye might remove them far from their border. Behold, I will raise them out of the place whither ye have sold them, and will return your recompense upon your own head" (Verses 6, 7).

The prophecies of Zechariah 12 and 14 have not been fulfilled yet either. They are future events. The presence of the Jews and their state in the land of Israel and in Jerusalem is a mandatory condition, in order to meet requirements of God's Plan. If Judah would not be living in the land of Israel before the future siege of Jerusalem by the heathen nations of the world, Zechariah's prophecies could have never been fulfilled. As we see, there are many Scriptural proofs of Judah living in the Holy Land before the final redemption and advent of the Messiah.

In 1949, just before the first elections to the Knesset, more than two hundred rabbis from all over Israel, who represented all religious groups and parties, signed an announcement, which began with these words: "We thank Hashem that we have been privileged, through His great mercy and kindness, to see the first buds of the beginning of redemption, with the establishment of the State of Israel."

The wars, modern Israelis have currently fought, according to the opinion of the Gemara in Megillah (17b), are "the wars of the beginning of the Redemption".

In many synagogues the special prayer-blessing has been recited for the State of Israel: "Our Father in heaven, the rock of Israel and its Redeemer, bless the State of Israel, the beginning of the sprouting of our Redemption."

God promised to Judah: "And thou, O tower of the flock, the strong hold of the daughter of Zion, unto thee shall it come, even the first dominion; the kingdom shall come to the daughter of Jerusalem" (Micah 4:8).

Here again God reaffirms that Judah will reestablish the old kingdom of David, which is the modern state of Israel with its capital in Jerusalem.

The Return of the Jews to the Promised Land in 1948 with the help of the UN was the first stage of the redemption, and was predicted by the Prophets and our Sages. The Ramban, R. Kalischer, and R. Kimchi (Radak) explained that before the final redemption, there will be a preliminary Jewish immigration to the land of Israel with the permission of the gentile nations.

The restoration of the exiles, the return of the Twelve Tribes to the Promised Land is a foundational corner stone of Messianic Judaism.

The Final Stage of Redemption. Will Israel repent on its own or it will be forced to repent by God or His Messiah?

The final stage of redemption does require national repentance and spiritual belief in the God of Israel (Isaiah 59:20; Jeremiah 29:12-13; Hosea 3:5; Deuteronomy 31:2).

There is another opinion of Rambam (Maimonides) that the Messiah will bring the Jews to repent, which is his task. The Ramban (Nachmanaides) on the other hand, said in his "Book of Redemption" that it is pertinent that at the time of their exile Israel will be sinning and transgressing, but even so, it was prophesied, "The punishment of your iniquity is finished daughter of Zion; He will no more carry you away into captivity" (Lamentations 4:22). This prophecy was meant that the length of the exile was predetermined, and God will redeem Israel unconditionally, regardless whether they repented or not, when the appointed time arrives.

R. Johanan said that "The son of David will come only in a generation that is either altogether righteous or altogether wicked."

It makes no big difference how they repent, by themselves or through the Messiah, but, as Rabbi Eliezer said, "If Israel repents, they will be redeemed, if not, they will not be redeemed" (Babylonian Talmud, Sanhedrin 97b). World redemption depends on redemption of the house of Israel. God has reaffirmed the future redemption of His people:

"At the same time, saith the Lord, will I be the God of all the families of Israel, and they shall be My people" (Jeremiah 31:1).

There are some theologians who teach that it is the task of the Messiah, ben Joseph or ben David, somehow, (some suggest forcefully, the others—by special qualities of his charismatic personality), to restore the Israelite nations to the God of Israel and make them be obedient to His Laws.

The others (Rabbi Eliezer ben Hyrcanus, Sanhedrin Chapter 11) say that the Ten Tribes would return based on the prophecy of Ezekiel 20:33,

"As I live, says the Lord God, surely with a mighty hand and with outstretched arm, and with fury poured out, will I be King over you."

These words were understood as if to say that the Almighty, in His time, will force the Israelites to repent and return.

We cannot agree with these ideas. The Ten Tribes in exile with the help of Judah and the Prophet Eliyahu, (Malachi 4:5-6), will find the way to reject sin, to repent of their idolatries, depart of evil and do good. They will learn to do righteousness and justice.

The God of Israel will turn His face to His repented children and send them the Messiah who will bring them home to the Promised Land. Contrary to the opinion of those scholars, the Messiah comes not to remove sin from the House of Israel; he will come when they already have rejected sin and proved themselves worthy for his coming. And because of it (their repentance and acceptance of the God of Israel), the Messiah might come much earlier than the appointed time.

It is true that Bible says that God first will send the Prophet Eliyahu to prepare the Israelite People for the coming of the Messiah. But it is not necessary to be that way. There is a Talmudic opinion saying that "If we will listen to God's voice, if we will prepare ourselves on our own, then Moshiach will be able to come 'today', immediately, without the Prophet Eliyahu having to come first to prepare us" (Siftei Tzadikim b'Haalotcha).

The Jewish Sages teach that every generation in which the Temple is not rebuilt is as wicked as the generation in which it was destroyed; for, had we been worthy, the temple would have been rebuilt in our days.

Many great Sages, including Rambam (Maimonides), were of the opinion that repentance must precede redemption, the coming of the Messiah. R. Eliezer and R. Yehoshua in Sanhedrin 97b debated whether the earlier stages of redemption require repentance. Both of them agree, however, that the final stage of redemption, when the Messiah will be revealed, certainly requires repentance. R. Yehudah in Yalkut Shimoni (2:595) categorically declares that repentance absolutely must precede redemption and **if Israel does not repent, it will not be redeemed.**

Two closest of R. Akiva's disciples, R. Simeon ben Yohai and R. Meir were of the same opinion, contrary to their teacher, that the Ten Tribes will repent and return to God of Israel in the Messianic Times (Sanhedrin 110b).

R. Teichtal in his work "Em Ha-Banim Semeichah" taught that the initial return of the Jewish People to the Promised Land does not require repentance and perfect faith. Then the prophet Eliyahu will come and lead the Israelites to repentance. The task of Eliyahu is: "he shall turn the heart of the fathers to the children, and the heart of the children to their fathers" (Malachi 4:5-6). When the Messiah comes, he will find all Israel repented, and he will proceed with the final reunification, ingathering, and redemption.

It is not the Almighty either who will enforce Israel to repent and return; rather they will do it on their own with the essential help of the prophet Eliyahu and the Jewish People, the keepers of God's Laws.

"Therefore, O house of Israel, I will judge you, each one according to his ways, declare the Sovereign LORD. Repent! Turn away from all your offenses; then sin will not be your downfall. Rid yourselves of all the offenses you have committed, and get a new heart and a new spirit. Why will you die, O house of Israel (Ezekiel 18:30-31)?

What we see from these words is that God does not enforce Israel to stop sinning although the Almighty could do anything He desires. It is His Divine Plan that Israel freely chose not to sin and come back to their loving Father—the God of Israel.

"Finally, they cried out to the LORD for help, saying, "We have sinned against you because we have abandoned you as our God and have served the images of Baal" (Judges 10:10).

"I will give them a heart to know me, that I am the LORD. They will be My people, and I will be their God, **for they will return to Me with all their heart**" (Jeremiah 24:7).

Acceptance of their guilt, rejection of sin and repentance—is all that God requires from His children Israel:

"The people of Israel said to the LORD, "We have sinned. Do to us whatever you think is right. But please rescue us today! Then they got rid of the foreign gods among them and served the LORD. And He could bear Israel's misery no longer" (Judges 10:15-16).

Our opinion is supported by the Scripture:

"And the Redeemer will come to Zion, to those in Jacob who turn from transgression, says the Lord" (Isaiah 59:20).

The other version of the same verse might be translated as, **"A Mashiach will come to Zion, and to those of Jacob who repent of willful sin."**

Another note worthy to mention here is that the Hebrew word Mashiach does not mean 'savior' or 'redeemer' as translated in English language everywhere. It simply means 'the anointed one'. The idea of innocent human or divine or semi-divine being sacrificing himself in order to save humanity from the consequences of Adam' sin is purely Christian and has no foundation in Judaism.

'Turn from transgression' has the same meaning as repent and reject sin. We have to reiterate once more that it is not God or the Messiah who stop 'those in Jacob' from sinning; the Israelites themselves 'turn from transgression' with the help of the Jewish People and the Prophet Eliyahu.

"For there shall be a day, that the watchmen upon the mount Ephraim shall cry: 'Arise you, and let us go up to Zion unto the Lord our God" (Jeremiah 31:6).

"I have blotted out, as a thick cloud, your transgressions, and, as a cloud, your sins: return unto me; for I have redeemed you" (Isaiah 44:22).

The People of Israel, the Ten Tribes, eventually will turn to their God,

"They will come and shout for joy on the heights of Zion; they will rejoice in the bounty of the LORD—the grain, the new wine and the oil, the young of the flocks and herds. They will be like a well-watered garden, and they will sorrow no more" (Jeremiah 31:12).

They will come together with the remnants of the Jewish People in the Diaspora, "In those days, at that time," declares the LORD, "the people of Israel and the people of Judah together will go in tears to seek the LORD their God" (Jeremiah 50:4).

If these passages are not speaking of the Ten Tribes of Israel and their future reunification with the Jewish People and ingathering in the Promised Land in the time of Mashiach, then what else are they speaking about?!

There are quite a few verses in the Hebrew Bible confirming what we just have said.

"When all these blessings and courses I have set before you come on you and you take them to heart wherever the Lord your God disperses you among the nations, and **when you and your children return to the Lord your God and obey Him with all your heart and with all your soul,** then the Lord your God will restore your fortunes and have compassion on you and gather you again from all the nations where He scattered you" (Deut.30:1-3).

"Incline your ear, and come unto me; hear and your soul shall live. Seek the LORD while he may be found; call on him while he is near" (Isaiah 55:3, 6).

"Return, you backsliding children, and I will heal your backslidings. Indeed we do come to You, For You are the LORD our God" (Jeremiah 3:22).

"I have no pleasure in the death of the wicked; but that the wicked turn from his way and live: turn you, turn you from your wicked ways; for why will you die, O house of Israel" (Ezekiel 33:11)?

Here we go. Israel has to repent on its own, out of love for their Creator!

'When you and your children return to the Lord and obey Him with all your heart and soul', 'come unto Me', 'return, you backsliding children',—all these words plainly imply a voluntary inner spiritual transformation of the Israelites from 'being Christians' to their Hebrew identity which undeniably means repentance and acceptance of the God of Israel and His Divine Laws.

"Come, and let us return to the Lord" (Hosea 6:1).

"Then I will give them a heart to know Me, that I am the LORD; and they shall be My people, and I will be their God, for they shall return to Me with their whole heart" (Jeremiah 24:7).

Where do we see in these passages that God forces the Israelites to repent? Quite the opposite, He asks them, He supplicates and pleads with them to return to Him; as a loving father, He even begs the children of Israel to repent and return to "the Lord your God, for He is graceful and merciful, slow to anger and of great kindness. Turn to Me with all your heart, with fasting, with weeping and with mourning" (Joel 2:12-13).

Redemption of the Israelites will follow by redemption of the whole world. The Ingathering of all the house of Israel is not a singular event, it cannot happen at once, and it is not spiritual at the beginning. As the dispersions of the Israelites and the Jews had happened in a few stages throughout the history: 741b.c.-721b.c., 597 b.c.-586 b.c., 70 a.c. and 135 a.c; the same way will the regathering and restoration of the Twelve Tribes be in a few stages, the first having been accomplished with the creation of the State of Israel in 1948.

Some theologians have compared this process with the analogy of the prophet Ezekiel's 'Valley of dry bones' (37:1-14). These bones are all the House of Israel, and they represent the two stages of Return. At the beginning, before the bones become alive, sinews cover the bones, then flesh, then skin, and finally, the breath of life. In other words, the first physical restoration of the Jews to the Land in unbelief will be followed by the second spiritual ingathering of the rest of the House of Jacob to the Lord in belief.

Rabbi Yehoshua, who lived in the first half of the third century and was called "Rabbi of the Talmud," and R. Kalischer, who lived many centuries later, (1795-1874), had taught that the initial stages of redemption do not require repentance. The final redemption, however, does require national repentance. R. Kalischer and R. Alkalai (1795-1874) viewed the development of rising nationalism (Zionism) among the Jewish people as one of the first stages in the process of redemption, which not require repentance. In their opinion, these actions of the Jewish people would accelerate the coming of the Messiah. Both of them had promoted Jewish nationalism, settlement of the Eretz Israel and the establishment there of agricultural communities. They felt that awakening Jewish nationalism with the help of nations (kings, Governments) to gather the scattered of Israel to the Holy Land will bring about the beginning of the Redemption process, which in turn would hasten the coming of the Messiah.

One more point of great importance is that all the house of Jacob, which, of course, includes Judah and Israel, will not know their God, until future events predicted by the Ezekiel 38-39 and Zechariah 12-14 come to pass. It means that the majority of the Jewish people do not know God today; neither do the rest of the Lost Ten Tribes of Israel. Here is the proof of it:

"Israel shall know that I am the Lord their God from **that day and forward**" (Ezekiel 39:22). Chronologically 'that day' will start after the armies of Gog will have been defeated.

The final reunification will also take place after the War of Gog and Magog: "Therefore thus saith the Lord God; now will I bring again the captivity of Jacob, and have mercy upon the **whole** house of Israel" (Ezekiel 39:25).

Obviously, all these events have to occur before the advent of the Messiah and the final redemption, as God had prophesied. True Zionism is based on Torah and justified by it! Here is another blow to the 'Torah Jews against Zionism'. God is not a human. He cannot make the false promises and mistaken statements! The Naturei Karta and Co. does. It is the will of God to have Jewish nation in the Promised Land prior to the Final Redemption and the Messianic Age!

CHAPTER III:
JEWISH UNITY 1. A BIT OF HISTORY

State of Jewish Unity during the Roman-Jewish War 66-70 a.c.

Jewish unity—a wishful thing. The Great Jewish Revolt of 66-70 a.c. against the Roman Empire. In the North, the Zealots under the leadership of John of Giscala and Simon Bar Giora at the battle of Beth Horon defeated the forces of Cestius Gallus, the legate of Syria.

The Romans regrouped. General Vespasian, appointed by Emperor Nero instead of Gallus, concentrated 60,000 troops, and successfully crushed the Jewish resistance in Galilee, Caesarea and the coast lands.

John of Giscala and Simon Bar Giora and their forces managed to escape to Jerusalem, the center of rebellion. John and Simon, both the popular Zealot leaders of the Revolt, desperately started fighting each other for the ruler ship of Jerusalem. Jerusalem's authorities and the fanatical Sikarii of Eleazar ben Simon took a part in this battle. Brutal civil war erupted as a result, which later proved to be disastrous. The rivals were not only trying to destroy each other,—they also burned their grain supplies to starve their opponents into submission. 69a.c. was a Sabbatical year, with less grain available, and the city was under the siege by the time the harvest began. The citizens of Jerusalem were terrorized by the Zealots and Sikarii. Many starved to death. Many tried to run away but were caught by the Romans and crucified around the city, five hundred a day.

To show how divisions and hatreds work, we shall take as an example one sad episode from the Zealot Temple Siege in 68a.c.

While Simon ben Giora and his soldiers were stationed outside the city walls, harassing the people, John of Giscala, within Jerusalem, had overthrown lawful authority and set himself up as a despotic ruler. He established his headquarters in the Temple. The former High Priest Ananus ben Ananus raised the citizens of Jerusalem against the Zealots who were in control of the Temple. John of Giscala and his comrades asked the Edomites for assistance. When they arrived, the Zealots opened the gate of Jerusalem to them, and the Edomites slaughtered ben Anan's forces, killing him as well.

Just before the Passover in 70 a.c. Titus began the siege of Jerusalem. At that time all the Jewish factions had realized the necessity of joining forces. They met the Romans with fierce resistance. There were no fewer than 600,000 men and women of every age engaged in the armed struggle, preferring death to a life that involved the idol worship and the expulsion from their country. Unfortunately, it was too late. The Romans succeeded. The Great Jewish Revolt was defeated. The Temple was destroyed. 1,100,000 Jews were killed during the siege, 97,000 were captured and sold to slavery, and many others fled to areas around the Mediterranean.

These events in detailed account come to us from the Jewish-Roman historian Josephus Flavius, former Jewish commander of Galilee, who wrote two books, "The Jewish War" and "Jewish Antiquities".

State of Jewish Unity in the Times of the Maccabees to the Time of the Bar Kokhba Revolt 132-135 A.C.

Perhaps in earlier period of history the Jewish nation had enjoyed peace and unity? Let us take a look at the time of the Maccabees. After the death of Alexander the Great (356-323 b.c.) and the 40 years of war between 'The Successors', his Empire broke up into four stable power blocks, the Seleucid Empire in the east being one of them. In 198 b.c. Antiochus III defeated the Egyptians and included Judea in his Empire. A process of Hellenization, started by Alexander, had intensified when Antiochus IV Epiphanes (215-146 b.c.) became ruler of the Seleucid Empire in 175 b.c. He decided to force the Jews to abandon their monotheism for the Greeks' paganism. In 167 b.c. Jews were forbidden to perform sacrifice. The Sabbaths and feasts were banned. The Holy Temple was defiled by erecting the Olympian Zeus on the altar, allowing the sacrifice of pigs, and opening the shrine to non-Jews. The possession of Jewish scriptures or performing circumcision was punishable by death.

Jews refused to abandon the religion of their fathers and worship pagan Greek gods. Mattathias the Hasmonean, a Priest from Modiin, and his five sons, sparked the Jewish revolt against the Seleucid Empire. Many Hellenistic Jews were killed by the followers of the Maccabees alongside with Greeks. After the victory, the Maccabees ritually cleansed the Temple and re-established traditional Jewish worship there and installed Jonathan Maccabee as a High Priest. The Jewish festival of Hanukkah celebrates the re-dedication of the Temple following Judah Maccabee's victory over the Seleucids. After almost 500 years of subjugation, in 142 b.c. Judea became free and independent again.

But tensions and rivalry among the Jewish factions, mainly Sadducees and Pharisees, had developed and threatened the unity of the kingdom. A bone of contention was the issue of the office of High Priest. The Hasmoneans had usurped not only the throne of Judah, but also the authority of High Priest. By Jewish tradition, the priesthood comes from the descendants of Aaron and the tribe of Levi.

During the reign of Alexander Jannaeus (103 b.c.-76 b.c.), the King of Judea and the High Priest, internal divisions had reached their apogee. His marriage to his brother's widow, which was forbidden by the Torah, added more oil to the fire. On one occasion, Jannaeus purposely incited the crowd to riot at the Temple against him, and soldiers at his command slew 6,000 people. This was the beginning of the Judean Civil War. The rebels, supported by the Pharisees, wanted to overthrow the bloody Hasmonean king and end Hasmonean Priesthood. The war lasted six years and took 50,000 Judeans lives.

Jannaeus succeeded in this war. Supported by Sadducees, he decided to take revenge from the rebels. In Jerusalem he crucified 800 Judeans and had the throats of the rebels' wives and children cut before their eyes while he was eating and drinking with his concubines.

These were the fruits of division and hatred!

During the period of the second century b.c. till the destruction of the Temple in 70 a.c. and dispersion in 135 a.c., the Jewish nation was bitterly divided on many rival factions. According to Josephus, there were the Sadducees, the priestly party, associated with the aristocratic groups of the Hasmonean "priests-kings." They rejected the Oral Torah (Talmud), and accepted only the written Torah, the five books of Moses which they interpreted literally. They didn't believe in the existence of an afterlife, resurrection of the dead, immortality of the soul. Basically, their priority was not religion but politics. They did not reject Judaism; they just could not accept Rabbinical Judaism the equivalent of what later became the Talmud.

Bitterly opposed to them were the Pharisees, scribes and sages, who at various times acted as a political party, a social movement, a school of Jewish thought. Conflicts between these two groups reflected many aspects of social and religious live: between wealthy and poor; Hellenization and Judaism; importance of the Temple's ritual versus importance of the Oral Law; recognition of only the written Torah versus additional interpretations of Tanakh by Rabbinical authorities. An untold toll of Jewish lives resulted from this rivalry. It is worth mentioning that the Sadducees, having being close associated with the Temple in Jerusalem, after its destruction in 70 a.c., vanished from history. Their opponents, the Pharisees, are the progenitors of today mainstream Rabbinical Judaism.

The Essenes, another Jewish religious group, flourished from the second century b.c. to the first century a.c. Philo of Alexandria (20 b.c.-54 a.c.), a Jewish philosopher, in his works noted that Essenes were very religious; loved God, esteemed honesty, piety, morality, and freedom. They didn't get married and lived in communal residence, sharing money, properties, food and clothing. Much of their time they spent studying Scriptures and Law according to philosophical and allegorical interpretations. They removed themselves from society, possessed no slaves, and rejected the use of weapons or participation in commerce. Josephus recorded that Essenes lived in large numbers throughout Judea in various cities, dedicated to asceticism, voluntary poverty, peace and abstinence from worldly pleasures. In their eschatological belief, the Essenes viewed themselves as the last generation before the coming of a long anticipated Teacher of Righteousness and Messiah. In 1947, in a cave near the Dead Sea, two Bedouin shepherds found the Dead Sea Scrolls, commonly believed to be Essenes Literature.

There was another group called the Zealots. It was a political party of freedom fighters in the first century a.c. who tried to raise the people of Judea in rebellion against the Romans and liberate themselves by force of arms. They also were defenders of the Law. The first Zealot in the Bible was Levi, the son of Jacob, who avenged the crime perpetrated upon his sister Dinah by killing the men of Shechem (Genesis 34:26). Another example is Phinehas, the son of Eleazar, the son of Aaron the priest, who killed Zimri the son of Salu for sexual intercourse with a Syrian woman (Numbers 25:11-14). Nobody tried to kill King Solomon for having 700 wives and 300 concubines from all countries of the world!

But the best example for 'Zeal for the Law' is Mattathias, who slew a Jew who was offering sacrifice to an idol. He was reported to have shouted, "Whosoever is zealous of the Law, and maintains the covenant, let him follow me!" That is how the Maccabees started their rebellion against the Seleucid Empire. The Hellenistic Sadducees and Jewish idolaters were targets of priority for the Zealots.

The Sicarii ("dagger-men") were a religious-political extremist group. They had branched out from the Zealots. They wanted to liberate Judea from Roman dominion and establish an independent theocratic state. They originated, as Josephus point out, in 6 a.c. when Judah of Galilee, their teacher and leader, led this religious sect in rebellion against the Romans. Judah was killed and his followers were scattered. Some 50 years later the Sicarii reappeared under Menachem, grandson of Judah. They fought not only against the Romans, but also against the Jewish high priesthood, which they saw as collaborators with the Romans. They also were against the Sadducees, Herodians, wealthy elite and idol worshippers. Terrorist acts, kidnapping and assassinations were their usual tactics. In the Jewish Revolt (66-70 a.c.) the Sicarii committed a series of atrocities in order to force the Jews to go to war. In Jerusalem, Menachem attempted to take over authority of the entire rebellion, and crowned himself in the Temple as the messiah-king. Most of the Jews were outraged, and Eleazar, the captain of the Temple guards, attacked and defeated the followers of Menachem who was captured, tortured, and executed. After the fall of Jerusalem and destruction of the Temple by Titus, about 900 Sicarii had managed to escape to the fortress of Masada, where they committed mass suicide in 73 a.c., preferring death rather than to submit to the Romans.

It was a unique time in Jewish history. The heroic epoch of the Maccabees, the Roman conquest, Jewish-Roman wars, destruction of the Second Temple, Bar Kokhba Revolt, Exile. The Jewish nation was deeply divided. Each party and sect had its own vision on political perspectives, eschatology and the Messiah. No matter how you look at it, religion played the most crucial part in these events of Judea's history. There was no peace, no unity, and no brotherly love among the Jewish People. Causeless hatred, evil speeches, jealousy, gossip and slander; religious terrorism of the Zealots and Sicarii, their fanaticism and intolerance, shielded by the name of God, were the main reasons contributing to destruction of the Second Temple and Jerusalem, sealing the fate of the Jewish nation. This is exactly what the sages teach: exile was caused by unwarranted hatred and the love of money.

"Why was the first Temple destroyed? Because of the three sins of which the Jews were guilty: Idolatry, sexual indiscretions and murder. The second Temple—when the Jews were involved in Torah, mitzvahs and acts of kindness—why was it destroyed? Because the Jews were guilty of harboring baseless hatred towards each other" (Yoma 9b)!

The Talmud calls the sins of hatred, quarrels, gossip and fighting 'unknown sins', because people who are guilty of them, do not realize that they are at fault and depict themselves as victims always blaming other parties as the abusers and hate mongers.

The Essenes were very religious too, but they chose no violence and no radical extremism in order to achieve their eschatological expectations. Tolerance, brotherly love, peace and deep faith in God of Israel were the principles of their daily life.

"That which is hateful to you, do not do to your fellow. This is the whole Torah." These words belong to the famous Jewish religious leader Hillel the Eldest (110 b.c.-10 a.c.). Born in Babylon, at the age of forty he moved to Jerusalem, where he lived in the time of King Herod. Gentle and patient, Hillel loved his fellow men, pursued peace and tolerance.

"Make the study of the Torah your chief occupation; speak little, but accomplish much; and receive every man with a friendly countenance", said Shammai (50b.c.-30c.e.), the most eminent contemporary and the Halakhic opponent of Hillel. He was a Jewish sage, an important figure in Judaism's core work of rabbinical literature, the Mishnah.

These men had organized two schools of thought, the Academy of Hillel and the Academy of Shammai. Each school assumed the personal characteristics of its founders, with Hillel representing the ideals of kindness, love, and conciliation; and Shammai, their opposites. Each of them served as a President of the Sanhedrin.

Despite many significant differences, controversies, and bitter fights over matters of Jewish Law, they got along pretty well, displaying love, friendship, and tolerance toward one another. The two groups even intermarried. Both schools greatly contributed to Halakha and Rabbinical Judaism.

CHAPTER IV:
JEWISH UNITY 2. SATMAR AND NETUREI KARTA

State of Jewish Unity in Modern Times

We are not finished with Jewish unity yet. Today Judaism is the oldest monotheistic religion with historical continuity lasting more than 3000 years. It is still bitterly divided into many rival parties, sects, and movements. Unity is a wishful thing. Bitter lessons of the past have not been learned.

Present Jewish religious movements basically consist of three large groups: Orthodox Judaism, Conservative Judaism and Reform Judaism. This division is based on interpretations and the way of observance of Jewish Law and acceptance of modernity.

All Jewish people are divided into two main groups: The Ashkenazis represent Jews from Central and Eastern Europe, namely from Russia, Poland and Germany. Sephardic Jews hail from Mediterranean countries, mainly from Spain and Portugal and also from North Africa, the Far East and Southern Europe. Their theology and basic Jewish practice are the same. They differ only in a number of ritual and cultural details.

In the State of Israel all of these religious movements of Diaspora Jewry exist, but Israelis classify themselves a little bit differently as "secular'," traditional" and "religious", or "Haredi".

There is no central religious authority in Judaism today to enforce the Jewish Law, as there was in history with special courts, so the practice of Judaism is mostly voluntary.

Haredi Judaism (Ultra-Orthodoxy) is a very conservative movement. Their lives are occupied by study, prayer and meticulous religious observance. According to them, Jews who do not keep the laws of Shabbat, the holidays, family purity, and kashrut are considered non-religious.

From Haredi Judaism springs Lubavitch Judaism with more liberal views on modernity; Hasidic Judaism is rooted in the Kabbalah, as interpreted by Rebbe Israel Ba'al Shem Tov.

There are also other movements such as Reconstructionist Judaism, Jewish Renewal, Humanistic Judaism . . . We try to chase the number of Christian denominations.

Satmar and Neturei Karta

Actually, this chapter began with a heading about another two Jewish organizations that branched out of Haredi Judaism. They call themselves Satmar Hasidim and Neturei Karta, the latter being the most radical group of Orthodox Jewry.

Satmar is a Hasidic movement of Hungarian and Romanian Jews. Their leader was Grand Rebbe Yoel Teitelbaum (1887-1979), who refined and officially formulated a vehement position against Zionism and the State of Israel. The followers are numbered close to 130,000 members, which makes Satmar one of the biggest and most influential Hasidic movements in existence today.

The Satmar group is a deeply divided by a 'family feud' on the issue of leadership between two brothers, Rabbi Aaron and Rabbi Zalman, the sons of R. Teitelbaum. Their 'cold war' has involved rabbinical courts, Beitei Din, litigation in the New York State Supreme Court, an Appeal Court in Brooklyn, and numerous disputes concerning the will of the previous Rabbi. Up until today, there is no official 'peace treaty' or any sort of reconciliation between the two sides and two brothers.

Neturei Karta (Guardians of the City) is not of Hasidic origin. They descend from Hungarian and Lithuanian Haredi Jews. The movement was formally formed in Jerusalem in 1938. It numbers approximately 5,000 from which around 140 are involved in anti-Israel activities. They also live in New York, London and in various cities of North America. One of the founders and the leaders of the fiercely anti-Zionist Neturei Karta was Haredi Rabbi Amram Blau (1894-1974). There are two branches of Neturei Karta nowadays: A largest and more moderate faction led by Rabbi Katzenellenbogen, and a smaller, but more radical faction led by Rabbi Hirsch in Jerusalem and by Rabbi Weiss and Rabbi Beck in New York.

Both groups are united in their ideological opposition to the Zionism and State of Israel, but their backgrounds are so significantly different that they cannot affiliate with one another.

They are two separate movements which have had disagreements.

An Initial Introductory Outline to the Three Oaths.
The Position of the 'True Torah Jews' towards the Zionists and their State of Israel

Basically, both movements have chosen the same theological arguments to fight against Zionists, namely the Three Oaths, mentioned in the Talmud (Ketubot 111a), based on a passage from the Song of Songs in the Bible. These Three Oaths are:

-Not to ascend to the Holy Land as a group using force;

-Not to rebel against the governments of countries in which we live;

-The Nations of the World should not excessively persecute the Jews in exile.

Since we have designated the Three Oaths as the subject of a separate chapter further on (Chapter VII, 'The Three Oats and Song of Songs'), we are not going to fully discuss it here. To explain it simply, what the anti-Zionists are saying is: It is forbidden by the Torah for the Jewish people to end the Exile, to rebel against the nations, to immigrate to the Holy Land by force en masse and to establish there a political State, until God decides the right time for these actions and sends the Messiah.

All these 'prohibitory proofs' were taken from the one and only source—the Three Oaths of Canticles (Song of Solomon), and they are highly obscure and allegorical in nature.

In their zeal against the Zionists, Naturei Karta not only denounces Israel's existence, but traditionally embraces its enemies.

During the Israeli war for independence, when on May 15, 1948, just one day after the creation of the state of Israel, Arab armies of Jordan, Egypt, Syria, Iraq, Lebanon and Saudi Arabia invaded the newly-born state, and Jews heroically fought against significantly larger Arab forces, sacrificing their lives, two rabbis of Jerusalem went out with a white flag to the Jordanian army, "showing that the true Jewish people were surrendering to them." The Zionists saw this act of treachery and fired at them. "Thank God, they missed",—the event is proudly described by Torah Jews against Zionism. Its activists organize protests and demonstrations in Jerusalem, in Gaza and the West Bank, in New York, Montreal and London. They portrait themselves as devoted Jewish champions for 'World Peace' and 'Universal Justice'. They have lobbied the USA government to use 'tough love' sanctions against Israel. They enjoy using the Internet, TV, interviews and all kinds of publicity to advocate their cause. They remind us of Jewish communists who applauded Stalin's executions of fellow Jews in the Soviet Union.

When the Palestinian Authority with Yassir Arafat formed a government, Rabbi Moshe Hirsch (1923-2010) endorsed it as a rightful ruler over the Land of Israel, including the modern-day state of Israel. He served in the Arafat government as Minister for Jewish Affairs, for which he was paid by the Palestinian Authority.

Rabbi Moshe Ber Beck, leader of Naturei Karta in the USA, forbids its members to live or even visit Israel, benefit from it or support it in any kind, including paying sale taxes. Even under the threat of torture or death, one can not violate these prohibitions. The Rabbi himself emigrated from Israel in 1973 and has no wish to come back. These teachings and actions are in contradiction to the Talmud and our Sages:

"In your own land, you may dwell in safety, outside your land there is no safety for you" (The Yalkut on Leviticus 25:18). "Anyone, who has the ability to come to Eretz Yisroel and does not, will have to account for his failure in the future world" (Rabbi Yosef Chaim Sonnenfeld).

"Jews who dwell outside the Land of Israel are idol worshippers in purity" (Talmud, Avoda Zara 8).

"In the Diaspora, whoever increases its settlement (by establishing a home, business, etc) adds to the destruction of the worship of God. But in the Land of Israel this same work is considered a mitzvah since it settles the Land" (The Chatam Sofer).

Torah Jews against Zionism have taken one passage from the Talmud (Ketubot 111a) and use it over and over again as a basic proof of their theological position. While there are dozens of Talmudic and Bible passages, speaking against their teaching, they just ignore them. They call everyone who happens to disagree with them, 'heretics' and 'Zionists', considering that only they understand the Scriptures and the ways of God. Rabbi Yisroel Dovid Weiss and some members of Naturei Karta in 2006 attended the International conference of Holocaust deniers in Tehran, where they embraced their friend, anti Zionist Jewish hater, president of Iran Mahmoud Ahmadinejad.

What do Neturei Karta and people like Arafat, Farrakhan, Duke, Nasrallah and Ahmadinejad have in common? Their common goal is to get rid of the Zionists and the State of Israel. Period. If the motives of NK are deeply rooted in religion, although they manipulated and ignore Scriptures in their way, the motives of the others are rooted in the anti-Zionism hatred, covered sometimes with politically correct anti-Semitism, where Jews and their State are demonized indiscriminately. They deny the right of the Jewish people to exist as a people because they are Jews. These individuals are pure racists.

Members of NK are often called self-hating Jews and anti-Semites. These labels are inappropriate. Being Orthodox Jews, they cannot be anti-Semite and self-hating Jews. Besides, by watching their live actions on videos and reading their views, it has not given an impression that they are suffered or depressed of being self-hated Jews. On contrary, they look proud and pleased with themselves as they are doing a superior God's work and justifiably called 'The True Torah Jews'. They, probably, not realize that while Jewish People are fighting for their survival, the "Torah Jews against Zionism' serve as a 'fifth column' that threatens the very survival of the State of Israel and Jews around the World. Their shameful behavior in the political sphere and especially collaboration with the sworn enemies of the Jewish people and the State of Israel rightfully deserved negative reactions of the vast majority of Orthodox Jewry:

"People should not in any way believe that NK is representative of Orthodox Jewry".

"A small sect of ultra-Orthodox, anti-Zionist rabbis, embracing Iranian president was 'horrific' and 'offensive'.

"It is deplorable, abhorrent and despicable that these people could associate themselves with this Hitler of our generation".

"Under no circumstances, should their garb and their calling themselves 'rabbis' deceive anyone. In fact, they are an insignificant group of unemployed parasites who represent nobody but themselves".

In a rare public statement, the Ultra-Orthodox congregation of Adass Israel Australia denounced the 'nefarious and totally irresponsible handful of Jewish charlatans who attended the recent Holocaust-denial conference of Jew—haters in Tehran': "We are disgusted and repelled by the treacherous and contemptible conduct this deranged and reviled group of misfits and desecraters of God's name, who in their boundless and obsessive craving for publicity habitually raise their ugly heads and besmirch the reputation and honor of all observant Jews."

Neturei Karta would not be so harshly condemned if they stopped using indecent political tactics, exaggerations and lies in the international press about Zionists and the State of Israel and, what is most important, if they would quit affiliation with enemies of the Jews.

41

Since NK try to portray themselves as righteous, religious Torah Jews, they ought to be kind, patient and loving individuals not only towards the Palestinians, Lebanese, Iranians and other 'oppressed' people, but firstly towards their brothers and sisters of the Jewish nation, to whom they belong. Hatred against the Zionists, the State of Israel and Israelis is not what the Torah teaches.

"Whosoever destroys a single soul of Israel, is guilty as though he had destroyed a complete world; and whosoever preserves a single soul of Israel, Scripture credit him as though he had saved a complete world" (Babylon Talmud, Tractate Sanhedrin 37a).

At a time when Jews all over the world face rising waves of anti-Semitism, when de-legitimization and destruction of Israel is a goal of the enemies of the Jewish state, it is more than disheartening to see Jews themselves adding to the vilification, embracing fanatical anti-Semites, and causing shame and pain to our people. This is especially distressing when it is done in the name of Judaism. There is no justification for this.

If you call yourself the True Torah Jews, we are speaking here of NK members, so live the Torah way, as majority of the Orthodox Jewry live: love your fellow man, do not do others that is hateful to you, be merciful and kind. That is what God wants to see in us. Our great Sages have shown examples of piety and righteousness: R. Hillel the Elder, R. Akiba, Baal Shem Tov, R. Schneur Zalman, R. Menachem Mendel Schneerson, and many, many more Tzaddiks.

Even if you think that you defend Torah against the Zionists, who, according to your opinion, violated the Three Oaths of Song of Songs by immigrating to the Promised Land and creating the State of Israel without permission of God, still your tactic of hate and intolerance towards your brothers and sisters, who happen to be members of the Zionist movement, and your collaboration with the evil enemies of the Jewish people, this attitude does not constitute the Torah way. On the contrary, these kinds of action are strongly condemned by the Torah and Judaism. Your anti-Zionist rhetoric is a stab in a back to the Israelis. It is a call for genocide of the most vulnerable part of the Jewish population, mostly refugees and their children. What service to the Jewish People can statements of the True Torah Jews, like this do: "We American Jews are thankful to be living under the trustworthy government of the United States of America and our honorable President Barack Obama and not under this traitor Netanyahu"?!

Rav Kook, one of the most celebrated and influential Rabbis of the 20th century, thought that the, "role of religious leaders is to help Zionists to find the spark of God in their souls, teach them Torah with love and kindness; in the end, they will understand that the laws of Torah are the key to true harmony, a light for the nations and bring salvation to the World."

Speaking of righteousness, Rav Kook said:

"The purely righteous do not complain of the dark, but increase the light; they do not complain of evil, but increase justice; they do not complain of heresy, but increase faith; they do not complain of ignorance, but increase wisdom."

In contrast to Rav Kook, the NK demands that all religious Jews, first and foremost Orthodox Jewry, must get out of the State of Israel, leave the state behind; do not participate in state affairs, do not support it, do not go there and do not live there. Let it self-destruct. If it becomes a danger for you—leave. The State will disintegrate itself from a "Jewish State" into a multinational melting pot. Let the Zionists face the wrath of God for violating the Three Oaths. In the beginning of their activities, the NK always maintained that the Zionists are primarily responsible for violating prohibitions against establishing a secular state while in exile. Now they go further saying that even if the State of Israel was entirely religious, it still violates the Three Oaths of Shir Ha Shirim, because all their actions are not approved by God.

Throughout history the God of Israel has used men of flesh and blood to fulfill His future Plans. Moses led the Israelites out of Egyptian slavery. Anointed king Cyrus freed Jews from Babylonian captivity. Theodor Herzl, Vladimir Jabotinsky and David Ben Gurion organized the Zionist Movement and created the State of Israel. The Zionists were agents in a Heavenly Plan to bring about spiritual Messianic Redemption to the People of Israel. The Jewish Scriptures are full of prophetic evidence, confirming that the establishing of the modern State of Israel in 1948 was in fulfillment of the Word of God, whether you like it or not!

God Predicts, Defends, and Blesses the state of Israel

Besides the questionable and highly obscure allegorical Three Oaths, Naturei Karta and Satmar lack solid Biblical proofs for their position. They just repeated say again and again that it is against the will of God to end the exile, to immigrate to the Promised Land, and build there a State of Israel. They cannot explain away the verses of the Bible which are predict, approve, and bless the creation of the State of Israel and the presence of the Jews in the Holy Land and in Jerusalem in order to fulfill the prophetic Word of God. Every Bible student knows that God promised to reunite and redeem all the House of Jacob in the End Time, when He will send the Messiah, son of David. But not many scholars know that prior to the final stage of redemption there was an ingathering of the Jewish remnants in the aftermath of the Holocaust and WWII to the Holy Land where the State of Israel had been created.

Our Biblical proofs are very easy to verify. Just take the Bible and look at the following verses:

Zephaniah 2:7; Zechariah 2:12, chapters 12 and 14; Isaiah 49:21; 56:8; 66:8; Hosea 1:7; 6:11; Micah 4:8; Joel 3:1,2, 6,7.

Commentaries to these verses were given in Chapter I. To show how effective our proofs, we may linger over the verse of Zechariah 12:2.

"Behold, I will make Jerusalem a cup of trembling unto all the people round about, when they shall be in the siege both against Judah and against Jerusalem." The prophet confirms the fact that "all the people of the earth be gathered against Jerusalem." (Zech.12:3) It is clear that this prophecy is a future event. It is also clear that the house of Judah, the Jews, must live in the Holy Land in order to fulfill the prophecy of Zechariah. The house of Israel, the "Lost" Ten Tribes, was not mentioned here, because the timing of this prophecy is before the redemption and reunification of both houses of Judah and Israel. The Jews and their State will already be in the Land of Israel, exactly as the prophecy predicted. The People of Israel (the Ten Tribes) will still be in exile, waiting for their awakening and coming of the Messiah, son of Joseph who will bring the whole House of Jacob to the Holy Land.

Satmar and the Neturei Karta often have criticized the Zionists for causing much anti-Semitism and enmity amongst the gentile nations of the world towards the Jews and their state.

What do you think? Will the nations of the world assemble their armies in the deadly siege against Judah-of-the-Israelis and Jerusalem in the last days because of love, or hate?! The Israelis-Arabs conflict in the Middle East surely has involved all the nations of the world. And if God had not allowed this situation, how would the prophecies of Zechariah have been fulfilled? It is not wise at all go against God and His Word! The Almighty knows what He is doing, and the Zionists and the State of Israel are important participants in His prophetic future.

The Geopolitical events of today's world inevitably indicate that the nations of the world will get ready to march against Israel and Jerusalem, and they will face their tragic end, as prophecy has assured us.

So, here is a question to Satmar and NK: If God prohibited the Jews to end the exile, to immigrate to the Land of Israel and establish their state before the coming of the Messiah, according to your opinion, how come that the same God in His prophetic Word told us that the house of Judah will already be placed in the Holy Land in order to meet the requirements of the prophecy? (Zephaniah 2:7; Zechariah 12:2 and many others).

The answer is simple. The Almighty God not only predicted and allowed the Jews to establish their State in the Land of Israel prior to the advent of the Messiah as the first stage of the final redemption, but He also blessed them and protected them. It is through the House of Judah, the suffering "servant of God," that God's Plan for the future final Redemption of all the families of Israel and, eventually, of the whole world, will come to pass, and ultimately usher Humanity into the Messianic Age.

The 'True Torah Jews against Zionism' have blamed the Zionists for all the misfortunes, that have befallen on the Jewish people, including the rise of the anti-Semitism around the world, violence, persecutions, and even the Holocaust. They paint a beautiful picture of how Jews lived in the world before the Zionists appeared. They were at peace with the nations of the exile, law-abiding loyal citizens, who "prayed for the welfare of the city." They enjoyed peace and prosperity. All they had to do was study the Torah, pray to God and patiently await for salvation. Their life in the Arab world was even better—pure paradise!

Anyone, who knows a little bit of history of the Jewish nation, understands that what NK says is not true. There were many Hitlers, Ahmadinejads, Hamans, Chmelnickis and Petluras in Jewish history. There were crucifixions, Crusades, Inquisitions, burnings alive, expulsions, blood labels, pogroms and massacres way before the Zionists come, so these accusations are baseless and shameful.

CHAPTER V:
HOLOCAUST.
"WELFARE OF THE CITY"

General Overview on the Holocaust

The Hebrew expression HA-SHOAH means the Catastrophe, the Disaster, and the Holocaust. The Satmar Grand Rebbe Joel Teitelbaum in his book 'Vyoel Moshe' wrote: "It is because of the Zionists that six million Jews were killed." He called Zionism 'the work of Satan', 'a sacrilege' and 'a blasphemy'.

"The Holocaust", he said, "was a direct result of Zionism, a punishment from God. Hitler's rise to power and atrocities committed by Nazis towards the Jewish nation were regarded by the Rebbe as Hitler being a messenger of divine wrath, an Angel of Death, sent by God to punish the Jews because of the apostasy of Zionism against the belief in Messianic redemption".

These outrageous statements have been vigorously supported by the Naturei Karta cult, the Torah Jews against Zionists and many other anti-Zionists elements.

When the Holocaust started, the Zionist organization could not really save the Jews of Europe, because the gates of Palestine had been shut by the British White Paper of 1939. The Revisionist Zionist movement began to organize immigration in 1937, both legal and illegal, from Austria and later from the free city of Danzig. At least 20,000 Jews were saved this way. The entire World was indifferent and coldblooded to the fate of the Jews. The United States and most European countries, including Great Britain, refused to accept Jews. They did not want to apply too much pressure on the Nazi Government to save the Jewish People from the gas chambers because they were afraid that Hitler might stop the mass annihilation of the Jews and let millions of them emigrate to America or England. These two countries of Manasseh and Ephraim respectively betrayed their brothers and sisters of the Jewish People in the time of need, and by their inactions in this critical situation, they helped to seal the tragic fate of the Jews.

The Ministry of Foreign Affairs of Britain and the State Department of USA silently agreed in the Bermuda Conference of April 1943 to let Hitler himself decide the fate of the Jews, rather than organize **unwanted mass immigration** of the Jewish People to their countries. The leaders of the West hide from their own people facts of the Holocaust. The information of how many Jews were killed had been kept in secret since 1941.

The American and the British Governments were saying that even if Hitler would let the Jewish People go free, there would not have been enough boats for their transportation; no food, houses and other living accommodations in their countries, which were deeply involved in the ongoing war. In fact, it was cheap rhetoric; there were plenty of empty ships good for human transportation; and it was proven that the consumer levels in the USA during the war were higher and surpassed that of the prewar period.

Magazines and newspapers did not report detailed stories of Nazi atrocities towards the Jews. In most cases the Western press had followed the example of the New York Times by placing short notices in the back pages of their publications that the majority of the readers could not find.

That is why there was no outcry of the American People; no meetings and protests of public organizations in defense of the Jewish People against the Nazi genocide.

In 1943 an eye witness testified about the concentration camps and the gas chambers before the USA Supreme Court in front of the

Justices. When he finished his testimonies, Associate Justice Felix Frankfurter, himself a Jew, said: "I understand that you think that your story is true, but I personally cannot believe in it."

John J. McCloy (1895-1989)

During the course of German atrocities towards the Jews there were some calls from political leaders and Jewish organizations to bomb the railways and communications systems serving the concentration camps in order to stop the gas chambers of Nazi killing machine.

The Assistant Secretary of War, John J. McCloy effectively blocked any decision for US Air Force bombing raids of the railways approaching the concentration camp of Auschwitz. In his opinion, it was not economically viable and rational to bomb the concentration camps rather than selected priority military targets. It was dangerous and not profitable for the Allies to bomb the gas chambers and save the Jews. Their planes flew over the concentration camps and bombed military targets in proximity of 1-2 kilometers and even caused some damage to the camps' structures as a result of these raids. Some experts say that if the Allies had have bombed the gas chambers and surrounding railways of just the three concentration camps of Treblinka, Sobibor and Oswenzim, the Nazi annihilation machine would have been interrupted for many months, and hundreds of thousands of people would have been saved. Seems, the cost of the weight of a few bombs had become more valuable than the lives of those defenseless victims. The Medal of Honor Mr. McCloy received as a rewarded from the USA Government, was deserved in the same way that the bloodiest terrorist of all times Yasser Arafat, deserved the Noble Prize for Peace he received in Oslo in 1994. The moral standards of John J. McCloy did not prevent him from pardoning convicted Nazi war criminals in the time when he served as High Commissioner in Germany (1949-1952). His sympathies for fascism were mentioned by many observers of his career especially in the light of his financial connections with J.P.

Morgan where his father-in-law Fredrick Zinsser was a partner. As a lawyer, he represented I. G. Farben and its affiliates. In 1936, he shared a box with Hitler at the Nazi Olympics in Berlin. Clearly, his decisions were racially and politically motivated.

Years later, answering an extensive criticism of his actions during WWII, John McCloy stated that the decision not to bomb Auschwitz 'lay with the British alone.' After that he changed position and said that the decision was President Roosevelt's, and he just followed the boss's order. After the war, the Marshall of the RAF Sir Arthur 'Bomber' Harris declared that "a rescue plan (of the Jews) was perfectly feasible, but I was never asked to undertake it".

According to the Constitution of the United State of America, helping the enemy during the war is considered as treason.

Jack Philby (1885-1960) and the Oil Weapon

It was another decisive factor which determined the policy of the United States and the Great Britain towards the Jews during the years of Holocaust (which still has continued to our days!). This factor is—oil discovered in South Arabia in 1938. There were three malicious, villainous, and evil men motivated by Anti-Semitism hatred and greed for money who drastically changed history and fully controlled geopolitics in the Middle East.

These men are:

Jack Philby (1885-1960), British intelligent officer. Fhilby become a very influential Chief adviser to the King of Saudi Arabia Ibn Saud. He held the keys of Palestine in his hands. Philby converted to Islam in 1930. Moved by hatred against the Jewish People, he was instrumental in preventing the immigration of Jews to Palestine and establishing their independent state.

He betrayed the interests of Great Britain, secretly helped to secure contracts of USA oil companies with Saudi Arabia, and double-crossed vital British economic interests in favor of Nazi Germany. With the help of Allen Dulles and Nazi intelligence, Philby did everything possible to sabotage the creation of a Jewish homeland. He invented 'Oil Weapon' policy and used it as an instrument in international politics, forcing Presidents and Prime-Ministers to bend to his will. By compromising the vital interests of Germany, Britain and America and blackmailing them with the 'Oil Weapon', Jack Philby together with Ibn Saud and the Dulles brothers made possible the British Government decision in the White Paper of 1939 that effectively closed the borders of Palestine for millions of Jews trapped in Europe. The Zionists who understood what this new Law meant expressed it this way: "It is a death sentence for millions of Jews trapped by the Nazi in Central Europe". Thus the fate of 6 million Jews was sealed. Hitler was given the green light, and the annihilations of European Jewry had begun.

Ibn Saud (1876-1953)

His full name is King Abdul-Aziz of Saudi Arabia. When oil was discovered in 1938, Ibn Saud, by the advice of his very influential friend Jack Philby, granted concessional authority over Saudi oil fields to American Oil companies. He also double-crossed and betrayed the interests of Great Britain by establishing mutually beneficial relations with Nazi Germany directed against Britain and the Jews in Palestine. Their partnership was cemented by their pathological hatred of the Jewish People. He wished that not one Jew should tread on Palestinian soil. To implement this policy, Ibn Saud also used the 'Oil Weapon'. Anybody who wanted to profit from Saudi oil had to support his policy—no Jews in Palestine. Middle East Oil was and continues to be the imperative factor in International politics, and the Governments involved hardly can deny it.

The first President of the USA, who understood after a meeting with Ibn Saud that the price for helping the Jewish People was too high and had to chose between the Jews and Arab Oil, was President Roosevelt. Suddenly his sympathies with Jewish aspirations to have their own homeland and state evaporated and the President chose oil. His new policy was neutrality for the benefit of Arabs. The same policy has been continued by President Obama in our days by appeasing the Arab world and betraying the USA's best ally and friend, Israel.

Allen Dulles (1893-1969)

Dulles was an American diplomat, spy, corporate lawyer, banker, and Government official. International intrigue, varied love affairs, and clandestine operations to topple governments all marked the life of Allen Dulles who is regarded as the keystone figure in the history of American intelligence. At the age of 23 he was working in Switzerland's diplomatic service when he ran across an application for a visa to the United States from the future leader of communist Russia Vladimir Lenin in 1916. Who knows how the events of the history could have change if that visa would have been granted by Dulles?

Later on Allen Dulles with his associates in the CIA learnt and practiced the art of changing Governments in Third World countries almost at will. According to the authors John Loftus and Mark Aarons, "The secret wars against the Jews", Allen Dulles is "one of the worst traitors in American history." Before and during WWII, Dulles played a significant role in financing Nazi Germany. The brother Dulles financial network included a wide range of the Third Reich corporations, American oil cartels, and Saudi Arabia. Allen Dulles with his friend Jack Philby, being "archetypical upper-crust" anti-Semites, who used their connections and influence, helped King Ibn Saud to implement his policy 'not one Jew in Palestine' by forcing the Great Britain to promulgate the White Paper in 1939. The mass immigration of the Jews to Palestine, the only one possible way to save them, was successfully prevented. There are also accusations of some authors that Allen Dulles was heavily involved in smuggling Nazi money back to his Western partners, in preventing the capture of Nazi war criminals, and arranging their emigration to the USA and Latin America.

According to the Constitution of the United State of America, helping the enemy during the war is considered as treason.

The Righteous Among the Nations

By contrast, there were two outstanding men who had helped the doomed helpless Jews more than any political leaders in the world. Not many people, particularly among the Jewish nation, know the truth.

Pope John Pius XII (1876-1958)

This Pope began his Papacy in 1939. There are many controversies connected with the role Pius XII played in the Holocaust years. Some people say that the Pope kept silence and did nothing to help the Jewish cause. They call him 'Hitler's Pope.' Others disagree saying that the Pope actively protested against the deportation of the Jews of Europe to the concentration camps and, in fact, saved more Jews than anybody else. The latest documents (1940-1945) revealed that Pope made every effort to "work diligently to save Jews from Nazi tyranny."

On 21 September 1945, the general secretary of the World Jewish Council, Dr. Leon Kubowitzky, presented an amount of money to the pope, "in recognition of the work of the Holy See in rescuing Jews from Fascist and Nazi persecutions."

After Pope's death in October 1958, Rabbi J. Stern stated that Pius XII "made it possible for thousands of Jewish victims of Nazism and Fascism to be hidden away . . ."

At the United Nations, Golda Meir, Israel's Foreign Minister, said, "When fearful martyrdom came to our people in the decade of Nazi terror, the voice of the Pope was raised for the victims. The life of our times was enriched by a voice speaking out on the great moral truths above the tumult of daily conflict."

Many Jews publicly thanked the Pope for his help. For example, Pinchas Lapide, a Jewish theologian and Israeli diplomat to Milan in the 1960s, estimated controversially in 'Three Popes and the Jews', that Pius XII "was instrumental in saving at least 700,000 but probably as many as 860,000 Jews from certain death at Nazi hands." Nobody knows exactly how many Jews were saved by this Pope.

William Zukerman, the former American Hebrew columnist, wrote that "no other leader did more to help the Jews in their hour of greatest tragedy, during the Nazi occupation of Europe, than the late Pope".

Jewish rabbis and Yad Vashem (the Holocaust History Museum) are very much inclined to honor Pius XII by posting his name as one of the 'Righteous among the Nations'. We think it has to be done!

Francisco Franco (1892-1975)

Another 'Righteous among the Nations' is His Excellency Generalissimo **Francisco Franco,** Spanish dictator, general and head of state of Spain from 1936 until his death in1975.

People misjudged this man, his life and deeds. Very few know that by refusing Hitler's request for Spain to join the Axis in the war in 1940 and not taking part in "Operation Felix" in the beginning of 1941to allow the German's troops to use the territory of Spain for capturing the strategically important naval base of Gibraltar and invading North Africa, Franco changed the course of WWII and History. Hermann Goering in Nuremberg jail: "Hitler lost the war when he refused the intention of immediately after the fall of France to involve Spain—with or without the consent of Franco—to capture Gibraltar and invade Africa".

Winston Churchill in his memoirs: "If Hitler had possession of Gibraltar, the outcome of the war would be different."

The borders of all European countries for escaping Jews were closed except for Spain which under Franco's directives accepted 40,000 Jews. The Spanish diplomatic missions in Hungary, Romania, Greece and France were instructed by Franco' Government to issue visas and passports to Jews running from Nazi atrocities.

What motivated this great man of Spain to be such a beneficiary to the Jewish People? Is it the blood in his veins of the famous Middle Age Rabbis Yosef, Yosia and David Pardo? Maybe he heard their voices to rectify injustice, to return them to Spain from where they had been forcefully expelled in 1492 as a result of the Spanish Inquisition under the leadership of Torquemada? A devout Catholic, Franco never pronounced the word 'Jew' publicly and avoided any discussions on this subject. The secrets of his personal life he took to the grave.

We hope that the name of Francisco Franco of Spain will be rehabilitated among the Jewish People and will be honorably placed in the Yad Vashem Museum as a Righteous man, a Friend of the Jewish nation.

The Role of Zionists before, during, and in the aftermath of the Holocaust

Even after the Holocaust, the British continued to hunt down and turn away boatloads of illegal immigrants whenever they could. For these evil deeds to their brothers in a desperate crisis, Ephraim, being modern England, will be accountable before the Almighty and the House of Judah in the due time. 250,000 displaced Jews, survivors of the Holocaust, were living in Europe in DPC (Displaced Persons Camps). After the War, the tiny Jewish community in Palestine and the struggling Zionist movement still managed to save few hundreds of thousands of Jews out of millions of European Jewry. But the fact is that nobody else saved more.

Before the Holocaust, the picture was different. Among all of Jewry, the leaders of Zionism somehow foresaw approaching disaster from the Nazi Germany. They responded to it by sending their emissaries to countries of Europe, mainly to Germany, Poland, Hungary and the Baltic with a strong message to obviate the coming danger by emigrating to their national homeland in Palestine, before it became too late. The Jews of Germany did not want to listen. They had quite opposite plans. Reform Judaism was born in Germany, where the Jews were very supportive of German nationalism. They wanted to assimilate to German society, claiming that they were loyal citizens 'of the Mosaic persuasion', who pray to God 'for welfare of the city' (Germany). The Zionists ideals of self determination as a Jewish nation and settling in the Promised Land scared them, because it would raise questions about their own loyalty. In rejecting Zionism, they went so far that they systematically removed all references to the Holy Land and Jerusalem from their liturgy. A significant contribution to the tragic finale of six million European Jewry and German Jews in particular, was due to a large segment of anti-Zionist Ultra-Orthodox Jews and their Rabbis. They ridiculed the effort of Zionists, called them bandits, communists, heretics. They instructed Jewish communities not to listen to Zionists 'propaganda' and patiently wait when God sends the Messiah to save them. Does it not resemble Satmar and Torah Jews of Neturei Karta today?

Beside the anti-Zionist Orthodox Rabbis, who actively blocked the Zionists rescue efforts in the 1930s, there was another faction of anti-Zionists, the Jewish Bund; it was particularly strong in Poland and the Baltic countries, and they also agitated together with the Jewish communists against the Zionist movement.

How can Satmar and Neturei Karta members dare to say that the Zionists did nothing to save European Jewry? They cannot accept the truth, to their great embarrassment, that the Zionists happened to be right in predicting the Holocaust, while Rabbis like themselves had done everything to deny it and prevent the Zionists effort to save as many Jews as possible through emigration to Palestine. Instead, Jews went to the gas chambers, because rabbis persuaded them listen to them, but not to the Zionists.

Vladimir Jabotinsky (1880-1940)

One of the leaders of Zionism, Vladimir Jabotinsky, who was deeply concerned about the situation of the Jewish communities in Eastern Europe during the 1930s, prepared an evacuation plan to Palestine for the entire Jewish populations of Poland, Hungary and Romania. Governments of all three countries approved this plan, but Polish Jewry, mostly religious, by advice and pressure of anti-Zionist Orthodox Rabbis and the Bund rejected it.

Jabotinsky repeatedly warned Polish Jews of the coming catastrophe. In August of 1938 he wrote them crying words from his heart, he supplicated, begged them to trust and listen to him, but his warnings went largely unheeded. Here is his letter:

". . . It is already three years that I am calling upon you, Polish Jewry, who are the crown of world Jewry. I continue to warn you incessantly that a catastrophe is coming closer. I became gray and old in these years, my heart bleeds, that you, dear brothers and sisters, do not see the volcano which will soon begin to spit its all—consuming lava. I know that you are not seeing this because you are immersed in your daily worries. Today, however, I demand your trust. You were convinced already that my prognoses have already proven to be right. If you think differently then drive me out from your midst. However, if you do believe me, then listen to me in this 11th hour: in the name of God let any one of you save himself as long as there is still time. And time there is very little."

And more: "What else I would like to say to you on this day of Tisha B'Av is whoever of you will escape from the catastrophe, he or she will live to see the exalted moment of a great Jewish wedding—the rebirth and rise of the Jewish State. I do not know if I will be privileged to see it, but my son will! I believe in this, as I'm sure that tomorrow morning the sun will rise."

Very sad words. You cannot read them without tears in the eyes. Especially, when the tragic faith of the Polish Jewry has known to the world. Jabotinsky was right. He did not live long enough to see his dream come true, the birth of the State of Israel, but his son did!

One of a few voices amongst Haredi Jews, who supported the Zionists, was the voice of righteous Ha Rav Kook:

"Come to the Land of Israel, pleasant brothers, come to the Land of Israel, save your souls, the souls of generations, the souls of our entire nation."

Strong words to Jews in Diaspora issued by Rabbi Atiya (1885-1970) in his book Lech Lecha:

"Wake up, dear brothers, rise up and come to Zion while the gates are still open, and God forbid, do not remain with those who tarry, lest it be too late and you will cry out, but not be answered."

The State of Israel was not created because of the Holocaust

Another false claim of "Torah Jews against Zionism" is that the State of Israel was created because of the Holocaust. Some of them even say that the Holocaust is a myth, invented by Zionists to justify their state. The United Nations had given the state to the Jews as a special favor, as an act of petty contrition in the aftermath of the Holocaust, they claim. They also try to convey an idea that the Zionists immediately after WWII brought hundreds of thousands of Jews from Europe to create the state of Israel at the expense of the Palestinians. This idea is wrong because most of the 1948 Jewish population of Palestine had arrived before the war. Certainly, the Holocaust helped to mobilize public opinion internationally in favor of the Jewish state, but it was not a crucial factor or necessary cause.

Contrary to the Arab and anti-Zionist propaganda, the State of Israel was not created because of the Holocaust. The right of the Jewish people to self determination was recognized in the League of Nations Mandate of 1922, giving Great Britain control of Palestine for the purpose of making a Jewish national home there.

This Mandate was based on the Balfour Declaration of 1917, where the British government "viewed with favor" the establishment of a Jewish National Home in Palestine. With the Holocaust or without it, sooner or later, the Jewish state would have been established in the Land of Israel! Why is that so? The answer is simple—thus said God! Jewish independence was on the horizon.

If it would not have been for the Holocaust, which annihilated six million European Jews, the majority of those victims would have become citizens of the young State of Israel. That was the original goal of the Zionists, their hope and strength—to bring European Jewry to Palestine, to their homeland. If it had happened, the State of Israel would be much stronger and prosperous today and would not have exacerbated the problems it faces, especially with the Palestinians.

The Ultimate Goals of Neturei Karta and the Torah Jews Against the Zionism

Satmar and Neturei Karta want the State of Israel to be dismantled, if possible, peacefully. But what if a peaceful solution is impossible? We get an impression that these people in their blind hatred against the Zionists would not mind even the forceful destruction of Israel with its grave consequences.

Of course, they cannot say it aloud for understandable reasons. All the Land of Israel, they continue, has to be returned to the 'legitimate owners'—the Palestinian people. They do not accept the notion of two independent states of Arabs and Jews living peacefully together, because they wish that the Palestinian Authority alone rule Palestine. Those Jews, mostly religious Orthodox, who lived there before the establishing of the State of Israel in 1948, might be allowed to live under the Palestinian Authority. The rest of the majority of the Jewish people, around five million, could ask the lawful Palestinian government permission to live in their country or even become citizens of the Palestinian state. If not allowed (as if there is any doubt!), the Jews would have to leave the Holy Land and return to the countries of their exile, where they would be supposed to live peacefully and in harmony with the nations, pray to God "for the welfare of the city" and patiently wait for the coming of the Messiah.

There is no worse anti-Semite than an anti-Semitic Jew. Nor is there a worse anti-Zionist than an anti-Zionist Jew. It is of them said Berl Katznelson, the Zionist leader of the old 30s:

"Is there any other people on Earth who is so emotionally confused that believes that everything his nation does deserves contempt and reproach, while every murder, rape, robbery, committed by their enemies fills their hearts with admiration and awe?"

These words are perfectly characterizing members of the "True Torah Jews" against Zionism of modern day.

We should ask the Torah Jews against Zionism: Is it OK before giving the Land of Israel to the Palestinians, to warn them that the Land transaction is temporary and they will voluntarily have to give it back to Israelites, when God sends the Messiah and redeems us?

They also assure us not to worry about the lives of the Jews because the Arabs are not as bad as we might think! The nations would not do us harm as they had done in the Middle Ages because all countries have become more civilized. Anti-Semitism and persecutions are past history. Furthermore, "the gentiles mentioned in the Bible and Talmud were murderous idol worshippers, whereas our gentile neighbors today are civilized and believe in the one God, Allah, for example." So, there is nothing to worry about! This is the program of the 'True Torah Jews against Zionism'. This is what they want. They are going even farther by stating that God wants it too. Their plans and actions conveniently shielded by God's name. God said that the Zionists are rebels and heretics, because they did not get permission to end the exile, to immigrate to the Promised Land and build there a state, therefore the Zionists shall be punished and their State of Israel must be dismantled (destroyed).

Is this really what God wants? Absolutely not! By quoting the Holy Scriptures above, we have already shown that there are many proofs in the Bible that God Almighty has predicted, protected and blessed the Zionists and the Jewish State of Israel as the first stage of redemption of Judah before the final redemption of all the families of the House of Israel. No wonder, the Satmar and Neturei Karta cult keep silence about these passages, as if they do not exist. The controversial allegorical Three Oaths of the Canticles, which are not even Halakhically binding, are all they have as a century old theological proof of their platform. This double standard characterizes their position all over, no matter which subject you touch. Their fanaticism and stubbornness remind us of the Zealots and Sicarii of Jewish history, whose religious fanaticism and intolerance caused the Jewish nation millions of lives, destruction of the Temple and a tragic 2000 years of Exile with its persecutions and unspeakable sufferings.

The activities of these 'Orthodox Jews against Zionism' such as collaboration with the Palestinians and embracing open enemies of the State of Israel, racists and Jewish haters, publicly burning the flag of the Jewish State, have given an impression that they are seeking a warranty for their future protection and well being from the Arab world, in case of Israel being dismantled or destroyed. They do not realize two things: firstly, that Israel cannot be destroyed, because God would not let it happen: "But Judah shall dwell forever, and Jerusalem from generation to generation" (Joel 3:20); "They and their children and their children's children will live there forever, and David my servant will be their prince forever (Ezekiel 37:25); "I will plant Israel in their own land, never again to be uprooted from the land I have given them" (Amos 9:15).

Secondly, the appearance of a new Hitler in the Arab world, be it Ahmadinejad or somebody else from Hamas, Hezbollah, the Muslim Brotherhood or the Palestinian Authority. There is no difference for them what kind of Jews they are facing: Zionists, Orthodox Torah Jews against Zionists, university and press intellectuals, international activists, Jews from left or right, old or young—as Hitler, they will kill all of them without discrimination.

'Welfare of the City'

"And seek the welfare of the city where I have sent you into exile, and pray to the Lord on its behalf; for in its welfare, you will have welfare" (Jeremiah 29:7).

Surprisingly, the Neturei Karta, on rear occasions, uses this application from the Tanakh to prove that Jews in Exile should be loyal citizens, praying to God for their countries (cities) welfare, obeying the laws, and patiently waiting for the coming of the Messiah. This passage is their cornerstone of "Foreign Policy" for the Jews in Exile to this day. In the best tradition of the Christian fundamentalists, Neturei Karta has taken this verse out of context, and presented it as a general guide of Jewish behavior in the Diaspora.

Here is the response to the "Foreign Policy" constantly advocated by NK:

"If a Jew will forget his origin and true identity and consider himself a full pledge citizen of the country of his exile, if he thinks that Berlin is Jerusalem . . , then a raging storm will uproot him . . . and destroy" (Rabbi Meir Simcha Ha Cohen).

Meanwhile, it was not even a prophecy. When king Nebuchadnezzar of Babylon (another example, as to how God uses Gentiles for His purposes) conquered Judea, destroyed the First Temple and led the Jews to the Babylonian captivity, there were two groups of prophets with two different opinions on the duration of the Exile. The Prophets Hananiah, Ahab, and Zedekiah prophesied that "Thus saith the Lord; even so will I break the yoke of Nebuchadnezzar king of Babylon from the neck of all nations within the space of two full years" (Jeremiah 28:11). These prophets were prophesying things people liked to hear, but they were not sent by God, and God caused them to die for telling the lies.

Jeremiah, being a true prophet of God, said that the Babylonian captivity would last seventy years (Jer.29:10).

Therefore, "build houses and live in them; plant gardens and eat the fruit of them; be increased there and not diminished; seek the welfare of the city where I have sent you in exile, and pray to the Lord on its behalf, for in its welfare you will find your welfare" (Jer.29:5-7).

Jews in the Diaspora have their Guide to the daily way of living among the nations, which is the Torah with its Ten Commandments. Instructions of Jeremiah 29:7 were given only to the captives in Babylon guiding them on how to behave during the prophesied seventy years of captivity. To apply these particular recommendations to all Jews throughout their 2000 years of Exile is absurd.

Who is the real Israel?

"The Zionists had no rights to call their state "Israel" because they are not representing Israel. We are the real Israel; we are the People of Israel because we are the true Torah believers," explain the Torah Jews against Zionism.

Being the true Torah believers, does not automatically make you an Israelite. You are a part of Israel because you belong to one of the Israelite Tribes, but the real Israel are the 'lost' Ten Tribes of Israel, as our great Sage Ramban explained in his work 'The Book of Redemption' (Sefer Ha Geulah).

"The overwhelming majority of the Ten Tribes had been exiled by the Assyrians and had never returned to the Promised Land though they were destined to do so in the future. The Ten Tribes", he said in 1260 a.c, "were still in Tserefath" (France and its neighborhood) and 'at the ends of the north,' meaning at that time the northern areas of Europe.

In Biblical history there were two periods of time when the name 'Israel' meant all twelve tribes of Jacob: When God revealed Himself to the Hebrew tribes on Mount Sinai, gave them the Heavenly Torah, and formed the nation called Israel; and the second time when God allowed His people to have human kings, and they organized themselves into the United Kingdom of Israel. Since Israel and Judah were defeated and exiled more than 2700 years ago, they still have remained two different entities, never been reunited, not synonymous nations, living in the four corners of the earth, having different cultures, history, languages, and religions. They will be one nation and one Kingdom again in the End Times when the prophecy of Ezekiel 37:15-29 will come to pass.

The first part of the 'Torah Jews' statement has some validity. Historically and scripturally the State of Israel should be called Judaea. The main reason for this is that the population of this state are Jews from the tribes of Judah, Benjamin and Levi, who in the past (930 b.c.-135a.c. with the exception from 586 b.c. to 142 b.c. and 63b.c.-135 a.c.) had their own state called Judaea. The Jews are not the Israelites of the Northern Ten Tribes, so the NK is right here. Obviously, the Israelites of the Ten Tribes are not the Jews! The Promised Land correctly bears the name 'Israel'.

The second part of their statement is completely wrong. They are not the Israelites of the northern Kingdom (the Ten Tribes in exile), because they are Jews from the tribes of Judah, Benjamin, and Levy from the southern Kingdom of Judaea. The name 'Israel' was given to Ephraim and Manasseh, who are the dominant leaders of the Ten Tribes of Israel (Genesis 48:16, 19). They guessed the first part rightly, but it was just a guess. They do not understand or ignore the difference between the Jewish People and Israelite People; between the ancient states of Israel and Judaea and the modern Judah-Israeli State of Israel. The Jewish People and the Israelite People at this point of time are not synonymous! They are different nations, living in very different portions of the Globe. God shows it very clearly and understandably in dozens of passages throughout the Torah and Tanakh. All our great Sages have known this. We slightly touched on this matter in our Introduction to this book, and we feel that the time has arrived to go to the next Chapter, where we are going to explain an additional clarification of the meanings of Judah and Israel (Ten Tribes).

CHAPTER VI:
JUDAH AND ISRAEL

Nahmanides and the Ten Lost Tribes of Israel

The greatest Jewish Sage of all time Nachmanides (Moshe ben Nachman 1194-1270) knew very well of the existence of the Ten Tribes of Israel in the exile. He was well aware of the difference between them and the two tribes of Judah and Benjamin known collectively as Judah, whose descendants are now to be found among the present-day Jews. Nachmanides pointed out in his book that the overwhelming majority of the Ten Tribes had been exiled by the Assyrians and had never returned to the Promised Land though they were destined to do so in the future. The Ten Tribes, he said in 1260 a.c, were still in Tserefath (France and its neighborhood) and 'at the ends of the north,' meaning at that time the northern areas of Europe. According to Nachmanides, chapter 37 of Ezekiel speaks of a future Redemption for both Judah and Israel. The two kingdoms will unite into one kingdom under the house of David.

That is how Ramban explained the history of Israel's exile:

"Let me clarify the matter for you . . . The kingdom of Israel included the ten northern Tribes. These were exiled by Sennaherib as it says, "For he rent Israel from the house of David; and they made Jeroboam the son of Nebat king: and Jeroboam drove Israel from following the Lord, and made them sin a great sin" (II Kings 17:11). "Until the Lord removed Israel out of His sight . . . so was Israel exiled out of their own land to Assyria unto this day" (17:12). This is a proof that all the Kingdom of Israel was exiled to Assyria but the Kingdom of David remained as it was until Nebuchadnezzar exiled them to Babylon. "There was none left but a tribe of Judah only" (II Kinds 17:18). The Kingdom of David included Judah and Benjamin, with Judah always being the dominant tribe. It is obvious from Scripture, continues Ramban that this term, i.e. **House of Joseph, applies to the Kingdom of Israel who are the Ten Tribes.**

"They should be ashamed not to recognize this fact! When was the House of Joseph like a flame devouring the stubble of Esau? (He comments on Obadiah 1:18). Not in Biblical times! The Ten Tribes had already been exiled and they are still in Exile from Canaan even unto Zarephath" (Rashi, Ibn Ezra, Radak and others say that Zarephath means France; Abarbanel says it means France and Britain).

Notice how this great scholar was upset with those people who could not understand the simple meaning of the Obadiah prophecies (1:18) being intended for the future. Instead, they dismissed them as having already been fulfilled in the past. We feel the same way, when the 'True Torah Jews against Zionism' tell us that the prohibitions of the Three Oaths of Shir-Ha Shirim should be applied against Judah, Zionists, Jewish state of Israel, because Judah is Israel; the Jewish people and the people of Israel are the same; therefore they sin a great sin before the Almighty for violating His Oaths to end the exile and establishing the State of Israel in Eretz Yisroel before the coming of the Messiah. We just repeat what Ramban said to his opponents:

"You are wrong and should be ashamed of your actions. All your theological dogmas are in errors!"

Historical and Scriptural views on the Division of the United Kingdom of Israel

In Scriptures the Division of the Tribes is very well explained. In the I Kings 11 God has decided to punish Solomon for his sins, "I will surely rend the kingdom from thee, and will give it to thy servant" (Verse 11). To Jeroboam (servant) God Said: "Behold, I will rend the kingdom out of the hand of Solomon, and will give ten tribes to thee" (Verse 31).

"So Israel rebelled against house of David unto this day"
(I Kings 12:19; II Chronicles 10:19).

The split of the United Kingdom of Israel into the two separate, politically independent states of Judea and Israel (the Ten Tribes) was initiated and designed by God Himself (1Kings 12:15, 24). He has specific reasons for doing this. In the End Times, when He will reunite, ingather and redeem all families of Jacob, we will fully understand in detail the Divine wisdom of the Creator's Plan.

Centuries before the Kingdom of Israel split, God told Jacob: "Be fruitful and multiply; a nation and company of nations shall be of thee, and kings shall come out of thy loins. Behold, I will make of thee a multitude of people" (Genesis 35:11; 48:4).

During the life time of the first kings of Judea and Israel, these two kingdoms were at bloody war: "And there was war between Rehoboam and Jeroboam all their days" (I Kings 14:29).

"And there was war between Abijah (King of Judah) and Jeroboam (King of Israel). And Abijah and his people slew them (The children of Israel) with the great slaughter: so there fell down slain of Israel five hundred thousand chosen men" (2 Chronicles 13:2, 17).

These wars had not been limited to only Judah and Israel. There had been wars among the other Tribes of Israel as well.

"Then Jephthah gathered together all the men of Gilead (Manasseh), and fought with Ephraim: and the men of Gilead smote Ephraim. And there fell at the time of the Ephraimites forty and two thousand" (Judges 12: 2, 6).

The Kingdom of Israel had lasted 209 years (930 b.c-721b.c.). Israel went into Assyrian captivity circa 721b.c. and somehow mysteriously disappeared from the face of the earth. They became known as the legendary 'Ten Lost Tribes of Israel'. Since then world history has been dealing with the nation of Judah, from the former state of Judea who later were called Jews.

Understanding the terms 'Judah' and 'Israel' (Ten Tribes)

The main reason we wrote this Chapter is to show that there is a huge difference between the house of Judah, the Jewish People, and the House of Israel, the Israelite People of the Ten Tribes. Despite the fact that these nations are of the same Semitic stock being twelve sons of the Patriarch Jacob, they are different nations now, living in the different countries of the World, having different histories, cultures, languages, traditions, and religions.

Most people do not understand the difference between the people of Judah and the people of Israel. Quite often we hear such expression as 'Moses led the Jewish people out of Egypt', 'The Torah was given to the Jews', or 'The Jews conquered the land of Canaan under the leadership of Joshua' and so on. These understandings are not Scriptural. In the Torah and Tanakh you never find such an expression as 'Jewish People.' The God of Israel has never said that Israel is Judah and Judah is Israel.

"Hear this word that the LORD has spoken against you, **O people of Israel,** against the whole family that I brought up out of the land of Egypt" (Amos 3:1).

"Now the length of time the **Israelite People** lived in Egypt was 430 years" (Exodus 12:40).

"But God led the people around by the way of the wilderness toward the Red Sea. And the **sons of Israel** went up out of the land of Egypt equipped for battle" (Exodus 13:18).

"These are the commandments and the judgments, which the LORD commanded by the hand of Moses unto the **children of Israel** in the plains of Moab by Jordan near Jericho" (Numbers 36:13).

'Say to the children of Israel', 'Speak unto all the congregation of the children of Israel, and say unto them'; 'Say to the Israelites'—that is how God called His People!

You cannot find the word 'Jew' in the Hebrew Bible before the Babylonian captivity (Esther 2:5)!

At that time the word 'Jews' was not even in existence! And in the beginning there was no Jewish state of Judaea, of course. The first Hebrews and the Israelites were not Jews, and they never called by the name 'Jews'.

In fact, the correct formulation should have been constructed as 'Moses led the Israelites (or Hebrews) out of Egypt'; likewise, 'The Torah was given to all Twelve Tribes of Israel' (not to Jews!).

The concept that the Ten Tribes of Israel have been lost 2800 years ago and therefore have no part in the World-to-Come, is wrong and has been rejected by God, the Sages of the Talmud and Rabbinical literature. Many Rabbis and scholars have misunderstood the teachings of Biblical Israel and the End Time Prophecies of Reunification, Ingathering and Redemption of all the Tribes of the House of Israel and have applied the fulfillment of all these future events to the Jews only. They teach that Judah is Biblical Israel, and all the future prophecies of reunification and redemption have been pertained to Judah only.

If the Church in their 'Replacement Theology' have rejected Israel and taken all the Heavenly blessings, the choosiness, the restoration, and the glorious Kingdom for themselves, as being 'spiritual Israel', leaving all the curses of the Bible to the 'earthy Israel; the Jews have done the same with the Ten Tribes of Israel. It does not matter whether it is the Christians replacing Israel or the Jews taking the name Israel instead of them, the result is the same: the Word of God is twisted and misinterpreted. And whoever is doing this, plays with dangerous fire, faces the wrath of the Almighty!

The Jewish people have not heard the awakening cry of their brothers and sisters of the Ten Tribes of Israel in Exile. How could they, if they have no knowledge of their existence? Hundreds of millions of Israelites have been replaced in popular consciousness by the Jews alone! The Ten Tribes are as though they were a fairy tale, a myth and a fantasy. The Jewish Rabbis are unwilling to hear the true story. They are increasingly against ingathering those people into the Land of Israel.

Rabbi Avraham Isaac Kook said that those Israelites who were assimilated in ancient times and their descendants have progressively been becoming more and more suited to receive the Divine Revelation of their Israelite identity. As time progresses, they will be yearning and striving to declare the name of Israel on their inheritance (Shemoneh Kevatsim, Kovets 8:205).

The religious and the secular leadership of Judah, instead of obstructing the greatest Prophecies of final Reunification, the last Exodus and Redemption of all the Tribes of Israel, which goes against the will of God, should open their hearts and spirits to the Israelites, go to them in the countries wherever they live in exile to bring them the Divine Light of the Torah and knowledge of the God of Israel. They have to do everything in their power to bring them to the God of their fathers, to His Laws, and to the Promised Land. Not as a Christian 'Joes' and 'Jacks' of Ephraimites or newly born Christian Zionists with 'Hebrew roots' and 'Israelite Tribal identity' who will make a phony Aliyah to the Land of Israel to missionize Jews and 'steal from the flock of the Almighty' as many individuals and organizations propagate; but rather Judah will bring back a newly repented nation of Israel whose hearts and spirits will have turned to the only God of the Universe, the God of Israel and His everlasting Torah.

The Ten Tribes of Israel in exile do not have to be converted to Judaism in the manner of Ruth: "Where you go, I will go; and where you live, I will live: your people shall be my people, and your God my God: where you die, will I die, and there will I be buried: the Lord do so to me, and more also, if anything but death part you and me" (Ruth 1:16-17).

There was a time when the Israelites had been in possession of all of it. There was a time when they had known their God and lived by His Divine Laws. It is they who received the Divine Revelation of the Torah from the hands of Almighty at Mount Sinai. They are still His chosen People. The Almighty has never broken the Covenant with them. As the loving father, He wants the children of Israel to repent and come back to Him.

"All who rage against you will surely be ashamed and disgraced; those who oppose you will be as nothing and perish. You, O Israel, My servant, whom I have chosen. Do not fear, for I am with you; do not be dismayed, **for I am your God**. I will strengthen you and help you" (Isaiah 41:8-11).

National repentance of the Israelites was experienced by them throughout their earlier national history.

"Finally, they cried out to the LORD for help, saying, "We have sinned against you because we have abandoned you as our God and have served the images of Baal" (Judges 10:10).

Judah and Israel need each other. That is what Almighty wants, and eventually that will be precisely done! (Jeremiah 3:18; Ezekiel 37:22-28).

"And I will say to them which were not My people, you are My people; and they shall say, You are my God" (Hosea2:23).

As evidences show, the Jewish People are not ready for this monumental task: To go to the Ten Tribes to teach them Torah and knowledge of the God of Israel in order to bring them back to the religion of their fathers and to the Promised Land. And, besides, the Ten Tribes are also not prepared to join the "two sticks" of Ezekiel and be re-united with the Jewish People. The "little sister" of Song of Songs 8:8 which was identified by the great Ramban (Nachmanides) as Israel in exile, is not ready for Redemption or, as it was put by the Father of all the Commentators Rashi, "she is not ripe for Redemption."

From ancient times the Ten Tribes were known as rebellious, violators of the Commandments, stubborn and hard-hearted people. They have worshipped idols, gods which cannot save, and brought forth the 'strange children' of mixed ancestry.

"They and their fathers have transgressed against Me even unto this very day" (Ezekiel 2:3). On top of it, there are the prohibitions of the Three Oaths against Israel going up to the Promised Land en masse without permission of God (Babylonian Talmud, Ketubot 111a). The Ten Tribes are obligated not to rebel against the nations of the world and make no forceful mass emigration to the Land of Israel, unless

God sends the Messiah whose task is to re-unite all the Twelve Tribes of Israel and bring them to the Land of their fathers (more has been devoted to this subject in Chapter VII: "Three Oaths"). But before the Almighty sends the Messiah, the Israelites should have repented in order to be worthy of his coming. As many great Sages have said, repentance must precede redemption.

"Then when they are exiled among the nations, they will remember Me. They will recognize how hurt I am by their unfaithful hearts and lustful eyes that long for their idols. Then at last they will hate themselves for all their detestable sins, and they will know that I am the Lord" (Ezekiel 6:9-10). That is what going to happen: This is the Divine destiny of Israel (the Ten Tribes).

There is an interesting opinion that the Messiah, son of Joseph, who according to the Talmud will arrive before the Messiah son of David, may be the political leader, a President of the United States, the country where the Tribe of Manasseh resides. With a convincingly new knowledge of Israelite Identity, he could completely turn around the whole issue of Awakening and Reunification, and move Prophecy ahead to Redemption and the Messianic Age (followed by the Wars of Gog and Magog).

The Almighty, since the separation of the United Kingdom of Israel, throughout the Hebrew Bible, has always threatened Judah and Israel separately. He has never stated that they are the same nations at this period of time as they had been in time of Moses when they received the Heavenly Torah on Mount Sinai and became one Israelite nation. There are dozens upon dozens of prophecies in Scripture saying that all the Tribes of the Two Houses of Israel will definitely repent, re-unite and be redeemed by the Almighty in the End of Times with the advent of the Messiah ben Joseph or ben David. Together they will usher in the wonderful Messianic World. All the great Sages, Rabbinical literature, and other related sources have pointed out that there will be a re-unification of the Twelve Tribes and the Final Redemption of Israel (Isaiah 11:13, 27:13 49:18-20; Jeremiah 3:18; 31:17-19; 50:4; Ezekiel 16:53-55; 37: 15-28; 47:13; Hosea 2:2-3, 23; Obadiah 1:18, 20).

The Ten Tribes did not die out and disappear from history. It is the Word of God that all Twelve Tribes of the House of Israel will be represented among the nations in the End Times. In spite of all of the above, the Jewish People (we are speaking of the majority in the State Israel and in the Diaspora) do not understand these prophecies. They do not want to hear about the existence of the Ten Tribes in exile, let alone mentioning a sharing of the **Biblical** Promised Land with them. They simply ignore the plain truth of the Bible.

"You would not even mention your sister Sodom in the day of your pride. Nevertheless, I will bring back and restore them by bringing back Sodom, with her daughters, and by bringing back Samaria, and her daughters: and I will bring those that return of thee in the midst of them" (Ezekiel 16:53, 56).

Yair Davidiy from Jerusalem, founder of Brit-Am / Hebrew Nations Organization and author of the book 'Ephraim. The Gentile Children of Israel', explained the matter this way: "This is the message for Judah. In order for Judah to realize herself and to bring back all her exiles and rehabilitate herself, Judah must also seek the Lost Ten Tribes and cause them to return! This is important to Judah for her own sake!"

Are the Ten Tribes Really a Myth and Fairy Tale?

To us, this situation is very upsetting. Most of rabbis and scholars believe that there is no such thing as hundreds of millions of Israelites from the Ten Tribes still in exile. They use the "Replacement Theory" which basically holds that the Ten Tribes is a myth and fairy story; that back in history the Ten Tribes had already returned to the Promised Land, (in the time of the Prophets Jeremiah, Ezra, and Nehemiah), and that the Jewish People, Judah, is the Biblical Israel representing all the Twelve Tribes, and that all future prophecies of the re-unification and redemption in the End Days pertain to them.

These people just simply have ignored the opinions of the greatest Sages such as R. Eliezer, R. Joshua, R. Shimon, R.Yehudah the Prince,

73

R. Nachmanides and many, many more, whose saying on the subject goes like this:

"The ten tribes are destined for the World to come" (R. Yehudah);

Israel will never be forgotten or rejected by God! God's Covenant cannot be broken! (Judges 2:1; Leviticus 26:44; Psalms 111:5; Jer. 31:36).

Rabbi Eliezer said (in respond to the negative position of R. Akiva): "Just like a day is followed by darkness, and the light later returns, so too, although it will become 'dark' for the ten tribes, God will ultimately take them out of their darkness" (Talmud, Sanhedrin 110b).

"He who scattered Israel will gather him, and will keep him as a shepherd keeps his flock" (Jeremiah 31:1).

"For thus saith the LORD; Just as I have brought all this great evil upon this people, so will I bring upon them all the good that I have promised them" (Jer. 32:42)!

The Mishnah, Tractate Sanhedrin 11:1 says: "All Israelites have a share in the World-to-Come, as it is says, "your people also shall be all righteous, they shall inherit the Land for ever; the branch of My planting, the work of My hands, that I may be glorified" (Isaiah 60:21).

"And I will cause the **captivity of Judah** and the **captivity of Israel** to return, and will build them, as at the first" (Jer.33:7)!!

"You are My servant. I have chosen you, and not cast you away. Thou art my servant, O Israel, in whom I will be glorified. Can a woman forget her sucking child, that she should not have compassion on the son of her womb? Yea, they may forget, yet will I not forget thee" (Isaiah 41:9; 49:3, 15).

After reading such strong assurances of Almighty, one never can accept negative statements of the skeptics, including R. Akiva, on the subject of the Ten Tribes of Israel.

R. Nachmanides answered those scholars who claimed that the Ten Tribes had already returned to the Promised Land in the times of the Prophets Jeremiah, Ezra or Nehemiah: "They are referred to in a general sense as from Israel (2 Chronicles 35:18) and not by their specific tribes since they represented only a **small portion** of their tribe. These are they who returned under Esra with the Jews from Babylon. They were not expressly mentioned by their tribes since they were attached to Judah. They all settled in the cities of Judah. **There was no Redemption for the Ten Tribes who remained in exile"** (Sefer HaGeulah, The Book of Redemption). That is why in the books of Ezra and Nehemiah only families of Judah, Benjamin, and Levy were listed.

R. Nachmanides gave a strict and clarifying answer to those who deny the existence of the Ten Tribes in exile: **"There was no Redemption for the Ten Tribes who remained in exile"!**

The Twelve Tribes of Israel will become again one nation and there will be one King, the Messiah son of David. The House of Israel will be no more divided into two nations. Together they will become one nation of Priests, a Light to the World. Together they will merit life in the Messianic Kingdom and in the wonderful, everlasting Heavenly World-to-Come, the ultimate destination for spiritually regenerated Humanity.

Despite all of the overwhelming evidence (especially the 'two sticks' of Ezekiel 37:15-28!), these people have rejected the plain truth of the Hebrew Bible and absolutely have not differentiated the meanings of the names Judah, Israel, Jerusalem, Samaria, Ephraim, Manasseh, Jews,—for them it all means Jews and nothing else. They ignore the simple and clear teaching of the Restoration of the whole House of Jacob in the End Time; they do not pay proper attention to the way how the Prophets of the Hebrew Bible have constantly made a careful distinction between the Kingdom of Israel and the Kingdom of Judah; between the Israelite People and the People of Judah. God has dealt with these two Kingdom and two nations completely separately throughout Scripture. And it will be that way until the advent of the Messiah and Redemption 'in the last days.'

The other scholars, even though they accept the concept of the existence of the Ten Tribes, for some strange, irrational reason call them 'Jews', as if they are indeed identifiable as the real physical descendants of Judah, Benjamin, and most of Levy who collectively have been known to the world as Jewish People. Of course, there is another understanding as to who might be called a 'Jew', beside being born of a Jewish mother, being converted according to Judaism or being the physical descendant of the citizens of Judaea, and that is abiding by the Jewish way of life and faith. The Ten Tribes have completely lost their Hebrew identity. They have forgotten the God of their fathers and His Divine Torah. They have worshipped idols, the 'gods which cannot save'. To call them 'Jews' under these circumstances is sacrilege and insult against the Jews who worship the God of Israel and live by His Holy Laws, who would rather sacrifice their life to keep their Jewish faith. It is very obvious that these criteria are not applicable to the Ten Tribes. To call them 'Jews' is incorrect and unscriptural.

This 'replacement theology' has taken deep roots among not only the Jewish religious communities around the world, but in the secular circles in Israel and in the Diaspora as well. It could not be more farther from the Biblical Truth!

God has always kept an eye on His people Israel in exile:

"And yet for all that, when they be in the land of their enemies, I will not cast them away, neither will I abhor them, to destroy them utterly, and to break My covenant with them; for I am the Lord, their God" (Leviticus 26:44).

Even after Israel went to Assyrian captivity, God reaffirmed that **"Mine eyes are upon all their ways; they are not hid from My face"** (Jeremiah 16:17).

"In every place where Israel was exiled the Shekhina (Divine Presence) was exiled with them" (Talmud, Megillah 29a; TJ, Ta'an. 1:1, 64a), as it is written in the Tanakh: "I shall become to them a small sanctuary in the countries where they shall come" (Ezekiel 11:16).

It is concerning Israel, the Ten Tribes in Exile, of whom the Almighty speaks:

"I the Lord have called thee in righteousness, and will hold thine hand, and will keep thee, and give thee for a covenant of the people, for a light of the Gentiles" (Isaiah 42:6).

God regards the house of Israel (Ten Tribes) "as a light to the Gentiles, as My salvation unto the end of the earth" (Isaiah 49:6). "You are My servant, Israel, in whom I will be glorified (Isaiah 49:3).

The time is coming when Israel, the servant of God, His 'first born son' (Exodus 4:22), "For I am a Father to Israel, and Ephraim is My firstborn" (Jeremiah 31:9), will totally repent and turn to the God of their fathers and will be rewarded for their righteousness: "And their seed shall be known among the Gentiles, and their offspring among the people; all that see them shall acknowledge them, that they are the seed which the Lord has blessed" (Isaiah 61:9).

In order for these prophecies to be fulfilled, the Ten Tribe of Israel will need to have repented, be reunited with Judah, and to have turned to God of Israel and His Immortal Torah. All of this will be accomplished in due time, in the 'days of Mashiah'.

Many people have not realized that Almighty has chosen the Israelites in the same way as He chose the Jewish People!

"This is what the LORD says, He who appoints the sun to shine by day, who decrees the moon and stars to shine by night, who stirs up the sea so that its waves roar—the LORD Almighty is His name: only if these ordinances vanish from my sight," declares the LORD, "will the descendants of Israel ever cease to be a nation before me" (Jeremiah 31:35-36).

Israel will not be forgotten nor rejected by God: "You are My servant. I have chosen you, and will not cast you away" (Isaiah 41:9).

In light of all of this, we would like to say to all those who confuse (whether by lack of knowledge or ignorance) the Israelite peoples, as something other than the Ten Tribes, together with the Jewish people: Be careful! Do not make this grave mistake. Listen to what God has said on this matter. Learn history and rethink your position.

This problem is not new. At the time of the prophet Ezekiel (592 b.c.) the Jews of Jerusalem turned away from the ten tribes of Israel in exile and spoke against their coming back to the land of their fathers. Listen how God rebuked them:

"Son of man, thy brethren, even thy brethren, the man of thy kindred, and all the house of Israel wholly, are they unto whom the inhabitants of Jerusalem have said, Get you far from the Lord; unto us is this land given in possession. Therefore say, thus saith the Lord God; although I have cast them far off among the heathen, and although I have scattered them among the countries, yet will I be to them as a little sanctuary in the countries where they shall come" (Ezekiel 11:15-16).

What does the Hebrew Bible Say of Judah and Israel?

In Scripture, God has carefully shown the difference between the house of Israel and the house of Judah, between the people of Israel and the people of Judah. Judge for yourself:

"And he shall set up an ensign for the nations, and shall assemble the outcasts of Israel, and gather together the dispersed of Judah from the four corners of the earth . . . Ephraim shall not envy Judah, and Judah shall not vex Ephraim"(Isaiah 11:12-13).

"In those days the house of Judah shall walk with the house of Israel, and they shall come together out of the land of the north to the land I have given for an inheritance unto your fathers"
(Jeremiah 3:18).

"For the house of Israel and the house of Judah have dealt very treacherously against Me, saith the Lord" (Jeremiah 5:11).

"And I will cause the captivity of Judah and the captivity of Israel to return, and will build them, as at the first" (Jer.33:7).

"Behold, the days come, saith the Lord, I will perform that good things which I have promised unto the house of Israel and to the house of Judah" (Jer. 33:14).

The best description concerning the destiny of Israel and Judah in the last days can be found in the famous 'Two Sticks' prophecy of Ezekiel 37: 16-24:

"And I will make them one nation in the land upon the mountains of Israel; and one king shall be king to them all; and they shall be no more two nations, neither shall they be divided into two kingdoms any more" (Verse 22).

These verses are convincingly clear and very understandable!

This reunification has never taken place in history, so it is definitely an event of the future. Until it happens, Judah and Israel will remain as two different entities. Is more evidence needed? With pleasure:

"Then shall the children of Judah and the children of Israel be gathered together" (Hosea 1:11).

"Therefore will I be unto Ephraim as a moth, and to the house of Judah as rottenness. When Ephraim saw his sickness and Judah saw his wound . . ." (Hosea 5:12-13).

Does anyone know that God speaks here of the Middle East 'Peace Process' between Israelis and Palestinians as 'Judah's wound'? What of the 'sick at heart' adulterous and godless Israel (Great Britain, USA, Canada, Australia, New Zealand and almost a good dozen of European countries, with the combined population of hundreds of millions of people)? It pictures the Godless and sinful Ephraim, the 'Lost Ten Tribes' of Israel in exile who lost their Israelite identity and knowledge of the God of their fathers and His Divine Laws and have worshipped the gods which 'cannot save'.

"And it shall come to pass, that as you were a curse among the heathen, O house of Judah, and house of Israel; so will I save you, and you shall be a blessing: fear not, but let your hands be strong" (Zechariah 8:13).

"And I will strengthen the house of Judah, and I will save the house of Joseph, and I will bring them again to place them; for I have mercy upon them: and they shall be as though I had not cast them off: for I am the Lord, their God, and will hear them" (Zechariah 10:6).

In all these passages the Almighty speaks separately of the house of Judah and the house of Israel. Nowhere in the Hebrew Bible does

God say that Judah and Israel are the same! By the way, when God mentions the names of Joseph, Manasseh, Ephraim or Samaria, this automatically means Israel, the 'lost' Ten Tribes of Israel in exile, to be more precise. **Ephraim or Manasseh are collective terms used in the Bible to identify the entire body of the Ten Tribes of Israel.**

When God speaks of the house of David, Judah or the house of Judah, Zion or inhabitants of Jerusalem, this automatically means Jews, the Jewish people. Sometimes the term 'Israel' might apply to all Twelve Tribes, depending on the context of the verses, as, for instance, in Ezekiel 38 and 39; or it could be applied to the Jews only (Ezra 2:2, 59-70; 3:1; Ezekiel 3:5; 8:10-12; 14:1). The term 'Judah' always means the Jews, i.e. Zephaniah 2:7; Zechariah 12-all.

Some people propagate the idea that the tribes of Israel are disappeared; assimilated with the nations of their exile; completely lost their identity; vanished; died out and unable to play any role in prophetic future; that God really does not care for their fate. They have been consigned to the realm of myth and fiction.

This is not true! God does remember His people. He has a Plan for the future reunification and redemption of all Israel, Judah and the 'Lost' Ten Tribes of Israel, in a Holy Land.

Just take a look at these passages of Hosea 1:10:

"Yet the number of the children of Israel shall be as the sand of the sea, which cannot be measured nor numbered; and it shall come to pass, that in the place where it was said unto them, you are not My people, there it shall be said unto them, you are the sons of the living God." Is it not impressive?

This prophecy will find its completeness during Ezekiel's 'two sticks' reunification with the advent of the Messiah. But until this happen, Judah and Israel will have continue remained two separate entities.

"Then shall the children of Judah and the children of Israel be gathered together" (Verse 1:11). Simple and clear! This will happen after the Almighty annihilates the evil hordes of Gog (Ezekiel 39:25).

Judah and Israel have their own uniqueness. Each one has its own task to perform. They need each other in these troublesome times. They have to learn and recognize their brotherhood. The sooner they repent and awaken to their Israelite identity, which means the acknowledgment of God of Israel as the one and only God Almighty of the Universe and His Divine Torah, and start helping and cooperating with each other, the sooner God will send the Messiah and redeem them.

Misconceptions in Identifications of Judah and Israel

Many people, especially after the establishment of the modern state of Israel in 1948, began to call the Jews 'Israelites', sincerely thinking that ancient Israelites are the same people as Jewish nation today. But they are not the same. Prior to the splitting in the ancient times of the United Kingdom of Israel, there were no Jews at that time, no Jewish nation. The Bible tells us that the people Moses led out from Egypt called themselves Hebrews: Abram the Hebrew (Genesis 14:3), Joseph the Hebrew (Genesis 39:14), God of the Hebrews (Exodus 5:3), or Israelites (Exodus 31:13; 33:5 and countless more). The very same people were recipients of the Torah on Mount Sinai. It is not correct to say that Torah was given to the Jews. In fact, the Torah was given to all tribes of Israel, to the Hebrew nation.

All Israelites are Semites because they are the descendants of Shem, one of the three sons of Noah. Although from Abraham came Ishmael (Arabs) and Isaac (through whom later on will descend the Israelites and Jews), Abraham himself was neither Jew (Israelite) nor Arab; he was just a Hebrew, named in the honor of his ancestor Eber. That is exactly what the Bible calls him—'Abram the Hebrew' (his name was not changed yet at this point to Abraham). It is of interest to take a look at this message of the Bible: "Sons were also born to Shem, whose older brother was Japheth; **Shem was the ancestor of all the sons of Eber**" (Genesis 10:21). For some reasons, the Scripture clearly states here that 'Shem was the ancestor of all the sons of Eber', indicating that this progenitor was so important, that all his descendants should have named after him. So, it was not a surprise that one of the 'sons of

Eber', Abraham, was named by his name, which cannot be revised and replaced by the word 'Jew' because it has nothing in common.

There is a Talmudic tradition, seemingly originated before the time of Moses, that God rewarded Eber for not taking part in the building the Tower of Babel as ordered by Nimrod (Genesis 11:4). For this reason God blessed Eber and his descendants and allowed them to use the original language which God gave to Adam at the Creation. This language is Hebrew. And as a special favor for his righteous deeds, God honored Eber's name by naming his offspring Hebrews. That is why all the sons of Eber are called 'Hebrews'. As it was shown, 'Eber', 'ha-ivri', and 'Hebrew' cannot be translated as 'Jew' because the correct translation is simply means 'Hebrews', the children of Eber. In the days of Abraham the term 'Jew' had never been used.

In Hebrew language the world 'the Hebrew' translated as 'ha-ivri', which could be understood as 'outsider', 'stranger', or 'one who crossed over' from another place. As it says in Genesis Rabbah, 'Abram separated himself from a word steeped in idolatry and polytheism by crossing over to worship one God, the Creator of all things'. Rashi commented the same way, and never translated 'ha-ivri' as 'Jew'. He even went farther explaining in details why Abram was called 'stranger' and 'outsider'. Abram was born east of Canaan in the city named Ur of Chaldea in Mesopotamia (Genesis11:28). Following God's command, (Genesis 12:1, 4), Abram crossed over the Euphrates River and become 'the stranger from the other side' among the people who dwelled in the land of Canaan. The other meaning of 'outsider' is that Abraham stood 'on the other side' in opposition to the entire pagan world.

Most commentators of the Bible have agreed that it is correct to consider Eber as the eponymous ancestor of the Hebrews.

Abraham 'the First Jew'

Some scholars simply disregard what we just said and insisting on calling Abraham 'the Jew' instead of Abraham 'the Hebrew'. They even specify that Abraham was 'the First Jew'. To say that Abraham was 'the First Jew', simply means that he descended from the Tribe of Judah, which is not the case because Abraham was born many hundreds of years before Judah. This is the narrowest interpretation. The other view of Abraham as 'the First Jew' may be rationalized with the fact that he was the Patriarch of the Jewish People and the Father of Judaism; that he was the first believer in a monotheistic God and entered into covenant with the Almighty and obeyed His Laws. All of this constitutes Judaism. First of all, Abraham was the Father not only of the Jews, but also of Israel (the Ten Tribes), of Ishmaelites, Edomites, and of many other nations. Secondly, the real Judaism began with the Divine Revelation at Mount Sinai, when God entered into Covenant and revealed to the Children of Israel (also called the Hebrews) the Ten Commandments with the rest of the Laws (613 in total). Moses and Aaron, in a broader religious sense, are the ones who we may also call 'the First Jews'. They for the first time in Hebrew history led Israel in worshiping God with all the precepts, rules and regulations required by the Laws of God (including circumcision, the main sign of the Covenant between God and Abraham). Some rabbis go to the extent of insisting that Abraham in his time knew and observed the whole Torah with all its Commandments, Sabbaths, Festivals, Kashrut, and so on, not only just circumcision. This is pure speculation. In the same way we could call the Patriarchs Heber and Noah 'the First Jews' because they eventually were also the progenitors of the Israelites (Jews and the Ten Tribes) and believed in the God of Israel. They were faithful, obedient and righteous men and 'walked with God'. That is why the Almighty honored and blessed them. He even established the Covenant between Himself and Noah as a perpetual token for all generations:

"And God said to Noah, This is the token of the covenant, which I have established between me and all flesh that is on the earth" (Genesis 9:17).

To 'walk with God' in the manner of the Patriarchs Enoch, Noah, and Eber, may we suggest, means to lead an upright and Godly life, purposeful, and dedicated to the true worship of God. They were all righteous in their conduct and obedient to the Laws of God in order to please their Maker (There is a Talmudic opinion that the Torah was in existence before the Creation of this World, Pesachim 54a; Nedarim 39b).

So would not all these three men, Enoch, Noah, and Eber be qualified too as 'the First Jews' in the manner of Abraham?

From the Patriarch Abraham came out many different nations. Three major monotheistic religions of Judaism, Christianity, and Islam sprang out of this progenitor (the Semites). Abraham is not only the Father of Judaism but Christianity and Islam as well. The New Testament and Koran are both attested to this truth. If it is alright to call Abraham 'the first Jew', would not it be correct also to call him 'the first Christian' or 'the first Muslim'?

Isaac also was neither Israelite nor Jew because the name 'Israel' was given by Almighty to his son Jacob (Genesis 35:10). Even then, when God changed the name of Jacob to Israel, Jacob could not have called 'Jew' because the Jews were destined to emerged much later from one of his twelve sons named Judah. Of course, the Israelites consisted of the twelve tribes, but nobody called at that period of time the separate tribe a nation, like Issachar nation, the nation of Reuben, nation of Joseph, nation of Simeon, or nation of Judah and so on. **They all were called Israelites or Hebrews**.

Judah became a nation after the division and establishing of their own state called Judaea. The term "Jew" also became known much later after the Babylonian captivity and the Greek domination over Palestine. According to some explanations, the word 'Jew' in Hebrew means 'Praise' (Genesis 29:35).

Therefore, if correctly applied, the Jewish People can be called 'the people of praise'.

Why would, after the separation, the northern kingdom call itself by the name of Israel? Because Manasseh and Ephraim were given this name by their grandfather Jacob-Israel's blessings (Genesis 48:16), and they were leaders of the rest of Israelite tribes. And why did the southern kingdom call itself Judaea? Because of Judah, who represented the most populous and dominant tribe, and was highly praised by his father and the brothers (Genesis 49:8). After the separation and exiles, Judah and Israel became absolutely different nations, living in different countries in the four corners of the earth. They have had their own histories, cultures, traditions, languages, and religions. Exactly, as the Bible predicted.

Same Brothers—Different Nations

Some people might wonder how that was possible that from the same father came different nations. The Bible answers this kind of questions by illustrating examples of Ishmael and Isaac, the sons of Abraham. Everybody knows that the Arabs (Ishmael) and the Israelites (Isaac) are completely different nations. Or that Esau (Edom) and Jacob (Israel), the twin-sons of Isaac and Rebekah, are also different nations today.

Here is how Scripture described the situation:

"And the children struggled together within her (Rebekah); and she said, if it be so, why am I thus? And she went to enquire of the Lord. And the Lord said unto her,

"Two nations are in thy womb, and two manners of people shall be separated from thy bowels; and the one people shall be stronger than the other people; and the elder shall serve the younger" (Genesis 25:22, 23).

The nations of Ishmael and Esau have one thing in common: they have hated Israelites from ancient times. Today they are the sworn enemies of Jacob's descendants and are still seeking vengeance and the destruction of Israel.

The Ten Tribes of Israel as 'being Christian'

How will the descendants of the Ten Tribes eventually reunite with the Jewish People? We have the answer to this complex question.

There are some scholars who envision the reunification of the Ten Tribes with Judah as 'being Christians'. They suggest leaving them alone as they are until the arrival of the Messiah who somehow at the End of Days will turn them from 'being Christians' to worshipping the God of their fathers, His Holy Torah and bring them back to the Promised Land.

We think that concept of "Israelites being Christians" is not correct and that the truth is not represented by "Lost Israelite identity" or "Hebrew roots": Their eyes and hearts still have not been opened to the Almighty God of Israel. They have continued to worship their Trinity God and Messiah Jesus. They preach the doctrine of 'no works' which is the direct rebellion against God's Laws. Even Jesus was against this teaching: "If you want to enter into life, keep the Commandments". How can they return to their Israelites roots without acceptance of God' Sacred Words and His Laws? The definition of sin is the transgression of these very Laws. Instead of surrendering, repenting and obeying these Laws, the Christians have decided to bypass and ignore them because, in their mind, salvation will come 'not through works and obeying the Laws of God but faith alone'.

Scripture and the Sages say this is not acceptable!

"There is a way that seems right to a man, but its end is the way of death" (Proverbs 14:12).

"Keep my Decrees and laws, for the man who obeys them will live by them. I am the LORD" (Leviticus 18:5).

"These gods, who did not make the heavens and the earth, will perish from the earth and from under the heavens" (Jeremiah 10:11).

Solomon (Ecclesiastes 12:12-14) concludes: "Fear God, and keep His Commandments; for this is the whole duty of everyone."

Who is God speaking about in the verses below?

"O My people! Those who lead you cause you to err, and destroy the way of your paths. Woe to those who call evil good and good evil" (Isaiah 3:12; 5:20).

And more:

"For the customs of the people are vanities. A tree from the forest is cut down and worked with the axe by the hands of the craftsmen. They decorate it with gold and silver; they fasten it with the nails and with hummers that it moves not" (Jeremiah 10:3-4). Is this not the Christmas tree, very familiar to all Christians, God speaks of and condemns here? Or consider another passage:

"What fools they are who carry around their wooden idols and pray to gods that cannot save" (Isaiah 45:20).

To 'bring the Israelites back' does not literally mean to bring them to the Promised Land only. Rather, turn them to the God of Israel and to His Divine Torah. We doubt very much that the Almighty will redeem those of the Ten Tribes who wish to remain 'being Christians.' Those who reject the God of Israel and continue worshiping false gods, who cannot save, and craven idols, "Will I number you to the sword, and you shall all bow down to the slaughter" (Isaiah 65:12). Why such a harsh punishment? "It is because these people abandoned the Covenant of the Lord the God of their fathers" (Deuteronomy 29:25). The explanation given is right on target!

This issue is very important. It is a matter of life and death. Here is no compromise. God warns those who 'forsake God of Israel and forget 'My Holy Mountain' (Isaiah 65:11), who wish to be remained Christians,

"My servants will eat, but you will go hungry; My servants will drink, but you will go thirsty; My servants will rejoice, but you will be sad and ashamed. And the Lord God will put you to death" (Isaiah 65:11, 15).

These are very strong words! Those Christians of the Ten Tribes of Israel in exile who understand and accept the prophecies of the Last Days, (especially prophecies of Israel being 'My Kingdom of Priests' and 'My holy nation'), and wish to fulfill them, better listen to what the Almighty God has said and obey His Divine Word.

"Turn to Me and be saved, all the ends of the earth, for I am God, and there is no other" (Isaiah 45:22).

It is mostly the responsibility and Divine Mission of the Jewish People to go to the Israelite Tribes in exile, wherever they live, and bring them the light of the Torah and knowledge of the God of Israel. It is their duty and destiny to do everything possible to awake this sleeping giant, Joseph, to their Israelite identity and bring them back to One and only Almighty God, God of Israel.

Therefore, Judah will bring to the Holy Land not 'Joes' and 'Jacks' of Joseph, the 'born again Christian Zionists', Jews lost to Christianity, Christians of the Ephraimites Tribers who found their Hebrew roots in order make a phony Christian Aliyah to missionize and steal Jewish People from the flock of the Almighty. Quite the contrary. 'Our' Judah will bring back the newly repented, the Torah accepting Israelites with a 'new heart' and a 'new spirit' who finally will get out of their 'graves' of exile and out of the chains of false religions. They will found the God of their fathers, the one and only Almighty God of Israel. As the Bible says: **"The children of Israel in the Last Days will seek the Lord their God" (Jeremiah 50:4-5).** 'The Lord their God' most definitely means God of Israel, not Jesus, Mohammad or anybody else.

The God of Israel has always remembered His People Israel and He has a beautiful future for them.

"For your maker is your husband—the Lord Almighty is His name; your Redeemer is the Holy One of Israel, the God of all the Earth. For a small moment I have forsaken you; but with great mercies will I gather you" (Isaiah 54:5, 7).

Yes, we would send Judah to the Ten Tribes to bring them the light of the Divine Torah with its everlasting Laws, with the knowledge of God that they might realize who they really are and be able to restore themselves to the point as they were at the Mount Sinai when the Creator revealed Himself to all Twelve Tribes of the Israelite nation and gave them His Holy Torah.

"Also for you, Judah, a harvest is appointed, when I return the captivity of My People" (Hosea 6:11). This verse is a direct confirmation of the Almighty that the rest of the whole House of Israel (Ten Tribes) will return and join their brothers—the Jewish People.

The People of Israel were designated by God to be unto Him "a Kingdom of Priests and a Holy Nation" (Exodus 19:6).

To achieve this glorious status and become what the Almighty wants them to be, the Israelites of the Ten Tribes cannot longer remain "being Christians". No matter how many Christian apologists may say that Judaism and Christianity are the similar religion, worshipping the same God; the truth is that these religions are very different, and they do not worship the same God. They never have.

To repent means to change one's way of thinking and behaving. In order to achieve this, the Ten Tribes have to be shown the truth of their Israelite origin and receive a clear explanation as to how they become what they are. It needs demonstrating to them that the reason they have forgotten their Hebrew origin and the God of Israel is sin and transgression of the God's Laws. Basically, they have violated Commandments # 1 and # 4. The First Commandment is: "You shall have no other gods before Me"; and the Fourth: "Remember the Sabbath day, to keep it holy" (Exodus 20:2-17).

"Keep My Sabbaths holy, that they may be a sign between us. Then you will know that I am the LORD your God" (Ezekiel 20:20).

This 'sign' has been lost by the Ten Tribes for more than two and a half thousand years. The Israelites have forgotten the God-given holy Sabbaths and replaced it by the meaningless Sundays. God foresaw what would happen to His people Israel in exile.

"And that which comes into your mind shall not be at all, that you say, We will be as the Gentiles, as the families of the countries, to serve wood and stone" (Ezekiel 20:32).

Nevertheless, the Almighty gives hope and courage to Israelites to repent and come back to Him.

"All who rage against you will surely be ashamed and disgraced; those who oppose you will be as nothing and perish. **You, O Israel, My servant, whom I have chosen.** Do not fear, for I am with you; do not be dismayed, **for I am your God.** I will strengthen you and help you" (Isaiah 41:8-11).

The Israelites will come to the Promised Land from the all corners of the World: "Behold, they will come from afar; some from the north, some from the west, and some from the land of Sinim" (Isaiah 49:12).

"I will say to the north, 'Give them up!' and to the south, 'Do not hold them back.' Bring my sons from afar and my daughters from the ends of the earth" (Isaiah 43:6).

More on Definition of Judah and Israel

The Judeans of old had acknowledged the existence of the Ten Tribes of Israel in their countries of exile. They perfectly understood the differences between their peoples. Modern Israelis however, citizens of the State of Israel, and the majority of the Jews in the Diaspora, have no knowledge of it and are indifferent on this matter. Supersessionism or "Replacement theory" is so obvious and convenient for them that they are satisfied with it and are not looking for any other options. Rabbis and scholars are especially to be found in the mainstream of this trend.

In the Hebrew Bible there are so many prophecies for the latter years, pertaining to Judah and Israel separately, that our conclusion cannot be wrong—Judah and Israel are not synonymous! They are two very distinct and separate nations. To understand and accept this Biblical truth is the key to understanding Bible Prophecy.

As Nachmanides says, it is obvious from the Scripture that the House of Joseph represents the Ten Tribes of Israel in exile who never have been reunited with the Jewish People, but are destined to return to the Promised Land and to be redeemed by the Almighty in the days of Mashiach. They should be ashamed not to recognize this fact!

In Zechariah 12 and 14 and Zephaniah 2:7 God speaks of Judah only; the name of Israel is not mentioned there. Why? Because the Bible is describing events before the reunification of Judah and Israel.

Meanwhile, in Ezekiel 38 and 39 God speaks of Israel after reconciliation and reunification of Judah and Joseph. So in this case 'Israel' means all Twelve Tribes of the house of Jacob.

All these prophecies are very well known to the students of the Bible. Nobody can deny their importance for future fulfillment.

We hope that the information we have provided in this work will be of sufficient help for many to understand one of the most important issues of Judaism—the definition of Israel and Judah, and their roles in future events concerning the Messianic Age and the World-To-Come.

Some skeptics say, 'Well, even if the lost Ten Tribes of Israel do exist, how we (or they) know, whether or not they are Israelites? There are no genetic proofs and no records to which tribes we (or they) may belong to.' We would advise them not to worry. God knows His children: He knows who they are, and where they are. As oil will not mix with others liquids, so Israel will not assimilate with other nations forever. It is written in Deuteronomy 29:29, "The secret things belong to Lord our God". In another place said: "It is the glory of God to conceal a matter; to search out a matter is the glory of kings" (Proverbs 25:2).

"For, lo, I will command, and I will sift the house of Israel among all nations, like as corn is sifted in a sieve, yet shall not the least grain fall upon the earth" (Amos 9:9).

God gives us a hint where the majority of the Ten Tribes of Israel are geographically located:

"They shall walk after the Lord; He shall roar like a lion: when He shall roar, then the children shall tremble from the west" (Hosea 11:10).

Manasseh and Ephraim eventually will have rejected God of Israel, while Judah still remained faithful:

"Ephraim compassed Me about with lies, and the house of Israel with deceit; but Judah yet ruled with God, and the faithful with the saints" (Hosea 11:12).

In this verse, as in any others quoted above, God shows the difference between the house of Israel and the house of Judah so convincingly clear that only stubborn and ignorant people can reject the plain truth of the Bible.

Where are the Ten Tribes Today?

Prophecy says that Israel will multiply as the stars of the heaven and as the sand of the sea shore, which undoubtedly means hundreds of millions of people; the house of Israel will spread abroad to the four corners of the globe; God will be always with Israel, and bring them to the Holy Land again; all nations of the world will be blessed through Israel; God will not leave Israel until everything written and spoken will be done. Clearly, God is not speaking here only about the Jewish people, whose total population in the world today is only 13,155,000, of which 5,634,300 live in the State of Israel, and the rest (6,444,000) are in the Diaspora, mainly in the USA. And the Jews have had no nations and kingdoms of their own, except for Judaea in the past and the modern State of Israel today. Meanwhile, God predicted to Israel that 'a nation and a company of nations shall be of thee, and kings shall come out of thy lions'; "I will make of thee a multitude of people" (Genesis 35:11; 48:4). Surely, this applies not only to Judah, but to all Israel. The total population of the house of Israel in the world, the so called 'Lost' Ten Tribes, is about 450,000,000 people! And the tribes of Israel have never been lost in the eyes of the Almighty God. These tribes are around us, some of them are among the mightiest countries of the world e.g. United States of America (Manasseh); others have lost some of their greatness such as Britain (Ephraim); while others are otherwise distinguished e.g. Australia, Canada, Belgium, Sweden, Switzerland, Finland. They are all Israelite countries, originating from Israelite Tribes. If somebody wants to know more about this subject, we gladly recommend visiting the **Brit-Am, Movement of the Ten Tribes of Israel, Web Site: //www.britam.org**

Brit-Am is headed by its founder, a very knowledgeable and dedicated man, the popular theologian and writer Yair Davidiy from Jerusalem.

All Scripture and the Sages say that the Israelite Ten Tribes eventually will return to the Promised Land and receive the Heavenly Torah once more. Whosoever does not accept this plain Biblical truth is guilty of denying the Word of God.

There are many people, Jews and Gentiles alike, who have understood these prophecies of the End of Days; who find and rightfully identify the countries of Israelite origin. They are feverishly working towards the awakening and reunification of all the families of Israel in order to fulfill the prophecies of final Redemption and the Messianic Age.

The Ten Tribes of Israel are still in the 'graves of exile', figuratively speaking. They have completely lost their Israelite identity. Their 'dry bones' (Ezekiel 37:1-14) are waiting for spiritual revival and restoration to their original faith of the God of Israel and His immortal Torah. The Almighty gives us assurance that His Words are holy and true:

"Judah and Israel will be "as though I had not cast them off" (Zechariah 10:6).

We are absolutely positive that it will exactly happen to Judah and Israel as God said it would!

Ramban (Nahmanides) explained that Israel had been exiled, separated from nourishment of the wisdom of Torah, from the Law, and he welcomed the idea that Judah, the keeper of the Law, should go to the Ten Tribes and awaken them to the knowledge of the God of Israel.

Today most of the World unjustly goes against the Jews. Anti-Semitism, hatred and racism have reached unprecedented levels. The very survival of the Jewish state of Israel is at stake. All people of good will, who believe in the Bible as the Sacred Word of the Almighty, should make a choice and stand firmly on the side of Israel. That is what God wants them to do. In turn, they will save themselves and help God to advance His Divine Plan for the World-to-Come, which would be absolutely impossible if Israel did not exist.

"I will bless those who bless you and curse those who curse you. All the families of the earth will be blessed through you (Israel)" (Genesis 12:3 I).

The Jewish People depend on their Israelite brothers and sisters. Judah cannot fight God wars alone. Judah and Joseph must reunite in order to face enormous challenges in these troublesome times of the end of our age. **"For a long time Israel had been without the true God, and without a teaching priest, and without Torah" (II Chronicles 15:3).**

Judah will be that 'Teaching Priest', a watchman for the house of Israel (Ezekiel 3:17), who perfectly understands the prophecies of the End Times. We sincerely hope and believe that this time will eventually come! Judah will be the watchman, who is destined, called by God to fulfill the Divine Mission—to bring his brothers and sisters of the Ten Tribes to the 'true God' of Israel; to His Torah and to the Holy Land.

"For Torah will go forth from Zion" (Isaiah 2:3).

The sooner they repent, the sooner they will be reunited and redeemed by the Almighty. Judah should prepare the state of Israel, its economy, infrastructure, defense, and agriculture in a proper way to accommodate of coming of hundreds of millions of their brothers and sisters from the Ten Tribes of Israel.

Judah once saved the life of Joseph by convincing his brothers not to kill him but rather sell him as a slave,

"Come, and let us sell him to the Ishmaelites, and let not our hand be upon him; for he is our brother and our flesh. And his brothers were content" (Genesis 37:27).

Now the time has come for Judah to repair all wrongdoings to his brother Joseph (the Ten Tribes of Israel in Exile) and bring him back to the rest of the family, to the Almighty God of his fathers, and to the Promised Land.

The Jewish People have to take the initiative, to awaken the giant Joseph. They must go to the Ten Tribes wherever they live, and bring to them the light of Torah and knowledge of the 'true God' of Israel. That is exactly what God wishes them to do:

"In those days the house of Judah shall walk with the house of Israel, and they shall come together out of the land of the north to the land that I have given for an inheritance unto your fathers (Jeremiah 3:18).

"Walk with the house of Israel" some translators understood as saying 'go unto'.

"Judah and Benyamin (i.e. the present-day Jews) are destined to go unto the Ten Tribes in exile and bring them back in order to merit with them the Messianic Era and life in the World-To-Come" (Yalkut Shimeoni, Song of Solomon 905).

"For on My holy mountain, on the high mountain of Israel," declares the Lord GOD, "there the whole House of Israel, **all of them**, will serve Me in the Land; I will accept you as fragrant incense when I bring you out from the nations and gather you from the countries where you have been scattered, and I will show Myself holy among you in the sight of the nations; and then you will know that I am the Lord" (Ezekiel 20:40-42).

Then, united together and redeemed by God, they will become again one nation and one Kingdom of Priests, a light to the World. Together they will merit the Messianic Era and life in the World-To-Come.

"Whosoever shall call on the name of the Lord shall be delivered" (Joel 2:32).

We apologize to our readers for the lengthy discourse on the subject of Judah and Israel. We feel it was necessary for two reasons. Firstly, it will help people better understand the Biblical prophecies of the End Times and the geopolitical development in the world today by learning the truth about the Ten Tribes of Israel and obligations of Judah towards their brothers and each other, because the Jews need Joseph, and Joseph needs Judah; secondly, it will help us to successfully argue against the Satmar and Neturei Karta theological position, rooted in the prohibitions of the Three Oaths of Shir Ha Shirim, which is the subject of the next Chapter.

CHAPTER VII:
THE THREE OATHS AND
THE SONG OF SONGS

Finally we have arrived at the Chapter concerning the Three Oaths. What are these Oaths? Where did they come from? How are they connected with the main theme of our work, the State of Israel and its prophetic future? What effect do they have on Judaism, Zionism and the Satmar and Neturei Karta movements? In this Chapter, we will try to give answers on these and many other related questions.

The Song of Songs and its Puzzles

Let us begin with the smallest book of the Bible, where the Three Oaths were found, the Song of Songs. It contains only 117 verses, but it is the most obscure, controversial and puzzling book of the Tanakh.

Some people believe that authorship of this book belongs to Solomon because the first verse of Chapter 1 says: "The Song of Songs, which is Solomon's." Others have argued that the correct translation of the title should read as 'which is for Solomon', as was common practice in ancient times. There is a solid tradition in the Talmud (Bava Batra 15a, based on Proverbs 25:1) that Hezekiah, King of Judea (715 b.c.-687 b.c.), was the author of the book. He has been greatly praised by the Bible:

"For since the time of Solomon the son of David king of Israel there was not the like in Jerusalem" (2 Chron.31:26).

There is also a suggestion that the book was written by God and dedicated to His love for Israel. There is no mention in the book about Solomon's ancestry, specifically, that his father was King David, as there is in his books of Proverbs and in Ecclesiastes. The name 'Solomon' is translated from the Hebrew 'Shlomo' and the expression could be read as saying "the King to whom peace belongs", and God is the source of all peace.

The time of this book is also in dispute. It varies from an earlier date circa 950 b.c. which is close to Solomon's time, to a very late 300-200 b.c., the time of an anonymous writer. Linguistic analysis points out that vocabulary of the book is derived from ancient Hebrew and from post-exilic languages, such as Persian, Greek, and Aramaic.

The title 'The Song of Songs' depicts supremacy, greatness, excellence over the 1005 songs Solomon wrote (I Kings 4:32), like similar titles such as 'the king of kings,' or 'holy of holies'. In Hebrew it is rendered as 'Shir ha-Shirim', in a short version of Latin it is called 'Canticles'. The Song of Songs is found in the last section of the Hebrew Bible, known as the 'Ketuvim' (Writings), where the special group of 'Hagiographa' books is located, such as Job, Psalms, Proverbs, and Ecclesiastes.

Disagreements about contents of this book have persisted up to this day. Some expositors taught that in the earlier history of Israel this book was the subject of literary interpretations only and understood it as a poem of love and marriage. In an ancient translation of the Hebrew Bible into Greek language, the Septuagint, by the seventy Jewish Elders in the time of the King Ptolemy II Philadelphus (285-246 b.c., Tractate Megillah 9), the predominant method of translation of the 'Song of Songs' was the literal one. Later on, in the time of the completion of the Talmud, (around the end of the 6 Century a.c.), the interpretation of the 'Songs' become mainly allegorical. The Sages had begun to violate the principal of literal translation of Scripture which says 'no verse of the Torah may be divorced from its plain meaning', (Babylonian Talmud: Tractate Shabbath, folio 63a), and universally cleaved to the method of allegorization of the 'Songs'.

"Those who recite a verse of 'Songs' as they would a common song, or who read its verses in inappropriate circumstances, bring evil to the world, because the Torah wraps itself in sackcloth, and standing before the Holy One, blessed be He, complains: "Master of the World, Your children have made me a harp on which mockers play" (Sanhedrin 101a).

Accordingly, the theme of the book was understood differently. Some Haggadic Midrashim translated it as the story about the Messiah, the time of the Third Temple, the history of Israel from the time of the Exiles to the future Messianic Age. Even some found the Prophet of Islam Muhammad in verse 5:16 of 'Songs'! There have been some theologians who understood the Song of Songs as referring to the Exodus from Egypt. Others pointed to events concerning the Torah on Mount Sinai where the God of Israel revealed Himself to the Israelite nation. Few insisted that the Canticles is all about the Tabernacle or the Solomon Temple in Jerusalem.

But most Jewish scholars have treated this book as explicitly religious, written in allegorical form and representing the relationship between God and Israel. It is interesting to note, that the name of God is never mentioned in the Song, and neither is it in the books of Esther or Ecclesiastes either. Nevertheless, it has been insisted that the book depicts the allegorical love between the Israelite People and God.

Others say that the book is a wonderful poem celebrating human love and sexuality. It is regarded as one of the greatest pieces of erotic literature ever written. Socrates called the Song "the erotic mania of the soul for the divine". Christians have interpreted it as an allegorical relationship between Jesus and the Church or Christ and the human soul, as husband and wife.

In Jewish mysticism, Kabbalah, in the book of Zohar, the Song became the most important Biblical text, not only regarded as sacred erotica, but profoundly linking to the entire Torah, reflecting on Jewish history beginning with the Forefathers, the exodus from Egypt, the subsequent defeat and exile, future redemption and restoration, and even the resurrection of the dead (Zohar, Parshat Teruma, Daf.143).

The Kabbalistic Sages viewed Shir-ha-Shirim as a craving dialogue between the rational soul and active intellect imprisoned within the human body, which is the obstacle in the path of their union with Hashem.

Some scholars insist that Song of Solomon is nothing other than a hymn, glorifying the ideal human love between King Solomon and a poor shepherd girl, Shulamite, before, during and after marriage. There are differences of opinion on the number and task of the characters involved. In addition to Solomon-lover and Shulamite-beloved; man is Solomon, woman is "Wisdom"; lover is Messiah, woman is Israel; the Lord is Lover, the Jewish people are the beloved; there is the Shepherd-lover in between, whom Shulamite chose over King Solomon despite all his riches and splendor. The young shepherd was victorious because he was the one 'whom my soul loveth', his true love satisfied her heart and soul, whereas the love of the King offered only pleasure and luxury for the bodily senses.

Others maintain that this is a true story of the first love between Solomon and Abishag the Shunammite, although they accepted parallel allegorical interpretation of God's love for His people, where God praises Israel and Israel praises God. Who was Abishag the Shunammite? Her story is recorded in the I Kings, chapter I:

"Now King David was old and stricken in years; and they covered him with clothes, but he got no heat. So they sought for a fair damsel throughout all the costs of Israel, and found Abishag a Shunammite, and brought her to the king. And the damsel was very fair, and cherished the king, and ministered to him: but the king knew her not" (Verses 14).

Young Solomon met and fell in love with beautiful Abishag in the palace of his father David. Since King David never had intercourse with her and had not married her, she was free, and Solomon, after getting rid of Adonijah, (fourth son of David and Haggith, who had plotted against Solomon and wanted to marry his father's concubine), made Abishag his wife.

According to one of the different opinions, the book may be regarded as a criticism against King Solomon who had 700 wives and 300 concubines in his harem (I Kings 11:3); against sexual exploitation of women and promiscuity; and as a triumph of true pure love and beautiful marriage over unfaithfulness, temporal bodily pleasure and broken dreams of the heart outside the marriage.

How Solomon could be the author of such a Divinely-inspired holy book, glorifying the institution of marital love, people argued, since he had the reputation of being a violator of the Ten Commandments, a sinner?

"For Solomon went after Ashtoreth the goddess of the Zidonians, and after Milcom the abomination of the Ammonites. And Solomon did evil in the sight of the Lord, and went not fully after the Lord, as did David, his father" (I Kings 11:5-6).

On the other hand, there is a Jewish belief that in no way can a profane person produces a holy book. The Canticles, the Holy of Holies, must have been written by a holy man, which is Solomon.

This book has also been considered as just a collection of ancient Near Eastern love ditties similar to Sumerian erotic passages, the Egyptian Ramesside love poetry, and the Syrian Wedding Songs, where the groom is presented as a King and the bride plays a role as the Queen.

If the Song of Solomon is just promoting human sexual love and marriage, sometimes passionately and frankly erotic; without well expressed religious or theological motives or prophetic insides, how come, then, that this little puzzling book, after long debate, was accepted by the Council of Jamnia (Yavneh) in 90 a.c. in the Bible canon and placed within the category of 'Wisdom' Sacred books in the Tanakh? The Song definitely entered the canon not only as a secular love poem. Something else had moved the wise men of Jamnia to render their decision.

What was it? Allegory? Yes, it is the allegorical interpretations of the text with Hidden meanings, which have little or no connection with the meaning of the words of the text translated. That is the answer! And here are some examples of it.

"Let him kiss me with the kisses of his mouth—for your love is more delightful than wine" (Song of Songs 1:2). This verse is explained as referring to Israel who at Sinai took upon itself to keep the revealed Torah, and God sent an Angel to kiss each Israelite. 'Wine' here symbolizes the Torah, which makes one spiritually rejoice in heart and brings delight and comfort to his soul.

"I am black but comely" (Songs 1:5). The interpreters understood: 'I am black through my own deeds or in my eyes, but comely through the deeds of the Patriarchs or comely in the sight of God'.

That is why Rabbi Akiba said: "Heaven forbid that any man in Israel ever disputed that the Song of Songs is holy" (The Mishnah Yadayim 3:5). "Anyone who would dare treat this book as a secular love poem forfeits his share in the World to come", concluded R. Akiva.

The Song of Solomon is the most difficult and intriguing book of the Old Testament. Rabbi Saadia explained:

"Know, my brother, that you will find great differences in interpretation of the Song of Songs . . . it resembles locks to which the keys have been lost."

Jewish Sages have interpreted the Song as allegorical love between God and Israel. The concept of identifying God as a husband and Israel as a wife is very well known in Hebrew Scriptures:

"For thy Maker is thine husband . . . For the Lord hath called thee as a woman forsaken and grieved in spirit, and a wife of youth . . . For a small moment have I forsaken thee; but with great mercies will I gather thee" (Isaiah 54:5-7).

"I will greatly rejoice in the Lord, my soul shall be joyful in my God; for He has closed me with the garments of salvation, He has covered me with the rope of righteousness, as a bridegroom decked Himself with ornaments, and as a bride adorned herself with her jewels" (Isaiah 61:10).

"They say, if a man put away his wife, and she go from him and become another man's, shall he return unto her again? . . . but thou hast played the harlot with many lovers; yet return again to Me, saith the Lord" (Jeremiah 3:1).

"Return, O backsliding children, saith the Lord; for I am married unto you" (Jeremiah 3:14).

These are just few examples of the typological expression of metaphorical relationship between God and the People of Israel, as human relationship between husband and wife. Despite the fact that some scholars have argued against allegorical interpretation, saying that the Song of Songs nowhere gives hint to an allegoric understanding and even using the allegorical approach, the result is so subjective, that there is no way to rightly identify correct interpretation. The text itself, they say, does not indicate that we should interpret this book differently than any other Bible book. Song of Song's events really took place, and Solomon and Shulamite were real historical personalities. All things are possible to those who allegorize.

Although the Canticles are accepted by most scholars according to the concept of an allegorical interpretation, the discussion has not reached an accepted consensus and has left other possibilities open.

No other book in the Scriptures involves so many controversies and variety of interpretations than the Song of Songs, which is Solomon's.

The Three Oaths

The verses of the Song of Songs that originated the Three Oaths are: 2:7; 3:5; 8:4. What are they saying?

"I charge you, O ye daughters of Jerusalem, by the roes, and by the hinds of the field, that ye stir not up, nor awake my love, till it please" (Songs 2:7). The wordings of verse 3:5 are identical to 2:7. The third verse of Oaths is Songs 8:4:

"I charged you, O daughters of Jerusalem, that ye stir not up, nor awake my love, until it pleases."

Whose words are these? Who is speaking in verses 2:7; 5:3; and 8:4? Many modern day commentators have understood that these "Chargers" belong to beloved Shulamite, the main female character, whose intimate thoughts, feelings and dreams are recorded 53% of the time, while the male lover speaks for 39% in the book. They interpret these passages literally, thinking that the main message here is human love between the lover and beloved:

"Daughters of Jerusalem do not arouse or awaken love until it so desires."

Love needs time. Do not rush it, do not excite it, and do not stir it up. Wait for the right time, no matter how long it takes. Let love take its natural course. To illustrate their point, they explain that as the gazelle is a member of the antelope family, and the hind is a female deer, both animals are very skittish, easily frighten, and if anyone wants to approach them closely, must exercise extreme patience and caution. And so too with love.

As our readers already have learned previously, from the same three verses of Song of Songs come the Three Prohibition Oaths, which are the subjects of our discussion here.

These Three Oaths are recorded in the narrative, Midrash Ketubot 111a of the Babylonian Talmud, containing a discussion defending Rav Zeira's decision to leave Babylon and go to the Land of Israel. They were taken from the Solomon's Song of Songs, and in large part consist of an exegetical analysis of the three verses of allegorical text translated as love relationship between God and Israel. Here are the quotes of the Oaths as they are conveyed in the Gemara (Talmud):

"What are these Three Oaths?

One, that **Israel** should not storm the wall (Rashi: forcefully return to the Land of Israel).

Two, the Holy One made **Israel** take an oath not to rebel against the nations of the world.

Three, the Holy one made the nations vow that they would not oppress **Israel** too much".

We ask our readers to note right away that in all the Three Oaths the name 'Israel' is written; there is no name 'Judah' mentioned at all. As we have explained elsewhere, Israel (the Ten Tribes) and Judah are not the same nations at this particular time and will continue to be different national entities until the Reunification and the Final Redemption (Ezekiel 37:19-28). The conclusion is: The Three Oaths are meant to be for Israel, not for Judah!

Does the Hebrew Bible support the Notion of the Prohibition Oaths?

Many students of the Bible wonder how it was possible from the simple words "Do not stir up nor awaken love until it pleases" to come up unexpectedly with prohibition Oaths? They say that such a rendering of the verses of Song of Songs goes against the literal meaning of the Bible. In many instances throughout the Scripture God has encouraged His People to end the exile, to emigrate to the Promised Land "en masse" and establish their own kingdom.

"Set up road signs; put up guideposts. Remember the highway, the road on which you traveled. Return, O Virgin Israel, return to your towns. How long will you wander, O unfaithful daughter? (Jeremiah 31:21-22).

This passage speaks of Israel. Where do we see prohibitions here? On the contrary, God exhorts and pleads with His People to return to Him and His Land. As loving father, with broken heart, He begs the children of Israel to listen to Him and return home because "The Lord has redeemed His servant Jacob" (Isaiah 48:20). It is up to the house of Israel to make her own decision whether to repent, end the exile, and return to the Promised Land and be faithful to God or not.

"Awake, awake, put on your strength, O Zion! Shake off your dust; rise up, O Jerusalem; free yourself from the chains of the bondage from your neck, O captive daughter of Zion" (Isaiah 52:1-2).

Seems, this is a direct command to Judah (Jerusalem, Zion) to end the imprisonment of the exile, to break the chains of slavery from her neck, deliver them from the bondage and proclaim liberty.

God unconditionally, whether they repent or not, says to the Israelites that the time of the exile is ended and the Divine Decree is no more in force.

"The punishment of your iniquity is finished daughter of Zion; He will no longer carry you away into captivity" (Lamentations 4:22).

The motives of these verses cannot be compatible with the prohibition of the Three Oaths!

"Turn, O backsliding children, for I am married unto you. Return, faithless people, and I will heal your backsliding. Behold, we come unto Thee; for Thou art the Lord our God" (Jeremiah 3:14, 22).

These verses definitely do not speak of a prohibition to end the exile and return to the Promised Land. Quite the opposite! They are pleading, exhorting, and even demanding the entire house of Israel to do so.

"Behold, I will open your graves, and cause you to come up out of your graves, My People. Then I will bring you back to the Land of Israel" (Ezekiel 37:12).

Here are the same motives of ending the exile and returning home to the Promised Land.

The Torah Jews against Zionism have taken these Oaths as a prohibition for the Jewish people to end the Exile, to emigrate to the Promised Land and build there a state before God allowed them to do so and sent the Messiah. This has been their theological base for more than a century without any significant changes.

What do the Sages Say?

There are a variety of opinions among Jewish Sages on this subject. The Rambam (i.e. Maimonides, 1135-1204 a.c.) may have considered the Oaths as a Divine Decree and as a warning that such actions to end the Exile would be unsuccessful in his time. Nevertheless, in his "Epistle to the Jews of Yemen" he interpreted the oaths metaphorically, not literally, and did not include them in the main work of his life, the Mishneh Torah as legally, Halakhically binding.

Rabbi Chaim Vital (1543-1620 a.c.), 16th century Kabbalist, said that, according to our Sages, the time of these Oaths had expired, because the Oaths were binding only for one thousand years.

The Ramban (i.e. Nachmanides, 1194-1270 a.c.) had never treated the Oaths as Halakhicly binding. On the contrary, he propagated an idea that Jews have to conquer and settle in the Land of Israel in every generation as positive commandment, and considered such actions as a great Mitzvah in the sight of the Lord.

"Living in Israel is equated with the rest of the Mitzvoth combined" (Numbers 33:53; Tosefta Avodah Zara 5, 2).

"A person should always live in Eretz Yisroel; anyone who lives in the Diaspora is as if he worships idols", concluded Ramban based on Ketubot 110a.

The Maharal of Prague (1525-1609 a.c.) is often understood as saying that the Oaths were legally binding and that Jews could not violate them even though the nations threatened to kill them with terrible tortures. There are some opinions of scholars and particularly of R. Menachem Kasher that the conclusions of the Maharal were understood wrongly, and the real position of the Maharal towards the Oaths is in a manner similar to that of Rambam: The Oaths are Divine decrees that exile cannot be shortened, and our effort to do so will only end in disaster. Such an event happened to the descendants of Ephraim, who tried to shorten the predestined time of exile in Egypt and to hurry the redemption.

A legend says that members of the Tribe of Ephraim, who were in Egyptian Bondage with the rest of Israel before the Exodus, miscalculated the Time of Redemption. God told Moses that the Israelites would be in Egyptian bondage for 400 years (Genesis 15:13). They thought the time had come 30 years beforehand and attempted to leave. They miscalculated the time of Redemption by counting from the day of God's Covenant with Abraham instead of the day of the birth of Isaac. The Philistines met them and killed many of them; so only ten were left to turn back.

The Satmar Rebbe (1887-1979) built a vehement position against Zionism and the State of Israel based on the Three Oaths which he evaluated as strict legal prohibitions for the Jewish people not to "ascend like a wall" to the Holy Land and establish in it their state. "It is the Zionists", he said, who are "guilty of the Holocaust and it is because of them that six million Jews were killed". His writings and leadership in this regard caused deep divisions and hatred among Jewry, mainly in Orthodox communities, where some radical Torah Jews of the Naturei Karta cult proclaimed the Jewish State of Israel and Zionists enemy #1, and have since done everything in their power to dismantle (or destroy) the state and send the Jewish population back to the countries of their exile, where they are suppose to wait for permission from the Almighty to end the exile and be redeemed.

For the Satmar Rebbe it makes no difference whether the Jews, in their unquenched longing for the land of their fathers, repent and turn to God, "Even if the whole Government were all pious, as men of old, any attempt to take their freedom prematurely would be to deny the Holy Law and our faith."

To back up this statement, the Satmar Rebbe and Neturei Karta have dug out Scriptural 'proofs' from one passage of the Prophet Jeremiah 27:22: **"They will be taken to Babylon and there they will remain until the day I come for them,' declares the LORD. 'Then I will bring them back and restore them to this place."**

The Torah Jews Against Zionists made these words sound like they speak of a strict prohibition against the Jewish People endeavoring to end the Exile, to emigrating to the Promised Land and building a State there, unless God Himself will 'come for them and restore them to this place'. On first sight this translation of the Prophet's message looks normal, providing that the reader is not familiar with the context of the whole story expounded in this Chapter.

What exactly are we looking for?

Not much.

Just for the simple meaning of the word 'They' at the beginning of the verse: Who or what are 'they'? Is the word 'they' pointing to the Jewish People or does it indicate something else? You do not have even to read all of Chapter 27 to see that a 'little trick' is being made with the meaning of 'they' as if it represents the Jewish People. This is an outrageous imposition! An analysis of the verses 27:18-21 reveals that the Prophet Jeremiah uses the pronoun 'they' as referring to the golden, silver, and bronze 'vessels which are left in the House of the Lord (the Solomon Temple), and in the house of the King of Judah, and at the Jerusalem' (Verse 18).

In order to properly understand verse 22 and the meaning of 'they', it has to be read in conjunction with verse 21which clarifies the questions and answers it:

"Yes, thus said the LORD of hosts, the God of Israel, **concerning the vessels** that remain in the house of the LORD, and in the house of the king of Judah and of Jerusalem; They shall be carried to Babylon, and there shall they be until the day that I visit them, said the LORD; then will I bring them up, and restore them to this place" (Jeremiah 27: 21-22).

The Prophet Jeremiah simply repeats a message from God to the Jewish People in Babylonian captivity: When the prophesied seventy years shall be over I will bring you back to the Promised Land (29:10) together with all the sacred treasures of the Temple that King Nebuchadnezzar had carried to Babylon (27:22).

In 2 Kings 25:13-17 all the treasures of the Temple that had been carried away by the King of Babylon are listed in detail. In Ezra 1:7 we read that indeed, 'Nebuchadnezzar had taken away from Jerusalem articles belonging to the Temple of the Lord and had placed them in the temple of his god'.

Moreover, we see clear confirmation from Scripture in several places that these vessels were returned to Jerusalem together with the Jewish People after seventy years had been expired:

"And the vessels also of gold and silver of the house of God, which Nebuchadnezzar took out of the temple that *was* in Jerusalem, and brought them into the temple of Babylon, those did Cyrus the king take out of the temple of Babylon, and they were delivered unto one, whose name was Sheshbazzar, whom he had made governor; And said unto him, Take these vessels, go, carry them into the temple that is in Jerusalem, and let the house of God be builded in his place" (Ezra 5:14-15).

What have these golden, silver, and brass 'Vessels of Ministry' to do with the Three Prohibition Oaths of the Song of Songs that have caused so much religious-political controversy, hatred, division, and animosity amongst the Jewish Communities?

This is not the first time we have caught the True Torah Jews Against the Zionism (another example of the same nature was described in Chapter V under the subtitle, 'Welfare of the City', Jeremiah 29:7). They have shamefully manipulated Scripture. In the best tradition of Christian fundamentalists, they have taken Biblical passages out of context, misrepresented the facts and wrongly translated the verses. They have done this for the one and only purpose: To prove their dogmatic (and mistaken!) ideas against the hated Zionists and their State of Israel.

The Religious Zionists have claimed: The Three Oaths were Aggadic (homiletic) Midrashim, they were not Halakhically obligatory. The fact the Jews have returned to the Promised Land and successfully established the modern State of Israel, which continues to exist today, is evidence that the Oaths were void and the Divine Decree has ended. The nations of the world violated their end of the Oath to not excessively persecute the Jews, therefore the validity of the other two vows was nullified, and the Jews were allowed to immigrate to the Land of Israel 'en masse'. The Jewish people could not be considered to have rebelled against the nations because the UN acknowledged the creation of the Jewish State of Israel. To put it simply, the Jews have not violated any of the Three Oaths of Shir-Ha Shirim.

The Anti-Zionists, of course, have denied everything stated above and maintained that the Three Oaths were Halakhicly binding, and therefore the Zionists were heretics and rebels against God.

"The Daughters of Jerusalem": They are not the Jewish People!

'I adjure you, O daughters of Jerusalem'. Who do they represent, these daughters of Jerusalem? Are they the Jewish People as Satmar and Naturei Karta claim? Do the prohibitions of the Three Oaths apply to them? The answer is—Not at all! In the book, there is a dialogue between the two main characters, God and His beloved, the House of Israel. The Song of Songs was written, when Solomon was the King of United Israel, prior to its division into the two separate, politically independent kingdoms of Israel and Judaea. Among the geographical references to the cities and towns in the book, there is no mention of Samaria, the capital city of Northern Kingdom of Israel, founded later by the Israelite king Omri (reigned 876-868 b.c.).

The 'daughters of Jerusalem' cannot be the Jewish People. They are, probably, the people of Israel, the Ten Tribes in exile (the reason we use the word 'probably' is that there is another meaning of 'daughters' as 'heathen nations destined to ascend to Jerusalem' or 'the righteous souls'). We have already explained that there is a huge difference between the Jewish people and the people of Israel. They are not synonymous at this point of time! In the Bible Judah is sometimes referred to as Israel but the Kingdom of Israel is never referred to as Judah. Jews are those who belong to Tribe of Judah. The people of the Tribes of Benjamin and Levy are also called 'Jews' because historically they joined the most populous and dominant Tribe of Judah and chose their faith and destiny as their own. In the same manner, among the multitudes of the Ten Tribes of Israel there are might be some insignificant elements of Jewish descent who historically for almost 3,000 years chose the faith and destiny of Israel and in the beginning of their exile identified themselves as Israelites, but as long centuries of their migrations and travails have passed, they have forgotten the God of their fathers, the Torah, and even their Israelite origin. It is alright to say that all Jews are Israelites; but not all Israelites are Jews! The conclusion is: The Ten Tribes of Israel in Exile are not the Jews. They are Israelites from the separated Northern Kingdom called Israel. They are not the physical descendants of Judah, Benjamin or Levy, and they have not lived a Jewish way of life, neither have they upheld the Jewish faith. If they were the same as the Jews, why would God, throughout the Scriptures, has called and dealt with them separately?

Now, let us go back to the Tree Oaths. We have learned that the 'Daughters of Jerusalem' could be explained, in addition to meaning 'the house of Israel', as also connoting 'heathen nations'. This resulted in even more various interpretations of the Oath verses. Many scholars think that these 'Daughters of Jerusalem' in the Song may be simply understood as maiden friends and companions of Shulamite or young women attendants of King Solomon's court.

Song of Solomon 1:5 "I am black, but comely, O you daughters of Jerusalem . . ." has been translated as: a) "Though I am black with sin, I am comely with virtue, O nations who are destined to ascend to Jerusalem"; or b)" I am black all the days of the year, and comely on Yom Kippur; or c) "I am black in this world, and comely in the World to come." **In all these verses, explained Rashi, 'the nations of the world' are figuratively referred to as 'daughters of Jerusalem'.**

The Targum, for instance, translated Song of Songs 2:7 as referring to Moses charging the Israelites in the desert after the return of the spies: "I adjure you, O assembly of Israel, by the Lord of Hosts, and by the strength of the land of Israel, that you presume not to go up to the land of Canaan until it be the will of Heaven . . ."

111

The tractate Kesubos 111a in the Talmud renders this verse as God speaking to Israel, adjuring Israel not to rebel against the yoke of the nations and not ascend 'as a wall' to the Holy land.

Rabbi Shlomo Yitzhaki (1040-1105a.d.), Teacher of Israel, the Father of all Commentators, better known by the acronym Rashi, explained the Song of Songs 1:5; 2:7; 3:5; 8:4 as being Israel speaking to the heathen nations (his opinion was supported by Sforno and Metzudas David):

"I adjure you, O nations who are destined to ascend to Jerusalem, lest you become as defenseless as gazelles or hinds of the field, if you dare cause hatred or disturb the love while it yet gratifies" (2:7; 3:5).

'O daughters of Jerusalem' might be also translated as, 'You nations in whose midst I dwell' (Rashi).

'If you will wake or rouse the love until it pleases', Rashi understood it as to say: 'If you will try to sway my Beloved's love for me by persuasion and incitement to abandon Him, while His love is still desirous of me', or 'Know, you nations: Although I complain and lament, my Beloved holds my hand and is my support throughout my Exile'.

What a difference of meanings is derived if one takes the 'daughters' as meaning the 'heathen nations'!

Jews will live in the Land of Israel and in Jerusalem prior the attack of the heathen nations of the World in the 'last days'

In verse 8:4 the adjuration sounds a little different. It lacks the previous the threat of making them as vulnerable as the "gazelles and hinds of the field," because the timing of this adjuration in this verse is closer to the Final Redemption, and its purpose is not to frighten the nations, but to let them know that whatever they plot, their efforts to disturb God's love for Israel are in vain (Divrey Yedidiah).

Rashi interpreted the meaning of 'gazelles and hinds of the fields' as follows: "If you keep the adjuration, well and good; but if not,—you will become ownerless and your flesh will become a pray like that of the animals of the field."

Targum explains that in verse 8:4 it is the Messiah talking to Israel before Redemption: "I adjure you, O my people of the house of Israel, why do you war against the nations of the earth to leave the exile? Stay here a little longer, until the nations who have come up to wage war against Jerusalem will be destroyed; and after that the Lord of the Universe will recall the love of the righteous, and it will be His will to redeem you."

This is quite an interesting translation! First of all, why would the nations wage war against Jerusalem and be destroyed?

By attacking God's chosen people, those nations directly attack God. And this leads to grave consequences. Against what nation in Jerusalem will they go? Arabs? Chinese? Europeans? Not so! The heathen nations of the world will wage war against Judah, i.e. the present Israelis who will happen to live in the Holy Land and in Jerusalem, right in the aftermath of 'Judah's wound', which may result from the iniquitous ongoing Peace Process. This is according to God's will as expressed in the Bible's prophecies of Zechariah 12 and 14; Zephaniah 2:7; Hosea 5:13 and many others.

Secondly, why will the nations be destroyed? Because God will protect Judah, His servant, against the murderous armies of God's haters, the same way as He will have protected re-united Israel at the dawn of the Messianic Age in the battles of Gog and Magog with the same results (Ezekiel 38, 39).

If God allowed the Jewish People to come back and live in the Holy Land and have their state and be part of His Divine Plan in future events in order to fulfill the prophecies, how can we say that the same God had imposed the Three Prohibition Oaths against Judah to do so?!

Remember, what the Messiah in the Targum said according to the commentary of Rashi to verse 8:4 of the Songs? "Stay here a little longer, until the nations who have come up to wage war against Jerusalem will be destroyed; and after that the Lord of the Universe will recall the love of the righteous, and it will be His will to redeem you."

These words were spoken to the Ten Tribes of Israel in exile 'to stay a little longer' (in exile among the nations) and patiently wait for the right time when God destroys the nations who will have ascended against Jerusalem (Judah). God will send the Messiah who will bring the Ten Tribes to the Promised Land to join with the rest of their brothers of the victorious Jewish nation (the Israelis) and redeem all of them on the Mountains of Israel.

As we can see, the allegorical interpretations of the Three Oaths by the Sages differ from each other and lead to various conclusions. It is not surprising, that the Ramban (Nachmanides) implicitly rejected the Three Oaths as Halakhically binding because to treat them as such would effectively nullify a Biblical commandment: "The Jew in every generation as a positive commandment has to attempt to conquer the Land of Israel" (Numbers 33:53).

Analyzing the Three Oaths, we suddenly discovered some very important details: 'Daughters of Jerusalem' are the same heathen nations, 'who are destined to ascend against Jerusalem to wage war' and be destroyed. This future event was precisely prophesied by God in Zechariah 12:2-3, 9 and 14:2-3.

"Behold, I will make Jerusalem a cup of trembling unto all the people round about, when they shall be in the siege both against Judah and against Jerusalem" (Verse 12:2).

In the next verse the prophet indeed confirmed that all heathen nations of the world will attack Jerusalem:

"And in that day will I make Jerusalem a burdensome stone for all people; all that burden themselves with it shall be cut in pieces, though all the people of the earth are gathered together against it" (Verse 12:3). God Himself will defend the Jewish people and Jerusalem.

"And it shall come to pass in that day, that I will seek to destroy all the nations that come against Jerusalem." (Zech 12:9)

From being a most excellent Song of human love, Shir Ha Shirim is changed into a book containing a deep prophecy, divinely connected to the prophetic Word, and the holiest book of the Bible.

"The entire universe is unworthy of the day on which the Song of Songs was given to Israel. All the Writings are holy, but the Song of Songs is the holy of holies," said Rabbi Akiva.

Speaking of R. Akiva, we found a Talmudic source in Melkita (Exodus), Shirata, Beshallal: t, #3:

R. Akiba said: "I will speak of the beauty and praise of God before **all** the **nations. They** ask Israel and say, "what is your beloved more than another beloved that "thou dost so charge us" (Canticles 5:9), that you die for Him, and that you are slain for Him' as it says, 'Therefore till death do they love Thee' (a pun on Canticles I: 3), and "For thy sake are we slain all the day" (Ps. XLIV, 22). "Behold", they say, "You are beautiful, you are mighty, come and mingle with us". But the Israelites reply, "Do you know Him: We will tell you a portion of His renown; my beloved is white and ruddy; the chiefest among ten thousand" (Canticles 5:10). When they hear Israel praise Him thus, they say to the Israelites, "We will go with you, as it is said, whither has your beloved turned him that we may seek him with you"? (Canticles 6:1). But the Israelites say, "You have no part or lot in Him,' as it is said, "My beloved is mine, and I am His" (Canticles 2:16).

By analyzing the words of this greatest Sage of Jewish Law and Tradition, we can easily see that the 'Daughters of Jerusalem' are, in fact, the 'nations of the world'. It is to them speaks R. Akiva!

"O daughters of Jerusalem, I charge you", with these words begins Canticles 5:8. It is they, the very same nations of 2:7; 3:5; 5:8, and 8:4 who ask Israel, "What is your beloved more than another beloved that "thou dost so charge us" (Canticles 5:9), "that you die for Him, and that you are slain for Him"?

The conclusion from the above is clear: the Three Prohibition Oaths cannot be applied to the Jewish People because their presence in the Promised Land and in Jerusalem at the End Time was predicted and blessed by Almighty God in many instances of Scripture.

Maimonides and his Letter to the Jews of Yemen

The Rambam (Maimonides) in his Epistle to the Jews of Yemen, "Iggeret Le-Teiman", (chapter 4, Kafach edition, page 55), wrote:

"Solomon, of blessed memory, foresaw with Divine inspiration, that the prolonged duration of the exile would incite some of our people to seek to terminate the exile before the appointed time, and as a consequence they would perish or meet with disaster. Therefore he admonished and adjured them in metaphorical language to desist, as we read, "I adjured you, O daughters of Jerusalem" (Song of Songs 2:7; 8:4). Now, brethren and friends, abide by the oath, and stir not up love until it please" (Ketubot 111a).

We would like to make a little comment on it. According to traditional rabbinical sources, King Solomon completed building the first Temple in Jerusalem in 960 b.c. In his dedication speech at the opening ceremony in front of the "assembled elders of Israel, and all the heads of the tribes, the chief of the fathers of the children of Israel" Solomon foresaw with Divine inspiration, that the Israelites for their sin and disobedience would be punished by God and sent into exile to the lands of their enemies. It was the best time for Solomon to make the People of Israel swear to abide by the 'prohibition' Oaths, if it would have been necessary. Instead, Solomon prayed to God in plain literal, not metaphorical or allegorical language, as follows:

"When Thy people Israel be smitten down before the enemy, because they have sinned against Thee, and shall turn again to Thee, and confess Thy name, and pray, and make supplication unto Thee in this house; Then hear Thou in heaven, and forgive the sin of Thy people Israel, and bring them again unto the land which Thou gavest unto their fathers" (I Kings 8:1, 33-34).

Solomon did not mention any prohibitions or oaths in his divinely inspired speech, nothing concerning rules and conditions of the exile. All he asked the Almighty to do was to listen to the repentance and prayers of the children of Israel in the time of need and forgive their transgressions, and restore them to the Promised Land. Not even a hint of how long the exile would be (compare the 'prolong duration of the exile' (!?) in the words of Rambam). There is no indication here as to whether Israel should end the exile on its own or wait for the Messiah. There is nothing that says whether they should emigrate to the Promised Land 'en masse' or like 'a door'. They are not told if they should be obedient citizens and 'pray for the welfare' of the countries of the exile, and not rebel against the nations. It also does not say whether or not the nations of the world were adjured not to oppress Israel too much. Solomon said nothing along these lines!

The old questions still have not been answered: When and where did the People of Israel or the Jewish People make these Oaths? Some rabbis answer that at the time of revealing the Torah on the Mount Sinai, all 'the Jewish souls', including the unborn Prophets, were present, even those of future souls who would ever live, and they swore to obey the Divine Laws of Torah. This is fine. But the problem is that there are no Prohibitions Oaths in the Tanakh to end the exile, not to emigrate to the Promised Land, and not to build the Jewish state of Israel! Furthermore, the scholars again and again confuse 'the Jewish souls' with the souls of the rest of Israel (Ten Tribes in exile), who are the overwhelming majority of the Hebrews, and they are by no means Jewish today. Why? Because the Ten Tribes are not the physical descendants of Judah, Benjamin, and much of Levy, known to the world as modern day Jews; and their way of life and faith are not Jewish. Simple and clear!

Even if the House of Israel accepted these Oaths, why and how could the Oaths have force on the Jewish People today? The Oaths can only apply to the people who undertake them, not to their generations for unlimited Centuries. Those Oaths cannot be imposed on unborn descendants of Israel who were not alive at the time of Moses (Yoreh Deah 228:35).

There are no proofs whatsoever that Solomon in his famous speech in an inauguration ceremony, dedicated to the opening of the Holy Temple, made the People of Israel swear to and accept these Prohibition Oaths. Even if Solomon meant them in his Song of Songs, how is it possible for these Oaths to be valid and have mandatory effect on the

Jewish People after 2,800 years? The Oaths are in force for those people who voluntarily accepted and kept them. For those peoples of future generations who have not accepted the Oaths and known nothing about them, they will have had no obligatory effect. They are just void.

If the Three Prohibition Oaths really had been in force as Halakhically binding Laws from the time of Solomon, our Sages would have known and obeyed them. There is not a slightest hint in the Talmud that this was ever so. Our greatest Rabbis Hillel, Johanan ben Zakkai, Eliezer, Joshua, Akiva, and Judah the Prince did not write anything on the subject of the Three Prohibition Oaths of Shir HaShirim. Rabbi Akiva, whom the Talmud praises as having had Divine Knowledge even higher than Moses, definitely knew nothing about these Oaths. Otherwise, he would have not raised the flame of the Jewish Rebellion against the mighty Roman Empire during the Bar Kokhba Revolt (132 a.c.-135 a.c.) which led to catastrophic destruction, massive slaughter, and 2000 years of cruel Exile. Rabbi Akiva was not alone. Almost all the Sages of the Sanhedrin and the Academy of Yavneh supported the armed rebellion against the Rome. It is impossible to countenance these Sages breaking Jewish Laws, if the Three Oaths would have existed as Halakha. The same applies to the Sages of the First Jewish-Roman War of 66 a.c.-70 a.c. when the Second Temple was destroyed by the Roman General Titus. Obviously, the Sages did not know of any prohibitions as not to rebel against the oppressing Roman Empire and not to seek Redemption through armed struggle without permission of God, who (according to the Oaths) was first supposed to send the Messiah to achieve these tasks.

And what about the Heathen Nations amongst whom the Israelites were to live in Exile? When and where did God make the heathen swear not to overly persecute Israel in their 'host' countries? Was it at the same time when the Hebrew nation received the Holy Torah on Mount Sinai? Or did Solomon somehow cajole the Heathen Nations into taking the Oaths not to overly oppress the Israelites? The Bible does not confirm this. The other nations were not present at the time. And how much does "overly" mean? Why would God impose such an obligation on the nations, if they know nothing about it? Certainly, one cannot find such information in the Tanakh.

But what we know for sure is that throughout the history of the Israelite and the Jewish Peoples the foreign Nations and Empires have brought much destruction and suffering on God's chosen People. This started with the Egyptians, Assyrians, Babylonians, Greco-Persians, Romans, Arabs, Muslims and continued with the never ending oppression of Russia, Nazi Germany, Europe and the most of the modern World. That is how the Nations of the World have kept the Third Prohibition Oath—not to persecute Israel in Exile too much. The actions of the Nations should have caused annulment of the Prohibition Oaths a long time ago!

'If two people made an oath to do a certain thing, and one of them violated the oath, the other is exempt from the oath'
(Shulchan Arukh Yoreh Deah 236:1).

The Talmudic and Midrashic sources indicate that this Law applies even when Oaths are between Jews and Gentiles.

Based on this, since the nations of the world grossly violated the Third Prohibition Oath of not persecuting the Jewish People excessively, the Jewish People have no more legal obligations to keep and abide by these Oaths because they have no Halakhic significance.

There is an opinion that the Oaths of Song of Songs were invented by the Amoraim Rabbis during the time of the compilation of the Talmud circa 500 a.c-600 a.c. The reason for this was to prevent future disasters brought on by rebellious wars against the nations of Exile and the appearing of false messiahs. They thought that this would help ensure the survival of the Jewish People and Judaism and would make life much easier in Exile. The events of WWII and its culmination with the Holocaust which annihilated six million Jews proved that the Three Prohibition Oaths of Songs has become irrelevant to the Jewish People.

Some scholars explain that the Prohibition Oaths are not the Commandments, but rather are part of the Jewish belief system derived from the Biblical prophecies of Exile as the punishment to the House of Israel for their sins; and His promises to send the Messiah and redeem them at the 'End of Days'.

In the verses of the Bible we will not find any direct prohibition to end the exile, return to the Promised Land or against establishing the Jewish State of Israel! On the contrary, the Hebrew Bible is full of God's passionate passages encouraging His People to end the exile, to repent and return to the God of Israel and to the Holy Land!

Rebbe Avnei Neizer (Stones of the Crown, 1870-1910) commented that since the Gemara (Talmud) was not clear about determining the precise definition and parameters of the term "not enslaving Israel too much", it could not be understood as having Halakhic force.

He also taught that 'The Daughters of Jerusalem' were 'the souls of the righteous.' The main point he made was that the Oaths were not meant as a Halakhic injunction because they were not worded in a Halakhicly mandated manner nor were they specific enough in definition, especially as applies to the third Oath given to the heathen nations of the world.

If we were to take the meaning of the "Daughters of Jerusalem" as being the 'heathen nations' of the world who are destined to ascend to Jerusalem and be destroyed by God, (R.Akiva, Rashi, Sforno, Metzudas David), there remains no validity for the Three Prohibitions Oaths to be applied against Israel in the Song of Songs. This conclusion would not take from the book its holiness and greatness at all. Despite this possibility, let us first examine an application of the "Daughters of Jerusalem" as meaning Israel.

'Do not Ascend as a Wall' and other Prohibitions

This is the first prohibition to Israel: Do not forcefully storm the wall, do not come back to the Promised Land "en masse." Or, as Rabbi

Chelbo said, "Do not ascend like a wall from the Exile. If so, why is the King Messiah coming? To gather the exiles of Israel."

Beside the fact that we already indicated that Israel is not Judah, that the People of Israel are not the same as the Jewish People (at this particular time until the reunification and final redemption: Ezekiel 37:16-28), the prohibition "do not ascend as a wall" cannot apply to Judah.

The grievous violations of the nations against the Jewish People, and the consequent Resolution of the United Nations, allowing the creation of the State of Israel, have nullified the Oaths. The Oaths were only in effect for a thousand years. At all events they are not Halakhically binding. Many great Sages of Israel have rejected them.

Moreover, the Hebrew Scripture have also rejected them! Regardless as to whom these Prohibition Oaths may or may not apply, to Judah or Israel (the Ten Tribes), according to Tanakh, there is no prohibition to end the exile, to emigrate to the Promised Land 'en masse' as a wall, or in a small groups as 'a door'. There is no prohibition that can be found in the Bible's verses against Judah establishing an independent State of Israel in the Holy Land. There are no such prohibitions applying to Judah, or to Israel, in the Hebrew Bible!

The Three Oaths Were Intended for Israel (The Ten Tribes in exile), not for Judah!

If there is any validity and Heavenly wisdom in these Prohibition Oaths, which we rather prefer to call 'the Divine Decrees', (and we incline to think there is), they might have been designed for Israel, the Ten Tribes in Exile, not for the Jewish People. And the time of their fulfillment is 'the days of Mashiach'. Scripture provides more than enough evidences that the Oaths are not applicable to Judah.

Just consider these points:

I. If the Prohibition Oaths are of Divine origin and apply to Judah only, how come that the same God throughout the Scripture predicted, allowed, blessed and protected the Jewish State of Israel?

"And the sea coast shall be for the remnants of the house of Judah" (Zephaniah 2:7).

"Also, O Judah, He hath set a harvest for thee, when I returned the captivity of My people" (Hosea 6:11).

"For behold, in those days and at that time, when I shall bring again the captivity of Judah and Jerusalem" (Joel 3:1).

Where do you see the prohibitions for Judah to end the Exile and return to the Promised Land in the Bible's passages like these?

And more:

"Awake, awake; put on thy strength, O Zion; put on thy beautiful garments, O Jerusalem. Shake off your dust, rise up, O Jerusalem. Free thyself from the bands of thy neck, O captive daughter of Zion" (Isaiah 52:1-2).

The Almighty is not only asking or trying to persuade the Jewish people to come back to the Promised Land, (not even mentioning the prohibition!); He encourages and demands for them to free themselves from the bondage of the Exile, proclaim their liberty and return to the Land of their fathers.

Actually, God appeals to Israel (the Ten Tribes) with the same message:

"Return thou backsliding Israel; and I will not cause Mine anger to fall upon you; for I am merciful. Only acknowledge thy iniquity. Turn, O backsliding children; for I am married unto you"

(Jeremiah 3:12-14).

"Set up road signs; put up the signposts. Take note of the highway, the road which you came. Return, O virgin Israel, return to your towns. How long will you wander, O unfaithful daughter?"

(Jeremiah 31:21-22).

By posting this question 'How long will you wander'? God shows that He has not imposed any length-of-time determined prohibition on His People against ending the Exile and returning to the Land of

Israel. On the contrary, He wishes them to return to His Land. It is up to Judah and Israel to wake up, repent of their sins and come back to the God of Israel and to the Holy Land. They have free will to make such a decision. The time is at hand.

And, indeed, the children of Israel will have heard their God:

"Behold, we come unto thee; for thou art the Lord our God. In those days the House of Judah shall walk with the house of Israel, and they shall come together out of the land of the north to the land that I have given for an inheritance unto your fathers" (Jeremiah 3:18, 22).

II. How it would be possible to fulfill God's prophecies of Ezekiel 38 and 39 and Zechariah 12 and 14, if Judah, the modern day Israelis, will not have been allowed by the Almighty to live in the Land of Israel and in Jerusalem? Is not something wrong here? Who is not telling the truth? God is not a human—He cannot make a mistake.

"God is not a man, that He should lie, nor a son of man, that He should change his mind. Does He speak and then not act? Does He promise and not fulfill"? (Numbers23:18).

The people are! Those of the 'most famous' radical sect of Orthodox Jewry—Neturei Karta and the Torah Jews against Zionism, are the ones not telling the truth. It is they who deny the legitimacy of the State of Israel and the rights of the Jewish people to end the Exile and emigrate to the Promised Land without special permission from God and arrival of the Messiah. It is they who do not want to recognize the Prophecies of the Bible according to which the Jewish People will successfully end the Exile and build the democratic Jewish State of Israel in the Holy Land. The establishment of the State of Israel in 1948 is the first step of the ingathering and redemption of the whole House of Israel. The God of Israel predicted it, defended it, and blessed it!

III. We do not have to forget that the main heroes in the Song of Songs of Solomon are Lover-God and Beloved-Israel. There is no name 'Judah' mentioned in the book, because the Song was written by the

King Solomon prior to the division of the United Monarchy into the two politically independent states of Judaea and Israel (circa 930 b.c.).

Just consider the wordings recorded in Talmud, Ketubot 111a:
"What are these Three Oaths?
One, that **Israel** should not storm the wall;
Two, the Holy One made **Israel** take an oath not to rebel against the nations of the world;
Three, the Holy One made the nations vow that they would not oppress **Israel** too much."
What do we see here? All the Three Prohibition Oaths apply to Israel, not to Judah! One cannot 'revise' the meaning of Israel being Judah because the context of the Oaths clearly indicates Israel, not Judah.

IV. "The daughters of Jerusalem". Who are they symbolizing? Are they the Jewish people as some theologians and the Torah Jews against Zionism together with the radical sect called Neturei Karta try to prove?
We do not thing so! The best translators and commentators of the Hebrew Scripture did not agree either! Rashi, Metzudas David, and Sforno, explained that "the daughters of Jerusalem" of 1:5; 2:7; 3:5; 8:4 of the Songs are the "heathen nations" who are destined to go up to Jerusalem, not the Jews! The same was confirmed by the Head of all Sages, R. Akiva.
V. How come that the Targum understood verse 2:7 of the Songs as "I adjure you, **O assembly of Israel**, by the Lord of Hosts . . ."? Moses is clearly speaking here of all Israel, not specifically of Judah.

VI. The same question may be raised on another place in Targum where the Messiah is talking to Israel before the Redemption, i.e. reflecting on verse 8:4 of the Songs: "I adjure you, **O my people of the house of Israel** . . ." Again, Israel is spoken of, not Judah.

VII. How come that Ramban (Nahmanides) interpreted "little sister" of verse 8:8 of the Songs as **Israel in Exile**, not Judah? And so did Metzudas David. And so did the 'father of all translators' Rashi explaining the verse 8:10 of the Songs as 'the little sister', **which is Israel**, proudly and reassuringly declaring, "I am a wall. I am ready for Redemption" (Artscroll commentaries on Shir haShirim 8:8).

VIII. How can we talk of the Talmudic prohibitions to end the exile, to immigrate to the Promised Land and establish the State of Israel, regardless as to whom those prohibitions applied (to Judah or to the Ten Tribes in exile), since the Torah and Tanakh are full of verses meaning the opposite of the Prohibitions, as we have conclusively demonstrated above??

The Holy Bible Versus Aggadic Midrash

The Sages of the Talmud have always taught that the process of regathering and redemption of the whole House of Israel is not momentary. It takes time and will be realized in stages. It will proceed in an orderly fashion; the way it has been designed by Almighty in His Divine Plan. There are many passages in Talmudic literature devoted to this theme.

Naturally, we have to answer the question: Do we give the same weight to Aggadic Midrash Ketubot 111a dealing with the Three Prohibition Oaths as you have to give to the Sacred Words of the Bible on the same subject? There is an interesting opinion in the Talmud, Erubin 21b (Soncino edition) which states: "My son, be more careful in the observance of the words of the Scribes than in the words of the Torah".

History shows that some scholars are more willing to reject God than the Talmud, as the trial of the great Rabbi Eliezer demonstrated when the Sages of Academy ignored the voice of Heaven that supported R. Eliezer Halakhah and chose the man-made exegetical decision of the majority (Talmud, Baba Metzia 59b).

"Never follow a crowd in doing wrong. When you testify in court, do not side with the majority to pervert justice" (Exodus 23:2).

The truth is that Judaism does not esteem the Talmud as being holier than the Bible. The Five books of Moses, the Torah, are considered as the most important book of the Tanakh among the Prophets and Sacred Writings because it is viewed as God Himself literarily speaking. There is a big difference between the Bible which is a Sacred Word of God, and the Talmud compiled by men, no matter how wise they are. The Divine Torah should be treated with great respect. One who sees someone carrying a Torah scroll must rise before it until the Torah scroll is placed in its position or until one no longer sees it (Kitzur Shulchan Aruch 28:3). In Judaism, from a legal perspective, the Biblical Laws are more important than rabbinical laws. When the question arises on a matter between the Written Law of the Bible versus Talmudic interpretation of the Oral Law, the final decision is on the side of the Bible.

Based on the above, it is our opinion, that the literal interpretations of God—inspired Biblical verses concerning the end of the Exile of Judah and establishing of the State of Israel in the Promised Land should have prevailed against the obscure, highly disputable and unreliable allegorical Prohibition controversies of the Three Oaths of Canticles in Tractate Ketubot 111a of the Babylonian Talmud!

Beside all of this, we still cannot see how the immigration of the Jewish people before the establishing of the State of Israel, during or after it, might be considered as a mass immigration of the house of Israel 'en masse' or as a 'wall'. Hundreds of books have been written on the subject of the immigration of Israel as a 'wall' and as a 'door' in connection with the Three Oaths of the Song of Songs. The 'Theory of replacement' has taken its toll as usual. Everybody seems to have forgotten that there are two main characters in the Song of Solomon. God praises Israel and Israel praises God. There is no name of Judah mentioned anywhere in the book! The Three Prohibition Oaths may have been designated only for Israel and for the particular time of the Final Redemption and Advent of the Messiah, son of Joseph.

Granted, Judah was part of the Twelve Tribes of the house of Israel before the United Monarchy split, but after the Northern Ten Tribes of Israel had gone into exile and disappeared until the appointed time to meet their future destiny, the two and a half tribes of Judah will remain a separate and different entity. Judah cannot bear the name of Israel, because it does not belong to him. This name belongs to Ephraim and Manasseh, the sons of Joseph (Genesis 48:5, 16). As we explained elsewhere, the Almighty will deal with Israel and Judah separately until the Final Redemption and Reunification in the end of Times, in a "Latter Days" and the Advent of the Messiah (Ezek. 37:24).

Nowhere in Scriptures did God say that Israel is Judah, and Judah is Israel!

An Analysis of Immigration to Israel as 'a Wall' and as 'a Door'

To demonstrate that claims against the Jews of immigrating 'en masse' or 'ascending like a wall' to the Holy Land makes no sense and does not stand up to criticism, all we have to do is to use simple mathematics. In the beginning of the 20th century, in 1919-1923, in the wake of WWI, 40,000 Jews arrived in Palestine, mainly from Russia. In 1924-1929, another 59,000 immigrants settled in Eretz Yisroel from Poland and Hungary. During 1929-1939, with the rise of Nazism in Germany, 250,000 immigrants arrived, mostly from Eastern Europe as well as professionals, doctors, lawyers and professors from Germany. By 1940 the Jewish population in Palestine reached 450,000.

As a result of Arab-Jews tensions, leading to a series of bloody Arab riots in 1929 and the "Great Uprising" of 1936-1939; and in order to please their oil rich Arab partners and protect their own oil interests in the Middle East, the British issued the White Paper of 1939, severely restricting Jewish immigration to a limit of 75,000 for five years.

Despite of the British effort to curb illegal immigration, during 14 years of its operation from 1933-1948, Aliyah Bet smuggled total of 110,000 Jewish immigrants into Palestine.

The largest immigration of the Jews was recorded in 1948-1950, when new waves of anti-Semitism and persecutions resurged in Eastern Europe, and in increasingly hostile Arab countries. The total numbers of refugees reached over 500,000 Jews.

If we look at the immigration by separate countries, the number of Jewish immigrants [compared to the numbers of Jews who stayed behind], are so small and insignificant, that one cannot call it ascending as 'a wall' or 'en masse'. The Jewish people did not return *'en masse'* to the Land of Israel, but rather through individual immigration as well as a series of the five Aliyahs. The Jews continue to individually immigrate to Israel today. There was never a point in history where a majority of world Jewry collectively migrated to the Land of Israel.

Let's take the former USSR, the larger contributor of immigrants, for example. In 1968 exit visas to Israel were given to 231 Jews; in 1972-31,652; in 1978-12,090; in 1984-340.

You cannot call it mass immigration, and by no means may immigration in stages by small numbers of people be described as 'ascending as a wall'. But this is only the first part of the equation. The second part is the following.

What is the population of Israel now? Before we answer this question, let us see what the Bible said on this matter.

God said to Abraham: "In blessing I will bless thee, and in multiplying I will multiply thy seed as the stars of the heaven and as the sand of the sea shore" (Genesis 23:17).

To Isaac God said: "And I will make thy seed to multiply as the stars of heaven (Genesis 26:4).

To Rebekah: "And they blessed Rebekah", and said unto her,

"Thou art our sister, be thou the mother of thousands of millions, and let thy seed possess the gate of those which hate them" (Genesis 24:60).

The promise of multiplication was reaffirmed by God to Jacob: a) 'And thy seed shall be as the dust of the earth'; b) 'and thou shalt spread abroad to the west, and to the east, and to the north, and to the south': c) 'and in thee and thy seed shall all the families of the earth be blessed.'

And more, which is very important for our discussion here:

"And, behold, I am with you, and will keep thee in all places whither you go, and will bring you again into this land; for I will not leave you, until I have done that which I have spoken to you of" (Genesis 28:14-15). In these two verses we have found a treasure-trove.

Remember, God changed the name of Jacob to Israel (Genesis 32:27; 35:10). So, we find that Israel will multiply as the stars of heaven and as the sand of the sea shore, which undoubtedly means hundreds of millions of people; that the house of Israel will spread abroad to the four corners of the globe; that God will be always with Israel, and bring them to the Holy Land again; that all nations of the world will be blessed through Israel; and that God would not leave Israel until everything written and spoken will be done.

Clearly, God does not speak here about the Jewish people, whose total population in the world today is 13,155,000, of which 5.634,300 live in the State of Israel, and the rest are in the Diaspora, mainly in USA-6,444,000. These numbers are not compatible with "the stars of the sky and the sand of the seashore". And the Jews have had no nations and kingdoms, except that of Judaea in the past and the modern State of Israel today. Meanwhile God predicted to Israel that "a nation and the company of nations shall be of thee, and kings shall come out of thy lions;" "I will make of thee a multitude of people" (Genesis 35:11; 48:4). Surely it is not referring to Judah, but to Israel!

All the Scriptures and Sages say that the Israelite Ten Tribes eventually will return to the Promised Land and receive the Heavenly Torah once more. Whosoever does not accept this plain Biblical truth is guilty of denying the Word of God.

Like Rabbi Chanina said in Gemara, the Holy One made Israel to take these Oaths. Israel was prohibited to ascend as 'a wall', 'en masse' to the Promised Land. Keep in mind that the population of the ten tribes of Israel is approximately 450,000,000 people, plus 13,000,000 million of Judah bringing the total of 463,000,000 million. The Jews, even including those who were born in the State of Israel, in numerous stages of immigrations, for one hundred and ten years in the 20th and the beginning of the 21st century have managed to bring 5.6 million people to the land of Israel. This makes only 0.12% of the total population of Israel. How in the world can one call this kind of immigration as 'ascending as a wall' or 'en masse'? It simply goes against logic and any kind of imagination!

Since we have established the truth that Israel, the Ten Tribes in Exile, and Judah, the Jewish nation, modern Israelis, are not the same people today and, in fact, are completely different nations, living in different countries of the world; having different histories, languages, cultures and religions; that God has separate Prophetic Plans for both entities; and He will deal with them in such regard until the End of Days; we feel that there is no need to continue our discussion against the Satmar group and Neturei Karta radicals because we have successfully made our case.

'The Little Sister' of the Song and Divine Decrees

Even if the 'Daughters of Jerusalem' in verses 1:5; 2:7; 3:5; and 8:4 of the Songs represent Israel (who is 'Beloved' then? Is not it commonly accepted that 'Beloved' is Israel?!), as in tractate Ketubot 111a, and not the 'heathen nations who are destined to ascend against Jerusalem', as R. Akiva, Rashi, Sforno, Metzudas David and others translated, or 'the souls of the righteous', as written in the holy Zohar Vayechy (242a); none of the Three Prohibition Oaths (Divine Decrees) can apply to Judah (1948 up to the modern days), because they were designed for Israel, the Ten Tribes in Exile (End of days, advent of the Messiah) which is not the same!

Song of Solomon 8:8, "We have a little sister, and she has no breasts; what shall we do for our sister in the day when she shall be spoken for?" Ramban interpreted 'little sister' as Israel in Exile, not Judah, and the Angels of Heaven asked, "What shall we do with her?" She is not ready for Redemption (she is not yet ripe for Redemption, Rashi); for she has been exiled from Eretz Yisrael, the Land of Life, and separated from the place of Torah. The Great Ramban knew precisely who the Ten Tribes are, and where they were living in Exile!

"For a long time Israel had been without the true God, and without a teaching priest and without Torah" (II Chron. 15:3). And without the great leaders like Moses, Aaron or David, we should add.

Metzudas David translated this verse differently: It is the Jewish People at the time of imminent Redemption who are asking this question about the fate of their brothers Israel, the Ten Tribes, who are still scattered in exile and unprepared for Salvation. He perfectly understood the subject of Judah and Israel! "By what merit, Israel asks, will they become deserving of Your deliverance at the predestined time?"

"If she be a wall," God answered. Rashi commented: "If Israel will gird herself with faith and act towards the nations as if fortified with walls of brass (Jeremiah 1:18), which they cannot infiltrate, then shall we be with her, and the nations shall have no power to rule over her."

And what was the response of 'the little sister'? In verse 8:10 of the 'Songs' Israel proudly and reassuringly declared, "I am a wall, and my breasts like towers." Rashi translated: "Your fear is unjustified. I comfort myself not like the 'door', but like the 'wall'. You thought me not ripe for Redemption, know that I am quite ripe: my synagogues and study-houses, which nurture Israel with words of Torah, are like towers" i.e. fortifying and serving as towers of strength for all (The art Scroll commentaries on Shir HaShirim 8:8-10).

Speaking of the terms 'door' and 'wall', we can assure our readers that in 1948 Judah did ascend to the Land of Israel like a 'door'(in small numbers), but the Ten Tribes of Israel in the future, when they will be ready ('ripe') and when the appointed time arrives, (advent of the Messiah), together with the remnants of Judah in the Diaspora, (Jeremiah 3:18), will definitely ascend to the Land of their fathers like 'a wall', ('en masse')!

The Three Oaths might be a future guidance for Joseph (Israel in exile), when they will awaken to their Israelite identity (with the help of Judah, Jeremiah 3:18; Ezekiel 37:22) and the Prophet Eliyahu (Malachi 4:5-6) who will turn the hearts of the fathers to their children, and the hearts of the children to their fathers, and turn to God with repentance and prayers. God will hear them and will send the Messiah, son of Joseph, who will successfully fight God's wars, defeat the forces of Edom (Europe, Turkey and surrounding Arab and Muslim nations), rebuild the Temple and resume sacrifices. He will bring the Tribes of Israel to expanded Biblical borders of the Promised Land for its purification and reunification with Judah. After his suffering and death ('suffering servant', Isaiah 53; Zechariah 10:10; Midrash Konen, BhM 2:29-30), will arrive the Messiah, son of David, 'the conquering King', who will complete the reunification and the final Redemption of the house of Israel. There is a Talmudic opinion that the interval between the two Messiahs will be 40 years. The other tradition says that after the death of the Messiah son of Joseph, there will be a period of forty five days during which first comes the Prophet Elijah, then the Messiah son of David.

Since the Three Oaths are not Halakhically obligatory and not a part of the Mishneh Torah, but a simple reflection of obscure and controversial prophetic disputes of the Rabbis (writings) about the future Exodus and Redemption of the whole House of Israel in the 'latter days', on which subject there are many different opinions of the Sages of the Talmud, they have no Scriptural legitimacy as Divine prohibitions against ending the exile, returning to the Promised Land and establishment of the Jewish State of Israel.

Similarities and Differences between the
First, Second, and Third Exoduses

If we look at the first Exodus from Egypt in Moses time, it is evident that the God of Israel gave clear directions as to how and when the slavery in Egypt would end.

"Fear not to go down to Egypt, for I will there make of thee a great nation. I will go down with thee into Egypt, and I will also surely bring thee up again" (Babylonian Talmud, Megillah 14a).

According to God Prophecy, the Israelites would be in Egypt for 400 years, "Then God said to Abram, "You can be sure that your descendants will be strangers in a foreign land, where they will be oppressed as slaves for 400 years" (Genesis 15:13); or 430 years, depending on if you reckon it from the birth of Isaac or of actual time of the Covenant of Pieces. "The time that the people of Israel lived in Egypt was 430 years" (Exodus 12:40). Furthermore, it was specifically prophesied in many instances that Moses would lead the Israelites out of Egypt, "So now, go. I am sending you to Pharaoh to bring My people the Israelites out of Egypt" (Exodus 3:10); at that exact point in time, "At the end of the 430 years, to the very day, all the hosts of the LORD left Egypt" (Exodus 12:41); even details of the Exodus were prophesied, such as the stubbornness of Pharaoh, ('But I know that the king of Egypt will not let you go unless a mighty hand compels him'); the ten plagues; the Covenant at Mount Sinai and final destination of the Israelites, "I will bring you up out of the affliction of Egypt unto the land of the Canaanites, and the Hittites, and the Amorites, and the Perizzites, and the Hivites, and the Jebusites, unto a land flowing with milk and honey" (Exodus 3:17).

The scholars, as far as we know, do not count all these detailed particulars and conditions of the First Exodus as Halakhically binding Laws. Rather, they have treated them as Divine Decrees, violation of which could bring grave consequences, as happened to the Ephraimites when they miscalculated the time of their deliverance and left Egypt prematurely thirty years ahead of the preordained time. This story is based only on the passage of 1 Chronicles 7:21, "And Zabad his son, and Shuthelah his son, and Ezer, and Elead, whom the men of Gath that were born in that land slew, because they came down to take away their cattle".

The Ephraimites, when they left Egypt on their way to the Promised Land, were met by a hostile army of the Philistines. They engaged in battle and were defeated by them. As a result, they lost 300,000 men (from one source) or 200,000 men (from the other source). Only ten Ephraimites, who escaped from the battle, returned to Egypt and told the rest of Israelites what had happened (Targum Rav Yosef on I Chronicles 7:21).

The Second Exodus, this time of the Jewish People from Babylon, former citizens of the defeated Kingdom of Judaea (with some elements representing a minority of the Ten Tribes of the Northern Kingdom), also have not had any Halakhically regulated Laws or Prohibition Oaths. It was a Divine Decree issued by the Almighty through the Prophet Jeremiah which plainly outlined God's plan concerning the captives of Judaea and Jerusalem whom King Nebuchadnezzar carried into exile to Babylon. Here is this Plan:

"Build houses and settle down; plant gardens and eat what they produce; marry and have children; Increase in number there; do not decrease. Also, seek the peace and prosperity of the city to which I have carried you into exile. Pray to the LORD for it, because if it prospers, you too will prosper. This is what the LORD says: "When **seventy years** are completed for Babylon, I will come to you and fulfill my gracious promise to bring you back to this place (Jeremiah 29:4-7, 10).

Some people of the tribes of Judah, Benjamin and much of Levi returned from the Babylonian captivity to the land of Judaea together with a few members (a minority) from the Ten Tribes of Israel exactly in the time and manner described in this Divine Decree.

The Third Exodus of the whole House of Israel which consist of the Twelve Tribes of Judah and Israel (Joseph) does not have such an impressive clarity and definition in Hebrew Scripture as the previous two

Exoduses had. It is impossible to find out how long this Exile suppose to last and exactly when it will be ended. No definite time is given whatsoever. Instead, all the Prophets have spoken of the indefinite times of 'the latter years', 'last days', 'end times'. Another given expression is 'in the days of the Messiah'. But when the Messiah will arrive, nobody knows, except God Almighty. He has decided to keep this mystery (and a few others) out of man's knowledge, as it written," The secret things belong to the LORD our God" (Deuteronomy 29:29).

There are many obscure, highly contested passages in the Bible regarding everything connected with the Third Return. The Sages of the Talmud have disputed whether the Israelites will have to have repented before the coming of the Messiah or the Messiah will cause them to repent after his arrival. There are thousands of opinions on the whereabouts of the Ten 'Lost' Tribes of Israel. Some say that the Ten Tribes have already returned in the times of the Prophets Jeremiah, Ezra, and Nehemiah and today are well represented among the Jewish People. Others insist that they have disappeared a long time ago, assimilated with the surrounding people and are not in existence any more, and God does not care about them. Many point out that the final reunification and redemption of Israel spoken of by the prophets, involve only the Jews of the Diaspora who are suppose to reunite in the future with the rest of the Jewish nation (Israelis). Nevertheless, one thing God has made clear: the Last and Final return to the Promised Land in the 'days of Mashiah' will involve and include all Judah and all the Ten Tribes of Israel, the whole House of Jacob. This is in contrast to the partial exodus from Babylonian Captivity in the Second Return.

"I will multiply people on you (Mountains of Israel), **all the House of Israel, all of it.** Then shall they know that I am the Lord their God, which caused them to be led into captivity among the heathen: but I have gathered them unto their own Land, **and have left none of them anymore there**" (Ezekiel 36:10; 39:28).

The creation of the Jewish state of Israel in 1948 also has caused hot debate among the scholars as to whether these actions were approved by God or they were illegitimate according to Scripture. We support the position of some rabbis and scholars that God predicted, blessed and defended establishment of the State of Israel and the return of Judah as the first step in the final redemption of the whole House of Israel. This return of the Jewish People to the Promised Land was partial because not all Jews returned. It was also the return of people who did not have a perfect faith in the God of Israel and were not obedient to the requirements of the Torah's Laws. Many well known Rabbis were in agreement that the initial stage of the Third Exodus of the Jews to the Land does not require perfect faith and repentance, e.g. (Abraham Isaac Kook (1865-1935); Yehuda Solomon Alkalai (1798-1878); Zvi Hirsch Kalischer (1795-1874).

Basically, they taught that even though Zionism is a political movement; it actually serves as a tool of God to promote His Divine Plan by initiating the return of the Jewish People to their homeland, which has to be cultivated and changed to become like the 'Garden of Eden'. R. Nahmanides was the strongest defender of the idea of Israelites settling on the Holy Land and counted these actions as great Mitzvoth in the sight of the Lord.

Incidentally, there is a Kabalistic teaching asserting that each verse in the Torah corresponds to a certain year of human history. Some rabbis have come to the conclusion that the creation of the State of Israel in 1948, which correspond to the year 5708 of the Jewish calendar, was predicted by the Torah. They even pin point this verse—Deuteronomy 30:3, "Then the LORD your God will restore your fortunes and have compassion on you and gather you again from all the nations where he scattered you".

Furthermore, the return of the Jews had the other Biblical goal: to prepare the Promised Land to accommodate hundreds of millions of their brothers and sisters of the 'Lost' Ten Tribes of Israel whose coming is 'at hand'. The Bible, in their words, spoke of the Zionists all along!

Others, on the contrary, have qualified these actions (end of exile, immigration to the Holy Land and organizing the state) as rebellion against God, called the people involved 'heretics', 'rebels', and Zionists. They want to dismantle (or destroy, whichever comes first) the State of Israel, give all the Land of Israel and authority to the Palestinians, and send the Jewish population back to the countries of their previous exiles. The main reason behind their position are those 'famous' Three Prohibition Oaths which we have been discussing here. In their opinion, the Third Exodus and creation of the State of Israel cannot possibly take place without permission of God and the advent of the Messiah. This group of rabbis and their followers has united in their effort with the enemies of the Jewish State acting as subverts within the Jewish nation allied with the Palestinians and others including Anti-Semite international elements around the world and have done everything in their power to realize their goals.

We think that, as in the previously discussed two Exoduses were no Halakhically mandated legal prohibitions and Oaths against ending the Exile, but only Divine Decrees. The same condition might be applied to the Third Exodus. Moreover, we think that those Divine Decrees of the Last and Final Exodus have been wrongly applied to the Jewish People. We have already explained elsewhere on a few occasions that the Prohibition Oaths (Divine Decrees) were designed for the 'Lost' Ten Tribes in Exile, aiming for a distant future of the 'End Days', the days of the Mashiach, and cannot be employed against the Jews (1948 and up), because Judah and Israel (Joseph) are not synonymous nations at this point in time, as they were in Moses time, and will continue be different entities until the arrival of the Messiah (Ezekiel 37:22).

Nowhere in the Jewish Bible does God say that Israel is Judah and the Jewish People are the same as Israelites of the Ten Tribes in exile. In Scripture the prophets consistently made a careful distinction between the House of Judah, who after the Babylonian captivity becomes known as the Jews, and the House of Israel, the Ten 'Lost' Tribes of Joseph, known as the Israelites. In other words, 'All Jews are Israelites; but not all Israelites are Jews'.

There are more than forty prophecies in the Hebrew Bible overwhelmingly speaking of reunification, ingathering and redemption of the whole House of Israel on the Holy Land. God's prophets were very much concerned with the future national restoration of the Tribes of Israel. They constantly make a careful distinction between the House of Judah and the House of Israel. It is vitally important to understand these differences in order not to be confused and misinterpret them. These prophecies cannot be ignored, spiritualized or misunderstood as if they apply to the Jewish People only. The Prophets have plainly expressed the will of the Almighty to restore His People Israel to the Promise Land. There is absolutely no reason to think that those prophecies will not be fulfilled: They are authoritative, trustworthy, and unconditional.

"Thus says the LORD, who gives the sun for light by day and the fixed order of the moon and the stars for light by night, who stirs up the sea so that its waves roar—the LORD of hosts is His name. Only if these ordinances vanish from My sight," declares the LORD, "will the descendants of Israel ever cease to be a nation before Me" (Jeremiah 31:35-36).

Whoever ignores or rejects these prophecies of the future Great Return of the whole House of Israel ("So then, the days are coming," declares the LORD, "when people will no longer say, 'As surely as the LORD lives, who brought the Israelites up out of Egypt, but, The LORD lives, who brought up and who led the descendants of the house of Israel out of the north country, and from all countries where I had driven them; and they shall dwell in their own land" (Jeremiah 23:7-8), is guilty of disobeying the sacred Words of God.

"But this shall be the covenant that I will make with the house of Israel; after those days, said the LORD, I will put my law in their inward parts, and write it in their hearts; and will be their God, and they shall be My people" (Ezekiel 31:33).

Unless and until all Israel repents, turns back to the God of their fathers, accepts His Divine Torah and is restored to the Land, with Judah and Joseph joined as one, there will be no Messianic fulfillment, no Redemption and there will be no realization of the Kingdom of God.

More Scriptural Proofs Concerning Jewish Immigration to the Promised Land and Creation of the State of Israel

As a matter of fact, when we speak of the Third Exodus, there is a visible division of the Scriptural passages outlining rules and conditions distinguishing between the return to the Holy Land of Judah and that of Israel. The Return of the Jewish People has been described more often and with greater clarity. It has not been confined to any particular time, repentance, Prohibition Oaths or with the advent of the Messiah. The physical return of the Jews to the Land was in fulfillment of numerous prophesies in the Bible, and it will accelerate the coming of the Messiah. Let us again take a look at Zephaniah 2:7:

"And the seacoast will be for the remnants of the House of Judah. For the LORD their God shall visit them, and turn away their captivity".

The Prophet here strictly speaks of Judah, not Israelites (the Ten Tribes). The 'remnants' indicate the tragedy of the Holocaust during WWII when 6,000,000 European Jews were killed by the Nazis. The 'seacoast of Canaan' is the geographical border of the territory allotted by United Nations to the Jews in their decision to partition Palestine in 1947.

That the Jews will return in small, insignificant numbers, who somehow would have managed to stay alive after the Catastrophe, speaks the Prophet Joel 3:5:

"For on Mount Zion and in Jerusalem there will be **those that shall escape.**"

It is not necessary to confine understanding of 'remnants' 'and those that shall escape' only to the tragedy of the WWII Holocaust. It is a widely accepted opinion that the two thousand years of exile with unparallel suffering and killing, when vast numbers of the Jewish People perished, are also included in the category of 'remnants'.

That God sets no time and no limit for the Jews to return and really wants them to come back, may be seen from Prophet Zechariah 2:7:

"Deliver thyself, O Zion, that dwellest with the daughter of Babylon."

In the prophecy of Micah 4:8 God promises to the Jewish People to restore statehood which shall resemble a continuation of the glorious Kingdom of Israel in the time of David and Solomon.

"And thou, O tower of the flock, the strong hold of the daughter of Zion, unto thee shall it come, even the first dominion; the kingdom shall come to the daughter of Jerusalem".

This prophecy found its fulfillment in 1948, when 'the daughter of Zion', the Jewish People, established after 2000 years of exile the Independent Jewish State of Israel in Palestine.

We can go on and on proving by Scripture that the Almighty wants the Jewish People to return to the Promised Land first, before arrival of the rest of the Ten Tribes of Israel.

The return of the Ten Tribes has been limited also to certain circumstances and conditions. Firstly, Judah has to return and prepare the Land for the vast multitudes from the Ten Tribes.

"Also, O Judah, He hath set a harvest for thee, when I return the captivity of my people" (Hosea 6:11).

'A harvest' here is directly connected with the Ten Tribes when God ends their exile and under the leadership of the Messiah they will come home to the Promised Land. Judah, as the host, will organize their settlement and accommodation.

"The Lord God which gathered the outcasts of Israel saith, **yet will I gather others to him, beside those that are gathered unto him**" (Isaiah 56:8). This is understood that God first will gather to the Holy Land the remnants of Judah, and then, when the appropriate time comes, He will gather the rest of the Ten Tribes together with the rest of the Jews in Diaspora.

"In those days the house of Judah shall walk with the house of Israel, and they shall come together out of the land of the north to the land that I have given for an inheritance unto your fathers" (Jeremiah 3:18).

Necessary Conditions for Fulfillment of the Prophecies of the Final Exodus

Before the Ten Tribes return, God wants them to reconcile their differences and enmity with the Jewish People:

"The envy also of Ephraim shall depart, and the adversaries of Judah shall be cut off: Ephraim shall not envy Judah, and Judah shall not vex Ephraim" (Isaiah 11:13).

At the present time, the USA, England, Canada, Australia, New Zeeland, South Africa and a good dozen of the European countries of the Israel's origin do not have friendly, brotherly relationship as perfectly outlined in this Biblical verse,

"Manasseh shall devour Ephraim; and Ephraim, Manasseh: and they together shall be against Judah" (Isaiah 9:21).

Note: Manasseh is America and Ephraim represents Great Britain. Judah is, of course, the Jewish People, modern Israelis, the citizens of the Jewish state of Israel.

Another necessary condition for their return is total repentance and acknowledgment of the God of Israel and His Divine Torah:

"And a Redeemer shall come to Zion, **and unto them that turn from transgression in Jacob, says the LORD**" (Isaiah 59:20).

"I will give them a heart to know me, that I am the Lord. They will be My people, and I will be their God, **for they will return to Me with all their heart**" (Jeremiah 24:7).

And lastly, the most important aspect of their return will be the arrival of the Messiah who the Almighty will send to reunite the whole House of Israel, bring them home to the Land of their fathers and redeem them. All of this will happen in the beginning of the Messianic Age.

"And I will make them one nation in the land upon the mountains of Israel; and one king shall be king to them all: and they shall be no more two nations, neither shall they be divided into two kingdoms any more at all. And David my servant king shall be over them; and they all shall have one shepherd: they shall also walk in my judgments, and observe my statutes, and do them" (Ezekiel 37:22, 24).

Yes, before the coming of the Messiah, the Israelites must repent and have perfect faith because the Final stage of the Third Exodus is a spiritual return to the God of Israel and to His Torah in order to be redeemed by the Almighty.

It is so evident that the Ten Tribes of Israel are the People to whom the Prophet Eliyahu will be sent; then the Messiah, son of David, will be revealed. With their help and the support of the Jewish Sages, the Ten Tribes of Israel will be awakened to their Hebrew roots which undeniably means acceptance of the God of their fathers, the God of Israel, His Divine Torah, and the Holy Land as their inheritance. Until all of this come to pass, the Ten Tribes have to abide to the rules and conditions of the Divine Decrees (the Three Oaths of Shir Ha Shirim).

Only this explanation is viable and sheds penetrating light on the thick foggy mist surrounding the mysterious and highly controversial Prohibition Oaths.

Opinions of the Sages Regarding the Three Oaths and the Term 'Jews'

As we pointed out, there are many Sages who accept the Three Oaths as strong Halakhically binding prohibitions; and there are Sages who equally reject them. Why we are suppose to believe and follow the opinions of R. Maimonides, R. Bahya ben Asher, R. Maharal, and R. Teitelbaum and ignore Sages such as R. Nahmanides, R. Alkalai, R. Kalischer, and R. Kook?!

Besides, in the Sages opinions on the Three Oaths, there is no differentiation between the nation of Judah and the Israelites of the Ten Tribes, a definition of which is very important from the Bible's point of view in dealing with the Prohibition Oaths. From all of the Sages, R. Nahmanides knew best the difference between Judah and the Ten Tribes of Israel, which he perfectly explained in his book 'Sefer HaGeulah' (The Book of Redemption). Jews, according to R. Nahmanides, are those who belong to the Tribes of Judah, Benjamin, and much of Levy, former citizens of the Kingdom of Judaea, including some insignificant number of people from the Ten Tribes who returned to Judaea from the Babylonian Captivity together with the Judah. They settled in the cities and the towns of the Jews and voluntarily accepted the destiny and faith of the Jewish People. This great Sage was very much upset and outraged with the people of his time who could not understand the difference between Judah and Israel. "It is obvious from Scripture", explains Ramban, "that the term 'House of Joseph' applies to the Kingdom of Israel who are the Ten Tribes". So many scholars and theologians have propagated the idea that the Ten Tribes of Israel became 'lost', assimilated, died out, disappeared from the face of the earth and human history and will not have any role in the eschatological future events.

Nahmanides answered them: You are wrong! The Ten Tribes are well and alive. They had been exiled and they were still in Exile from Canaan even unto Zarephath (France, Britain, and northern Europe). He categorically declared that the Ten Tribes never came back to the Promised Land and had never been redeemed by the Almighty. He said that, according to Scripture, Joseph is destined to return and will join the rest of the whole House of Israel in the 'Days of Mashiah'.

It seems that for some Sages it is appropriate to call the Ten Tribes of Israel in exile 'Jews', the same way as they call Jews of Judah by this name. To call Israelites of the Ten Tribes 'Jews' would be appropriate if there would have been reliable profs of (a) their direct physical descent from Judah, Benjamin and Levy, collectively known to the World as a modern-day Jews; or (b) if the 'Lost' Tribes of Israel would have practiced Judaism as their way of life and faith. Since it is obvious that these two conditions have nothing to do with and are not applicable to the House of Joseph, to call them 'Jews' is both incorrect and unscriptural. And it is also offensive to the 'real' Jews who keep the

Laws and practicing Judaism as a way of everyday life according to the Heavenly Torah and often even sacrifice their life in order to maintain the faith and believe in the God of Israel.

If the rabbis would 'straighten' out their position in calling the Israelites of the Ten Tribes 'Jews', and would call them what they really are according to Scripture, there would not have been confusion and disagreements as to whom those Oaths (Divine Decrees), might or might not be applied: Everybody would have understood that the Oaths were designed for the Ten Tribes and for the time of 'the latter years', when the Messiah will have been revealed (not in 1948!).

Jewish anti-Zionists should Revaluate their Position

In Chapter I, where we discussed the Zionists and their State of Israel, we have proved in detail from Scriptures that the Almighty God prophesied and blessed the immigration of the Jewish People to the Promised Land and establishment of the State of Israel as the fulfillment of the Divine Plan of the Almighty. This will be the first stage of Return and Final Redemption of the whole House of Israel. Meanwhile, there is not a single word in the Hebrew Bible suggesting that Israel (the Ten Tribes) rebelled against the nations of the exile, immigrated to the Holy Land as a 'wall', 'en masse' or restored the Kingdom of Israel without the permission of God who will send the Messiah to accomplish all these tasks. Nothing of this has yet transpired. The Last Exodus of the house of Israel (the Ten Tribes) and the rest of Judah definitely will take place in the not so distant future, (Jeremiah 23:7-8), as will everything else, prophesied by our Creator, the God of Israel.

Those Jewish anti-Zionists, who called themselves the 'True Torah Jews', ought to revaluate their positions and re-examine the Torah and Scriptures more carefully in a new direction, rather than spend their time on the political front, organizing demonstrations against Israel and its leaders, embracing the enemies of the Jewish people and the State of Israel, endangering the lives and well being of the Jewish nation, to whom they belong.

We hope, that this work will help them to understand God's Plan for the 'End Times' and through an act of repentance before God and the people they have offended; with their new knowledge and love of God, they will go to their brothers and sisters of the Ten Tribes of Israel to bring them the light of the Torah, to help them to awaken for their and our glorious Divine Destiny—the last Exodus, Reunification and the Final Redemption on the Mountains of Israel.

CHAPTER VIII:
THE STATE OF ISRAEL,
ITS FRIENDS AND ENEMIES

The Birth of the New State of Israel and the Response to it by its Arab Neighbors

The 14 of May 1948 is the day of birth of the new state—the Jewish Democratic State of Israel. The establishing of the State was based on the United Nations General Assembly Partition Plan Resolution 181 on November 29, 1947. One day before the expiration of the British Mandate of Palestine, the Jewish Agency proclaimed independence of the state which they named Israel.

"Eretz Israel [Hebrew: The Land of Israel] was the birthplace of the Jewish people. Here their spiritual, religious and national identity was formed. Here they achieved independence and created a culture of national and universal significance. Here they wrote and gave the Bible to the world", says Declaration of Independence. Throughout forceful exile from their land for almost two millennia, the Jewish people had never lost faith and hoped to return to the Promised Land. In every generation they have longed and prayed to God to bring them back to their ancient homeland and restore their independence and political freedom. Finally their nightmare of homeless life, persecutions and unspeakable suffering had come to the end, and the centuries long dream of possessing their own land, the land of their fathers, where they can live freely and safely, become a reality.

The sovereignty and right of self-determination of the Jewish people to be masters of their own fate, like all other nations in their own sovereign State, had been achieved.

"Accordingly, we, members of the People's Council, representatives of the Jewish Community of Eretz-Israel and of the Zionist Movement, are here assembled on the date of the termination of the British Mandate over Eretz-Israel and, by virtue of our natural and historic right and on the strength of the Resolution of the United Nations General Assembly, hereby declare the establishment of a Jewish State in Eretz-Israel, to be known as the State of Israel," continues Declaration. "Israel will be open for Jewish immigration and for the ingathering of the Exiles; it will foster the development of the country for the benefit of all of the inhabitants; it will be based on freedom, justice and peace as envisaged by the prophets of Israel; it will ensure complete equality of social and political rights to all its inhabitants irrespective of religion, race or sex; it will guarantee freedom of religion, conscience, language, education and culture; it will safeguard the Holy Places of all religions; and it will be faithful to the principles of the Charter of the United Nations," read Ben Gurion. "We offer peace and neighborhness to all neighboring states and their people, and invite them to cooperate with the independent Hebrew nation for the common good of all.

Placing our trust in the Rock of Israel, we affix our signatures to this Proclamation at this session of the Provisional Council of State. On the soil of the homeland, in the city of Tel-Aviv, on this Sabbath eve, the 5th day of Iyar, 5708 (14th May, 1948)".

The United States Government in its memorandum titled 'Recognition of new states and Governments in Palestine', dated 11 May 1948, stated: "The Arab and Jewish communities will be legally entitled on May 15, 1948 (the date of expiry of the British Mandate) to proclaim states and organize governments in the areas of Palestine occupied by the respective communities."

Well, the neighboring nations had rejected the decision of the UN and the good will extended to them in the Israeli Declaration. On the following day the Arab armies of Syria, Egypt, Iraq, Transjordan, and Lebanon launched an attack against the newly-born state of Israel. Saudi Arabia sent military troops to operate under Egyptian command. What was the purpose of this attack? The Arab countries had voted against the United Nations resolution to partition Palestine into Jewish and Arab states with a Corpus Separatum for Jerusalem, which allotted to Jews 16.3 percents of the original territory of the British Mandate; they didn't want Jews in Palestine, and they intended to destroy the new Jewish state and establish Arab rule over all of Palestine. They spoke of "driving the Jews into the sea" and ridding Palestine "of the Zionist Plague". Azzam Pasha, the General Secretary of the Arab League, on the eve of the Arab army's invasion, declared: "This will be a war of extermination and momentous massacre which will be spoken of like the Mongolian massacres and Crusaders".

The King of Egypt, Faruk I, planned to take control of Arab Palestine by installing his poppet, Nazis collaborator and Jewish-hater Mohammed Said Haj Amin el Husseini, the mufti of Jerusalem, as king of a new Palestinian nation. However, the Jewish fighters miraculously won the war, which concluded with the 1949 Armistice Agreements, but it did not mark the end of the Arab-Israeli conflict.

History of the Refugees

During the War of Independence approximately 725,000 Palestinian Arabs fled or were expelled from their homes. David Ben Gurion did not agree with that number, "The refugee issue is one of the biggest lies, even among our own people. I have all the figures. From the area of the State of Israel, only 180,000 Arabs left in 1948. There were 300,000 Arabs all together in Israel and 120,000 remain."

There are many historical sources indicating that the leaders of the Arab countries encouraged and facilitated the flight of the civilian population from Palestine and made them refugees. Those leaders had told the Palestinians that the Arab armies in a short period of time would destroy the Jews and their state, and then the refugee would be able to return in peace and safety. The Arab leaders of Haifa were very proud that they had evacuated city and moved the Palestinian population out of the country. In April 1948, as recalled Golda Meir, she met with the refugees and begged them not to leave and not to be afraid for their safety. She warned them that if they fled they would be risking poverty, humiliation and an uncertain future. They did not listen. The Anti-Jewish propaganda of their leaders and the fear that the Arab world would count them as a traitors, determined their choice to flee.

The Palestinians commemorate every May 15 as Nakba Day, meaning 'disaster', 'catastrophe'.

The refugee status of the Palestinians and their descendants has remained one of the crucial problems in the ongoing Arab-Israeli peace negotiations up today. The entire world knows about the Palestinian refugees.

But what about the Jewish refugees? This is not a well known story. Yes, there were Jewish refugees right after the War of Independence. After their defeat, the Arab armies returned home, the governments had returned home. Their Governments began to put the guilt for all their humiliation and misfortune in war on the Jews living in their countries. Any Jew who sympathized with the Zionists or the State of Israel might be killed or jailed. In Iraq, for instance, all the anger and blame was turned against the Jewish community. Black lists of the richest and most prominent Jews were composed. State propaganda called them "Zionist spies". They were rounded up, arrested and jailed as enemies of the Arab people, accused of having committed treasonable offences, for which the punishment was death. Many of them were publicly executed by hanging, a spectacle that the Arab public enjoyed.

The Jewish 'Nakba' cost the lives of thousands of people. Anti-Jewish riots, pogroms and slaughters, the confiscation of properties and money, and mass deportations took place in most of the Arab and Muslim countries in the late 1940's. It is estimated between 800,000-1.000,

000 Jews were expelled or left their homes in Arab countries because of persecution and anti-Semitism. The Governments of the Arab League countries coordinated their policies towards the expelling or forceful deportation of the Jewish population.

This part of Jewish history, however, has been ignored by the Arab countries and the West. The United Nations has increasingly become pro-Palestinian, and the majority of resolutions of the General Assembly are unjustly directed against Israel. International peace activists and organizations for Human Rights and Global Justice have acknowledged the Arab Nakba with all its consequential human suffering, immorality, and need for restoration and compensation, but they somehow have "overlooked" and silenced the Jewish Nakba, as if it never happened. Jewish refugees had been victimized and had suffered not less than Arab refugees. There is adequate documentation for this.

Speaking of compensation, it is estimated that losses sustained by the Palestinian Arab refugees reached $3.9 billion, whereas losses of the Jews who fled Arab countries amounted to $6 billion.

It is the Arabs who rejected the UN Partition Resolution calling for the establishing of Arab and Jewish States. It is the Arabs who did not want to share the Land and live peacefully together with the Jews. It is the Arabs who started the war in order to destroy the young State of Israel and throw the Jews out of Palestine. After WWII, the Jews literarily had no home, nowhere to go. The European countries of their exile robbed them of their properties and did not welcome them back. They had one dream and hope—to settle in their historical, God-given Promised Land, the Land of their fathers, where they can live in peace and security, as other nations do. It is because of the Arab aggressiveness, hatred and intolerance towards the Jews in Palestine and in the surrounding countries of the Arab-Muslim League; it is because of the violence and animosity of their Governments and leaders, the Arab and Jewish Nakbas occurred as a direct result of Arab actions.

Let us see now how Israel dealt with the Jewish Nakba.

Israel's population in 1948 was about 800,000, and its territory was only 8,019 square miles. It is 32 times smaller than the state of

Texas. Territories possessed by the 35 Arab-Islamic states surrounding the Middle East, are 1,107 times larger than the State of Israel. As a result of the War of Independence and due to persecution and anti-Semitism, hundreds of thousands of Jews were expelled or left their homes in Arab countries. Most of these refugees, approximately 680,000 from the Arab lands, eventually immigrated to Israel. The People of Israel and its Government did not leave the Jewish refugees to rehabilitate themselves on their own: They did everything possible (and impossible) in their power to bring their unfortunate brothers and sisters to the land of their fathers; they provided foods, shelters, medical services, schools for children, and jobs. In 1948-1949 the Israeli Government airlifted 50,000 Jews from Yemen; in 1949-1951, 30,000 Jews fled Libya straight to Israel; in 1950-1952, 130,000 were airlifted from Iraq. Despite the necessity of living their property behind, 90% of the Jewish population opted to leave hostile Arab countries. They were temporarily settled in numerous tent cities and transit camps, which existed up to 1963. The refugees were gradually absorbed and integrated into Israeli society without help from the United Nation's various refugee organizations.

Contrary to the Palestinians and their supporters in the Arab-Muslim world, the Israeli Government has not turned the tragic plight of the Jewish refugees, their human rights violations and sufferings into political game for the purpose of bargaining to achieve some material and immoral goals. The Jewish nation has mobilized all its internal resources and those of the Diaspora, with the help of friends of the Free World, to accept and settle all the refugees on their historical, God-given Promised Land. There is a huge difference in the way the two nations have handled their refugees. The Arab countries have done nothing to solve their refugee problem despite their vast lands and resources. This simply is not in their political interests. They have used the refugee status of the Palestinians as a tool in their political games in the ongoing Peace Process negotiations; to mobilize world opinion against the Zionists and also to heat up hatred of the Arab population towards the Jews; and to keep up the flame of perpetual war against Israel.

The Political Situation in the Middle East Aftermath of the Arab-Jewish Wars

And the Arabs lost the war. Victorious Israel gained 18% more of the land than the UN Partition Resolution allotted it. The Gaza Strip was occupied by Egypt; the West Bank and East Jerusalem were occupied by Jordan. So, what happened with Palestinian self-determination and national independence? Did the Egyptians or Jordanians accommodate them with their aspirations? Did they take care of the Palestinian refugees, most of who were born in Arab countries? After all, they are naturally related to the Palestinian brothers by race and religion.

Egypt and Jordan possessed the occupied territories from 1949 to 1967. No effort was made to help the Palestinians with an independent state or even autonomy. On the contrary, King Abdullah I of Jordan (reign 1946-1951), grandfather of King Hussein, preferred a Jewish state to a Palestinian Arab state. Even after the war, when he conquered the West Bank and East Jerusalem, King Abdullah I had not recognized and tried to suppress any sign of the Palestinian independence. Instead, he wanted to be ruler of the annexed territories, and the Palestinians had to become citizens of the Jordanian State. The Palestinians were shocked. On July 20, 1951, while visiting the Al-Aqsa Mosque in Jerusalem, King Abdullah was assassinated by a Palestinian. Abdullah's grandson, King Hussein, (reign 1952-1999), continued the policy of King Abdullah I. In September 1970 Jordan crashed PLO fighters all over the country using the regular army and tanks. Later Arafat claimed that the Jordanian Army during 'Black September' killed between 10,000-25,000 Palestinians. Others reported that the numbers were ca.10, 000, including civilians.

The reason behind this cruel war was the fact that King Hussein did not want an independent West Bank under the PLO administration because it would threaten the sovereignty of his Hashemite Kingdom. As the King admitted, the Palestinian problem spelled "life or death" for Jordan and would remain the country's overriding national security issue. Besides, on September 1, 1970 several unsuccessful attempts to assassinate King Hussein were made, supposedly by the Palestinians.

Syria, together with the Palestinian Liberation Army, whose headquarters were located in Damascus, tried to intervene on behalf of the PLA fighters. When the Syrian Army with more than 200 T-55 tanks were about to cross Jordan's border, and the Palestinian militants rebelled inside the Jordan, King Hussein asked the USA and Great Britain to intervene on his side to attack Syria. "Situation deteriorating dangerously following Syrian massive invasion", in a panic he said in telegram to the USA, "I request immediate physical intervention both by land and air . . . to safeguard sovereignty, territorial integrity and independence of Jordan. Immediate air strike on invading forces from any quarter plus air cover is imperative". Tensions and hatred among Palestinians and Jordanians were so bad that members of Fatah declared that they preferred to die in battle, rather than surrender to the Jordanian dictates. And, in fact, when the Jordanian forces overcame the last pockets of the Palestinian uprising, seventy two PLA fighters fled to the West Bank and surrendered to IDF soldiers. Moreover, there are some transcripts of diplomatic communiqués show that the King requested Israeli intervention against Syria and the Palestinians as well! Good examples of 'brotherhood' in the Arab-Muslim world!

Jordan's occupation of East Jerusalem and the West Bank was brutal. They forcefully expelled Jews from East Jerusalem and destroyed or desecrated all Jewish holy sites. The life of the Palestinians in 20 UN refugee camps in the West Bank was unbearable, and they rioted against Jordanian occupation on few occasions: in December 1955; in April 1957; in April 1963; in November 1966 and April 1967. We have already mentioned the events of September 1970, known as 'Black September'. King Hussein had used the regular Jordanian army with tanks and machine guns, killing thousands of Palestinians.

The Egyptian occupation of the Gaza Strip was not better. There were 9 UN refugee camps that were exceedingly overcrowded with the Palestinians living in deplorable conditions. Egypt did not recognize the Palestinian rights of self determination and independence, refused to absorb any refugees, denied them passports, and forbade traveling and working in Egypt. Unemployment was very high, and the standard of living was very low both in the occupied territories of the West Bank and in Gaza.

It is interesting to note that the UN and the World had not cried aloud against the Egyptian and Jordanian occupation. Nobody at that time had invented the 'legitimate rights and national aspirations' of the Palestinian Arabs. It was only when the Jews took control over Gaza, the West Bank and East Jerusalem, as a result of a defensive war against aggressive Arab nations, that the situation changed dramatically, with the UN and Arabs wanting to stop the Israeli occupation and provide the Palestinians with an independent state.

On the other hand, the Arab-Israeli conflict has motivated radical Islam to unite against the Israel and the West, which Israel with its democratic and cultural values represents in the Middle East. The Arabs have used the Palestinian question as a political weapon and a convenient propaganda tool against Israel and the West. Bin Laden of the Al-Queada, Saddam Hussein of Iraq, Yassir Arafat of the PLO, Colonel Gaddafi of Libya, Mahmud Ahmadinejad of Iran,—are just a few of the anti-Zionists Jew-haters and racists who want to annihilate the State of Israel and the Christian West and establish a Muslim World Empire with a theocratic Islamic Government and Shariah laws. A gigantic clash between the two world largest civilizations in the world, Islam and Christianity, has begun, and tiny Israel happens to be just in the center of this battle.

The Peace Process

The Peace Process is a series of negotiations in the Israeli-Palestinian conflict between parties trying to solve all their problems in order to achieve a permanent true peace. This process has been going on and off for a good number of years, despite ongoing wars, terrorist attacks, retaliations, intifadas and the settlement activities.

The Palestinian side considers the year 1948 as the beginning of their dispute with the creation of the state of Israel. Therefore, they do not recognize the Jewish state's right to exist and want to destroy the Israeli state and get rid of the Jews. They also want to take back possession of the land and see the return of their refugees. Only after these goals are achieved, would they exercise the right of self determination and establish a politically independent Arab state in all the territories of the Palestine with its capital in Jerusalem. It was only in the late 1960th that the PLO and Yassir Arafat under international pressure changed their position and begun accepting the proposal to negotiate the two states solution. But another Palestinian group in Gaza, Hamas, still denies the right of the Jewish state to exist, and aim for the violent destruction of it.

The Israeli side says that the conflict had started later, in the 1967 Six Days War, instead of in 1948, when the United Nations Resolution allowed the establishment of the Jewish state. The Jews agreed with the UN Resolution, they did not conquer the land with the force of arms; the territory was allotted to them by the UN.

The International history of wars shows that countries that have defended themselves against aggressors, and were victorious, have not returned the captured lands. In 1967 it was Israel that was attacked by the Arab armies wanting to annihilate the Jews.

Again, the Jews miraculously won the war, and the Arabs became the victims. Israelis did not mind giving some control of the occupied territories to the PLO, provided that they would manage the violence and prevent terrorist attacks against the State of Israel. It is only after the Oslo Accords of 1993 and the 2000 Camp David Summit, that the Israeli had begun negotiating the possibility of the two states planned solution. It is commonly acknowledged by Israelis that the Palestinians in their negotiations ask too much and offer little or nothing in return, and often they conveniently forget their promises. The Palestinian leaders publicly, when they are facing Western diplomats or the mass media, affirm that they have changed their position and accept the right of the Jewish State to exist, but when they speak to the Arab audiences back home, they ignore all promises made, and renew the use of dangerous inflammatory rhetoric encouraging terrorism and advocating the violent destruction of Israel.

One of the most significant participants in the peace process between the Israelis and Palestinians is the USA. The American Government, since the creation of the State of Israel, has been the strongest supporter and a friendly ally of the Jewish state. Their financial and military help to Israel exceeds amounts to any other foreign country. Recently, beginning from 2002, America together with the European Union has been contributing one billion dollars yearly as financial assistance to the Palestinian Authority. On the other hand, a profound dependence on Middle East oil and unprecedented pressures from American oil cartels and its magnates, directs the policy of the USA Government towards appeasement of the Arab world and serves against the vital interests of Israel, quite often jeopardizing their lives and security.

As a mediator in the negotiations, the USA maintains that it is imperative for Israel, in order to achieve peace, to give up some land conquered in the 1967 war to the Palestinians; and the PA in return has to stop all terrorist activities and accept unconditionally Israel's right to exist. All American Presidents, at least in the past two decades, have accepted the plan of the two states final solution for the secure and peaceful future of the Israeli and Palestinian peoples.

There are many concerns and obstacles that need to be overcome before a true and lasting peace might be achieved. Israel's main concern is security, while the Palestinians want politically independent statehood. Questions of the Palestinian refugees; 500,000 thousand Jewish 'settlers' living in Occupied Palestinian Territories; terrorism; the status of Jerusalem; Gaza; the West Bank; the Golan Heights; safe borders; mistrust and hatred,—all of this has to be solved through negotiations.

One of the strongest instruments America and the International Community have applied to move the Peace Process ahead is the concept of 'Land for Peace'. The first time it was used was in Israeli's

Peace Treaty with Egypt in 1979, when Israel gave up Sinai for a comprehensive peace agreement, and the USA rewarded both parties with economical assistance. Will this Treaty be sustained and upheld after the 'Arab Spring' and depositing of the former President of Egypt Hosni Mubarak?

The Arab Spring or Democratic Revolutions in the Arab Countries

The Year 2011 will be remembered as the most crucial year in recent history, comparable for its importance with 1917 of the Russian Great October Revolution; or with the year of 1991, when with the collapse of the Berlin Wall, countries of the former Soviet Union and its satellites, fell down like domino chips.

Fanatics of the Muslim Brotherhood would not hesitate, they are ready and waiting for the opportunity to grub power in Egypt and join with the radical Islamists of Iran and Turkey to wage a final war against the West and Israel.

We do not share the over welcoming empathy of the Western Powers towards countries of the 'Arab Spring' in their fight for freedom and democracy. Although these people are united in a struggle against hated and bloody dictators, our prognosis, based on past history and the prophetic word of the Bible on the future, have led us to believe that after the post-revolutionary euphoria has settled down, these countries will still have neither freedom nor democracy. America, Canada, Great Britain, and the rest of the Western countries of Israelite origin by supporting the 'Democratic revolutions' of the Arab world have helped Radical Islamic Iran gain control over them. They will be eventually commandeered by extremists, religious fanatics, and terrorist organizations like Al-Qaeda, the Muslim Brotherhood, Hezbollah and Hamas, whose goal will be to move them into the Iranian sphere of influence; to destroy Israel; to establish Theocratic governments with Shariah Laws; with the ultimate aim of reunification of all the

Arab-Muslim countries into a single Islamic World Caliphate in the war against the 'infidels' and the capture of World dominion.

Biblical verses do indicate that Egypt will fight on the side of the 'King of the South', which is Iran, and will be attacked by the forces of the 10 European kings which is the 'King of the North' or, in modern language, is the Holy Roman Empire of the European Union lead by Germany (Assur).

"And at the time of the end shall the king of the south push at him: and the king of the north shall come against him like a whirlwind, with chariots, and with horsemen, and with many ships; and he shall enter into the countries, and shall overflow and pass over. He shall stretch forth his hand also upon the countries: and the land of Egypt shall not escape" (Daniel 11:40-42).

The life span of the King of the South's Empire will be short lived. The military response of the King of the North will be devastating. All the Middle East will be under the occupation and full control of the European Union.

In our view, those countries who were involved in the 'revolutionary democratic movements of the 'Arab Spring' eventually will be drawn into something like the1979 Revolution of Iran and themselves become radical Muslim republics that will be aligned with the Muslim Republic of Iran against the West and Israel. The deposed president of Egypt Hosni Mubarak said of the revolutionaries fighting for 'freedom', 'democracy', and 'equality': "They are talking about democracy, but the result will be extremism and radical Islam".

The liberal Western press, the politicians and the diplomats assured the public that the religious Islamic parties and particularly the Muslim Brotherhood would have no chance to winning the elections in the post-revolution Arab countries and would not play any significant role in politics. Their analysis turned out to be wrong. The Islamic parties have gained the political control in the countries of the Arab revolutions. Just take a look at the new Egyptian Parliament chosen in the November 28, 2011-January 11, 2012 elections. There are 508 seats in the Parliament, ten of which are distributed by Government appointment. From an available 498 seats, in first place with 47.2% (235) of all seats and gaining an outstanding victory came the Freedom and Justice Party, an Islamist political party tightly link to the Muslim Brotherhood of Egypt. The second victorious party was the Islamic Block of Al-Nour party with 27.8% (127 seats).

With 75% Islamist representatives in the Parliament one cannot expect Egypt to become a western style secular democracy, where freedom, equality and human rights will be protected and guaranteed. The post-revolution states of Egypt and Libya are moving towards becoming radical Islamic countries, having a Theocratic religion rule of state-religion with Sharia Law as the Supreme Law of the land.

The People of the Arab word do not know democracy, they are not ready for it, and they do not wish to have it. A recently conducted survey revealed that 95% of Muslims in Egypt want to play an active role in politics; 77% of Egyptians support the re-establishing of the Caliphate; 82% want to endorse death by stoning the adulterers and cutting off the hands of thieves and robbers.

They would rather have an Islamic way of life with its Sharia Laws, allowing stoning to death for adulterers and for those who leave the Muslim religion; cutting off the hands of thieves, and the segregate of women from men. They strongly approve terrorist organizations such as the Muslim Brotherhood, Al-Qaeda, Hezbollah, and Hamas and support of their struggle against Israel, including suicide bombings and the killing of civilians. One outcome in the aftermath of the Arab Revolutions is certain: There will be new waves of Anti-Semitism, blood libels, charges of an 'international Zionist conspiracy', inciting Jewish hatred and extreme violence against the State of Israel and the West.

The newly elected Islamist—dominated Parliament of Egypt has not waited a long time to express its ideological views on Israel. "Revolutionary Egypt will never be a friend, partner, or ally of the Zionist entity, which we consider to be the number one enemy of Egypt and the Arab nations", they declare while calling upon the Egyptian

Government to expel Israel's ambassador and to stop exporting oil and gas to Israel.

Doctor Mohammed Badie, leader of the Muslim Brotherhood, in his weekly address to party activists criticizes the peace treaty with Israel; he says that it was 'a mistake' and 'surrender', and he calls for abrogating the Camp David agreement and severing political and economical relations with Israel. He defines Israel and the United States as the prime enemies of Egypt and predicts victory over them with the help of Allah. The immediate goals, he says, should be to liberate Palestine from the Jews, recapture Jerusalem and the Golan Heights and bring the 'final solution' to the Zionists.

Once again, man makes plans, but God decides what actually will happen. Iran defies the international community and refuses to stop development of its nuclear military program. Its irrational 'push' against the industrialized countries of the West and use of the 'Oil Weapon' policy to choke Europe, will cause the King of the North, which is modern day European Union under the leadership of Germany, to strike as lightning. They will act against the King of the South which is Iran and Co. (Daniel 11:40-41).

Once more, our conclusion is affirmed by Scripture:

"He will gain control over the gold, silver, and treasures of Egypt, and the Libyans and Ethiopians will be his servants" (Daniel 11:43).

The fact that Egypt and Libya are mentioned as defeated servants in the victorious campaign of the King of the North (EU) against the King of the South (Iran) indicates that these countries will have been allied with the Islamic Republic of Iran. It has been reported that Muslim terrorists from Libya, Egypt, Iran, Palestine and Al-Qaeda from Pakistan and Iraq had deeply penetrated the Libyan movement and were playing important role in it.

For us it will not be a surprising if that the actions of the USA and NATO turn out to have brought more evil than good. Time will show.

Also, it is worth mentioning here that "Edom (Turkey), Moab, and the majority of the children of Ammon", both of the latter two representing today the Hashemite Kingdom of Jordan, "shall escape out of the hand of the King of the North" (Daniel 40:41). It seems that at the time of the European Union attack on Iran and its allies, Turkey and Jordan will have not joined the Islamic Republic and will not have fought on their side.

This means that the prophesied events of the battle between the Kings of the North and of the South will have taken place before the ultimate destruction of the sinful people of Edom as predicted (For Edom: Isaiah 34:5, 8; Obadiah 1:18; Ezekiel 25:12-13; For Moab: Jeremiah 48-all; and for Ammon: Zephaniah 2:8-11). The fatal end of these countries will happen during the time when God will ask Israel to bring the 'fist of My judgment' on these nations (Isaiah 11:12-14; Zechariah 12:6).

The same analysis applies to Syria. This nation was not mentioned concerning the conflict between the resurrected 'Holy Roman Empire' (EU) and the Muslim countries headed by Iran. Today events in Syria, the mass uprising of population and bloody confrontations with the Assad regime expected to end soon, will possibly result in fall of the authoritarian Government.

Syria will meet its destiny later on when, for its aggressiveness and hatred against the Jews, she will have faced the wrath of God's Judgments from the hands of Israelites (Jeremiah 49:24, 26-27; 51:20; Isaiah 17:1).

Regarding the Federal Democratic Republic of Ethiopia, which previously was a monarchy for most of its history; it is not clear yet how and when she will have become the ally of radical Islamic Iran. Most likely, Ethiopia will follow the pattern of its neighbors 'revolutions for freedom and democracy', in order to fulfill the Prophecy.

Turkey has also endured dramatic political and religious changes in recent years, but their revolution is a quiet one and initiated from the top. It was the Government of the Islamist Prime Minister Erdogan and his Justice and Development Party (AKP) that transformed this secular pro-western republic envisioned by its founder Kemal Ataturk, to the Muslim Republic of Turkey. They have severely disrupted their previously friendly relationship with Israel, USA, NATO and the West. They have become best friends with Iran, Syria, and Lebanon and have supported all terrorists' organizations in the Middle East who fight against Israel. From the most reliable ally of Israel in the Middle East Turkey has become the most antagonistic and is now a sworn enemy of the Jewish People and their State. This unexpected and sudden transformation of Turkey can be explained only by the Bible.

Our understanding of the origin of the People of Turkey is that their progenitor was not Japheth, as it was for the rest of the Turkic People of Central Asia, but Esau.

Yes, the same well known Biblical Esau who later was called Edom, the 'famous' twin brother of our Patriarch Jacob (Genesis 25:23-26). Through Esau's first born son Eliphaz and his son Teman (from whom the name Ottoman originated), grandson of Esau, came the Edomites, the modern day People of Turkey.

"You will live by the sword and you will serve your brother. But when you grow restless, you will throw his yoke from off your neck,"—thus Isaac blessed Edom before his death (Genesis 27:40).

When the Kingdom of Israel existed, Esau served his brother Jacob for most of the time. When Esau became stronger and had 'grown restless', he did exactly as the prophecy said: "In the time of Jehoram, Edom rebelled against Judah and set up its own king" (2 Kings 8:20). The Edomites Ottoman Empire later ruled (i.e. 'lived by the sword') the Land of Israel for four hundred years. This occurred while Israel having been defeated and humiliated was exiled to various countries of the world. Finally, in 1917 the Turkish Empire together with her ally Germany was defeated by the descendants of Jacob-Israel who were now called Great Britain and America.

It well may be, as suggested in the Talmud, that some elements of Edom's ruling elite could have been found in Europe, in Italy, Spain and Germany specifically. Scripture, however, indicates that Edom is modern Turkey!

As mentioned by the theologian writer Yair Davidiy from Jerusalem, "Esau was red and hairy. From a physical anthropological point of view the most hairy people in the world are the Turks. The early Turks were also described by others as red-haired. Later they intermixed with other peoples and largely lost this quality. This is interesting because there are those who identify the Turks with Edom".

Come, and Let Us Cut Them off from Being a Nation

"They have said, Come, and let us cut them off from being a nation; that the name of Israel may be no more in remembrance. For they have consulted together with the one consent: they are confederate against you: the tabernacles of Edom, (first on the list!), and the Ishmaelites; of Moab, and the Hagarenes; Gebal, and Ammon, and Amalek; the Philistines with the inhabitants of Tyre; Assur also is join with them" (Psalms 83:4-8). All the Arab countries surrounding Israel are well presented in this murderous coalition!

We can easily recognize today the countries of that confederacy who are going to attack Israel in order to 'cut them off from being a nation'. They are: The Palestinians of Gaza and the West Bank, Saudi Arabia (the Ishmaelites), Lebanon (Gebal and Tyre), Jordan (Ammon and Moab), Syria (the Hagarenes), Turkey (Edom and Amalek), and Germany (former Assyria with some elements of Edom). It is also include the terrorist organizations of Hamas, Hezbollah, the Muslim Brotherhood, Al-Qaeda and the other Jihadists of all kind, names and colors, who are under the control of the radical Islamite State of Iran. They will definitely have taken part in this bloody crusade. The very first in the list is Edom-Turkey. He has never forgotten nor forgiven that in ancient time Jacob had "took away my birthright and stolen my blessing" (Genesis 27:36). An ancient hatred towards his brother Jacob, a thirst for revenge and an irreconcilable wish to kill his brother, all of these will move Turkey to play a major role in the confrontation with Israel and fulfill the prophecies of the End Times. That this prophecy aims for the future, we may easily attest to the fact that such alliance of the participants in the plot Against Israel has never happened in the past history. This is commonly accepted view.

Some scholars and the Sages of Talmud believe that Edom represents the ruling classes, nobles and aristocracy of the European countries such as Italy, Germany, Spain, Portugal and the other 'non-Israelite sections of Europe'. Obviously, there is no country in existence today by the name of Assyria. In our opinion an ancient Assyria (Assur) is modern Germany!

If such is the case, how is it possible that Psalm 83 listed Edom, i.e. many non-Israelite countries of Common Market of Europe separately from Assur-Germany who 'is also joined with them'?

Psalm 83:
5 For they have consulted together with one consent;
They form a confederacy against You:
6 The tents of Edom and the Ishmaelites;
Moab and the Hagrites;
7 Gebal, Ammon, and Amalek;
Philistia with the inhabitants of Tyre;
8 Assyria also has joined with them;
They have helped the children of Lot. Selah

How may one speak of the fourth beast or the ten kings of the Prophet Daniel 7:23-24 which is the present-days resurrected Holy Roman Empire (the European Union) separately from its heart and soul, the organizer and undisputed economical, military, and political leader—Assur-Germany? Is not something wrong here? Such an interpretation of the Nations involved in a 'crafty counsel' against Israel definitely does not fit the Biblical description. How can Assur—Germany be regarded as a different entity to Edom, as a helper to him and secondary in significance to this military plot of the Nations against Israel ('they have helped the children of Lot'), if Edom is himself a part of Europe, and an integral part and essence of Germany?! It just simply makes no sense. What Psalm 83 says is that Edom is a different entity from Assur-Germany though in this planned attack they appear as allies pursuing a common goal to destroy Israel. This kind of military alliance between Edom (the Ottoman Empire) and Germany (Assur, the former Assyrian Empire) had also occurred during the WWI and can be explained only, beside the strategically motivated friendly cooperation, by mysteriously belonging to the same blood-related family of Edom. Their relationship has become more and more closed over decades. Germany promoted and absorbed a huge population of Turkish Diaspora which became the largest ethnic Muslim minority.

These ancient enemies of Israel, Esau and Assur, were defeated mainly by the allied forces of Israel (Joseph): Great Britain, USA, Canada, Australia, New Zealand and others. This trend will have exactly repeated in the time of the fulfillment of prophesy written in Psalm 83. The forces of Edom—Turkey will again form the military alliance with the forces of Germany-Assur to attack Israel.

As we will learn later, Assur far from being only a secondary helper in this war campaign will have become the military Head of all these nations. This conclusion may be derived from the Prophet Daniel 11:41when the King of the North (Assur) 'shall overthrow many countries but these shall escape out of his hand: Edom, Moab, and Ammon'. These are precisely countries that allied with Assur in Psalm 83.

It would not be the first time in history that the children of Esau (Edomites) and the children of Lot (Moab and Ammon) have attacked the children of Jacob (Judah). They are well known enemies of Israel from ancient times.

"So Saul took the kingdom over Israel, and fought against all his enemies on every side, against Moab, and against the children of Ammon, and against Edom" (1 Samuel 14:47).

This 'famous trio' of nations attacked Judah and inhabitants of Jerusalem in the time of King Jehoshaphat but 'The Lord set ambushments against the children of Ammon, Moab, and mount Seir (Esau) and they were smitten" (2 Chronicles 20:22).

Many scholars are quite amazed by the fact that Ezekiel 38 and 39, in describing the wars of Gog and Magog against Israel, does not mention the Semitic nations as participants of these military campaigns. There is no Edom (Turkey), nor are Ammon and Moab, all from the Semitic stock of Nations, mentioned. Do you wonder why? Because those Semitic nations who 'plotted with one consent' against Israel in Psalms 83, will have already been soundly defeated by Israelites with the help of the Almighty. The wars of Psalms 83, Isaiah 11, Zechariah 12 and 14, which are speaking of the prophesied defeat of those nations, will occur before the wars of Gog and Magog, that is why the Arab Semitic countries will not be physically able to join Gog's hordes and that is why their names are not mentioned in the prophecies of Ezekiel. God knows precisely what and how the events of the future are going to transpire according to His Divine Master Plan!

The fact is that Iran, Egypt, Libya and Ethiopia are not mentioned among the nations attacking Israel in Psalms 83; and Edom-Turkey with their historical 'friends' Ammon and Moab (Jordan) are not present as a participant in the wars between the King of the North and the King of the South in Daniel 11. This indicates that these wars will be different, and that Turkey in the End Times will not be allied with the radical Muslim countries of Iran and Egypt, but rather with Europe, Germany, to be more specific. This conclusion is based on Psalms 83:8 which says: "Assur (Germany) also is joined with them".

We have written about these matters more extensively in Chapter XIV, 'The Wars of Gog and Magog'. We shall deal separately in another place with Assur (Germany).

Today International geopolitical events in the World indicate that we are approaching the End Times of the Bible. The nations of the World are preparing to march against Judah and Jerusalem. Anti-Semitism is on a rise all over the Globe: in Russia and Europe (especially in Germany and France); even amongst our traditional friends in America and Great Britain. The events of recent days and the mass uprisings in Arab and Muslim countries go in line with Prophecies of 'the Latter

Years' which eventually will culminate in the Wars of Gog and Magog of Ezekiel 38 and 39 and the Siege of Jerusalem of Zechariah 12 and 14.

America and Europe are now welcoming these uprisings of the 'Arab Spring' as a movement for Freedom and Democracy. They had acted the same way in Iran by helping to deposit and humiliate their former friend, the Shah of Iran, Mohammad Reza Pahlavi during the Revolution (mass uprising) in 1979, which ultimately paved the way for establishing the Islamic Republic of Iran under the leadership of Ayatollah Khomeini; followed by 8 years of the Iraq-Iran War, which killed millions on both sides. The West has already forgotten that the Iranian revolution initially started with a secular liberal government and loud promises of freedom and equality. It took only a few months and a general national referendum to transform 'democratic' Iran into the Islamic Republic. **Sunnis and the Shiites in unison have declared that Islam is their choice.** It could hardly be otherwise because in the 'people's revolution' the People are Muslims. They are Islamists, and the tenets of their religious beliefs inevitably require and lead them to establishing Muslim Theocratic Republics with the Sharia laws. Of course, this comes with the need to return to Islam all lands previously ruled by the Muslims in the period of their conquest and glory.

Everyone knows what a danger Iran and its president Ahmadinejad represent today. It is not a secret that Iran is preparing for war. Despite ongoing international protests and sanctions, Iran has continued its effort to build nuclear weapons. Seems, the West have not learned the lessons of the past. They have been acting in the same way with the dictators they have cultivated: They support them as long as the oil flow to their countries is secured; and betray them in crises as we have witness today. Saddam Hussein of Iraq, Hosni Mubarak of Egypt, Muammar Gadhafi of Libya were all domesticated friends of the West.

At this very moment, while we are still preoccupied with the writing of this book, most of the evil men listed above are no longer around. Yassir Arafat died on November 11, 2004 in Paris. The cause of death is unknown. Some people say that Arafat was poisoned by the

Mossad or by his rivals from the PLO. Others are saying that he died from AIDS contracted through his homosexual activities. Bin Laden of Al-Qaeda, America's most wanted terrorist, was killed on May 2, 2011 in Abbottabad, Pakistan, by US Navy Seals. Saddam Hussein was sentenced by Iraq's court and executed by hanging on December 30, 2006. Colonel Gaddafi, deposed from power, lost a civil war, and finally was couth in a sewage pipe in his home town of Sirte and brutally killed by the rebels on October 20, 2011.

The Fanaticism of Islamic Nations will Ignite World War III

All these 'Revolutions' will have ended with the rule of radical Islam and the spirit of bloody Jihad. They will unite with the Islamic Republics of Iran and Turkey and other Muslim—"stan" countries of Southern Russia against Israel and the West.

"The Fanaticism of Islamic nations, whose leaders do not believe in Almighty God, will ignite World War III", said Nostradamus in 1555 a.c.

Israel will be in the center of a gigantic clash of the World's largest civilizations: The Christians versus Islam. The citizens of Israel, the Israelis, will be the most vulnerable because they will be surrounded by Arab and Muslim nations who are their sworn enemies.

Egypt is steadily moving towards becoming one of the most hostile enemies of Israel. With the deposing of President Mubarak, who somehow had been able to maintain peace between Egypt and Israel for 30 years, the true signs of the new revolutionary Egypt have started to appear. The Egyptian pipe line which brings Natural gas so essential to Israel through the Sinai Peninsula has been bombed five times already since the revolution begun. Hamas terrorists from Gaza on August 18, 2011, launched a sophisticated attack on a resort near Eilat, killing eight Israelis and wounding dozens. They penetrated the borders of Israel from Egypt's Sinai territory.

After seven months of post-Mubarak Egypt, on September 9, 2011a mob of anti-Israel protesters besieged and broke into the Israeli embassy in a way that reminded to us of the events when Iranian protesters during the revolution of 1979 took over the American embassy in Tehran. Only this time, fortunately, nobody was killed and no hostages were taken. In the same way as it happened in Tehran, Israel had to evacuate their diplomats by flying military jets into Cairo. Some observers say that Egypt's Supreme Council of the Armed Forces allowed this happened. Who knows what would have happened if Washington had not intervened and warned the military commanders of Egypt of imminent retaliation?

These are just the first fruits of 'free and democratic' Egypt. More definitely will come after the Muslim Brotherhood has consolidated its power in Egypt and joined the Muslim Republic of Iran.

It is wrong to conclude that the Arab Spring will bring to the Middle East Peace, Freedom, Democracy, Human Rights and the end of anti-Israel hostility. There are opinions among politicians that the 'Arab Spring' could easily turn into an 'Islamic Winter' with autocratic regimes and Sharia Laws instead of pro-Western style liberal democracies with free economies and human rights guarantees. The evidence has shown that animosities against Israel are on a rise, and the fight against the Jewish state, which all Arabs see as a scapegoat of all their problems, serves as a unifying factor among the post-revolutionary Arab countries. As a result, one can expect that the Muslim leadership of Egypt will soon abrogate the Peace Treaty with Israel, cut off the oil and gas supply and incite the Arab countries to attack and destroy Israel. American guarantees will not help, and Sinai with Gaza will not be returned to Israel for violation of the Peace Treaties.

The worse-case scenario was repeated in Iraq when American troops in 2003 under President George W. Bush invaded the country with the pretense that Saddam Hussein was endangering the World by the possibility of employing weapons of mass destruction (WMD). Saddam Hussein was deposed and hanged. The weapons of mass destruction were not found. The association of Iraq with Al-Qaeda was not proven. The casualties of Iraq were more than one million violent deaths. This war cost the USA 4478 soldiers killed in violent death and 33169 wounded. And the total cost to the US economy is estimated at a devastating three trillion USA dollars! Meanwhile, according to American Community Survey (ACS) for 2009, 14.3% of the USA population had an income below poverty threshold; 18.9% had income less than 125% of the poverty line, compared to 17.6% in 2008. The number of Americans living in poverty increased to 42.9 million. Were the USA Governmental actions to engage in this useless war justifiable? With a poor and failing economy at home? With millions unemployed and living in poverty? On top of it, the Government of Iraq insisted on a full withdrawal of all American troops (40,000) by December 31, 2011 and categorically denies permission to the USA to maintain a military base with 3.000-5.000 soldiers stationed on their territory after 2011. In the light of all the effort and sacrifices made by the American People, this is quite an unexpected attitude and shows ingratitude on the part of the Republic of Iraq

In our Introduction to this Book we wrote of this situation:

"All the effort that has been made in the Iraqi war in terms of death sacrifices and the money spent, ultimately will be nullified, because the radical Islamists aligned with Shiite Iran will take over to rule a 'Democratic' Shiite Iraq."

It is obvious that all the American involvement in the war in Iraq will be nullified. As soon as the last USA soldier leaves Iraqi soil, the Islamic Republic of Iran will move in and fill the void.

Latest reports on Iraq by the Human Rights Watch say that after the withdrawal of American troops, the Shiite-led Government of Prime Minister Nuri al-Maliki has revived the Saddam Hussein policy of a 'police state', excessively using security forces against Sunnis, dissidents, harassing protesters and journalists, and even killing and torturing detainees held in secret prisons.

Land for Peace and the Prisoner Exchange

For thousands of years the Land of Israel was possessed by many great Empires of the World but it had never been divided.

After the Turkish Ottoman Empire and their ally Germany were defeated in WWI, the League of Nations in accordance with the Sykes-Picot Agreement of 1916 gave the Imperialistic powers of Great Britain and France a mandate to rule the Southern portion of the Ottoman Empire. This divided the Arab region into different zones of influence. Lebanon and Syria were given (mandated) to France. Palestine was mandated to Great Britain in order to keep it as a refuge for the Jews, who had been scattered around the world. Britain violated this mandate.

In 1923 Britain 'chopped off' a huge chunk of the mandated territory originally proposed as a Jewish Palestinian homeland and assigned 75% of it to a newly created entity called "Trans-Jordan" which in 1946 was renamed "Jordan". The remaining 25% was supposed to belong to the Jewish homeland but the Arabs did not want to share even this portion of the land with the Jews: Their ultimate goal was to drive the Jews out of Palestine and repossess all of Palestine for themselves.

The price paid to Great Britain for all these treacherous actions was 'black gold'-Oil. The Almighty had foreseen this and warned the nations of grave consequences: "I will also gather all nations, and will bring them down into the valley of Jehoshaphat, and will plead with them there for My people and for My heritage Israel, whom they have scattered among the nations, and parted My land" (Joel 3:2).

This Land belongs to God. He had given it to His people Israel for ever. He said to Abraham: I will give to you and to your descendants after you, the land of your sojourning, all the land of Canaan, for an everlasting possession" (Genesis 17:7-8).

No human government or coalition of governments has the right or authority to change the Will of God and to cede portions of the Land of Israel to anyone else.

God is angry with the nations for scattering 'My people' among the nations and the partitioning of 'My land.' God keeps a record of how the nations have treated the Jews throughout history. He is going to punish those who have persecuted them and divided God's Sacred Land; the nations that have defended God's chosen People and the Land of Israel will be rewarded by the Almighty. It is up to all nations to determine their future destiny: To be destroyed or to be blessed. **It is impossible to fight against God and His People Israel.** The Pharaoh of the time of the First Exodus from Egypt learned this lesson (Exodus 14:30). So did Haman, the Agagite, in the time of the Persian king Ahasuerus (Esther 7:10).

The President of Egypt, Anwar Sadat, realized this truth and signed Egypt-Israel Peace Treaty in 1979, for which he payed with his own life at the hands of Islamic fundamentalists in 1981.

"The sons of your oppressors will come bowing before you; all who despise you will bow down at your feet and will call you the City of the Lord, Zion of the Holy One of Israel" (Isaiah 60:14).

Throughout the years of negotiations between Israelis and Palestinians with the help of the brokers of America, the European Union, Russia and UN no results of any significance have been achieved. Why? Because nations in search for peace are looking to men, who sometimes happen to be enemies, instead of trusting in the Almighty God of Sinai. Examples include Madrid Conference of 1991, the Oslo Accords of 1993, the Hebron and Wye Agreements of 1966-1999, the Camp David Summit of 2000, the Road map of 2003, the Israel-Hamas ceasefire of 2008, the Direct Talks of 2010. There is still no peace in the Middle East.

Succumbing to International pressure, mainly from the USA and Britain, in 1995 Israel unilaterally withdrew (the 'Disengagement Plan') from the Gaza Strip, abandoning all its settlements and military installations, ending the 38 years of Jewish presence in Gaza. Israel undertook responsibility for supplying the Gaza residents with water, electricity, communications, sewage network and even freedom from taxes on imported goods from Israel, while goods exported from Gaza to Israel are taxed by the Arabs.

The Under-Secretary-General for Political Affairs of the UN, Ibrahim Gambari, told the Security Council: "Israel has demonstrated that it has the requisite maturity to do what would be required to achieve lasting peace. Prime Minister Sharon should be commended for his determination and courage to carry out the disengagement in the face of forceful and strident internal opposition".

How did the Palestinians (Hamas) welcome and appreciate this good will gesture of the Israelis? Chaos and political struggle between Hamas and Fatah erupted as soon as Israeli had completed the withdrawal. Both factions were using automatic machine guns and grenade-launchers against each other, killing more than 600 Palestinians; and, of course, they did not forget to systematically attack Israel by launching Qassam and Katyusha rockets from the Gaza into Israel or sending the suicide bombers. In these attacks, they do not aim at Israeli soldiers or military installations, quite the opposite. They want to kill as many civilian, including children, as possible. Actually, children and students are their first priority targets. The more they kill, it seems, the happier they are. Any successful terrorist operation against Israel results in celebrations on the streets of Gaza and the Arab world. To do their bloody assaults, they do not hesitate to hide their deadly rockets in the midst of the public places such as schools, hospitals, markets, and mosques. They do not care of lives of their own people, using them as shields, as long as they save their own skin. The children and women are used as suicide bombers.

On very rear occasions we may hear World condemnations of such deadly attacks against Israel. However if Israel, God forbid, retaliates against the terrorists, and by mistake or accident kills a few civilians, all the International community in unison instantly condemns Israel as the 'bad guy'. Such incidents only occur in the first place because the terrorists hide amongst civilians. Everyone knows that Israel does everything possible to avoid civilian casualties. This is what is called the impartiality, justice and 'love' towards the Jewish people. The withdrawal from Gaza by Israelis was taken by the Palestinians, and especially by Hamas and other terrorist organizations, as weakness and defeatism, and as signification that terror and suicide bombers work effectively against Israel.

Giving land away for empty promises of peace will not bring true peace in the end. You cannot buy true Peace or Love for money or gifts. These things cannot be bought or sold. Real Peace may be achieved only if both sides are sincerely dedicated to it. The same goes for Love, which becomes a happy blessing when the lovers are totally devoted to each other. The policy of appeasement will not lead to Peace; on the contrary, it will produce a greater appetite in the more aggressive partner who will take it as a sign of weakness and surrender.

Somewhere in the desert of Sinai is Mount Sinai where the God of Israel revealed Himself to the Hebrews, formed Israel as a nation and gave them the immortal Torah. To give away such a Holy historical land is a sacrilege. America and Britain, both being the Israelite nations of Manasseh and Ephraim respectively, forced the Israeli Government to give Sinai back to Egypt. God definitely would not approve this action! That is why all these three countries will be punished by God (Hosea 3:5).

The same goes with the prisoner exchanges. For one or a few soldiers (alive or dead) Israel has set free hundreds of terrorists on whose hands is the blood of many innocent citizens of Israel, including the children and women. These freed criminals are gladly taken in by Hamas and other 'Jihadists' for the purpose of continuing to kill and terrorize the Israeli population. Jewish Law prohibits such practice, especially at time of war: "Captives should not be ransomed for more than their value, for the sake of the general welfare", teach the Rabbis of the Talmud. Otherwise, terrorists would make kidnapping a lucrative business. The present kind of trade however will only encourage them to do more kidnapping (Shulchan Aruch, Yoreh Deah 252:4).

The story of Rabbi Meir of Rothenburg, known as the Maharam (1215-1293 a.c.) is very revealing in this context. Kidnapping has been

an old and profitable business, especially against Jews. The Emperor
of France Rudolf I, in need of money, captured the seventy years old
R. Maharam, who was a well-known and respected Sage in the Jewish
communities. Rudolph put him in prison and demanded a huge
ransom for his release. Despite the fact that the rabbis and leaders were
ready to pay necessary money to free him, R. Maharam did not permit
them to do so. He wished to serve as an example not to encourage
enemies to imprison any other Jewish rabbi and/or leader in the future.
As a result, he remained in prison for another seven years and died in
captivity. The demand of the Emperor-terrorist was not satisfied and
Jewish Law was upheld.

The Wall

Here is another example, The Wall. To protect its citizens from
the Palestinian terrorist attacks, especially from the suicide bombers,
the Israeli Government has decided to build a barrier between Israel
and the West Bank. Israel was compelled to do this because the live
in the country had become unbearable under everyday bloody attacks
of the terrorists. Neither the United States, nor the European Union,
nor the United Nations, nor Russia,—nobody was able to help Israel
prevent the attacks. The Wall-barrier has indeed reduced the number
of terrorist attacks significantly; from 46 attacks in 2002, to 24 attacks
in 2003 (before construction of the Wall), to 1 attack in 2007 and 2
attacks in 2008 (after construction of the Wall). The terrorist leaders
of the al-Aqsa Martyr Brigades, Hamas, and the Palestinian Islamic
Jihad have themselves admitted that they are less able to conduct the
operations in Israel because of this Wall. Israelis say that the Wall has
not only saved the lives of citizens, but also serves as a guarantee against
attempts to undermine the political process of peace negotiations
between the Israel and the Palestinians. It helps neutralize the terrorist
activities and prevents them from disrupting the Peace Process and
holding it hostage.

There are many walls and barriers that have been built by many countries all over the Globe. South Korea protects herself from the North Korea by a barrier. India built a wall on 3,300 km. long to separate herself from Pakistan. Saudi Arabia has a particularly sophisticated security wall to prevent the Yemenite infiltration. It runs on Yemenite territory, in some places as deep as 7 km. which makes the local tribes angry. When construction is completed, it will have cost a half-billion euro. Saudi Arabia also built an ultramodern 900 km. barrier on its northern borders with Iraq. Turkey built a barrier against the Greeks on the Island of Cyprus. Thailand separated itself from Malaysia. Pakistan has a 2,400 km. barrier on the border with Afghanistan. Uzbekistan set up a wall along its borders with Tajikistan. The United Arab Emirates is setting up a barrier on their border with Oman. Kuwait strengthens its 215 km. border with Iraq. Ireland has a barrier to separate Catholics from Protestants. The USA constructed a wall to separate its border with Mexico, to protect itself against poverty-stricken Mexican workers and their families from illegal immigration.

This list could go on and on. Various walls and barriers have been built by the countries of the world and are accepted as the norm of our time. It is only when Israel constructed its defensive security Wall that the entire World unanimously expressed outrage against Israel, and called it "the Wall of Shame". The United Nations, the Red Cross, Human rights organizations, Amnesty International, the World Council of Churches, the International Court of Justice, Pope Benedict XVI and his bishops, our 'friends' from Naturei Karta, leftists intellectuals and the Torah Jews against Zionism (Have we missed someone?),—all denounce Israel. They falsely alleged that Israel is a violator of human rights and international laws, and is guilty of the crime of apartheid.

They disregard the fact that the number of Jewish victims in the years 2002-2008 dropped from 451 to 7, which is a reduction of 98.5% in deadly terrorist attacks. How can you justify walls to prevent the poor workers illegally entering the country for the economical reasons, as in USA or Saudi Arabia, compared with a Wall which prevents bloodshed and saves the citizens of the country?! Nations with walls on their own have thrown stones at Israel, while being themselves guilty of the 'crimes' they say Israel commits!

The morality of World opinion loses its weight and polarity when it comes to judging Israel. They have rarely missed an opportunity to show how much they 'love' the Jewish people.

Even the head of the Roman Catholics, Pope Benedict XVI and his bishops, who are supposed to obey and respect the sacred Word of God printed in the Holy Bible that the Promised Land was given by the Almighty to His people Israel forever, when it come to Israel's actions, speaks otherwise. The Pope just recently stated: "Israel cannot use the biblical concept of a Promised Land or a chosen people to justify territorial claims" (October 23, 2010). One of the bishops commented: "There are no longer a chosen people. All men and women of all countries have become the chosen people. The concept of the Promised Land and the justification of the return of Jews to Israel cannot be based on sacred Scriptures".

The Synod obviously took the side of the Palestinians who are 'suffering the consequences of the Israeli occupation: the lack of freedom of movement, the wall of separation and the military checkpoints'. The Vatican, who claims that its Christian religious roots lie in the inerrant Hebrew Bible, has ignored the will of God that the Holy Land belongs to the Jews. It has clearly taken a biased position against Israel. Why would the Vatican support the Palestinians and insist on the creation of a politically independent state? Do they really want to end the Israeli-Palestinian conflict and establish a justifiable and comprehensive peace between these people? The answer is, No! The Roman Catholic Church has its own agenda in the Holy Land, which is the ownership of Jerusalem. This ancient city is of great importance to Vatican. They call it holy. It is the place where Jesus had his ministry, the birth place of the Apostolic Church, the history of early Christianity. That is why throughout history they (through the Crusaders) fought bloody wars against the Arab-Muslim world to liberate Jerusalem from infidels and keep this Royal city for themselves. The Pope knows that the Catholic Church cannot wrestle Jerusalem from Israel in open military confrontation because the Israelis are too strong. The time of Crusades is over. So, they have left off the tactic of a close fisticuffs battlefield confrontation and instead let the international pro-Muslim community of the UN and the Palestinians do the dirty work for them. That is why the Vatican insists on a two States solution. They think, if the Palestinians will be given rights in Jerusalem, they too will gain. The Catholic Church is an integral part of the resurrected Holy Roman Empire, which is the European Union under the leadership of Germany today. Germany through diplomatic effort as the member of Quartet on Peace Process negotiations or by the might of Empire, any which way comes first, will try to gain control. The Church hopes it may possess, through Germany, Jerusalem in the future.

Their position is not based on God's Bible. It is obviously not kosher and not holy. They have forgotten one thing: Whoever goes against Israel goes against God. History and the Scriptures have proven this many times. And in the near future those nations will be given a powerful lesson in God Almighty's Judgments!

Hamas

In 2000-2004 Hamas had accounted for 425 terrorist acts, in which 377 Israelis were killed and 2,076 were wounded.

Hamas security forces systematically arrests and tortures Gazan citizens who oppose their rule or sympathize with Israel. After the take—over on July 2007, Hamas military courts have convicted to death penalties in unfair military proceedings numbers of Gaza residents for charges of treason and collaboration with the Israelis or with opposing parties, including Fatah of PA.

Political leader of Hamas, Ismail Haniyeh, said:

"We will never recognize the usurper Zionist Government and will continue our Jihad-like movement until the liberation of Jerusalem". At least they do not hide their plans!

In their Charter Hamas declares that their goal is to replace the State of Israel with a Palestinian Islamic state on the territory that now belongs to Israel, the West Bank and Gaza. They call their political-religious struggle against Israel a humanistic movement. The Charter says that the Arab-Israeli conflict is an inherently irreconcilable struggle between Muslims and Jews, Islam and Judaism. The Charter also says that it is not a national or territorial conflict but a conflict between believers and infidels. It is stated that the only way to conduct this struggle between "truth and falsehood" is through Islam and by means of Jihad (holy war), until victory or martyrdom.

"The time will not come until Muslims will fight the Jews (and kill them); until the Jews hide behind rocks and trees, which will cry: Oh Muslim! There is a Jew hiding behind me, come on and kill him!" These are the anti-Semitic motivations and ideology of Hamas.

PLO

The Palestine Liberation Organization was created in 1964 with the purpose of liberating Palestine from the Zionists through armed struggle. Its leader Yassir Arafat (1969-2004) was well known as terrorist #1in the world, who later 'transformed' himself to peacemaker and as a 'reliable' partner in the peace process between the Israelis and Palestinians. His PLO was also undoubtedly one of the terrorist organizations most known to the world.

A tragic-comedy has been played in the ongoing peace process negotiations, when, as Netanyahu said, "I think the central problem of the terrorism that we see today is that we have created a situation where we rely on the Palestinian Authority to be our subcontractors to fight terrorism".

In its Charter the PLO confirms that "the establishment of Israel is fundamentally null and void", "the armed struggle is the only way to liberate Palestine", "it is a national duty to purge the Zionist presence from Palestine", "the liberation of Palestine will liquidate the Zionist and imperialist presence".

Despite many promises to change the wordings of the Charter and to accept unconditionally Israel's right to exist, the PLO still has not done it up today. This fact shows, once again, their insincerity in dealing with Israel and the West. In their defense, the PA has said that with the establishment of the Palestinian state, the Charter will be replaced by a new constitution with an acknowledgement of Israel's right to exist. In other words, give us a state, and then we might say that you have the right to exist.

In 1993 Yassir Arafat admitted that "The PLO recognizes the right of the state of Israel to exist in peace and security". But this statement mainly was for the West, for him it was meaningless, because he never seriously considered true peaceful coexistence between the Palestinian and Jewish peoples.

Chairman Arafat viewed the peace process as a series of stages. The first stage is to establish the Palestinian state on the territories of Gaza and the West Bank. The second stage is to take over Jerusalem. The third and final stage is to build and reorganize their military forces and join together with armies of the Arab nations in the battle to destroy Israel. This is the long-term strategy of the PLO. Its leaders, when they are speaking to Arab audiences, have not hidden their ultimate goal to recover all the land of Israel from the Jews. In 1980 Arafat openly said, "Peace for us means the destruction of Israel". Most of the Arab countries have denied the right of the Jewish State to exist and have continued their preparations for its military destruction.

Palestinian Television, owned by the Palestinian Authority, often has made anti-Israel remarks, such as "Israel should not exist", "Israelis stolen our land", "Allah wants all Jews to be killed", "Jews have to return to their original homeland in Ethiopia and Europe". Every Gallup Poll said that the majority of the Palestinians do not want the Jews and their state in Palestine. No recognition. No peace. No negotiations. No Israel. Their text books for 12th grade Palestinian students are full of anti-Semitism, denial of the right to exist of the State of Israel and contain incitement to commit violence and terrorism against the Zionists and their state. They have brainwashed students with such false claims as that the Arab people lived in Palestine since ancient times before the Israelites appeared, therefore they have more right to the Land than the Jews. They are also taught, for instance, that Haifa is a Palestinian seaport; the Galilee, Nazareth and Beit She'an are regions in Palestine; the refugees must return to Palestine under the "banners of glory, jihad and struggle."

Senator Hillary Clinton had a chance to review the Palestinian Media Watch report containing analysis of eight text books for 12th grade students, published in 2007. She said that the books, which she called "child abuse" and the "glorification of death and violence", caused her to express skepticism about whether Palestinian Authority Chairman Mahmoud Abbas is a fair partner for peace. Time is flying fast, so do opinions. Now Madam Clinton has become the USA Secretary of the State, and together with President Obama renews the old policy of pressurizing and 'twisting hands' towards the Israeli Government for the sake of moving the Peace Process ahead. They hope to accomplish their goals and reach true permanent Peace in one year. Former Senator Clinton it seems has forgotten her skepticism about the Palestinian Authority and its Chairman.

Benjamin Netanyahu perfectly understood the position of the PA and its President, "Our enemies do not want an Arab state next to Israel. They want an Arab state instead of Israel". One could not say it better!

Israel cannot handle a small 'Gaza state'. How would they deal with a politically-independent 'big Arab state' on the West bank? Should Israel just rely on a white piece of paper with the signatures of Arab leaders who traditionally disregard promises and peace treaties, and still have not accepted the right of the Jewish People to live in the Holy Land and have their own state?!

Many Israelis, including Netanyahu, foresaw the consequences of withdrawal from Gaza as disgraceful capitulation to terrorist violence, sending a message that the Arab terrorism is being rewarded. The Withdrawal is viewed as disadvantage to real peace.

"I do not know when terrorism will erupt in full force, said the Prime Minister in 2005, right before the pull-outs;—my hope is that it will not ever. But I am convinced today that the disengagement will eventually aggravate terrorism instead of reducing it. Only we in the Knesset are able to stop this evil."

The Israeli Government and the Knesset decided otherwise, but reality shows that Netanyahu has been right. Gaza has become exactly what he predicted—a welcoming 'nest' for terrorism, an Iranian proxy right at the doorsteps of Israel. They have smuggled into Gaza a stockpile of rockets and the various arsenals of weaponry, and established a close relationship with another terrorist organization which, which is also controlled by Iran and Syria-Hezbollah in Lebanon.

Today's situation in the Middle East shows how right Netanyahu was in his predictions. "You have to understand", explained the Prime Minister to the members of the Knesset in March, 2012, "that the main source of Gaza terror is coming not from the Palestinians but their real boss Iran. Who gives rockets and money? Iran. Who trains them and creates an infrastructure of terror? Iran. Who gives the orders? Iran. Can you imagine what would happen, if Iran achieves their goal and builds the nuclear weapons? Many people say that I try to scare our society. I heard the same words from the same people when I warned the Government against giving away Gaza. I told them that rockets will immediately fly against our cities Beer Sheba, Ashdod, and Ashkelon. The bloody terrorist attacks will be intensified. Was I wrong? You are saying that the Palestinians might be upset and the Peace Process be disrupted. What Peace Process? Do we really have a Peace Process? Unless we decisively resolve the Iranian issue, the threat to our State and to the Jewish People will still remain".

To win a war and secure its existence, Israel must directly deal with the nuclear threat of Iran.

Israel with its compromising policy about giving away the Land of God for an elusive peace, pressurized by America and other International 'partners', in a way has helped Hamas to organize a terrorist state that planning and dreaming to annihilate the Jewish state; who will not accept any peace agreement; who openly declare that they will not stop their armed struggle until the last Jew in Palestine is killed. And on top of all this, the Israelites have supplied their sworn enemies in Gaza with food, water, energy, medications and other important goods of human necessity. Instead, why not quit to feed and cure them. Let them to build their own economy and learn how to feed and provide medical treatments to the people of Gaza themselves. Maybe they will learn something else besides launching rockets and bloody terrorist attacks against Israel?

The World already has forgotten Israel's unilateral withdrawal from Gaza, and increasingly criticizes Israel, no matter what they do to keep the Peace Process alive. It is the time to change the rules of the Palestinian game and start conducting themselves according to plain reality. The aggressor cannot be rewarded for his evil actions, but has to be rebuffed in a way that any thought of war or victory would no more come to his mind. They need to be aware of the grave consequences for their behavior. Then, and only then, may the two sides negotiate the Real Peace!

In the time of Ezra and Nehemiah, when the Jews returned from Babylonian captivity and started rebuilding Jerusalem, enemies from surrounding nations (Arabs) tried to do everything to prevent their effort. That is what Nehemiah told them:

"The God of Heaven will make us prosper, and we His servants will arise and build; but you have no portion, no right, and no memorial in Jerusalem" (Nehemiah 2:20).

These words today most aptly apply to the Palestinians who have continued to do malicious acts against the Israelis just as their predecessors had done, and have become 'splinters in the eyes and thorns in the sides' of Israel.

183

CHAPTER IX:
THE BIBLICAL PERSPECTIVE ON
THE PEACE PROCESS

The Peace Treaty and History of the Participants

There cannot be true peace in the Middle East between the Arabs and Jews in our days. That is what the Bible says. Real Peace will eventually come, when God will have redeemed all Israel and sent the Messiah, son of David. Then all the nations of the world will be redeemed and will start serving Almighty God, and true Peace will descend upon mankind. All the nations of the world will acknowledge the God of Israel, as the only God of the Universe, and then the Messianic Age will come.

Meanwhile, let us examine the Scriptures on the particular subject of Peace in the Middle East. First of all, to make a long lasting, comprehensive, true Peace between the Arabs and Israelis, requires full genuine commitment of both parties to pursue this noble goal with honesty, integrity and, if necessary, with sacrifices.

More than anything else in the world Israel wants Peace. Israelis are "literally dying for real Peace". They did not come to the Promised Land by force. They did not conquer the land by military adventure. After WWII and the disasters of the Holocaust, Jews had nowhere to go, except to their historical land of their fathers—the Land of Israel. They had lived in this land since the time of Joshua (1385 b.c) for a good 1,500 years until destruction and exile in 70 and 135 a.c. Before that they had had their glorious statehood, the United Kingdom of

Israel, ruled by the most famous Kings David and Solomon; their history, culture, the immortal Book of Books, the Bible, is well known to the World. Even after the Romans exiled them from their land, Jews were still present in Palestine, sometimes in small numbers, sometimes in large. In a.c. 614-617, for instance, Jews controlled the majority of the land and were dominant in Jerusalem. During the Crusader and Mameluk (Muslim slave controllers of Egypt) rules, Palestine was still dominated by Jewish culture and customs. The British Council in Palestine, James Finn, in 1857 reported:

"The country is to a considerable degree empty of inhabitants and therefore its greatest need is that of a body of population."

In his 'The Innocents Abroad' (1867), Mark Twain described the desolation of the Land in these words: "Palestine sits in sackcloth and ashes. Over it broods the spell of the curse that has withered its fields and fettered its energies . . . Palestine is desolate and unlovely . . . It is a hopeless, dreary, heartbroken land."

In these words evaporates the Palestinian claim of having had a significant Arab population, a thriving Palestinian culture, a verdant Land and so on. The Land of Israel for 2,000 years had been scarcely populated by men and beast and laid abandoned as a desolate waste. It is not an accident that not one nation of the world made Palestine their home state. God had secured and kept this Land for His people Israel, when they return from the exile again.

"But ye, O Mountains of Israel, ye shall shoot forth your branches, and yield your fruit to my people of Israel; for they are at hand to come. And I will multiply men upon you, all the house of Israel" (Isaiah 36:8, 10).

Jerusalem's population in 1785 C.E. was between 12,000-14,000 people. Hebron had approximately 850 inhabitants and Bethlehem 600. The Arabs called this land 'Southern Syria' and wanted it to become a part of 'Greater Syria', which would include Lebanon, Iraq, and Transjordan. They viewed themselves as an integral part of Syria, connected with it by national, economic, religious, linguistic, natural and geographical bonds. And because of this, they never sought to be a politically independent entity. They believed that there are no differences between Syrians, Lebanese, Palestinians and Jordanians and that they are all the same people.

"There is no such country as Palestine! 'Palestine' is a term Zionists invented! There is no Palestine in the Bible. Our country was for centuries part of Syria", a local Arab leader explained to the Peel Commission in 1937.

That is what the President of Syria, Hafez Assad, told to PLO Chairman Yassir Arafat:

"You do not represent Palestine as much as we. Never forget this one point: There is no such thing as a Palestinian People, there is no Palestinian entity, there is only Syria. You are an integral part of the Syrian people; Palestine is an integral part of Syria. Therefore it is we, the Syrian Authorities, who are the true representatives of the Palestinian People".

Only after the 1960^s did they begin to call the land 'Palestine'. The Jews and Christians always referred to the land as 'The Holy Land', 'the Land of Israel', or 'Palestine'.

"It is common knowledge that Palestine is nothing but Southern Syria", said Ahmed Shuqeiri, an official of the PLO, to the UN Security Council.

The Total population of Arabs, Jews and Christians in the time of the Turkish Ottoman Empire was not more than 200,000. Meanwhile, the Jewish population in the Palestine before the Roman expulsion, according to Josephus Flavius, was around 2,500.000. Between 1850 and 1918 the Arab population reached 550,000. The real reason for the Arab increase was Jewish immigration. The Jews created agriculture, built industry, infrastructure, hospitals and schools, provided jobs. The life of the Palestinians improved tremendously. Tens of thousands of Arabs from many surrounding Muslim countries immigrated to Palestine to benefit from these economical opportunities. In 1934 alone, approximately 33,000 Arabs left the Hauran Province in Syria for a better life in Palestine. That is why the UN, after considering all these facts, plus the Balfour Declaration and the San Remo Conference of 1920, partitioned the Land in order to establish a Jewish state alongside a Palestinian state, to live together in peace and harmony. The Jews accepted this decision. The Arabs rejected it. They rejected Israel's offers for peace in 1967 and in 1978. They rejected Ehud Barak proposal for a Palestinian independent state in 2000 and the peace package of Ehud Olmert in 2008. They do not want a Jewish state in Palestine. They do not want to share the Land of Israel with the Jews. They do not want Jews around. Period.

How can you make a real lasting Peace between the two nations, when one is sincere, shows its value of life and readiness to make necessary sacrifices, and, in fact, already has demonstrated it by giving away 'Land for Peace'; whereas the other side is cheating, asking too much and giving nothing in return, full of hatred, intolerance and aims for the destruction and annihilation of the other? How can one trust such a nation? And for how long has the World to pretend that this has been otherwise and play a cheap immoral political game with the so called Peace Process? How long can Israel sustain this torture under Global pressure to pursue the Peace process which continues to sap their strength and never will bring them peace and security? America and the rest of the 'Quartet' in an effort to appease the Palestinians and the Muslim world in general, have imposed outrageous, draconic demands on Israeli's Government, forcing them to make dangerous, self destructing decisions.

Israel feels that America has abounded her. The years of close relationship, when both countries had shared democratic values, enjoyed brotherly cooperation and military alliance, these years are gone. Now we have been witnessing "a new beginning" promised by President Obama—a new relationship between the USA and the Muslim world. The first priority of the USA is securing its own oil interests.

America's brotherly relationship with Great Britain also has deteriorated in our days.

"They shall eat every man the flesh of his own arm: Manasseh, Ephraim; and Ephraim, Manasseh: they together shall be against Judah" (Isaiah 9:20, 21).

Does not it make you wonder and shake to see how these powerful prophesies, made 2,700 years ago, show us precisely in detail situation of the World today?!

Our readers know that these three brothers (Manasseh and Ephraim are actually the nephews of the sons of Jacob), represent Israelite countries in Exile, identified by America, England and the modern Israelis, half of whom have ended their exile and become citizens of Israel while another half still lives in Diaspora.

God foretold this situation thousands of years before it happened in amazing detail,

"Then I cut asunder Mine other staff, even Bands, that I might break the brotherhood between Judah and Israel" (Zechariah 11:14).

Christian Zionism. Pastor John Hagee

The Western World, which is mainly Christian, estimated at more than one billion and a half in population, accepted the Jewish Bible as a Holy Book, the inerrant Word of God. Every Christian student of the Bible knows that there are plenty of passages in the Torah and Tanakh speaking on behalf of God, that Almighty has chosen the people of Israel as 'My people' and has given the Holy Land ('My Land') to Israel forever.

God said to Abram," And I will make of thee a great nation, and I will bless thee, and make thy name great, and thou shalt be a blessing: and I will bless them that bless thee, and curse him that curseth thee: and in thee shall all families of the earth be blessed"

(Genesis12:2, 3).

The best known 'Christian advocate' for the Jewish people is Pastor John Hagee. This is what he said:

"It is unscriptural to go against Israel, because by doing so, one, in effect, is poking God in the eye, which is not very wise to do (Zechariah

2:8)! I want to be blessed, not cursed, by God (Genesis 12:3). It is not possible to say, "I am a Christian" and not love the Jewish people."

Doctor Hagee is also one of the leaders of Christians United for Israel (CUFI). Here are some of his remarks made in August 2010 to the 5th annual CUFI Summit in Washington:

"Our world is divided into two groups: those who support Israel and those who not. There is no middle ground. No matter how much noise Israel's opponents make, America's Christians stand with Israel. I stand here as Israel is surrounded and hounded, boycotted and threatened. I stand here with a strong message of solidarity with you, my Jewish brethren, the apple of God's eye.

"At this difficult juncture in our history, permit me to say something to you straight from the heart. Please know that what I say is a sentiment shared by millions of Christians across America and around the world. When all the world is against Israel, we proudly proclaim: "Ani Yisraeli—I am an Israeli".

"Israel's enemies are our enemies. Israel's fight is our fight. If a line has to be drawn, then let it be drawn around both of us—Christians and Jews, Americans and Israelis. We are one. We are united. We will not be defeated. In the end, when the last battle has been fought, the flag of Israel will still be flying over the ancient walls of Jerusalem. Israel will prevail! Ani Yisraeli—I am Israeli."

God has blessed Pastor Hagee for his deep understanding of the Scriptures, his unprecedented bravery and unconditional love for God's chosen people.

The numbers of Christian 'Biblical advocates' for the Jewish people and the State of Israel are constantly growing. Among the most prominent Christian Zionist leaders are Billy Graham, Pat Robertson and Jerry Farwell.

There are many people who sincerely think that America's position towards the Israelis goes against the teachings of the Bible, because to go against Israel simply means going against God. Some religious leaders and theological authors directly connect natural turmoil and politico-economical disasters in the USA with the way they treat Israel. This is exactly what the Bible teaches!

Israel the Chosen

God has a Plan for ingathering, reuniting and redeeming all the families of Jacob in "latter years" on the Mountains of Israel with the advent of the Messiah son of David.

The establishment of the Jewish state in the Land of Israel in 1948 with its capital in Jerusalem is the first stage of God's Plan before the final stage of Redemption. In previous chapters we have shown to our readers proof of this in detail by quoting the Scriptures.

Why, then, do the majority of Christians disregard the Word of God and take the side of the Palestinians against the Jews? Pope Benedict XVI and his bishops have blamed the Israelis for using the Bible to justify their rights to the Holy Land. Is this not ridiculous? Due to their anti-Semitic sentiments they are ready to ignore the sacred Scripture for the sake of advancing their political agendas against the Jews. Instead of helping the Jewish people in fulfillment of the prophecies of the last days, as God has required, they have acted against God and His people. The answer is simple: They are guilty of anti-Semitism and jealousy of the fact that God chose Israel, instead of them.

Christians often explain their position by saying: "Look, what these evil Jews have done to the poor Palestinians. Is it justice? Is it what God wants?"

We can confidently and proudly answer to them: Yes, that is what God wants! This is His command and wish to give the Promise Land to His people Israel, whether you like it or not (Genesis 12:7; 13:15; 17:8; 26:3-5; 35:10-12)!!

Speaking of being chosen, it was not Israel's decision, but God's.

"And the Lord said unto Abram, for all the land which thou seest, to thee will I give it, and to thy seed for ever. And I will establish

My covenant between Me and thee and thy seed after thee in their generations for an everlasting covenant, to be a God unto thee, and to seed after thee" (Genesis 13:15).

To Abraham's son Isaac God said:

"I will make your descendants as numerous as the stars in the sky and I will give them all these lands. And through your offspring all the nations of the earth will be blessed" (Genesis 26:4).

To Isaac's son Jacob, whose name later was changed to Israel, God said:

"I am the Lord God of Abraham your father, and the God of Isaac: the land whereon you lying, to you will I give, and to your seed. And, behold, I am with you, and will keep you whithersoever thou go, and will bring you back into this land; for I will not leave you, until I have done that which I have spoken to you of" (Genesis 28:13, 15).

Israel being chosen is not a license for special privileges or racial superiority. On the contrary, it is a heavy burden and entails additional responsibilities towards God and fellow men. God has elevated Israel above the nations to be a holy people, a light to the world, and He has severely punished them for their transgressions throughout the ages.

"You only have I chosen of all the families of the earth: Therefore will I punish you for all your iniquities" (Amos 3:2).

Having being chosen by God has brought much grief and suffering upon the Jewish people. One survivor of the Holocaust expressed his feelings this way, "I wish God never had chosen the Jews. Could He not choose any other nation instead?"

"You have been set apart as holy to the Lord, and He has chosen you from all the nations of the earth to be his own special treasure. The Lord did not set His love upon you, nor choose you, because you were more in number than any people; for you were the fewest of all people: but because thou art a holy people unto the Lord thy God and the Lord loved you" (Deuteronomy 7:6-8; 14:2).

Talmudic tradition says that the Lord offered the Torah to all nations, but they all refused to accept it, except Israel. On an individual level, any Gentile who devotes his life to the study and observance of the Torah ranks as high as the High Priest. Our Sages have said that it was the intention of God that all humans be descended from the same progenitor, Adam (the fully developed image of the Creator) so that nobody could claim superior ancestral origin.

God has appointed all the House of Israel, including the Ten Tribes in exile, for a special mission:

"I have formed Israel for Myself that they will declare Me before the whole world. I will make you to be a covenant for the people and the light for Gentiles, that you will bring My salvation to the ends of the earth. And the Gentiles shall come to thy light, and the kings to the brightness of thy rising" (Isaiah 42:6; 43:21; 49:6).

The paradox is that among jealous Christian anti-Semites are a multitude of people of Israelite origin who have completely lost their national identity, and even in their wildest dreams could not imagine themselves being the chosen people of God in the same way as the Jewish people are. Is it not of them God speaks in Isaiah 45:20?

"Gather together and come, you fugitives from the nations. What fools they are who carry around their wooden idols and pray to gods that cannot save".

And, besides, who are you to judge the Almighty God?! You have chosen a dangerous path in going against the living God and His Wisdom. You know very well that God cannot stand two-faced Pharisees of the people, when they use the name of God for their dirty political goals, which have nothing in common with God and His prophetic Plan. The reason why you, being representatives of the Ten Tribes of Israel in exile, behave this way is:

"They will not frame their doings to turn unto their God: for the spirit of whoredom is in the midst of them, and they have not known the Lord" (Hosea 5:4).

"Your watchmen are blind: they are all ignorant, they are all dumb dogs, they cannot bark; sleeping, lying down, and loving to slumber. Yea, they are greedy dogs which can never have enough, and they are shepherds that cannot understand: they all look to their own way, every one for his gain, from his quarter"

(Isaiah 56:10-11).

"O My people! Those who lead you cause you to err, and destroy the way of your paths . . . Woe to those who call evil good, and good evil" (Isaiah 3:12; 5:20).

All your human imaginations of Global Peace, Universal Justice and Human Rights are nothing to compare with what God has in mind concerning His future Messianic Kingdom on Earth and His highly spiritual heavenly World-to-Come.

"For My thoughts are not your thoughts, neither are your ways My ways," said the Lord. "For as the heavens are higher than the earth, so are My ways higher than your ways, and My thoughts than your thoughts".

'Replacement Theology'

The same sick feelings of anti-Semitism and jealousy had motivated the early fathers of the Church to revise the Jewish Bible and come up with the "Replacement Theology". They said that God had rejected Israel for not accepting Jesus Christ (their Messiah), and had bestowed all the blessings of the Bible on Christians. Therefore, the Christians become 'Spiritual Israel', whereas the Jews ('Natural Israel') are convicted to damnation and to all curses of the Bible. Such an attitude has contributed to 2,000 years of hatred and bloody persecution of the Jewish people by the Christians. The 'New' Covenant has superseded the 'Old' Covenant. 'New Israel of the spirit' has superseded 'Old Israel of the flesh'. The Church replaced the Jews as God's chosen people and the Jews have no further role to play in God's designs.

The majority of Bible loving Christians and Churches who know that Scripture is full of God passages of blessings and prophetic future to His People Israel (the real Israel, not 'spiritual' or replaced one!), are keeping silenced and do not like speaking on this matter.

This incredibly arrogant claim of 'Replacement Theology', embraced by Christian Church, has been around for 1,700 years. The good news is that after creation of the State of Israel in 1948, its miraculous victories in the wars that followed, and the recapturing of the East Jerusalem in 1967, which again became the sacred undivided capital of the Jewish nation, many Christians have changed their mind about Israel. They have recognized the Biblical significance of reborn Israel. They have seen prophecies fulfilled; and they have rejected Replacement Theory as anti-Semitic, anti-Biblical, and as a great sin against God and His people Israel. The number of such Christians grows every day. There are more than 50 millions of them, mainly in the English speaking countries of Great Britain, America, Canada, Australia and others. They call themselves 'Christian Zionists' and unconditionally support Israel any which way they can.

The third international Christian Zionist Congress, held in Jerusalem in February 1996, proclaimed:

"God the Father, Almighty, chose the ancient nation and people of Israel, the descendants of Abraham, Isaac and Jacob, to reveal His Plan of redemption for the world. They remain the elect of God, and without the Jewish nation (we shall correct: and without the 'Israel nation') His redemptive purposes for the world will not be completed".

To end this subject, we say, that any person, knowledgeable in the Bible's verses, may just laugh at the absurdity of 'Replacement Theology'.

Beside, the adherents of the 'Replacement Theology' seem not to understand, or ignore the fact, that at the time of Christ (30-33a.c.) there was no Israel in Palestine to reject Jesus, but only the Jews. As a matter of fact, Israel, the Ten Tribes in exile, accepted the Christ before anybody else! Our readers have learned already that the terms "Israel" and "Jews" are not synonymous. They are absolutely different nations at this point of time (since circa 930 b.c. until the End Times).

The Lost Ten Tribes of Israel are still in Exile, waiting to wake up to their Israelite roots, to reunite with Judah in the Holy Land and be redeemed by the Almighty. Ironically, they are the ones who have worshipped Christianity. They are destined to reject it in the near future, when they will learn of their Israelite identity with the help of the Jewish people and the soon coming Prophet Eliyahu. The light of God's Torah will open their eyes, as Prophecy has predicted (Ezekiel 37:22; Malachi 4:5).

We sincerely believe that the time has arrived for mainstream Christians, descendants of Joseph and other tribes of Israel in exile today, wherever they are, to awake to their Israelite identity, repent and acknowledge the God of Israel; and start helping Judah in his lonely fight against an unjust and corrupt World, to bring God's Plan to a glorious conclusion.

The Peace Process in Relation to the Sickness of Ephraim and the Wound of Judah

Now let us return to the Peace Process. Why do we think that peace negotiations will collapse and there will be no peace in the Middle East? Because the Bible prophesied so! Representatives of Israel, the Palestinians, the USA, the EU and anybody else involved may sit at the bargaining tables, talking peace and security, but there will be no peace, no security. On the contrary, wars and destructions will come instead.

"When Ephraim saw his sickness, and Judah saw his wound, then went Ephraim to the Assyrian, and sent to king Jareb: yet could he not heal you, nor cure you from your wound" (Hosea 5:13).

What is the sickness of Ephraim? Ephraim is the son of Joseph who originally settled in the British Islands together with his brother Manasseh, who later separated and immigrated to America. The sickness of Ephraim is that of Joseph. Joseph represents the Ten Tribes of Israel in exile, mainly Great Britain and the USA. So, what is their sickness? First and foremost, Joseph has forgotten the God of Israel, become unfaithful to His Laws which He had given to Moses on Mount Sinai for all Israelites, and started to serve Baal, the false god of the Canaanites, whose name simply means 'lord' or 'master'. Later in the next Chapter we will explain how and why the apostasy of Israel began (in relation to the Holy Land and Peace Process).

After Israel's exile by the Assyrians and their subsequent migration to West and Northern Europe, the Israelites accepted and started worshipping another religion—Christianity. Their God had strongly warned them no to do so: "Thou shalt have none other gods before Me". Not in the heaven above, nor in the earth beneath.

"Hear, O Israel: The Lord our God is one Lord. Thou shalt not bow down thyself unto them, nor serve them: for I the Lord thy God am a jealous God" (Deuteronomy 5:7, 9; 6:4).

They have not listened. Idolatry is the main reason for Israel's sickness. Another important part of it is the loss of the indentifying sign of Israelite identity, which is the Sabbath:

"Also I gave them My Sabbaths, to be a sign between Me and them that they might know that I am the Lord that sanctified them. But the house of Israel rebelled against Me: they walked not in My statues, and they despise My Judgments" (Ezekiel 20:12, 13).

"Surely My Sabbaths you shall keep, for it is a Sign between Me and you throughout your generations that you may know that I am the Lord who sanctifies you" (Exodus 31:13).

The emperor Constantine in 321a.c. issued an edict where he abolished the fourth Commandment of God and changed the day of worship to Sunday instead of Saturday. It was accepted by the Christians as a norm of the day, and, indeed, they have honored Sunday as if it is "the seventh day God blessed and sanctified" (Genesis 2:3). God's holy Sabbath was replaced with the pagan day of the Sun-Sunday. This is one of the reasons, why the Israelites, the Ten Tribes in exile, lost their identity: It was because the Sabbath, the very day of the Sign that identifies the Creator, God of Israel and those who worship Him, was purposely taken away and substituted by a meaningless Sunday.

All these belies the famous sayings that "All Scripture is given by inspiration of God", "Scripture cannot be broken". It would seem that, "They love the praise of men more than the praise of God."

God Almighty says: "Blessed is the man who obeys My Commandments and keeps from defiling the Sabbath" (Isaiah56:2).

Christianity has disregarded these sacred words of the Almighty and proclaimed a doctrine of 'no works', meaning that salvation will come not by obedience to God's Laws and good deeds, but by faith alone. Even the Patriarch Abraham, who Scripture calls God's friend, was tested by his willingness to sacrifice his only son Isaac and prove his obedience to God 'by works' (Genesis 22:15-18).

By rejecting God's Laws, Christianity has committed a great sin and become a dead, apostate religion. The definition of sin is transgression of the Law. Therefore, the Almighty will judge them accordingly for the false teachings of a 'counterfeit Christianity', spiritual abominations, and unwillingness to repent.

"There is a way that seems right to a man, but its end thereof are the ways of death" (Proverbs 16:25).

All the sins committed by inhabitants of the ancient cities of Gomorrah and Sodom, as described in the Bible, have been inherited by the nations of Israel today. Primary, it is impiety, paganism, atheism, blasphemy, adultery, sodomy, homosexuality, bloodshed, lack of compassion, cruelty, violated marriages, arrogance of wealth, and disrespect for the laws of Nature, lust for every possible pleasure,—name it. That is what God calls Ephraim's sickness.

"Thy princes are rebellious, and companions of thieves; everyone loveth gifts (bribes), and followeth after rewards; they judge not the fatherless, neither doth the cause of the widow come under them" (Isaiah 1:23).

That Ephraim is Israel can be seen from many Biblical passages:

"I know Ephraim, and Israel is not hid from Me: for now, O Ephraim, thou committest whoredome, and Israel is defiled"

(Hosea 5:3).

And what is the cure for Judah's wound? It is translated as an abrasion needing a bandage, a remedy, a pressing together and binding up of a wound. It is figurative expression, an epithet for the real problem of Judah, which is the ongoing Peace Process. It has weakened the Israelis politically, morally and even militarily. This wound is incurable. The real disease of Judah is spiritual, an apostasy from God. They do not look for a balm nor seek the right remedy. To fix their problems, they look to men, even to their enemies, as Assyria in the past, which is now modern Germany. It would seem that Judah and Ephraim have forgotten their history. Assyria destroyed Israel and sent Ten Tribes into exile. Judah 'played the harlot' with her 'lovers' i.e. Assyrians, who 'discovered her nakedness, and poured their whoredome upon her' (Ezekiel 23:5, 8, 9).

The historical trend has continued. Judah still follows her 'lover', even after 6 million Jews have been killed in the Holocaust. Germany has become one of the most anti-Semitic countries in Europe. Israel increasingly seeks for Germany to be her ally and protector in the Middle East Peace Process, in spite of the 'special' relationship of Assur-Germany with Israel.

Germany as a Peace-maker will take over leadership of the Peace Process, which is going to be disastrous due to the 'Counterfeit Peacemaker'.

America is also getting weaker due to idolatry, moral decay, and lack of will power to act decisively on international arena; and absence of great and faithful leaders. As descendants of Israel, mainly represented by the Tribe of Manasseh, they broke the direct command of God not to chose their King (or President) from the strangers, but only from the 'brethren' (Deuteronomy 17:15). For their unfaithful behavior God subjected them to many curses outlined in Leviticus 26 and Deuteronomy 28. God is going to punish America for her sins:

"Behold, I, even I, am against thee, and will execute judgments in the midst of thee in the sight of the nations" (Ezekiel 5:8)

Soon the USA will be forced out of the peace negotiations as the most influential leader and broker. This role will be taken by the European Union, which is mainly represented by Germany. It sounds paradoxical, but the fact is that the Israelis and Palestinians both want the EU (Germany) to be a new mediator in the ongoing peace negotiations.

As pointed out in Hosea 5:13, Judah and Ephraim will go for help to Assyria, which is Germany today, but it will not 'heal you, nor cure you of your wound'. No matter how many bandages may be applied to heal Judah's wound, be it the 'help' of America or their old 'lover' Assur-Germany; be it the Peace Process or Land for Peace, nothing will help, just as it did not help in ancient times:

"At that time did king Ahaz (of Judea) send unto the kings of Assyria to help him and Tilgath-pilneser king of Assyria came unto him and distressed him, but strengthened him not" (2 Chron.28:19, 20).

King Ahaz gave to the Assyrians a lot of gold and silver from the House of the Lord, but the Assyrian king did 'help him not'.

'Whitewashers'

There are many prophesies in the Bible on the subject of Peace, that are very much applicable to the Peace Process of today between the Palestinians and the Jewish people. This prophesies will answer with clarity why we do not believe in Peace Process.

"They offer superficial treatments for My people's mortal wound. They give assurances of peace when there is no peace."

Or another interpretation of the same verse:

"They treat My people's wound as though it was not serious, saying, "Everything is alright! Everything is alright!" But it is not alright" (Jeremiah 6:14).

There are many leaders heavily involved in the Peace Process. This includes the Israeli Government, which has acted like the false and lying prophets of old, prophesying things God never told them. They are trying to fix that which is unfixable, and say what people like to hear. They have pretended to be physicians, and they slightly have cured the wound superficially, but not thoroughly. They have not sufficient qualification to fundamentally examine the wound, to find a proper remedy needed for complete and healthy recovery from the disease.

"For they have healed the wound of My people lightly, saying, "Peace, peace", when there is no peace" (Jeremiah 8:11).

"The way of peace they know not; and there is no judgment in their doings: they have made them crooked paths; whosoever goes therein shall not know peace" (Isaiah 59:8).

The leaders of Israel continually have told the Israelis soothing words of peace and security, but they really do not know what the root of their problems is:

"They keep saying to those who despise Me, 'The Lord says: "You will have peace". And to all who follow stubbornness of their hearts they say, "No harm will come to you".

God is angry with these leaders, for they are telling lies, things He never told them:

"For who has stood in the counsel of the Lord, and heard His word? Behold, a whirlwind of the Lord is gone forth in fury. The anger of the Lord shall not return, until He has executed, and till He has performed the thoughts of His heart: in the latter days you shall consider it perfectly" (Jeremiah 23:17-20).

The fact is that God reminds us that these prophesies will be perfectly understood in the latter days. An examination of our time shows that they appropriately apply to the present-day situation in the world, and particularly the Peace Process. They also indicate that we are now living in the End Times.

The Prophet Ezekiel compared the Peace Process with the wall, which builders reinforced by covering it with whitewash.

No matter how much land Israel would give to the Palestinians, no matter how many settlements would be dismantled, no matter how many refugees would be allowed to return,—any peace agreement they might achieve, would not stand the trials of daily politico-religious turbulence in the region, and would collapse the same way as the wall covered by whitewash.

"Precisely because they have misled My people, saying, 'Peace', when there is no peace, and because, when the people build a wall, these prophets daubed it with whitewash. Tell these whitewashers that their wall soon falls down. A heavy rainstorm will undermine it; great hailstones and mighty winds will knock it down" (Ezekiel 13:10, 11).

God Himself will deal with these leaders-whitewashers of the Peace Process, especially those International Brokers of the Quartet, the architects and the builders of artificial 'wall-peace'.

"So will I break down the wall . . . Thus will I accomplish

My wrath upon the wall, and upon them that have daubed it with whitewash, and will say unto you, 'The wall is no more, neither they that daubed it" (Ezekiel 13:14, 15).

The Peace Process in the Middle East is not God's Plan for the Future World. Otherwise, why would Bible tell us that soon all the nations of the world will go to war against the modern State of Israel and Jerusalem (Zechariah 12:2, 3; 14:2)?

How can we speak of Peace in the Middle East, if God predicted WWIII when the hordes of Gog and Magog will attack Israel (Judah and the Ten Tribes) and find their tragic end in the "latter years" (Ezekiel 38 and 39)?

Is the situation really so bad, and the wound of Judah incurable? Not so! Judah will turn to the God of Israel, and his 'spiritual wound' will be healed. Judah will finally realize that only God can heal his wound, only in God can he find real Peace and Security. This is how the prophets described it:

"Lord binds up the breach of His people, and heals the stroke of their wound" (Isaiah 30:26).

All the problems of Ephraim and Judah are due to apostasy, to falling away from God, and He will punish them with the Peace Process for their sins. Here is what God says of it:

"Why do you cry out over your wound, your pain that has no cure? Because of your great guilt and many sins I have done these things to you" (Jeremiah 30:15).

God calls the Ten Tribes of Israel to repent and return to Him, "I have no pleasure in the death of the wicked; but that the wicked turn from his way and live: turn you, turn you from your wicked ways; for why will you die, O house of Israel" (Ezekiel 33:11)?

Here comes the good news:

"But I will restore you to health and heal your wounds"

(Jeremiah 30:17).

"Israel shall be saved in the Lord with an everlasting salvation; you shall not be ashamed nor disgraced ever again" (Isaiah 45:17).

What about the enemies who wanted to destroy Judah and Israel? The God of Israel Himself will take proper care of them! The fate of these nations is very clearly outlined in Zechariah 12 and 14 and in Ezekiel 38 and 39. What is said, basically, is that Almighty God will fight the war on the side of Israel, and will be their Protector and Savior.

"But the Lord will be a refuge for His people, a strong fortress for the people of Israel" (Joel 3:16).

Nobody can withstand the wrath of God! The nations will be taught a powerful lesson. The Prophet Jeremiah described this punishment particularly well:

"All they that devour thee shall be devoured; and all thine adversaries, every one of them, shall go into captivity; and they that spoil thee shall be a spoil, and all that prey upon thee will I give for a pray" (Jeremiah 30:16).

The History of Israel clearly indicate, that when the Israelites listened to God, obeyed His Commandments and Statues, then God blessed them, lead and protected them in all their ways. But when they went astray from God and His Laws, worshiped idols and did detestable abominations, and became wicked as the heathen nations around, God turned His face from them and severely punished them for their sins.

Judah's solution to the Peace Process is to stop trust in men, be it America, Germany, Russia, United Nations, or the Palestinians (especially!). The Jewish people have to repent, turn to God, and reunite with the Ten Tribes of Joseph and then, with the help of the Almighty God of Israel, everything will be all right!

"In God I trust; I will not be afraid. What can man do to me" (Psalms 56:11).

CHAPTER X:
DRIVE THEM OUT!

Canaanites and Israelites

When, where and why did Israel's problems of idolatry, breaking of the Covenant and betrayal of God's trust originate? It started right after Moses' death at the age of 120, when the Israelite's tribes under leadership of Moses' successor Joshua (1450-1370) begun the conquest of Canaan, the Promised Land. God said to Israel:

"I brought you up out of Egypt into this land that I swore to give to your forefathers. I will never break My covenant with you, and you shall not make any covenant with the inhabitants of this land; you shall throw down their altars: but you have not obeyed My voice: why have you done this?" (Judges 2:1-2).

It is a very interesting passage. Why would God prohibit Israel from being friendly with the people of Canaan? Why were the Israelites obligated by God to drive them away from the Promised Land and break down their altars, smash the sacred stones and cut out the images of their goddess Asherah? Because those people were God-haters, idol-worshippers and evil-doers! They were opposite to everything God loves.

"You must destroy all the people the Lord your God hands over to you. Show them no mercy, and do not worship their gods or they will trap you. On account of the wickedness of these nations the Lord your God will drive them out before you, as He swore to your fathers, to Abraham, Isaac and Jacob" (Deuteronomy 7:16; 9:5).

It is for the love of Israel's forefathers and for the wickedness of those nations God was doing this. And, indeed, God had given into Israel's hands many nations: the Girgashites, the Hittites, the Amorites, the Canaanites, the Perizzites, the Hivites and the Jebusites. God hated them for their idol-worshipping, and didn't want Israel to be defiled with their pagan gods.

The Israelites had failed to observe God's Commandments. They conquered the Promised Land, but they did not drive the inhabitants of this land out. Instead, they made the Canaanites and other people pay tribute to them. After Joshua at the age of 110 and all his generation had died out, a new generation grew up, who did not know the Lord or what He had done for Israel. And they began to do the things that God had prohibited them to do. They abandoned the Lord, and started worshipping the Baals and Ashtaroth. They took daughters of the peoples they had left around to be their wives, and gave their daughters to their sons. And the Israelites were 'trapped'.

"So the Lord burned with anger against Israel and said: "Because this nation has violated My covenant and has not listened to Me, I will no longer drive out the nations that Joshua left when he died. I will use them to test Israel by them, whether they will keep the way of the Lord to walk in it as their fathers did, or not"

(Judges 2:20-22).

Centuries after the time of Judges, at the request of the Israelites, God granted them a King:

"The Lord said to Samuel, listen to the voice of the people, for they have not rejected you, but they have rejected Me from being King over them" (1 Samuel 8:7).

God Commanded to Drive Them Out!

Israel still had not changed its attitude towards God and His Commandments. God's warnings had been transgressed in every detail. The children of Israel had defiled themselves with the surrounding nations and their pagan gods. Even King Solomon, wisest amongst men, in order to please his foreign wives, had begun worshipping Ashtoreth the goddess of the Sidonians, and Molech the detestable god of the Ammonites. The people of Canaan were constantly causing the Israelites many problems: wars and oppression, the sin of idolatry, assimilation, apostasy from God and Torah and, this resulted finally in exile from the Holy Land.

"If you do not drive out inhabitants of the land, those you allow to remain will be like splinters in your eyes and thorns in your sides. They will constantly fight with you over land in which you live. And as I plan to do to them, so I will do to you"

(Numbers 33:55-56).

Wow! That is exactly what happened to the Israelites. Because they disobeyed God's command and did not drive out the inhabitants of the land, all the House of Israel were forcefully expelled from the Land, precisely as the Lord foretold. Obviously, God has promised to bring them back again, provided that they will have learnt their lesson and will correct their behavior in the future.

Our reader might ask what connection this story has to do with the modern State of Israel and the ongoing Peace Process between Jews and Palestinians? Surprisingly, the answer is: There is a direct connection! We are now living in the time when the Bible's Prophecies slowly but surely, here and there, are becoming a reality.

The creation of the State of Israel in 1948 is one of the most important prophesies ever fulfilled in our time. The real question now is: Should the Israelis follow the ancient command of God to "throw all inhabitants of the land of Israel out without mercy and destroy all their sacred altars, stones and images of pagan gods which cannot save," or not? First of all, there is no such thing as 'ancient commandments' of God as we may see from these Scriptural verses:

"My covenant will I not brake nor alter the thing that is gone out of My lips. All He does is just and good, and all His commandments are trustworthy. They are established forever and ever, to obey with faithfulness and uprightness. I have known from my earliest days that your Laws will last forever. All Thy commandments are Righteousness" (Psalms 89:34; 111:7, 8; 119:152, 172).

When Balak asked Balaam to change God's blessings towards Israel and, instead to curse them, Balaam answered:

"God is not a man, that he should lie, nor a son of man, that he should change his mind. Does he speak and then not act? Does he promise and not fulfill" (Numbers 23:19)?

The prophet Malachi confidently said that God has not changed. He is the same yesterday, today, tomorrow and forever. "For I am the Lord, I change not" (Malachi 3:6).

Are the Palestinians Really Canaanite Philistines?

Secondly, are we dealing with the same people in Palestine today who lived in the Canaan for more than 3,000 years ago, mainly the Philistines? Well, the Palestinian Arabs claim that they are direct descendants of the ancient Philistines who lived in Canaan before the Israelites moved in. Their motives are well understood in the light of the political battle for the Land's more rightful ownership in the Peace Process negotiations.

Most scholars believe that the Canaanites, who are also called Phoenicians and Philistines, are not Arabs, and have nothing in common with them. The Philistines are not even a Semitic people. They are the descendants of Ham through his son Mizraim.

"Mizraim was the father of the Ludites, Anamites, Lehabites, Naphtuhites, Pathrusites, Casluhites **(from whom the Philistines came)** and Caphtorites" (Genesis 10:13-14).

They were invaders from the Aegean Sea, the Island of Crete and Anatolian areas in the 12 Century b.c. The Canaanites and Israelites were the people who had dwelled in this land long before the Exodus from Egypt. If the Palestinians were these 'Sea People' as they pretend to be, they might have some justifications to claim the Island Crete from the Greek authorities as the homeland of their origin.

"Did I not bring Israel up from Egypt, **the Philistines from Caphtor**" (Amos 9:7)?

'Caphtor' denotes the ancient name of the Island Crete where the descendants of Caphtor, the son of Mizraim, were settled shortly after the Flood. They invaded Canaan, destroyed the people who lived there, the Avvites, and settled in their territory.

"The Caphtorites coming out from Caphtor destroyed the Avvites and settled in their place" (Deuteronomy 2:23).

The Philistines, the Sea People, are extinct. They have vanished from history. Any Palestinian Arab (Shem) link and identification with the Philistines (Ham) is false. Their origin, culture and language are completely different. The Philistines were invaders from the Sea in ancient times (circa 12 Century b.c.). Meanwhile, the Arabs invaded Palestine from the wilderness during the Arab's conquest under Mohammed in the seven Century a.c. That wilderness is the Arabian Peninsula, the Arabs homeland.

Prophesy said that Ishmael will live to the East in the presence of all his brother Israelites (Genesis 16:12; 25:18). Not all the land of Arabia is their homeland. In Southern Arabia there are no people of Ishmael descent at all. In Northern Arabia the Ishmaelite mixed with and assimilated with the Kushite and Semite peoples, who lived in Arabia before Ishmael (Genesis 10:7); with the Midyanites (who were their brothers through Qeturah, the wife of Abraham after the death of Sarah) and with other tribes living in that area. They intermarried and mixed with the Midyanites so massively that even the Biblical verses do not distinguish between them: The Ishmaelites called Midyanites, and the Midyanites called Ishmaelites.

"And the Midianites sold Joseph into Egypt unto Potiphar"
(Genesis 37:36).

"And Potiphar, an officer of Pharaoh, captain of the guards, bought him of the hands of the Ishmaelites, who brought him in Egypt" (Genesis 39:1).

That this identification is not a mistake, one can see from Judges 8:22, 24. Therefore, to say that all the Arab people are descendants of Ishmael is wrong because Arabs had existed long before Ishmael was born.

King Shalmanezer of Assyria called them Misuri, which means Egyptians. Well, Hagar, the mother of Ishmael, was an Egyptian, and she found him a wife who was also from the land of Egypt (Genesis 21:21). Ishmael's daughter by the name of Bashemath or Mahalath married the oldest son of Isaac-Esau (Genesis 28:9; 36:3). Before his death at the age of 137, Ishmael and his youngest brother Isaac buried in the cave of Machpelah which is near Mamre (Genesis 25:9) their father Abraham who died at the age of one hundred and seventy five.

The Israelites and the Philistines had been living in the Land of Canaan, the Promised Land, since the time of Abraham the Patriarch of the Hebrews and Abimelech the king of the Philistines. There had been a Peace Treaty between them (Genesis 21:32). Later on, after the Exodus from Egypt, God had used the Philistines as an instrument to punish and test His People Israel. The Philistines became brutal oppressors, mortal enemies and a constant plague to the Israelites.

In the time of King David, the Israelites defeated the Philistines and subdued them (2nd Samuel 8:1). The Kerethites and Pelethites were also Philistines who came from the ancient homeland of Crete. They were loyal to David and even served as his bodyguards. As far as the Bible is concerned, the Philistines were later destroyed and vanished from the face of the earth, as the prophets of God had prophesied.

"I will turn my hand against Ekron, till the last of the Philistines is dead" (Amos 1:8).

"Gaza will be abandoned and Ashkelon left in ruins" (Zephaniah 2:4).

"The word of the LORD that came to Jeremiah the prophet against the Philistines, before Pharaoh smote Gaza. For the day has come to destroy all the Philistines and to cut off all survivors who could help Tyre and Sidon. The LORD is about to destroy the Philistines, the remnant from the coasts of Caphtor" (Jeremiah 47:1, 4).

Many Bible scholars are of the opinion that the prophet speaks here of Pharaoh Necho who was defeated by the Chaldeans in the battle of Carchemish in 605 b.c. On the way back to Egypt, Necho attacked and destroyed the Philistines of Gaza. This was in the time of Josiah, the King of Judaea.

The last time the Philistines are mentioned in the Scripture is Zechariah 9:6, "Foreigners (a mixed race, Hebrew word 'mamzer' possibly connoting a bastard people) will occupy the city of Ashdod. I will destroy the pride of the Philistines".

Could it be that these 'foreigners, mixed race, bastard people' represent the modern day Palestinians who have falsified a claim to inheritance as if they were the rightful heirs of the ancient Philistines?

Palestine and the 'Palestinian People'

There was no name 'Palestine' until the time of the Romans when Emperor Hadrian renamed the Roman province of Judea, 'Palestine'. Never before in the History had the Land of Canaan or the Land of Israel been called Palestine. The change of name was intended to take revenge from the Jewish People for their stubbornness and for the Bar Kokhba rebellion against Rome (132-135 a.c.).

The same goes for the 'Palestinian People': Not one Empire who ruled Judaea at one time or other (Assyrians, Persians, Greeks, Romans, Arabs, and Ottomans) ever mentioned in their historical records the existence of a 'Palestinian People'. This nation was invented after the 1967 'Six Days War' by the political leaders in the Arab world, the UN and others Anti-Semites and Jew-haters as a tool in their fight against Israel. In fact, the Palestinians are mainly 'fresh' immigrants (from the last 100 years or so) who came from all the surrounding Arab countries. Historically they had called themselves Jordanians, Lebanese or Syrians. They thought of the Land as being an integral part of Syria. There are many known documents confirming this.

Of course, there are some diverse versions concerning the origin of the Palestinians. A few scholars think that the beginning of the Palestinians may be traced to the King of the Assyria Sennacherib (705-681 b.c.). This monarch removed the defeated people of Israel (the Ten Tribes) from the Northern Kingdom and resettled its territory with settlers, "from Babylon, and from Cuthah, and from Ava, and from Hamath, and from Sepharvaim, and placed them in the cities of Samaria instead of the children of Israel; and they possessed Samaria, and dwelt in the cities thereof" (2 Kings 17: 23-24).

Others say that the so called Palestinians are nothing other than 'fresh' immigrants of Arab descent from the surrounding countries of Egypt, Syria, Jordan, South Arabia, and Lebanon. This immigration originated not so long ago, in the first decades of the Twentieth Century. Prior to this Palestine was sparsely populated with nomadic groups such as the Bedouins and had lain waste for centuries.

"The area was under populated and remained economically stagnant until the arrival of the first Zionist pioneers in the 1880's, who came to rebuild the Jewish land. The country had remained "The Holy Land" in the religious and historic consciousness of mankind, which associated it with the Bible and the history of the Jewish people. Jewish development of the country also attracted large numbers of other immigrants—both Jewish and Arab. The road leading from Gaza to the north was only a summer track suitable for transport by camels and carts . . . Houses were all of mud. No windows were anywhere to be seen . . . The plows used were of wood . . . The yields were very poor . . . The sanitary conditions in the village [Yabna] were horrible . . . Schools did not exist . . . The rate of infant mortality was very high . . . The western part, toward the sea, was almost a desert . . . The villages in this area were few and thinly populated. Many ruins of villages were scattered over the area, as owing to the prevalence of malaria, many villages were deserted by their inhabitants".

—The report of the British Royal Commission, 1913—

Never in history had there ever been a Palestinian State in the Land of Israel. No one ruling Empire that conquered the Land of Canaan, throughout two millennia had acknowledged the existence either of such a State or of a distinct Palestinian nation with its own culture, language, or religion. The Palestinians later invented this myth to justify the Arab occupation of Gaza, the West Bank, and a future wishful ownership of Jerusalem. Their fairy-tales of Jerusalem as the third most sacred place, the third holiest city after Mecca and Medina for Islam because the Prophet Mohammed (in his dream) had flown to heaven from the Mosque on Temple Mount, are a continuation of the same myth. Needless to say, the El Aksa Mosque on the Temple Mount had not existed while the Prophet of Allah was alive. It was only built after his death in (632 a.c.) by Khaliph Abd El Malik approximately sixty years later. And, besides, the presence of an Islamic Mosque in Jerusalem, when the City was under the rule of the Byzantine Christians (Crusaders), would have been impossible.

There are some other opinions that the Palestinians are the modern day descendants of the Edomites, the Canaanites and the Philistines. The vast majority of the house of Esau migrated to the north and west to various countries of Europe (Italy, Germany, and Spain). Another more prominent branch, the tribe of Teman settled in Turkey and gave rise to the 'Ottoman Empire'. There is evidence that some of the remaining descendants of Esau (the Idumaeans) intermarried with the Canaanites, Philistines, Ishmaelites, Moabites, and Ammonites and have remained living in the territory of Gaza and West Bank. The Bible says that Esau, their forefather, married two Canaanite women and another one from Ishmael (Genesis 26:34; 28:9). In the time of the Babylonian King Nebuchadnezzar, when his army besieged Jerusalem, the Edomites joined the enemy against their brothers, the Jews, and committed deeds of merciless inhuman cruelty.

"Remember, O Lord, what the Edomites did on the day Jerusalem fell. "Tear it down," they cried, "tear it down to its foundations!" (Psalm 137:7).

"For your violence against your brother Jacob shame shall cover you, and you shall be cut off forever" (Obadiah 1:10).

This kind of brutal behavior and atavistic animalistic hatred towards the children of Jacob has been peculiarly characteristic of the descendants of Esau today. All successful terrorist attack against Israelis, in which many civilians and especially children or students have been killed, has led the Palestinians to celebrate in the streets with joy and happiness. They also were celebrating and dancing after the catastrophe of 9/11when 3,000 innocent civilians in the USA had been killed by the fanatics of Al-Qaeda.

There is evidence in Scripture that these people of Edomites descent (the Palestinians) together with other elements from the surrounding nations violently seized and apportioned between them the Land of Israel at one time or other time on a few occasions. As soon as the Israelite Tribes were defeated and forcefully taken to Exile, the surrounding nations had begun to annex their land and settle on it.

"Concerning the Ammonites, thus said the LORD; Has Israel no sons? Has he no heir? Why then does their king inherit Gad, and his people dwell in his cities"? (Jer.49:1).

The Edomites have performed these actions of occupying the Land of Israel whenever they possibly could. This Land has never belonged to the children of Edom. They are foreigners and illegal occupiers of the Land of Israel. God is going to punish Edom (the modern day Palestinians of Gaza and the West Bank) and his 'friends' the Ammonites and the Moabites.

"Surely in the fire of my jealousy have I spoken against the rest of the nations, and against all Edom, which have given my land into their possession with the joy of all their heart, with spiteful minds, to cast it out to plunder. Therefore thus says the Lord GOD; I have lifted up my hand, surely the nations that are about you, they shall bear their shame" (Ezekiel 36:5, 7).

This 'trio' of malicious nations will regret very much what they have done to the People of Israel in the time to come and they 'shall bear their shame'.

In the time of the Messiah son of Joseph, at the dawn of the Messianic Age, the Tribes of Israel will have applied 'the fist' of God's Judgments against the aggressive surrounding nations. They will have defeated and expelled them out of the Promised Land.

This will be done in accordance with the wish of God:

"No longer will the people of Israel have malicious neighbors who are painful briers and sharp thorns. Then they shall know that I am the Lord God" (Ezekiel 28:24).

Halleluiah! Finally the People of Israel will be able to live in the peace and security they have dreamed of for a long, long time.

Actually, for God it does not matter what names these tribes, people and nations previously or currently bear. God judges people not for their names but for their moral and spiritual values, for their faithfulness and deeds. Scriptures clearly tells us why God ordered the Israelites to rid the Promised Land of these people: It was hatred of the God of Israel, worship of gods which cannot save, and wickedness. All these things are an abomination in God's eyes. He does not want His Holy Land to be polluted with idolaters, who definitely will become a 'trap' for His people Israel and constantly will fight for the land, as happened in the past. God loves Israel. He does not want to see them as sinful and fallen away nation.

"Since you are precious and honored in My sight, and because I love you, I will give men in exchange for you, and people in exchange for your life" (Isaiah 43:4).

The Land of Israel-Palestine now, basically, is occupied by the two peoples, the Palestinians and the Jews. Should the Israelites drive out the Palestinians from the Promised Land, as God commanded?

The answer is dependent upon whether this nation is idolatrous and wick or not; whether they worship the God of Israel as the only Almighty God of the Universe, or they worship other pagan gods, "which cannot save." The God of Israel is very jealous God. He cannot stand idolaters; neither among His people Israel, nor among those who pollute His Holy Land.

The Religion of the Palestinian Arabs

The religion of the Palestinian Arabs is Islam. They have often maintained that Islam worships the same God as the Jews and Christians. The only difference is in the name. Allah is the same God as the Almighty God of the Bible. Our Gods and religions are almost the same, they say.

Is it so? Of course, not! They are as different as heaven and earth. Allah is not the same as the God of the Bible and never has been. Allah is the demon god of the Moon who was worshipped by Akkadians, Sumerians, Egyptians, Assyrians, Babylonians, Chaldeans and all the Arabia Peninsula as a supreme deity under various names many hundreds of years before Muhammad. The Moon in Islam is considered the holiest object in the sky among astronomical planets and stars. It is the guiding light of all Islamic traditional ceremonies, rituals and festivals.

Archeologists have found temples of the Moon-god all over the Middle East from the mountains of Turkey to the banks of the river Nile in Egypt. They have also discovered plenty of artifacts from pre-Islamic times, with the symbols of a crescent moon and stars such as nowadays sit on top of minarets and mosques, and decorate Islamic flags, graveyards and monuments. Their holiest temple, the Kabbah, in Mecca is the ancient place where pre-Islamic Arabian tribes worshipped Allah, the male lunar god, who was the husband of the female solar god, and the stars were considered to be their children (daughters). It was also the house of 360 idols, demons, jinni and other pagan gods and spirits, whom the merchants of Mecca worshipped. Jews and Christians have rejected Allah as a false god. The Hebrew Bible strongly warned the Israelites not to worship other gods, especially the powers of heaven, and not to serve them. (Deuteronomy 17:4; 2 Kings 21:3) "I will consume those who go up to the roofs and bow to the sun, moon, and stars" (Zephaniah 1:5).

Isaac versus Ishmael

Here we have in Islam another version of 'Replacement Theology'. This time it is produced not by Christians, but by Muslims. They have the same motives to rob the Israelites of their God, of being chosen and of the blessings of the Bible. They wish to bestow all of it on the Muslims. They have the same arrogance, intolerance, anti-Semitism and jealousy. The consequences include fanatical hatred, Jihad and bloody terrorism.

How could the Muslims have worshipped the same God as the Jews, if the Bible explicitly said that the Almighty chose Isaac instead of Ishmael, and Abraham blessed Isaac with the firstborn blessings, and sent Ishmael with his mother away to Arabia?

"He that shall come forth out of thine own bowels shall be thine heir" (Genesis 15:4). In this verse God confirms that the heir of Abraham will be his own son, not Eliezer of Damascus, the steward of the house.

"And God said, Sarah your wife shall bear you a son indeed; and you shall call his name Isaac: and I will establish My covenant with him for an everlasting covenant and with his descendants after him" (Genesis 17:19).

"Your son Isaac is the one through whom your descendants will be named" (Genesis 21:12).

God has established the Covenant for ever with the descendants of Abraham, Isaac and Jacob, not with the Ishmaelites.

Muhammad and his followers decided to revise the Hebrew Bible by stating that Allah had chosen and blessed Ishmael as heir of Abraham. Also they created a new story that it was Ishmael who God ordered Abraham to sacrifice, not Isaac. They have accused the Jews of misrepresenting history, corrupting the Bible, and taking the religious prerogative of God for themselves as the 'Chosen People'. Somehow they have forgotten the simple fact: Fifteen centuries before the Koran was written, the Hebrew Bible had already been in existence and God was worshipped by the Israelites.

Meanwhile, it is the Koran that lacks the truth of divine revelation; it is full of historical inaccuracies and anachronisms; it misplaces historical personalities and the chronological order of events (cf. Sura 25:57-61); it promotes the treatment of women and unbelievers as sub-humans; it commands conversion by force and the propagation of bloody Jihad-'holy war': All of it shows 'the gross ignorance of the self-styled Arabian prophet'.

The Holy Bible, the most precious Book in the World, the brilliant work of God Almighty, has perfectly accomplished its purpose of life and salvation from the first verse of Creation in the book of Genesis to the last words of the prophet Malachi. This immortal Book is perfect, full of Divine Wisdom, morality and God's inspiration. It contains many detailed prophecies which amazingly found complete fulfillment in the past, in our days, and, no doubt, will come to pass in the future. There is no error in the Bible, and this is a sure indicator that the Scriptures are beyond the possibility of having been produced by human hands.

God does not need people to revise His sacred Words or add some new 'revelations' of other gods, which 'cannot save', be it Son of God or Allah, the pre-Islamic moon god or any other deities and idols.

The Muslims have shown no respect for the God of Israel or for His Prophets. According to them, the last and final divine revelation was given to Muhammad (570-632a.c.); therefore these new revelations supersede and nullify the God of the Bible, His Covenant, Laws and the Prophets. The Koran, they say, is the final book given by God and has to be accepted by the whole world. Their ultimate goal is world sovereignty by means of the subjugation of all infidels (unbelievers), if not by persuasion, then by sword. It is not a religion of peace and tolerance. It has become more aggressive and violent, with the spirit of Jihad as the way and duty of the every Muslim.

The vast majority of peace-loving Muslims have been terrorized and kidnapped by a minority of jihadist fanatics who value death more than life. The majority cowardly follow them being scared to raise any voice of protest.

"Believers (Muslims), take neither Jews nor Christians to be your friends: they are friends with one another. Whoever of you seeks their friendship becomes one of their number, and God does not guide (those Jewish and Christians) wrongdoers"

(Koran, Sura 5:51-5:74).

Islam is not a religion based on the Hebrew Bible and Prophets. It is nothing else than a revival of the ancient cult of the moon god with all its pagan symbols and ceremonies. In other words, 'There is no God but Allah, and there are no prophets but Muhammad'. They made the pagan lunar god, al-ilah, who all Arabs had worshipped before Muhammad, the supreme God 'Allah'. The pilgrimage to Mecca, running around the temple of the Moon god, called the Kabbah; praying toward Mecca several times a day; kissing the black stone; fasting in the month which begins and ends with the crescent Moon; throwing stones at the devil,—all of this was practiced by the pagan Arabs for many centuries the same way as it is today by the Muslims.

At least the Christians gave a reason as to why God 'rejected' Israel—for not accepting Jesus Christ (their Messiah). The Muslims do not give any such explanation, except that Allah revealed himself to Muhammad as the Supreme God of the Universe and appointed him to be his only Messenger. The Jewish and Christian religions were abolished and superseded by Islam.

The real reason however may be found deep down back in the Biblical story of God's decision to make an everlasting covenant with Isaac, not with Ishmael, the first born son of Abraham. The bitterness of Ishmael accumulated over centuries has grown into hatred and an urge for revenge. Muhammad gave the solution: A new God and a new religion, where Muslims are the chosen people and the Jews are rejected. Ancient brothers have become enemies, and Ishmael still wants to kill Isaac.

We are not going to analyze here the Islamic religion in depth nor criticize the personal life and deeds of it founder because is not the theme of our work. It is worth mentioning however Maimonides opinion of Muhammad as 'the madman', 'possessed', a 'wicked impostor pretending to be a prophet'.

The Messianic Kingdom and Islam

As in Judaism and Christianity, the religion of Islam has much developed and has adopted eschatological teachings concerning the Messiah and the Messianic Kingdom. The Israelites have been waiting for the promised Messiah, a man from the House of David, the future King of Israel who will reunite all the Tribes of Israel and bring them home to the Holy Land for God's Redemption.

The Christians have been expecting the Second coming of their Messiah, Jesus Christ, son of God who will establish God's Kingdom on Earth.

The name of the Muslim Messiah is Muhammad al-Mahdi. He is the twelfth Imam, the ruler anointed by Allah, a descendant of the Prophet Muhammad, a great spiritual leader and savior. Among the Shiite believers there is a widely accepted legendary story that the twelfth Imam, son of the eleventh Imam, has been alive and in hiding since he was five years old (13 century). He is supposes to supernaturally reveal himself just before the Day of Judgment or the End of the World.

His appearance will be preceded by three years of horrendous world chaos, bloody wars, unparalleled suffering, tyranny, deaths, and oppression. As in the Messianic history of Judaism and Christianity, there have been quite a few imposters in the Islamic Messianic sphere claiming to be the hidden Imam, Muhammad al-Mahdi. The tasks of the Messiah of Islam are almost identical to the tasks of the Israelite or Christian Messiah: Peace, Justice, and Harmony.

The President of the Islamic Republic of Iran, Mahmud Ahmadinejad, is a strong Shiite believer in the coming of the twelfth Imam. He claims that he was "directed by Allah to pave the way for the glorious appearance of the Mahdi" and personally deeply commits to preparing world conditions for the appearance of Muhammad al-Mahdi in the way prophesized.

Those conditions are: wars, massive slaughter of populations, infectious diseases, starvation, World disorder, chaos. Ahmadinejad claims profoundly that it is his destiny to hasten the coming of the twelfth Imam. That is why Iran under his leadership has defied the International Community and is moving ahead with their plans for developing nuclear weapons of mass destruction. That is why Iran threatens to close the Strait of Hormuz and use the 'Oil Weapon' against Europe and USA. That is why they arrogantly announce their intention 'to wipe Israel off the map and have boldly challenged the Great Satan—America and the West. Ahmadinejad hopes that this kind of escalation of confrontation will bring about the necessary conditions: These include risks of energy crisis, global financial and economical instability, and even World War III. He thinks that his actions by bringing the World to bloody carnage and the death of millions of people will accelerate the coming of Muhammad al-Mahdi who will establish World Order and Peace.

Israelites must obey God and Drive the Palestinians out of the Holy Land

The answer to the question, "Should the Israelites drive out the Palestinians from the Promised Land as God commanded?" has not been given yet. So, what is the answer? Yes, the Israelites must obey God and drive the Palestinians out of the Land!

Why? For the same reasons God commanded the Israelites to destroy the heathen peoples in the time of Joshua: idolatry, worshipping pagan gods which 'cannot save', evil-doing. We are talking of the people of Canaan, the youngest son of Ham, whose descendants settled in the Land of Canaan, which is now called Palestine or the Land of Israel. Those people were cursed by God for indecent behavior by their father Ham towards the Patriarch Noah (Genesis 9:25). The three sons of Noah were born prior to the Flood and inherited all the evil inclinations and violence of the very people God destroyed. They were spared only because of the righteousness of Noah.

"Come you and all your house into the ark; for you have I seen righteous before Me in this generation" (Genesis 7:1).

The Bible describes the episode when Noah became drunk and fell asleep naked in his tent. His son Ham saw and 'uncovered the nakedness of his father', whereas his other sons 'Shem and Japheth took a garment, and walked backward and covered the nakedness of their father; their faces were turned away, and they did not see their father. When Noah awoke from his wine and knew what his youngest son had done to him, he said: "Cursed be Canaan; a slave of slaves he be to his brothers" (Genesis 9:25).

We do not know exactly what Ham did to his father, whether it was a malicious act of homosexual nature, or he castrated his father, thus preventing him from having a fourth son (Canaan was the fourth son of Ham), or a lewd delight in exposing his father's nakedness, but by the gravity of the curse we can conclude that it was not a harmless, inoffensive act of an innocent man. It definitely reminds us of the perverted sins of Sodom and Gomorrah (Genesis 19-all) and the prohibitions of Leviticus 18.

"You shall not uncover the nakedness of your father.

You shall not lie with a male as one lies with a females; it is an abomination" (Leviticus 18:7, 22).

On the other hand, Shem and Japheth had not participated with their brother Ham in "uncovering the nakedness" of their father, on the contrary, they condemned Ham and did everything to respectively protect the integrity of their father. In this very condensed story one question still remains as a big puzzle: Why was Canaan cursed instead of Ham? God knows the answer. The Bible does not directly reveal the reason. But in reality, the people of Canaan became synonymous with God-haters, idol worshippers, cruel murderers, sex perverts, bloody persecutors and oppressors of God's people Israel. The Canaanites were considered worthless sinners among the nations, abominations in the sight of the Lord.

The Land of Israel, 'My Land', is a Holy Land. God does not want His Land to be polluted with all these abominations. The Palestinians fit exactly the above descriptions of wickedness and idol worshipers. On top of it all there is radical Islam with its bloody terrorism, fueled by the spirit of Jihad; a fundamentalist ideology of intolerance, the use of physical force and violence against Governments, institutions and individuals who do not share their views on Islam.

"Fight and slay the pagans (infidels) wherever you find them, and seize them, beleaguer them, and lie and wait for them in every stratagem of war" (Koran, Sura 9:5).

Remember, God said, "On account of their wickedness I drove those nations out of this land. If you disobey My command and will not drive the inhabitants of the land out, they will harass you", and we may add continually fight for the land, and torture you with the 'Peace Process'. This is an exact characteristic of the Palestinians today! "They shall be irritants in your eyes and thorns in your sides; they will trap you with their idolatry: moreover it shall be that I will do to you as I thought to do to them". If you do not get rid of them, I will exile you again!

No, this is not going to happen anymore. The Israelites have learned their lesson:

"They shall not defile themselves anymore with their idols, nor with their detestable things, nor with any of their transgressions" (Ezekiel 37:23).

Israel will listen to God, and never again will be uprooted from the Holy Land.

"I will plant Israel in their own land. They will never be uprooted from the land I have given them" (Amos 9:15).

Again and again God has reiterated His uniqueness and Oneness: "Hear, O Israel: The Lord our God is one Lord."
(Deuteronomy 6:4)
"But I am the Lord your God. You must acknowledge no God but Me, for there is no other Savior. (Hosea 13:4)

God's first commandment is against idolaters because in His sight this is the heaviest sin of all sins.

"I am the Lord, which is My name! I will not give My Glory to another, nor My praise to graven images" (Isaiah 42:8).

This is the main reason why the Palestinians should be driven out of the Land of Israel, which in the turn will end the Peace Process and heal Judah's spiritual wound forever (Hosea 5:13).

Can the Israelis alone drive the Palestinians and the other people out of the Promised Land now? We think they cannot. There are many internal and international obstacles that will prevent the Israelis from accomplishing this task successfully. God's multiple prophecies of future defeat and subjugation of the Philistines, Moabites, Ammonites and Edomites will not come to fruition until one more condition will be met: reunification of the "Lost" Ten Tribes of Israel with Judah. When the strongest superpower in the World, this sleeping giant, Joseph, fully awakens to his Israelite identity and acknowledges his God and Savior, the God of Israel, they will finally reunite with their brothers of the Jewish nation. This reunification of all the families of Jacob will be the beginning of a new Messianic age of Liberation and Redemption. Their unity will be much stronger than before, when Moses led them from out of Egyptian bondage. Everything we are saying here was expressly prophesied by God:

"He will raise a banner for the nations and gather the exiles of Israel; He will assemble then scattered people of Judah from the four quarters of the earth. Ephraim's jealousy will vanish, and Judah's enemies will be cut off; Ephraim will not be jealous of Judah, nor Judah hostile toward Ephraim" (Isaiah 11:12, 13).

Who could stop such a superpower? Nobody! And here we go:

"They shall fly upon the shoulders of the Philistines towards the west; together they will plunder the sons of the east; they will possess Edom and Moab, and the sons of Ammon will be subject to them" (Isaiah 11:14).

United Israel's armies under the leadership of the brilliant Commander-in-Chief Messiah son of Joseph will conduct this attack swiftly and decisively. They will have a convenient military base right in the land of Israel, where the Palestinians will be on their west, and the rest of the enemies will be on their east. They will deliver a terrible blow to these nations and subjugate them. The land of Israel will be restored to its Biblical borders from the Nile to the Euphrates Rivers.

"Rise and thresh, O daughter of Zion, for I will give you horns of iron; I will give you hoofs of bronze and you will brake to pieces many nations" (Micah 4:13).

Divine Vengeance Against the Heathen Nations

God has given more details for His vengeance against those nations:

EDOM (Turkey, Amalekites, and Palestinians of the West Bank)

"The Lord has a day of vengeance, a year of recompense for the cause of Zion. For My sword has drunk it's full in the heaven; behold, it descends for judgment upon Edom, the nation I have marked for destruction" (Isaiah 34:5, 8).

"And the house of Jacob shall be a fire, and the house of Joseph a flame, and the house of Esau for stubble, and they shall kindle them, and devour them; and there shall not be any remaining of the house of Esau; for the Lord has spoken it" (Obadiah 1:18).

"Because Edom acted revengefully against the house of Judah, and has incurred grievous guilt in taking vengeance on them, therefore I will raise My fist of judgment against Edom. I will wipe out its people with the sword. I will make a wasteland of everything from Teman to Dedan" (Ezekiel 25:12, 13).

MOAB (Jordan)

"The calamity of Moab is near to come, and his affliction hastens fast. We have heard of Moab's pride, for his pride is very great. We know of his lofty pride, his arrogance, and his haughty heart. There shall be no more praise of Moab. Moab will be destroyed, her little ones will cry out. I will put an end to Moab, for the people offer sacrifices at the pagan shrines and burn incense to their false gods. Woe be unto you, O Moab! Your cities will fall, and your strongholds will be seized, and the hearts of the mighty men of Moab in that day will be like the heart of a woman in labor.

And Moab shall be destroyed as a nation because he magnified himself against the Lord (Jeremiah 48-all).

AMMON (Jordan)

"The days are coming, when I will sound the battle cry against Rabbah of the Ammonites; it will become a desolate heap of ruins, and the neighboring towns will be burned. Then Israel will drive out those who drove her out. I will bring terror on you, every one of you will be driven away, and no one will gather the fugitives. I have heard the taunts of Moab and the insults of the Ammonites, who mocked my people and made threats against their land. Surely Moab will become like Sodom, and the Ammonites like Gomorrah. The remnant of my people will plunder them, and the survivors of my nation will possess them. This is what they will get in return for their pride, for insulting and mocking the people of the Lord. The Lord will terrify them as He destroys all the gods in the land. Then nations around the world will worship the Lord, each in their own land" (Zephaniah 2:8-11).

PHILISTINES (Palestinians of Gaza)

"Because the Philistines have acted in vengeance and took revenge with malice in their hearts, and with ancient hostility sought to destroy Judah, therefore I will raise My fist of judgment against the Philistines, and I will cut off the Kerethites and utterly destroy their people who live by the seacoast. I will execute great and terrible vengeance to punish them in My wrath. Then they will know that I am the Lord" (Ezekiel 25:15-17).

"Ashkelon will see it and fear Gaza will shake with terror, as will Ekron, for their hope will be dashed. Gaza's king will be killed, and Ashkelon will be deserted. Foreigners will occupy the city of Ashdod, and I will destroy the pride of the Philistines"
(Zechariah 9:5-6).

DAMASKUS (Syria)

"Damascus has become feeble, and all her people turn to flee and panic. Fear, anguish, and pain have gripped her as they grip a woman in labor. I will kindle a fire in the walls of Damascus, and her young men will fall in the streets and die. All her soldiers will be killed" (Jeremiah 49:24, 26, 27).

"Look, the city of Damascus will no longer be a city but will become a heap of ruins" (Isaiah 17:1).

All these vows and great destructions God will inflict by the hands of His people Israel who will act as 'the blacksmith who fans the coal into flame and forges a weapon' for utter destruction.

"You are My war club, My weapon for battle—with you I shatter nations, with you I destroy kingdoms" (Jeremiah 51:20).

Looks like nuclear weapons will be used, otherwise how will such a huge modern city Damascus of Syria or Rabbah (Amman) of Jordan 'become a heap of ruins'? Lebanon, Syria, Jordan and the Palestinians will be destroyed by fire.

Moab and Ammon are brothers, the sons of Lot, nephew of Abraham. Their origin is given in Genesis 19:30-38. Lot and his two daughters were the survivors of the destroyed cities of Sodom and Gomorrah. They lived in a cave. In order to preserve seed from their father, the sisters decided to make their father drunk with wine and sleep with him. So they did as planned: And Lot was so drunk that he 'perceived not when they lay down, nor when they arose'.

That is how Moabites and Ammonites were born. They are of similar stock to the Israelites, but from ancient times developed hatred and animosity towards Israel (Deuteronomy 23:3-5). Together with Edom these three nations attacked Judah, and were destroyed by God who made them fight and kill each other. "Children of Moab and Ammon turn against Edom, utterly to sly and destroy them; and after every one helped to destroy another" (2 Kings 20: 22, 23). Their ancient lands in these days are in part of Jordan, along the east shore of the Dead Sea, east of the Jordan and south of Gilead.

No weapon turned against Israel will succeed. And any voice of protest or accusation against Israel will be refuted and silenced in judgment:

"This is the heritage of the servants of Lord, and their vindication is from Me" (Isaiah 54:15-17).

'Have I Pleasure in the Death of the Sinner'?

God's prophecies are certain. They are the most powerful proofs of the veracity of the Bible. Nobody can prevent them. They definitely will come to pass, unless . . . Unless what? Unless the nations, facing 'the fist of God's judgments', repent of all their wrongdoings before God, reject the idolatrous religion of Islam, and acknowledge the God of Israel as the One and True God Almighty of the whole Universe.

Is this scenario possible? We think it is. God has no pleasure in the death of sinners. He wishes that all people be righteous, obedient to His commandments, live happily in peace, prosperity, and harmony. And serve God.

"Have I pleasure at all that the wicked should die? And not that he should return from his way and live (Ezekiel18:23)?

Of course not! God wants wicked people to stop sinning, come back from their evil ways and live.

Remember, God pleaded with His people Israel the same way, with the same message, "Turn! Turn from your evil ways! Why will you die, O house of Israel" (Ezekiel 33:11)?!

The Arab world, and especially that of the Palestinians, should stop for a moment their daily activities, take a good breath and plunge deep into thought about their future. It is impossible to go against God Almighty and His people Israel. History has proven that all the prophecies of the Bible are true and have been fulfilled in every detail; so the rest of prophecy aimed at the future will definitely come to pass. The fanaticism of radical Islam, the bloody violence of the Jihad spirit, their hatred and lust for vengeance eventually will lead them to doom and destruction as the Biblical verses above surely have demonstrated. You have only one hope: Turn and pray to the God of Israel that He may forgive your wickedness that you and your children may live.

"If at any time I announce that a nation or kingdom is to be uprooted, torn down and destroyed, and if that nation, I warned, repents of its evil, then I will not destroy it as I had planned"
(Jeremiah18:7, 8).

What a golden, beautiful opportunity for sinful nations to repent and turn to the true God who can save!

Nineveh put on Sackcloth and Repented

The best example of this is the story recorded in the book of the prophet Jonah. Inhabitants of the great ancient city of Nineveh had sinned very badly, and their wickedness had come up before God. So, He sent Jonah to Nineveh to announce His judgment of destruction on the city and its inhabitants, unless they heed the warnings of the prophet and repent.

"So Jonah arose, and went unto Nineveh, according to the word of the Lord. When Jonah entered the city, he shouted to the crowds: 'Forty days from now Nineveh will be destroyed!"

The Ninevites believed God. Probably, the stories of Sodom and Gomorrah were very well known to them. They declared a fast, and all of them, from the greatest to the least, put on sackcloth to show their repentance. The king and his nobles issued a decree throughout the city: 'No one should eat and drink; everyone must wear garments of mourning and urgently pray to God; and must turn from their evil ways and their violence. Who knows? Perhaps even yet God will change His mind and hold back His fierce anger from destroying us".

When God saw what they had done and how they had put a stop to their evil ways, He had compassion and did not bring upon them the destruction He had threatened. That is how the great city Nineveh was spared by God (Jonah 1:2; 3:2-10).

What a wonderful story! Any individual sinner, city, or nation can be forgiven by the Merciful God of Israel, if they follow the example of the great ancient city Nineveh in their sincere and total repentance and turn to Him.

Do the Arabs have a Chance to be Saved?

The Israelite and Palestinian peoples came from the same Semitic stock, from the same ancestral father Abraham. They are brothers, and should live together in a happy brotherhood as good and decent peace loving neighbors. We think that it is Islam—the root of all problems which has divided the two nations apart and made them sworn enemies. Hatred, lust for revenge, bloody wars—all of it is the product of Islam.

It is not the battle between Jews and Arabs, as the International media tries to make us believe. The real battle is between Judaism and Islam. Judaism does not intend to conquer and convert all the World. Islam does. Judaism does not teach violence, terror, death. Islam does. Judaism does not avenge itself against the nations for not accepting their God, Torah and Prophets. Islam does.

One of the dogmas of Islam which prevents the peaceful coexistence of Palestinians and Israelis is the underlying teaching of the Koran that any land captured by Muslims, cannot be given back to infidels, even if they were the lawful owners. Muhammad himself originated this doctrine, as if it was Allah's command to never give up sacred Muslim territory and to fight for it until victory or martyrdom. This is the reason why the Arab Muslims have rejected the two state solution and are most reluctant to sign any peace agreement with the Israelis. The people of Israel (in their mind) have been cursed by Allah and are doomed for destruction. The Muslim religion is categorically against any Jewish presence in the land of Israel, and they may never quit their jihad-like struggle until the last Jew is killed, or they be soundly defeated and dispossessed from the land.

There is only way to stop the ancient hatred and bloodshed in the Middle East between the Arabs and Jews (and between the Arabs and the rest of the World) and establish a real and true Peace among the nations, and that is for Islam to be rejected as the false, hateful and idolatrous religion of the god Allah who cannot save, and turn to God Almighty, the One and Only God, who can save, the God of Israel.

"And the Lord shall be King all over the earth: in that day there shall be one Lord and His name one" (Zechariah 14:9).

"It shall come to pass in the last days, that the mountain of the Lord's house shall be established in the top of the mountains; and all nations shall flow unto it. And many people say, come you to the house of the God of Jacob; and He will teach us of His ways, and we will walk in His path; for out of Zion shall go forth the law, and the word of the Lord from Jerusalem" (Isaiah 2:2-3).

Idolatry will be utterly abolished by God for ever (Isaiah 2:18).

"And I will set My glory among the heathen, and all the heathen shall see My judgment that I have executed, and My hand that I have laid upon them. And the heathen shall know that I am the Lord, the Holy One in Israel" (Ezekiel 39:7, 21).

"Look unto Me, and be you saved, all the ends of the earth: for I am God, and there is none else. Unto Me every knee shall bow, every tongue shall swear. The people will declare, "The Lord is the source of all righteousness and strength". And all who were angry with Him will come to Him and be ashamed" (Isaiah 45:22-24).

The God of Israel personally calls upon all the nations of the World, including the Arabs, to reject idolatry and wickedness and turn to Him to be saved:

Turn! Turn you from your evil ways; for why will you die, O house of Ishmael?!

Will it really happen that the house of Ishmael shall reject Islam and turn to the one and only true Almighty God of Israel? Despite our wishes that they do so, the Bible's verses have informed us that the scenario will go in the opposite direction, leading to the 'Troubles of Ishmael', and culminating in their defeat in the wars to come.

At the battle of Jerusalem in 'the latter years', the besieged Israeli forces will destroy surrounding attacking Arab and Muslim nations, as the Bible describes:

"The House of the Judah shall devour all the people round about; on the right hand and on the left hand" (Zechariah 12:6).

The same story is told by the Prophet Isaiah:

"They shall fly upon the shoulders of the Philistines towards the west; they shall spoil them of the east together: they shall lay their hands upon Edom and Moab; and the children of Ammon shall obey them" (Isaiah 11:14).

We have already demonstrated above in detail why, who and how these nations be defeated and subjugated at the appointed times.

There is quite an interesting story in Islamic tradition about ancient cities of Sodom and Gomorrah which resembles the Biblical story of Genesis18:19. It says that in the time of the Prophet Lut people in the area of the Dead Sea were wicked on an account of murder, robbery, homosexuality and other despicable acts. Being the only righteous man, the Prophet Lut preached to his people to stop sinning, repent and turn to Allah. They received many warnings to reject their evil behavior or they would face the wrath of Allah. They did not take the words of the prophet seriously. They even intended to violate three young men (angels) sent to the Prophet Lut by Allah. These angels set the Prophet Lut with a few believers aside and save them. The angel Jibrail lifted the towns with his wings and turned them upside down smashing them into the earth and destroying all their evil inhabitants. That is how the Dead Sea was formed, the lowest point on Earth.

Muslims should heed this story and that of Nineveh and correct their idolatrous and wicked ways. However, Biblical verses say that this is not going to happen. In their unquenched hatred and vengefulness against the Jewish People, the Arab and Muslim nations will secretly plot an ultimum military attack against Israel in order to wipe them off from the face of the earth.

"They have said, come, and let us cut them off from being a nation; that the name of Israel may be no more in remembrance. For they have consulted together with one consent" (Psalms 83:4-5).

Who are these nations? As usual, the same ancient sworn enemy nations, mostly of Semitic stock: "The tabernacles of Edom, and Ishmaelites; of Moab, and the Hagarenes; Gebal, and Ammon, and Amalek; the Philistines and Assur" (Psalms 83:6-8).

Instead of repenting of all their evil and turning to the Almighty for forgiveness and be saved, as the people of ancient Nineveh did, these nations will have decided to fight against God and His people Israel. Their tragic defeat and miserable fate are well described in the Hebrew Scripture.

We shell shed more light on this subject in detail when we deal with the Wars of Gog and Magog from Ezekiel 38 and 39 in Chapter XIV.

CHAPTER XI:
THE DAY OF THE LORD

Alas! For this Day is Great

What is going to happen to Israel? Will it survive all the coming calamities, wars and destructions? Will Israel fulfill its Divine destiny of becoming a nation of priests, the light to the World? When and how will the Messianic World come? What does the day of the Lord mean and when will it come?

Only God can answer on these questions. Let's see what His Word says in the Hebrew Bible. People have the tendency to ignore and bypass all the negative, dark sides of the future. They picture it as a continuous chain of merry and happy sunny days under the blue sky. They associate it with flowers, divine music, complete physical and spiritual satisfaction, the greatest pleasures, loving and being loved, comfort and enjoyment of life. This is the paradise that everyone would wish to partake of.

Well, Scripture has drowned quite a different picture of future events. All the prophets have pointed to the special Day of the Lord, when the World will experience a time of great calamities and destructions, such as never before in the ages of human history. "Alas! For the day is great, so that none is like it."

There are different understandings on the time duration of the Day of the Lord. Some people believe that it is literally one day of God's judgment. Others identify it as a span of time, much longer than one day, a specific period of time sufficient for the fulfillment of God's will on earth. Many scholars say that the day of the Lord is the entire seventy weeks of the prophet Daniel 9:24, or a seven years end-time period of Great Tribulation, or even a millennia of reign of the Messiah. How they can equate the Messianic Time of peace, redemption and knowledge of God with the day of God's wrath is beyond our comprehension. The day of the Lord simply means a period of time determined by God during which He personally intervenes directly or indirectly in human affairs in order to accomplish His Divine Will.

Strangely enough, in the Hebrew Bible the Day of the Lord sometimes describes Divine Judgments which occurred in the past (Isaiah 13; Ezekiel 30), but most of the time those Judgments pertain to the future, to the latter years of our age (Ezekiel 39; Zechariah 14). The Day of the Lord is not only a time of punishment, but is also a time of Salvation. Accordingly, those people who have done wrong, the evil-doers and idol worshippers, do not want to see the judgments of the Day of the Lord because they know that this day will bring destructions, calamities and severe punishment upon them. For the righteous and the believers the Day of the Lord shall bring joy, happiness and blessings.

The nations shall be in sorrow and distress. Terror, misfortune and miseries of wars, terrible infectious diseases, darkness and gloom shell descend upon the earth.

"How awful that Day will be! None will be like it. Time of trouble for Jacob—but he will be saved out of it"

(Jeremiah 30:7).

In this terrible Day of 'darkness and of gloom' God will inflict judgments on all inhabitants of the earth, including Judah and the rest of the house of Israel.

"The Day of the Lord is awesome, a dreadful thing. Who can possibly endure it" (Joel 2:11)?

When will the Day of the Lord come? It might be much sooner than most people expect. The Scriptures do not exactly reveal the day or the year. But they have indicated that it will be in the End of Days, in the latter years. There is a sense of imminence and nearness in the passages of the Day of the Lord:

235

"For the day of the Lord is near" (Ezekiel 30:3).

"For the day of the Lord is coming. It is close at hand"
(Joel 2:1).

"Be silent before the Lord God! For the day of the Lord is near" (Zephaniah 1:7).

"The great and terrible Day of the Lord is near and coming quickly. A day of bitter tears, a day when even strong men will cry out" (Zephaniah 1:14).

Will all the House of Israel be Saved?

'The house of Israel will be saved out of it'.

"Then the Lord will be jealous for His land and will have pity on His people" (Joel 2:15). Will all the House of Israel be 'saved out of it'? We do not think so.

More detailed information is given by the prophet Daniel 12:1. According to him, not all the House of Jacob will be saved, but only those 'children of your people' whose names shall be found 'written in the Book'. God in heaven has a Book of Life, where the righteous and the holy people from all the nations who are chosen to be worthy of salvation, have been registered. No deed of corruption, fraud, cheating, money, influence,—nothing can change God's decision.

"Neither their silver nor their gold will be able to save them on the day of the Lord's wrath" (Zephaniah 1:18).

Wealth will be worthless in the day of wrath, but righteousness delivers from death. It is important to realize that not all Israel will be saved, but residue, only those, whose name will be written in the Book of Life by God in Heaven.

"In that Day the branch of the Lord will be beautiful and glorious; the fruit of the land will be the pride and glory of the survivors in Israel. Those who are left in Zion, who survived in Jerusalem, will be called holy and recorded among the living" (Isaiah 4:2, 3).

Many of the House of Jacob will have perished: These include those who forsook the Lord and His Holy Land; who worshiped idols from wood or stone, the gods which cannot save; those who rejected the calls of God and perpetually did evil, "Therefore will I number you to the sword, and you shall all bow down to the slaughter" (Isaiah 65:12).

"Though your people, O Israel, be like the sand by the sea, only a remnant of them will return. Destruction has been decreed overwhelming and righteous" (Isaiah 10:22).

Scripture even gives the exact proportion of people who will be perished:

"And it shall come to pass, that in all the land, saith the Lord, two parts therein shall be cut off and die; but the third shall be left therein. They shall call on My name, and I will answer them; I will say: 'It is My people', and they shall say: "The Lord is my God" (Zechariah 13:8, 9).

Whosoever shall Call on the Name of the Lord shall be Delivered

Even though the Day of the Lord is very terrible and awful, God has still called His People to repent and turn to Him: "Turn ye to Me with all your heart, and with fasting, and with weeping, and with mourning: whosoever shall call on the name of the Lord shall be delivered" (Joel 2:12, 32).

God will spare from the house of Israel those with a pure language, who will obey the Lord and serve Him with one consent; an afflicted and faithful people who trust in the name of the Lord. The Day of the Lord is a call upon the nations of the World to repent and correct their evil ways of living and turn to the God of Israel to be saved before it is too late. Otherwise they will face the wrath of God's Judgments poured out on them in the form of terror and destruction as when 'The heavens and the earth will tremble and the stars will withhold light'. Seek the Lord, seek righteousness and humility, if you wish to avoid unprecedented punishment and receive the overwhelming blessings of God.

"The remnants of Israel shall not do iniquity, nor speak lies; neither shall a deceitful tongue be found in their mouth: for they shall feed and lie down, and none shall make them afraid. Sing, O daughter of Zion; shout, O Israel; be glad and rejoice with all thy heart, O daughter of Jerusalem. The Lord has taken away thy judgments, He has cast out thine enemy; the king of Israel, even the Lord, is in the midst of thee: thou shalt not see evil anymore"

(Zephaniah 3:13-15).

We cannot start analyzing God's passages about Israel's prophetic future without first dealing with the soon coming wars of Gog and Magog prophesied by Ezekiel 38 and 39 and Zechariah 12 and 14—the siege of Jerusalem. The future fate of Israel depends totally on the outcome of these wars.

CHAPTER XII:
HOW THE EARTH WAS
RESETTLED

The Mysterious 'Sons of God'

To better understand alliances of the nations, their races and the lands of their dwelling, let us explain how the resettling of the Earth developed.

The descendants of Adam and Eve had begun to multiply on the face of the earth, as God commanded. The people of those generations decided to reject God and His Laws and live according to their own sinful inclinations and pleasures. All flesh had corrupted its way upon the earth.

"And God saw that the wickedness of man was great on the earth, and every imagination of the thoughts of his heart was only evil continually" (Genesis 6:5).

It would seem, the downfall of mankind began at the time when **"The sons of God saw that the daughters of men were beautiful, and they married any of them they chose"** (Genesis 6:2).

This verse of the Bible is one of the most puzzling in Scripture. Scholars have been arguing for a long time on defining who these 'sons of God' and 'daughters of men' were. Basically, there are two answers. The first one goes like this. Since we have learnt that before the 'sons of God' started the business of taking the 'daughters of men' to be their wives, there had lived two groups of people on the Earth. The descendants of Cain and the descendants of Seth. They both came from the seed of Adam and Eve. Cain is the one who killed his brother Abel and for that reason was cursed by God. He settled in the land of Nod, east of Eden, got himself a wife and begat sons and daughters.

Meanwhile, "Adam knew his wife again; and she gave birth to a son, and called his name Seth: For God, said she, hath appointed me another seed instead of Abel, whom Cain slew. A son was also born to Seth, and he named him Enos. At that time people began to worship the LORD" (Genesis 4:25-26).

So, the theologians have decided that from these two groups of people the descendants of Cain were called the 'sons and daughters of men'; and those who came from the seed of Seth were called 'Sons of God'.

This is the one view of the discussed verse. The second explanation goes in the opposite direction. While both sides agree that 'daughters of men' represent humans, regardless of whether they are the seed of either Cain or Seth, the identification of the 'sons of God' has caused much controversy. Those who disagree that the term 'sons of God' refers to humans, have come up with the idea that 'sons of God' are the fallen Angels who rebelled against the Almighty: As punishment, they were thrown out from Heaven and sent to earth after being stripped off those spiritual divine attributes they had possessed. They were given the ability to be like mortal humans, to be visible, eat, drink and produce offspring. Their children were called Nephilim. They were the mighty giants who were of old, 'men of renown' (Genesis 6:4).

The proponents of this idea say that if the 'sons of God' had been ordinary people, their children would have been normal humans, not 'mighty giants' called Nephilim. The concept of the fallen Angels may be hinted at in Scripture. It was believed in by Josephus Flavius, Philon of Alexandria, and even recorded in the Apocrypha and Pseudepigrapha of the Old Testament, the Books of Enoch and Jubilees. This is what these Books said on the subject:

"And it came to pass when the children of men had multiplied that in those days were born unto them beautiful and comely daughters. **And the angels, the children of the heaven**, saw and lusted after them, and said to one another: 'Come, let us choose us wives from among the children of men and beget us children" (Enoch 6:1).

"And it came to pass when the children of men began to multiply on the face of the earth and daughters were born unto them, that **the angels of God** saw them on a certain year of this jubilee, that they were beautiful to look upon; and they took themselves wives of all whom they chose, and they bare unto them sons and they were **giants**. And lawlessness increased on the earth and all flesh corrupted its way" (Jubilees 5:1).

The Essenes of Qumran in the Dead Sea Scrolls have supplied us with an ancient text, the Genesis Apocryphon, which contains the story of Angels interbreeding with the daughters of men.

The defenders of the theory that the 'Sons of God' were only humans argue that when God decided to destroy the human race in the Flood, He did not blame the Angels or any other spiritual beings for the downfall of man but strictly placed the guilt of it on the very men He had created:

"So God created man in His own image; in the image of God He created him; male and female He created them" (Genesis 1:27).

"The LORD saw how great man's wickedness on the earth had become, and that every inclination of the thoughts of his heart was only evil all the time. And the LORD said, "I will wipe this human race I have created from the face of the earth" (Genesis 6:5, 7).

Also, they point out, that those who believe in the theory of 'sons of God' as literally being the fallen Angels, were condemned in the second Century a.c. by Rabbi Simeon bar Yochai and find no support in Rabbinical Judaism. Well known Rabbinical Sages of Middle Ages such as Rabbi Yitzchaki (Rashi) and Rabbi Moshe ben Nachman (Nachmanides) agreed with this position. In their view the 'Sons of God' represent pre-Flood nobles and leaders: military chiefs, kings, or magistrates.

Which group of scholars is right and which is wrong, is not the subject of our discussion here. The flow of our story has to continue.

The Wife of Noah

God regretted that He had made man, and it grieved Him at His heart. Then He decided to annihilate men and all He created by Flood.

"I will destroy man and every living substance that I have made" (Genesis7:4).

God spared only Noah for his righteousness and his family of seven people for his sake.

There are some interesting opinions of the Sages concerning the wife of Noah. In the book Sefer Yasher (Hebrew for 'upright account') and in Midrash Bereshit Rabba 23:3 it says that Na'amah, the sister of Tubalcain, (Genesis 4:22), was the wife of Noah. The Bible does not confirm that. Nahmanides asked: "Why mention a name, if we do not know who it is?" The name Na'amah means 'the pleasant one', 'fear and beautiful'. No wonder that the Greek and Arab writers later compare her beauty with that of Venus and Minerva. The Targum of Jonathan ben Uzziel portraits her as a composer of funeral songs and lamentations. Some scholars picture her as an upright and chaste woman. Others say that she was a source of all the evil spirits in this World. There are speculations that Na'amah was the lover of Ham. She was with him in the ark during the time of the Flood and led him into adultery.

It is obvious that her name is mentioned not only on account of her personal charms. Every word in Scripture has its purpose and significance, including the mention of her name.

While it is clear that Shem, Ham and Japheth, the sons of Noah, were spared because of the righteousness of their father and as direct descendants of his seed in the same manner as the daughters of Lot were saved at Sodom and Gomorrah; Na'amah, being from the family of Cain, and otherwise predestined to be destroyed by the Almighty, was saved from the Flood due to her own righteousness and merit. She became the second Mather of the human race after Eve. This principal is confirmed very well by the Bible:

"As surely as I live, says the Sovereign LORD, even if Noah, Daniel, and Job were there, they would not be able to save their own sons or daughters. They alone would be saved by their righteousness" (Ezekiel 14:20).

Because Na'amah was from the seed of Cain, her name as the wife of Noah was not revealed in Scripture as were the names of Eve or Sarah, the wives of Adam and Abraham. But her redemption is the proof that not all the seed of Cain perished in the Flood. Believe it or not, we are the descendants of this woman whose name was mysteriously honored in Genesis 4:22.

Note: There is another woman with the same name, Na'amah, an Ammonitess who mentioned in the Bible. She was the wife of King Solomon and the mother of King Rehoboam (1 Kings 14:21; 2 Chronicles 12:13). It is directly from the offspring of this line that the future Messiah will come (1 Chronicles 22:9-10).

Nevertheless, an outcome of this mixing of the bloodlines between the seed of Seth and Cain later on resulted in rebellion at the Tower of Babel; the evil sins of Sodom and Gomorrah; the sworn enmity among Ishmael and Isaac, Esau and Israel (here lies an explanation of the two different enemy-nations in the belly of Rebecca); and the forced Exiles of the Tribes of Israel to the lands of their enemies. The consequences of this 'unholy' union have been manifested in our ungodly, highly corrupted, unjust, and violently evil World.

The Offspring of Noah

Noah was five hundred years old before the devastating Flood. He begat three sons: Shem, Ham, and Japheth, from whom all the earth was repopulated. It is worth mentioning that the all predecessors of Noah begat their children at the ages of 65, 70, 80, 90 or so, way before the age of 500. The Sages explained that all the children of one hundred years and older would have perished in the Flood. The sons of

Noah were born shortly (less than one hundred years) before the Flood. Rabbinical tradition says that in the eyes of Heaven (as distinct from civil authorities) in some respects a person is not entirely culpable for sins committed before the age of twenty. According to this tradition, the cutting-off age prior to the Deluge was a hundred years. God made it this way to prevent tragedy and sadness for the righteous Noah who did not deserve being liable to lose his children. It was not said of Noah that 'he begat sons and daughters' as it was said of everyone else in the genealogical line from Adam to Lamech, his father. Scripture says that Noah had only three sons who became the progenitors of the whole Earth:

"These three were the sons of Noah, and from these the whole earth was populated" (Genesis 9:19; 10:32).

We may confidently regard Noah as the second (after Adam) father of the Mankind. There is no certainty who is the oldest son amongst the three. When Scripture speaks of Noah' sons, Shem is placed first in the list, then follow Ham and Japheth (Genesis 5:32; 9:18; 10:1). It would seem, the oldest of the three here is Shem (Genesis 10:21). The youngest son of Noah would be Ham (Genesis 9:24). When Scripture speaks of genealogy, the order of their names is drastically changed in reverse order, placing Japheth at the head of the list, as if he was the first born of Noah: Japheth, Ham and Shem (Genesis 10:2, 6, 21).

In an ancient Jewish work of the second century B.C., called the Book of Jubilees or the Lesser Genesis (Leptogenesis), more light is shed on the order of birth of these three main progenitors, descendants of Noah: Shem is the oldest; he was born in the year 1205 after the Creation. The second is Ham, born in 1209. The youngest is Japheth, born in 1211 (Book of Jubilees 4:33).

Japheth

The etymology of the name Japheth has a few meanings; one of them (the most popular), based on Genesis 9:27, translates it as 'May

God shall make Japheth 'wide', 'enlarge; or 'extend' him. This was an indication that his descendants will be more populous than those of Shem and Ham; other sources interpreted the meaning of his name as 'fair', being white skinned in color. The Targum of Jonathan renders the translation as "God shall beautify Japheth".

From the seventy linguistically different nations who settled the earth after God's dispersion from the tower of Babel, Japheth's descendants contributed to fourteen progenitors. The territory of their settlement is called 'The Northern Zone'. This is north of Asia Minor, (Turkey), the northern Mediterranean and Europe. Japheth is called 'the father of the Indo-European family of nations'.

Out of fourteen progenitors of Japheth came these nations: Greeks, Romans, French, Italian, Spanish, Portuguese, Slavs, Russians, Bulgarians, Poles, Slovaks, Croatians, Indians, Iranic, Medes, Persians, Afghans, Kurds, Turks, Germans, Scandinavian, Anglo-Saxons, and others.

The late author Dr. Ernest L. Martin had quite an interesting opinion that the descendants of Japheth are not European peoples, at least not on the massive scale as many thought they were and that Japheth is not 'the father of the Indo-European race'. He thought, rather, that Japheth is 'the father of the Mongoloid type people of 'Yellow" race'. In modern day terms, they are the Asian nations such as China, Japan, India, Korea and many others of the regions of Southeast Asia, the Far East and Oceania. Dr. Martin does not reject the possibility that Meshech and Tubal could represent Russia, Eastern Europe and Central Asia. He is also not denying the fact that after the dispersal of the human race in the aftermath of the rebellion at the Tower of Babel in 1656 b.c. the descendants of Japheth went originally to Europe and gave their names to the nations and geographical locations they then dwelt in. That is why ancient historians confused the identifications of those nations and national geography before the Greek domination of the world and the times of the Romans. Later on, continues Dr. Martin, under the massive push of hordes of Assyrians, Israelites (the Ten Tribes) and other Semites migrating from the Eastern Mediterranean and Mesopotamian

Alexander Zephyr

areas to Europe, the Japhetic nations had to move further to the north and eastward into Asia. Thus Gomer, Javan, Togarmah and Kittim left Europe and went into China, where they settled and gave their name to the region. 'Cathay' is the name of China in their own language (after the word 'Kittim'). In the writings of the medieval traveler Marco Polo and the Persian astronomer Nazir al-Din-al-Tuzi in 1272 we are told that China was known to outsiders by the name of 'Cathay', 'Kitai', 'Cataya', 'Cathayan', 'Khitayns', which all very closely resemble the name 'Kittim'.

There is no consensus amongst scholars as to which modern day countries represent which descendants of Japheth.

GOMER (means 'complete')

Gomer is the first son of Japheth, the father of Ashkenaz, Riphath and Togarmah (Genesis 10:2-3). Josephus Flavius said: "Gomer founded those whom the Greeks now call Galatians, but were then called Gomerites" (Antiquities of the Jews 1:6).

In Islamic folklore, there is the story that Gomer lived up to a 1000 years, as did Nimrod, son of Cush.

Hippolytus of Rome in c. 234 a.c. said that Gomer is the ancestor of the Cappadocians, neighbors of the Galatians. Anatolian Galatia is in the modern territory of Turkey and was the home of the Gomerites (Celts).

Theophilus Evans, the Welsh antiquary, in 1716 said that Gomer was one of the ancestors of the Welsh people.

Talmudic sources point out that Gomer together with Ashkenaz gave rise to the people of modern Germany.

Other sources said that from Gomer came out the Armenians, Cimmerians, Scythians, Welsh, Irish, Huns, Germans, Franks, and Turks. Well known ancient historians such as Herodotus, Strabo, and Plutarch indicate that Gomer settled in Europe, north of the Baltic Sea and in the Crimea. Anciently, Gomer was identified with the

246

Cimmerians (Gimirru, Gimmerai) who dwelt on the Eurasian Steppes, in Southern Russia, Crimea and Ukraine. The Scythians chased them out into Armenia and Minor Asia (Turkey).

We read all kind of stories and identifications about Gomer, but nobody (except Dr. Martin and S. Collins and just these two as far as we know) has connected this first born son of Japheth, a warlike ally of Gog and Magog (Ezekiel 38:6), to the most populous and mighty country of the world—China!

The rest of the six sons of Japheth produced the following peoples and countries:

MAGOG—Scythians, Slavs, Russians, Bulgarians, Bohemians, Poles, Slovaks, Croatians.
MADAI—Indians, Iranians, Medes, Persians, Afghans, Kurds.
JAVAN—Greece, Romans, French, Italian, Spanish, Portuguese.
TUBAL—South of the Black Sea, city of Tbilisi in Georgia (the Caucasus Theory);
—Eastern Siberia, city of Tobolsk (Russian Theory).
MESHECH—Russia, city of Moscow.
TIRAS—Thracians, Teutons, Germans, Scandinavians, Anglo-Saxons, Jutes.

These are the seven sons of Japheth and their generations today.

Gomer begat three sons: Ashkenaz, Riphath and Togarmah (Genesis 10:3).

ASHKENAZ—the name may be derived from the Assyrian "Ishkuza" and also is identified with the Scythians ('Saka'), and the Sarmatians. In Rabbinic Literature Ashkenaz is believed to be the ancestor of the Armenian, Germanic, Scandinavian, and Slavic peoples. Ashkenaz and his father Gomer are closely identified by most expositors with the progenitors of the German people.

RIPHATH—('a crusher'). Josephus said: "Ripath founded the Ripheans, now called Paphlagonians" (Antiquities 1:6:1). Paphlagonia was a province in Asia Minor. Later they migrated to north-west Russia, to the Baltic Sea and the Gulf of Finland. The Carpathian Mountains may be named after them. Their descendants today are known as the Finno-Ugric people: Baltic Finns, Estonians, Karelians, Mordvinians, Komi, Udmurts, Hungarians, Ostyaks, and Mansi. There are also the Ural-Finno-Ugric people west of the Ural Mountains (Altai) which undoubtedly derived its name from Riphath.

Some researchers have found linguistic connections between the ancient Sumerians and the Ural-Altaic people.

TOGARMAH—Armenians, Georgians, the people of the South Caucasus (Kakheti, Leketi). Others add Germany and Turkey. The historians Josephus (37-c.100 a.c.), Jerome (c.347-420 a.c.) and Isidore of Seville (c.560-636 a.c.) said that Togarmah was the father of the Phrygians. Phrygia was a kingdom in the west central part of Anatolia, in what is now modern-day Turkey.

Saint Hippolytus (c.170-c.236 a.c.), Eusebius of Caesarea (c.263-c.339 a.c.), and bishop Theodoret (c.393-c.457 a.c.) regarded Togarmah as the father of the Armenians.

The territory of Togarmah in the 'last days' was spoken of by the Prophet Ezekiel 38:6 when he prophesied that "the house of Togarmah of the north quarters" will join together with Gomer's bands in the invading armies of Gog against Israel.

These are the sons of Gomer and their generations today.

JAVAN begot four sons: Elishah, and Tarshish, Kittim, and Dodanim (Genesis 10:4)

ELISHAH—Some speculate that he is an ancestor of the 'Almanim', possibly a reference to Germanic tribes (Alamanni); others say that he founded the Portuguese people under his actual Biblical name (Lisbon and Lusitania), when he came to the Iberian Peninsula with his uncle Tubal. The Cypriots are also suggested to be descendants of Elishah because in ancient times the island was known by the name of 'Alashiya'. The most popular identification of people descended from Elishah are the Greeks ('Hellas' is a form of the word Elishah).

TARSHISH—A lot of speculation is to be found regarding efforts to rightfully identify the offspring of Tarshish today. In Scripture, King Solomon traded with Tarshish. They brought him ivory, apes, and peacocks (2 Chronicles 9:21; 1 Kings 10:22). Tarshish should therefore be identified with some kind of 'exotic' country like India where the national bird is the peacock. Josephus identified Tarshish as the city of Tarsus in southeastern Asia Minor (Antiquities 1:6-1). This historical city was located in south-east Turkey, 20 km. inland from the Mediterranean Sea. Some scholars point out that 'ships of Tarshish' were either of Tartessos (in Spain) or Sardinia. Jewish tradition reflected in the Targum of Jonathan linked Tarshish with Carthage in North Africa. Other suggestions include the Etruscans, the Phoenician cost, Spain, Lebanon, the Dutch, Sri Lanka, the Filipinos, and even Britain.

KITTIM—'invaders'. This is no exception. As elsewhere, there is no unanimous answer. In ancient times the island of Cyprus was called Kition or Citium (in Latin). That is why Josephus identified Kittim with Cyprus. In Talmudic literature Kittim was sometimes used to apply to the Assyrians, Macedonians or Romans. Because the name of 'Kittim' may be pronounced like the names of the ancient Hatti (Khatti) people, Kittim has been identified as the same people as those of the Hittite Empire. Dr. Martin connected Kittim with China. In the Dead Sea Scrolls of Qumran, the Essenes referred to the Kittim as being the descendants of 'Asshur'.

DODANIM—There is a commonly accepted opinion that he was the progenitor of the people on the island of Rhodes. The Dodanim (who are also called Rodanim) were considered to be either Greeks or kin to the Greeks.

These are the descendants of Japheth who became the most populous people on the face of the earth as was prophesied in Genesis 9:27, "God shall ENLARGE Japheth".

HAM (in Hebrew connotes 'hot' or 'burnt', 'dark', 'black skinned').

HAM—(Cham, Kham) is the second son of Noah and the father of Cush, Mizraim, Phut and Canaan. After the Babylonian dispersal the descendants of Ham went along the Mediterranean and settled in North Africa, South Arabia and in the Land of Canaan. The Geographical area occupied by Hummites is the so called 'Southern Zone.'

CUSH—The generally accepted view is that he founded the black African people of Ethiopia. He begot Nimrod ('let us rebel')

who became the King of Babylon, therefore it is safe to say that Cush is the progenitor of the Babylonian people too (Genesis 10:8, 10). Some scholars think that Sudan is also of Cush. Others have opined, based on Genesis 10:11, that Asshur is also descended from Cush. We think that this assumption is incorrect because the Biblical narrative in these verses deals with the descendants of Ham's oldest son Cush and particularly of his son Nimrod. To say 'out of this land went forth Ashur and built Nineveh' and so on, makes no sense. The story is about Nimrod, not Ashur. The name 'Ashur' will appear later in Genesis 10:22 where he is shown as the second son of Shem. It is Nimrod who went forth from the land of Shinar and built Nineveh, and the cities Rehoboth, and Calah. It is Nimrod who invaded Assyria with his army and established the first world Empire with its capital Nineveh. That is why Assyria is called 'the land of Nimrod (Micah 5:6). There is a story that the name of the city of Nineveh came from Ninus, the son of Nimrod; others say that Ninus and Nimrod are the same person.

MIZRAIM: These are the people of Egypt. From his descendant Cashluhim came the Philistines (Genesis 10:14).

PUT—(Phut) Lybia.

CANAAN—the Philistines.

There are historians who say that Hanaan (Canaan), as a nation, does not exist today, but has vanished from the history. The modern day Palestinians insist that they are the direct descendants of the Philistines, and that the Land of Palestine belongs to them. They confidently claim that they are Muslims of Arab descend from Semitic stock. But the fact is that the Philistines came out of Canaan and Mizraim, the sons of Ham! Originally they settled in Egypt and the Augean Sea coasts and islands (e.g. Crete), but later on (12 Century b.c.) the Philistines invaded the Land of Canaan, destroyed a people called Avvites, and settled in their territories (Deuteronomy 2:23; Joshua 13:3; 1 Chronicles 1:12). All the nations descended from Ham's thirty progenitors are called Hamitic nations. They are not Arabs and they are not Semites! They have nothing in common with the Semites, because they belong to a different branch of the Human family. In addition, the Canaanite branch was severely cursed by God for the sin of Ham, their father.

'And God said, "Cursed be Canaan; a servant of servants shall he be unto his brethren" (Genesis 9:25).

Basically, Ham's descendants are: Egyptians, Ethiopians, Libyans, Canaanites, Yemenis, Sudanese, Babylonians, Mayans, Aztecs and others. There are speculations that the Yellow Mongoloid race of nations, including China, is of Hamitic origin, particularly, from the Sinite, son of Canaan (Genesis 10: 17). Other sources say that China originated from a mixture of Semitic and Japhetic peoples. We very much doubt these ideas. The Mongoloid race of nations, especially China, has a huge population, and fits more the blessing of enlargement given to Japheth, rather than to Ham.

SHEM (SEM) means 'name', 'fame', 'renown'.

Twenty six progenitors descended from the oldest son of Noah, Shem. The geographical regions of their settlements are the Northern area of the Persian Gulf, the lands of Syria, Chaldea, Palestine (together with Canaanites, Phoenicians, Hittites) and parts of Assyria, Persia, and the Arabian Peninsula. This constitutes the so called 'Middle Zone'. Their attributed colors of skin are 'white' and 'olive'.

Shem begat five sons: Elam, Asshur, Arphaxad, Lud, Aram (Genesis 19:22).

Elam—('eternity'), Arabia;

Asshur—('strong'), Assyria, who became modern day Germany (!);

Arphaxad—Israelites (Hebrews), Ishmaelites, Ammonites, Moabites, Edomites;

Lud—('strife'), Lydians and other related groups in Asia Minor;

Aram—('exalted'), Aramaic people: Armenia, Mesopotamia, Syria.

Some expositors believe that the whole of the European peoples descend from Shem. Others claim that the Anglo-Saxons are the descendants of Shem. It is also said that Tuitsch, a German patriarch, is none other than Shem himself, implying that Germany is a country of Semitic origin. The Muslims insist that Shem was the father of the Arabs, the Jews, the Persians, and the Greeks. There are many different theories, including those which said that the descendants of Shem possessed the territories from the Orient to India and the Caspian Sea. Pakistan, India, Bangladesh—are descended from Shem through Joktan and his son Ophir. Even nations in Africa, such as Yemen (in South Arabia opposite Africa), Eritrea and Ethiopia are claimed to be of combined Hamito-Semitic ancestry.

The Curse of Ham

In Scripture there are few hints as to how God differentiates between the descendants of Japheth, Ham and Shem. It is commonly agreed by scholars that Japheth is associated with light colored skin or reddish-white. (Proponents of the Mongoloid Theory changed Japheth's color from 'fair' or 'reddish' to a 'Yellow skin race'). Ham was given very dark or black skin colors. Shem is distinguished by tawny-white, medium dark or olive colors.

To understand the significance of the future prophetic role in the World of the descendants of Japheth, Ham and Shem, we have to look at the tiny story of the 'Curse of Ham'. We will also learn the blessings of God given to Japheth and Shem.

Everyone knows the story how Noah got drunk and fell asleep naked in his tent. Ham, the father of Canaan, saw the 'nakedness of his father' and told about it to his brothers Shem and Japheth. They took a garment and covered the 'nakedness of their father' without looking at him. When Noah awoke and knew what Ham had done, he said: "Cursed be Canaan; a servant of servants shall he be unto his brethren" (Genesis 9:25).

This story is short but encapsulates much meaning. What was so bad about what Ham had done that Noah cursed him with such a grievous punishment? And why was Canaan, the fourth son of Ham, cursed instead of his father? The Bible verses are silent about these details. We ought to remember that Japheth, Ham and Shem were born before the Deluge. They had inherited the sins of the people God destroyed. They were spared by God only because of their father's righteousness (Genesis 7:1). According to the story, Shem and Japheth were good and obedient sons of Noah, and treated him with the utmost respect and honor. Noah was for them a model of spiritual and moral guidance. Ham was quite different. The evil inclinations of sinful behavior had overcome all the goodness emanating from his father's righteousness, making him capable of uncovering 'the nakedness of his father'.

There are many opinions of scholars trying to answer questions concerning the expression, "When Noah awoke and knew what his youngest son had done." Really, what did Ham do to his father? What does it mean 'Uncover the nakedness of his father'? It must have been something more important and grievous than just simply (and innocently) having seen his father without clothes.

One source says that Ham brutally sodomized his father, using the drunkenness of Noah ('passed out') as a convenient condition to fulfill this malicious act. To 'uncover the nakedness' is very closely linked to Leviticus 18 as a prohibition against having sex with relatives: "None of you shall approach to any that is near of kin to him. Thou shalt not uncover the nakedness of thy father" (Leviticus 18:6, 7).

God's Law also prohibits homosexuality:

"Thou shalt not lie with man as with woman: it is an abomination" (Leviticus 18:22).

Others came up with the idea that Ham castrated his father in order to prevent him from having a fourth son. And there is another speculation that Ham had intercourse with beautiful Na'amah, Noah's wife, his mother, and as a result a fourth child was born by the name of Canaan. It is not an accident that the Bible emphasizes the fact that **"Ham is the father of Canaan"** on a few occasions (Genesis 9:18); that later on the Canaanites will reject settlement among their brothers beyond the River Nile in Egypt and on the Island of Crete in the Mediterranean Sea and go live in the Land of Canaan (Palestine) in order to meet their enemies of the house of Israel who would rule over them and fulfill the prophesy (Genesis 9:25).

Why would Moses specify in Genesis 9:18 that 'Ham was the father of the baby Canaan'?

"The sons of Noah who came out of the ark were Shem, Ham and Japheth. Ham was the father of Canaan"

It would seem there was a need to tell the readers of the Bible who the father of this boy was. Of course, if Scripture had told us that the mother of Canaan was Ham's wife, we would not have cause to speculate. We would be satisfied with the information provided.

Actually, if this was the case, there was no need to say "Ham is the Father of Canaan". It would have been naturally understood. Besides, Ham had other sons who were born before Canaan: Cush, Mizraim and Put. What was so special about the youngest, to point out specifically the name Canaan? No other babies born after the Flood were given such prominence as was Canaan. Concerning Shem and Japheth it was not said at all at this moment which sons they were fathers to. Moses deals with the genealogy of Shem, Ham and Japheth in another place, Chapter 10 of Genesis. It is also should be pointed out that the verse which we are discussing in Genesis 9:18 precedes the main story of the tragic events that resulted in 'curse of Canaan' (Genesis 9:21-25). We think that Moses had a reason to clarify this issue about the newly born boy because it had become evident to the Noah family who the mother and the father of this boy were.

Some theologians think that Noah cursed the youngest son of Ham because Ham himself was the youngest among the children of Noah. In other words, Canaan was heavily cursed by Noah only by his misfortune to be the youngest son without any guilt on him. Others suggest that there is nothing extraordinary in this story besides the fact that Ham simply violated Noah's privacy by entering his tent and looking at his father's naked body. Some speculate even further saying that Ham witnessed sexual intimacy between his drunken father and his mother. There is even a suggestion that Canaan at the time of the tragedy of 'uncovering the nakedness of Noah' was old enough to commit sin against his grandfather and followed in the footsteps of his father Ham. These explanations do not make too much sense and do not make the situation clearer. It is not even certain whether Canaan had been born at the time that Ham 'uncovered the nakedness of his father'.

According to the narrative of the Bible, "Now these are the generations of the sons of Noah, Shem, Ham, and Japheth: and unto them were **sons born after the flood**" (Genesis 10:1). It is hard to imagine that these events, when Noah 'after the Flood, began to cultivate the ground, and he planted a vineyard when he drank some of its wine, he became drunk and lay uncovered inside his ten', happened after the elapse of the space of time sufficient for Canaan to have grown up to a mature age.

In our opinion, the whole story of Ham's crime and punishment is directly connected with the 'love affair' triangle of Noah, his beautiful wife Na'amah, and their son Ham, when disgusting and shameful adultery was committed between mother and son, and, as a result, baby Canaan was born, the son of harlotry. In modern terminology day the word 'Canaan' would be replaced by 'bastard', meaning an illegitimate child born as a result of unfaithfulness. This sinful act of adultery might have signified the meaning of uncovering the nakedness of his father or mother which in Scripture is connected with sexual activity regardless who is involved: mother or father.

"You shall not uncover the nakedness of your father, which is the nakedness of your mother; she is your mother, you shall not uncover her nakedness. The nakedness of your father's wife shall you not uncover: it is your father's nakedness" (Leviticus 18:7, 8).

This fragment of the story is reported in Scripture for a reason. Moses wanted to show that the evil act Ham did to his father happened after the Flood. Just as the pre-Flood generations were wicked and sinned against their Creator, so was this to be continued by the new generations after the Deluge. Human nature and the attitude of men towards God had not changed.

It is of interest to consider the verse of the Prophet Zechariah 9:6. [This is the last time in Scripture that the name 'Philistine' is mentioned]:

"Foreigners (a mixed race, Hebrew 'mamzer', possibly connoting a bastard people) will occupy the city of Ashdod. I will destroy the pride of the Philistines".

Could not this 'mixed race, bastard people' represent the remnants of Edomites, Philistines, Canaanites, and Ishmaelites who modern day Palestinians try to represent by counterfeited claim of their inheritance to be rightful heir of these ancient peoples? They are more likely from the Edomites, whose progenitor Esau intermarried with the cursed Canaanite people. Actions of adultery are strongly prohibited by the Bible. The explanation provided might be of satisfactory to answer the questions: Why did God curse Canaan for the sin of his father Ham? Why did God curse the Canaanites, a nation, for the sin of one man?

Noah had reason to curse Canaan because God showed him what kind of people would come from Canaan who was born as a result of illegal adultery between mother and son: They would become the most evil and the worst idol worshippers, murderers, sex perverts and moral degraders, heavily linked to the overwhelming sins of Sodom and Gomorrah. In the course of history they were to become mortal enemies to, and brutal oppressors of, God's People Israel. That is why the Almighty commanded the Israelites to destroy the Canaanites.

"You must destroy all the people the Lord your God hands over to you. Show them no mercy, and do not worship their gods or they will trap you. On account of the wickedness of these nations the Lord your God will drive them out before you" (Deuteronomy 7:16; 9:5).

It is of important to notice that the 'Curse of Canaan' was limited to the people of Canaan only. The other descendants of Ham were blessed to become 'servants' in the sense of providing a high technological service to humanity.

God Blessed Japheth and Shem

God blessed Japheth with the 'enlargement' of his descendants who have truly become the most populous people in the World. Some commentators' say that this 'enlargement' applied not only to the physical characteristic but it also pertains to the intellectual ability of the Japhetic nations, perfectly expressed in philosophy, art, literature and music. The brightest manifestation of it is Greek culture which has enlightened the World aesthetically.

Unfortunately, Japheth in the End Times will be persuaded by Edom and allow himself to join the forces of Gog and Magog in the battle against Israel. Instead of serving God, he will choose to fight Him and His people Israel. His end will be a devastating defeat and massive slaughter. His own actions will condemn him to the tragic, disgraceful finale described in Ezekiel 39:17-20. The House of Israelites will show a last respect to Japheth by organizing the expanded burial of his multitudes on the Holy Land.

The blessings, God bestowed on Shem, are different in nature. They are spiritual. Canaan is to be 'servant of servants'; Japheth is to be 'Enlarged'; Shem is to be "Blessed be the Lord God of Shem" (Genesis9:26). To Ham and Japheth it was not said: "God of Ham" or "God of Japheth".

Shem is given spiritual supremacy among the nations, religious leadership. And as a result, the three greatest monotheistic religions on earth sprang out of Shem (Semites): Judaism, Christianity and Islam. By this blessing to Shem God is ensured that holiness and righteousness will be preserved through Shem, Abraham, Moses, and David, from whose seed the Messiah will come.

Only to the Israelites was given the Divine Mission to spiritually transform the ungodly World and lead it in Holiness and Righteousness to the acknowledgement of the One and only God of the Universe, Almighty God of Israel.

"You only have I chosen of all the families of the earth" (Amos 3:2).

"And you shall be to Me a kingdom of priests, and a holy nation" (Exodus 19:6).

"I will make you to be a Covenant to the people and the Light for Gentiles, that you will bring My Salvation to the ends of the earth" (Isaiah 49:6).

Because of Israel and through them, all inhabitants of the Earth will be blessed:

"And all peoples on earth will be blessed through you" (Genesis 12:31).

Israel's mission is not only to become holy and be the light to the Gentiles, but they have to show an example of it to the World and enlighten all the peoples to worship the God of Israel and His immortal Torah, in order to merit together life in the wonderful, highly spiritual World-to-Come.

To conclude this subject, we will use the wordings of Genesis19:32:

"These are the families of the sons of Noah, after their generations, in their nations: and by these were the nations divided in the earth after the Flood".

CHAPTER XIII:
WILDERNESS OF THE NATIONS

What is the 'Wilderness of the nations' of Ezekiel 20:35? Is it a real physical place or something of allegorical, symbolic, or spiritual nature?

I
The Physical Aspect

Let us examine the 'Wilderness' as the real geographical place.

To better understand the subject, we may find some key explanations in the verses of Ezekiel.

"I will bring you out from the nations and gather you from the countries where I have scattered you . . . And I will bring you into the wilderness of the Peoples, and there will I enter into judgment with you face to face. Like as I pleaded with your fathers in the wilderness of the land of Egypt, so will I plead with you, said the Lord GOD. And I will purge out from among you the rebels, and them that transgress against me: I will bring them forth out of the countries where they sojourn, and they shall not enter into the land of Israel: and ye shall know that I am the LORD" (Ezekiel 20:33-36, 38).

These verses were quoted as a future reference for our discussion. One important clue here is the fact that the Prophet compares the coming purifying of Israel in the 'Wilderness of the Peoples' to a real historical event. This was the 'wilderness of the land of Egypt, which is known as a desert of Sinai. Is there any similarity in judgment? Yes, there is.

"Your dead bodies shall fall in this wilderness . . . Doubtless you shall not come into the land, concerning which I swore to make you dwell therein, except Caleb the son of Jephunneh, and Joshua the son of Nun" (Numbers 14:29-30). Children under the age of twenty of the convicted generation of the desert were to be allowed to enter the Holy Land.

The judgment of God in the 'Wilderness' of Ezekiel is almost the same. The unbelievers and sinners will be purged out and go to the slaughter (Numbers 14:38). All of them will be brought out of the countries of their exile, but they will not enter the Promised Land, except those righteous believers with a 'new spirit' and a 'new heart'.

We cannot doubt or speculate on the 'Wilderness of Egypt'. This event is well known and generally accepted by the World; everybody knows the geographical location of the Sinai desert, the story of Exodus, the Divine Manna, receiving the Torah on Mount Sinai, and the conquest of Canaan. There were no other people or nations in the 'Wilderness of Sinai' to witness how God judged the Israelites. As Rashi puts it, "When I took you from Egypt, I took you through the wilderness which has nothing, not even any nations, so that no one see your shame as the rebellious ones among you were punished".

In the 'Wilderness of the Peoples', on the contrary, all the nations of Israelite exile will witness the judgments of God. As Radak explains, these judgments will teach all the nations powerful lessons, "The tribulations of the desert cause the nations to see and take heed".

Many scholars think that the prophesy of Ezekiel in the 'Wilderness of the Peoples' was fulfilled in the time of the Babylonian Return. Is it so? No, it is not! A careful and detailed analysis of the plain literal verses of Ezekiel 20:32-38 leads to the conclusion that this prophecy has nothing to do with the time of the Babylonian Return. It rather aims at the future Restoration and Redemption of the whole House of Israel in the days of the Mashiach and the beginning of the Messianic Era.

From Biblical and Rabbinical sources we know that God initiated the Babylonian Return by limiting it to seventy years, (Jeremiah 29:10), and after the expiration of those years, He appointed His special man,

King Cyrus of Persia, to free His People and let them go to the Promised Land to rebuild the Temple and Jerusalem. King Cyrus in 538 B.C. issued a Decree and set the captives free according to the wish of the Almighty. There were no judgments of God at that time. He did not say to the Judeans, "What you have in mind will never happen. You think that you want to be like other nations, like the different people in other countries. You want to serve wood and stone." He did not pass the captives under the rod, and did not bring them into the bond of the covenant. The rebels and transgressors against God were not purged; and the words "I will bring them forth out of the countries where they sojourn, and they shall not enter into the Land of Israel" could not have applied to the Judeans because they had not then sojourned in many countries of exile on the first place, and there had not been preset criteria as to who can enter the Land of Israel and who cannot (Ezekiel 20:32-38).

All these judgments of God were designed for the Lost Ten Tribes of Israel in Exile, who have lost their national Hebrew identity and have forgotten the God of their fathers and His live-giving Torah and have become idolaters as the people of the countries wherein they have dwelled. The time of their fulfillment is the future Restoration of the whole House of Israel in the days of the Messiah.

Meanwhile, in the time of the Babylonian Return, Jews and an insignificant number of other people from the Israelite Tribes, voluntarily, on their own will, enthusiastically decided to return to the Holy Land because they were true believers, faithful to the God of Israel and to His Laws. The vast majority of the captive Jews had decided of their own free will to stay in Babylon. That is why we consider the Babylonian Return as a Return to God in belief in comparison to the Exodus from Egypt and the modern return of the Jews (1948) to the Promised Land. This latter Returns were plagued with disbelief e.g. in the First Exodus from Egypt there was continuous rebellion in the desert; and the later creation of the Zionist State of Israel was seen as providing only a save heavens to the Jewish People after the disasters of the Holocaust.

The future 'Wilderness of the Peoples' should be compared to the Wilderness in the Exodus from Egypt: A common denominator of both wildernesses is the fact that they serve as jumping-off grounds, springboards for the Israelites on their way to the Promised Land. As the Biblical commentators correctly noted, "From the Wilderness they will enter the Land of Israel". If in the judgment of the Egyptian Exodus Wilderness the time of the wandering of the Israelites in the Wilderness before they were allowed to enter the Holy Land was forty years, in the judgment of the 'Wilderness of the peoples' no certain time is given whatsoever. We can only guess that these prophesies will happen in the 'End of Times', in the 'days of the Mashiach'. In any event, the judgment of the 'Wilderness of the Nations' should precede the prophecies of the 'Two Steaks' of Ezekiel 37:21. This will finish the business of reconciliation and reunification of the whole House of Jacob, "And say unto them, thus says the Lord GOD; Behold, I will take the children of Israel from among the nations, where they are gone, and will gather them on every side, and bring them into their own land".

Also, as in the case of the 'Wilderness of Egypt', when God created Israel as a nation, in the 'Wilderness of the Peoples' He will reconstitute the repented Israelites as a nation of the whole House of Israel again.

These points, in our view, have established similarities between the two wildernesses which, on first sight, might point out or give some hints that the 'Wilderness of the Peoples' is a physical place like the 'Wilderness of the Egypt' was, only a different location.

II
Spiritual Reality

Now let us analyze the 'Wilderness of the Peoples' as the Spiritual meaning.

'I will bring you to the 'Wilderness of the Peoples' does not indicate any particular geographical place. What it says is that God will bring the Israelites among the strange various nations as into a wilderness and execute judgments upon them 'face to face'. This wilderness does not indicate any physical geographical locality, or duration of time of the judgments. Being in 'the Wilderness of the Peoples' may be comprehended as representing the duration of time from the rejection of Israel and its punishment by Exile to their future restoration.

Why does the Prophet Ezekiel call the nations, where the Israelites live in exile, 'the Wilderness'? Our understanding goes like this: the Israelites of the Ten Tribes are the Chosen People of God, the same way as the Jewish People are also Chosen. A huge difference is that the Ten Tribes of Israel lost their national identity and forgot the God of their fathers. The Jewish People, on the other hand, are the only ones from the whole House of Israel who know their identity and keep the Torah. Both sections have a Divine task to perform. The Almighty will have prepared the glorious future for both of them. The prophecy of the 'Wilderness of the Peoples', it seems, applies only to the Ten Tribes, because Judah (or at least half of Judah) will have already been dwelling in the Promised Land.

Are not the wildernesses or deserts denoted as dry sand and fruitless soil which cannot bear fruit, nor produce anything useful for men—crops or vegetables (a land not sown, Jeremiah 2:2) and where there is not enough water to support life? We may symbolically or by way of allegory or metaphor, in the manner of the Prophet Ezekiel, explain the meaning of this. The Heathen nations of the world where the Israelites were forcefully exiled to are the 'wilderness' because they are idol worshipers. They do not know their Creator, the God of Israel. Their corrupted spiritual soil (and souls) cannot produce the holiness and righteousness required by Scripture. The absence of living waters which is the Torah, the Word of the living God, makes those nations a symbolic 'Wilderness'.

That is why God warned the Israelites: "And that which comes into your mind shall not be at all, that you say, We will be as the Gentiles, as the families of the countries, to serve wood and stone" (Ezekiel 20:32).

The destiny of Israel is better than this. They will become a holy nation of priests, a light to the Gentiles. They will bring salvation and the glory of the God of Israel to the ends of the Earth (Isaiah 49:6). All of this will happen in the time of the Messianic Age.

There are many instances in the Bible where the prophets use expressions such as 'the wilderness' or 'the desert' which symbolically represent Israel.

"I will make her like a desert, turn her into a parched land, and slay her with thirst. Therefore I am now going to allure her; I will lead her into the desert and speak tenderly to her" (Hosea 2:3, 14).

The next passage from the book of Ezekiel is very impressive and confirms even more that we are on the right track:

"And now she is planted in the wilderness, in a dry and thirsty ground" (Ezekiel 19:13). This means that Israel shall be exiled to the countries where is no true God of Israel, no Divine Torah—just dry deadly sand of idolatry and no life giving water, nor the reviving spirit of God. These are the harsh realities of the life of Israelites in Exile.

Why would the Prophet Ezekiel use all kinds of symbols, metaphors, allegories, and other symbolic language in his prophetic Book? This is a good question. But, on the other hand, why not? All God's prophets have used these techniques in order to properly and forcefully interpret their nightly dreams, God's revelations, and awesome prophetic visions.

Just compare, for instance, this Biblical passage:

"Behold, the days come, saith the Lord GOD, that I will send a famine in the land, not a famine of bread, nor a thirst for water, but of hearing the words of the LORD. And they shall wander from sea to sea, and from the north even to the east, they shall run to and fro to seek the word of the LORD, and shall not find it" (Amos 8:11-12).

Is not the Prophet describing here a spiritual famine and thirst, the Wilderness of the nations, the subject we are discussing?!

On the same theme of spiritual famine speaks this passage:

"For a long time Israel was without the true God, without a priest to teach and without the law" (2 Chronicles 15:3). Is not this a perfect

265

description of 'The Wilderness of the Peoples' of the countries of Israelite exile?

There are plenty of similar figures and symbols throughout the Book of Ezekiel that cannot be translated literally. One cannot find a confined geographical place of the 'Wilderness of the Nations', the same way as there is not a specified physical location of the 'Field of the Dry Bones' (Ezekiel 37:1); or 'The Valley of the shadow of death" (Isaiah 9:2). Who can positively identify the precise locations of those 'graves' of Israelite People? Are they in North America or England, the homeland of the sons of Joseph? Or, are they in Europe where the rest of the Tribes are residing? None of these is correct. The 'graves' (whose inhabitants shall be brought to life) of God's People Israel are in 'The Wilderness of the Nations', which are the heathen countries where Israel has been dwelling in Exile.

'The Wilderness of the Peoples' does not denote a specific geographical locality but rather a state of negative spirituality and lack of Godliness.

We would like to present another example of highly symbolical and allegorical expression which could help us shed more light on the discussed matter, and this is the passage of Ezekiel 37:12, "Behold, O my people, I will open your graves, and cause you to come up out of your graves, and bring you into the land of Israel" (Ezekiel 37:12). Many scholars think that Ezekiel speaks of resurrection of the dead. This is not the case. 'Graves' here is a metaphor, a symbolic expression of the 'Exile', to which the Israelites were forcefully subjected. The exile and captivity were always considered by the Jewish People as 'like death and the abyss' (Mid. Ps. to 71:4). We can easily substitute the term 'graves' for the 'Wilderness of the Nations' because these symbols connote almost the same meaning. If the 'graves' means the hardship of the Exile with its unspeakable suffering and persecutions, with oppression and prison like conditions; the 'Wilderness' for the Israelites also represents a spiritual death in idolatrous countries without the knowledge of the true God of Israel and His life-giving Torah.

So, why are we looking for a particular geographical location for 'The Wilderness of the Nations'? Ezekiel uses this metaphorical symbol to show the spiritual emptiness of idolatrous nations who do not know the Almighty God of Israel and His Immortal Torah. That is why God wants His People Israel to get out of this 'Wilderness'!

Likewise, why are we trying to interpret the metaphorical expression of 'open graves' as a real physical resurrection of the dead as if the Prophet had not meant a literal resurrection at all?

The 'dry bones' of Ezekiel 37:1 are also not to be understood as a resurrection of the dead, but rather as the two stages of return of the Israelites to the Holy Land and to God Almighty. The first stage is return to the Land in unbelief, represented by sinews, flesh, and skin (1948, Zionists, the modern State of Israel); the second stage of return is in belief to God, represented by the breath of life, which is the holy spirit of God (Ezekiel 37, the advent of the Messiah, and the Messianic Age).

Under layers of strange symbols, metaphors, hyperboles, fictional figures, fantastic dreams and visions, the Prophet Ezekiel persistently insists on the one and the only idea of Restoration and Redemption of the whole House of Israel which, finally, will culminate in what was described by Ezekiel 37:16-28.

There are multiple symbolic and poetical expressions like the similes 'new spirit', 'new heart', 'My sheep', 'feed in a good pasture', 'the dead will rise', 'I write My Laws in their hearts', 'clean water', 'dry bones', 'open graves', and 'The Wilderness of the people'. All of these served the Prophet as powerful tools to convey his ideas to readers as forcefully and clearly as Divine Providence wished.

Wait a minute! But what do the Sages of Talmud say? Surprise, surprise: The Rabbinical Authorities, basically, have confirmed what we just said. Rambam (Maimonides) in Moreh Nevuchim (Guide for the Perplexed 2:46) believes that the 'open graves' in the prophecy of

Ezekiel is not a physical resurrection of the dead, **but rather symbolic and in line with other prophetic visions often used by Ezekiel throughout his book** (!).

Rabbi Yehudah in the Talmud (Sanhedrin 92b) says exactly the same. In his opinion, **the entire episode of the 'dry bones' is a parable, a metaphor. Ezekiel did not mean an actual physical resurrection of the dead to eternal life** (!).

Conclusion: 'The Wilderness of the Nations' of Ezekiel 20:35 is nothing else but a metaphoric expression of the godless nations who do not know the Creator of the Universe, the Almighty God of Israel and His Divine Torah. In contrast to the historical 'Wilderness of Egypt', 'The Wilderness of the Nations' simply means the nation's spiritual barrenness, fruitlessness or wilderness.

CHAPTER XIV:
THE WARS OF GOG AND MAGOG

This is not an easy subject to understand. Before, when we were preoccupied with the Three Oaths of the Song of Songs, we thought that the Songs was the most difficult, mysterious and controversial book of the Tanakh. Now, we have since become deeply involved in trying to unlock puzzles of the prophetic texts concerning Gog's wars, we have come to realize that these prophecies contain no less (if not more!) complications and mysteries than the Songs of Solomon. There are so many controversies about the timing of these wars, their consequences, geographical locations, identity of the participants, especially of Gog and Magog, on how many nations will be involved, how many wars will be fought, their purposes, type of weaponries used, the prime target of the attack, what roles Judah and Israel will play, and much, much more.

Steven M. Collins and his Theory

One of the best experts on the Jewish-Israelite movement, and particularly on the Wars of Gog and Magog described by the Prophet Ezekiel 38 and 39 is the Christian theologian, Biblical Scholar, and esteemed author Steven M. Collins. He provides excellent commentaries on a daily basis connecting geopolitical events in the present World with prophecies concerning the future Wars of Gog and Magog.

In his work, 'What Ezekiel 38-39 Reveals about a Future WWIII', the author begins with an analysis of the three prophecies of Ezekiel

37, 38 and 39. Chapter 37, Steven Collins said, contains two separate prophecies, called 'Dry Bones' and 'Two Sticks'. Chapters 38 and 39 consist of one prophecy each of the future war of Gog and Magog. All three prophecies have their own distinct subject, different time-settings, and chronologically are not linked with each other.

In his opinion, the 'Dry Bones' prophecy of Ezekiel 37:1-14 concerns the resurrection of the 'whole House of Israel' which will occur one thousand years after the advent of the Messiah.

Another distinct prophecy of the same Chapter 37:15-28 'Two Sticks' prophecy, is a prediction of the complete and final reunification of all the tribes of Jacob under the leadership of a resurrected King David which is going to occur at the beginning of the Messianic Age.

Concerning the third prophecy of Ezekiel 38 and 39, the Gog and Magog War, he came up with a very bold and well argumented theory, basically saying that this war begins at the earlier stage of the redemption, "in the latter years", at the end of our current age, prior to the reunification of the whole house of Jacob and advent of the Messiah, before the Messianic Age begins.

All three prophecies are not chronologically sequential, they are in three different 'Biblical ages', and they are written in reverse time order: the Gog and Magog War, reunification of the 'Two Sticks', and (after an interval of one thousand years) a general mass resurrection of the 'Dry Bones'.

The geographical target of attack of the armies of Gog will not be the Land of Israel, where the modern 'tiny' Jewish state presently exists (Zephaniah 2:6-10), but rather the countries of West Europe, the USA, Canada, Australia, New Zealand and other territories, where the so called "Lost Ten Tribes of Israel" in exile are residing. Steven Collins identifies Gog as a chief prince of Meshech and Tubal, leader of Russia, and the 'land of Magog' as that part of Asia which is within the modern territory of Southern Russia.

According to Steven Collins, 'Gomer and all his bands' became most populous China; 'Togarmah of the north quarters and all his bands' is interpreted as a group of people closely related ethnically to the Chinese and located to the north of China's mainland: Mongolia, Siberia, Manchuria and North Korea. All of this is in accordance with his statement that Japheth's descendants were to be found in the Oriental regions of Asia. From what the Bible reveals, concluded S. Collins, it will be an alliance of Russia, China and Iran along with other Communist or East-bloc nations and radical Islamic nations in South-Central Asia and North Africa.

In his explanation as to why the target of Gog's attack will be the countries of the West, North America, and NATO, rather than the Jewish state in the Land of Israel, Steven Collins pointed out that there is no recollection of Judah in the prophecies of Ezekiel 38 and 39 as, for instance, in Zechariah 12 and 14. When God speaks of Judah, he means the Jewish nation, the modern Israelis; and when God speaks of Israel, He means the Ten Tribes of Israel in exile. Therefore, since Judah and Israel will not yet have been reunited and will live separately in different countries of the World as distinct entities, and only the name of Israel is written in the prophecies of Ezekiel, it means that the subject of Gog's attack will be the countries, where the Ten Tribes of Israel live. The Prophecy is therefore primarily directed at the modern nations of the tribes of Ephraim and Manasseh which are Great Britain and the USA.

Quite an interesting explanation is given by the author on the matter of the "Mountains of Israel" which in the Scriptures are positively connected with the Land of Israel on multiple occasions.

God said to Gog: "After many days you shall be visited: in the latter years you shall come into the land that is brought back from the sword, and is gathered out of many people, against the mountains of Israel, which have been always waste: but it is brought forth out of the nations, and they shall dwell safely, all of them" (Ezekiel 38:8).

In the opinion of Steve Collins, the 'Mountains of Israel' "cannot possibly be the Israeli nation for two reasons: (1) they are not high enough to be true mountains and (2) they have most assuredly not been "always waste." But if one flies over the Rocky Mountains of North America, it could be seen how high they are and there is no sign of human habitation over much of its expanse". So, the 'Mountains of Israel' in the Prophecies of Ezekiel "describes North America, not the Israeli nation".

The nation which is "brought back from the sword, and is gathered out of many people", continues the author "is the United States of America, the melting pot nation".

How does he explain away such a descriptions of Israel's condition as "they shall dwell safely, all of them" (Verse 8); or "dwelling without the walls and having neither bars nor gates" (Verse 11)?

"Well", he said, "after winning the Cold War, the Western nations of the house of Israel implemented rapid disarmament which dramatically reduced their military forces and their capabilities. By accident or design, the East Bloc nations have, by 'losing' the Cold War, succeeded in weakening the West's defense of its own homelands." It certainly does not make one believe that 'Israel will dwell safely, all of them'!

And what about the Arab countries? Will they take part in Gog's alliance against Israel? Mr. Collins thinks that there are two possibilities. "Since Ezekiel 38:2-6 states clearly that the attacking evil alliance of Gog and Magog will include 'bands' and 'many people' who are not named, it allows the possibility that the Arab nations will be allied with Russia, China and Iran". The second possibility, is that the Arabs are the descendants of Abraham, of the same Semitic stock as the Israelites; they 'have a great deal of oil wealth and are closely linked to America, Great Britain and the Western nations via economical and commercial ties' and through the democratic values planted by America and the West in countries like Iraq, Kuwait, Lebanon, etc.; plus "the fact that Iran (Persia, historical enemy of the Arabs) is allied to Russia, can also be a reason why the Arabs would NOT be part of the Russia-Chinese-Iran alliance."

Another participant in Gog's bloody attack against the nations of Israel is Esau, son of Isaac, the oldest brother of Jacob, whom the Bible names Edom. S. Collins believes that the descendants of Esau through his oldest son Teman (Genesis 36:34) become the Ottoman Empire and the modern day Republic of Turkey, because "the consonants of

Teman and Ottoman are identical". Turkey is a member of NATO and, as such, is allied to the West and Europe.

"However, there is one branch of Edomites family called Amalekites, which historically is intensely hostile to Israel; they likely will be allied with the armies of Gog and Magog at the end of this age."

Mr. Collins concluded that, since the Semitic and Caucasian nations are descended from Abraham, and the prophecy of Ezekiel 38 and 39 does not mention a single Semitic nation in the offensive alliance of Gog's armies, "it allows the possibility [another one?!] that all modern nations, descended from Abraham, will be on the same side" with Israel. Wow! This is a very interesting and important observation!

This, in short, is the theory of Steve Collins concerning the War of Gog and Magog as described in Ezekiel 38 and 39. Do we agree with his ideas? Regarding some aspects of his thoughts, Yes; but for key points of his theory, we do not.

Before we are going to put forward our reasoning, we would like to introduce to our readers to a few versions and interpretations from different sources on the subject of the prophecy of Ezekiel 38 and 39 which describes the Wars of Gog against Judah and Israel in the latter years. Nobody argues about the timing of these wars in general, because the prophet Ezekiel clearly states that Gog's attack will occur 'after many days', 'in the latter years', 'it (the attack) shall be in the latter days' (Ezekiel 38:8, 16). Even so, there are still a few misunderstandings in relation to Redemption, Reunification, Advent of the Messiah and the Messianic Age events as to the following: Whether the Wars of Gog will have begun before reunification of Judah and Israel? Will the Messiah (son of Joseph or son of David) have been revealed and the Messianic Age have started? Will the armies of Gog have initiated this attack on Israel after those events? A clarification of these matters is very important for understanding the true meanings of the Prophecies of Ezekiel.

Rambam (Maimonides), the great Jewish Sage, in Hilchos Melachim (Laws of the Kings of Israel and their Wars,12:2) advises us not to go into a deep detailed study on the subjects of the Wars of Gog, the coming of the Messiah and other sequences of future eschatological events. The "knowledge of these matters leads neither to fear not to love of God." We shall not be able to understand the exact meaning of many obscure passages of Scripture until the time of their occurrence. It is enough to know future events in accordance with what Prophecy revealed in general, without going beyond the plain meaning of the verses. "The detailed studies of these matters are in no way Principles of Faith," concluded Rambam. Well, despite this, we will try to go into some deep detailed study of Ezekiel 38 and 39 to satisfy our curiosity and in order to counter the arguments of other theories. We have nothing to lose: 'knowledge of these matters lead neither to fear not to love of God and in no way are principals of the faith'.

Gog from the Land of Magog

Who is this mysterious Gog, ruler from the land of Magog and the prince of Rosh (or just chief prince) of Meshech and Tubal, around whom so many tragic events will culminate in the End Times? Gog is a personality, a future demonic king, a despot and a tyrant. Many Bible expositors think that King Gyges (716-678 or 687-652 b.c.) of Lydia, in western Anatolia (the modern Republic of Turkey) was that legendary Gog of the Bible. The ancient Greek philosopher Plato (428-347 b.c.) related a myth about Gog, who was a shepherd for the Lydian King Candaules (735-718 b.c.). While in the field, Gog found in a cave a golden ring which could make him invisible any time he put it on his finger. So, the legend goes, Gog went to the palace, became invisible, seduced the queen, killed the king and made himself the ruler of Lydia. His country was called Gygea or Gog's Land.

Some scholars believe that Cambyses (530-523 b.c.), the king of Persia, or Antiochus Epiphanes (175-163 b.c.), the king of Syria, is represented by Gog from the land of Magog.

Others speculate that the Septuagint translation of Amos 7:1 with a connection to Proverbs 30:27 pictures Gog as a 'king of locusts', leading his hordes in attack on Israel in the latter years.

"Thus the Lord showed me, and behold, a swarm of locusts were coming, and behold, one of the young devastating locusts was Gog, the King" (Amos 7:1)

Christians point out from Revelation 9:3-11 that Gog of Ezekiel 38 and 39 is the 'Angel of Abyss', whose name is Abaddon in Hebrew or Apollyon in Greek, who is also called the 'Prince of Hell' and 'Destroyer'.

Those who prefer the Russian theory that Gog will lead the former Soviet Union forces allied with China and Iran, together with another group of nations, put forward the candidature of Vladimir Putin as a future candidate for the personification of Gog.

There are adherents of the Common Market of Europe theory, saying that Gog will come from a newly resurrected Holy Roman Empire who will ally with other enemy nations in wars against Israel. The role of Gog is given to a future leader of Germany, "a little horn", who will become the main force behind the European Union.

This 'king of fierce countenance', described by Prophet Daniel, is extremely crafty, cunning, deceitful—and bloody-individual, who will preach peace but practice war (Daniel 8:23-25).

Gog is also the attributed name of an Angelic being, a Principality, given charge over the land of Turkey, in a similar way to the 'Prince of Persia', 'Prince of Greece', or Michael, one of the chief Princes, who was given charge over Israel" (Daniel 10:12-21).

There is also an opinion that Gog and Magog are the Ten Lost Tribes of Israel trapped behind the legendary Gates-barrier built by Alexander the Great in the Caucasus Mountains to prevent them from invading the nations of the south.

The Khazars who lived between the Caspian and Black Seas were also associated with Gog and Magog by Christian and Muslim writers. Ahmad ibn Fadlan, the Arab traveler, noted in his writings that Gog and Magog were ancestors of the Khazars.

A Georgian chronicle too identifies the Khazars with Gog and Magog, describing them as "wild men with hideous faces and the manners of wild beasts, eaters of blood."

Another opinion says that the place of Gog may possibly be in Georgia of the former USSR whose capital is Tbilisi (indicating a connection with Tubal, son of Japheth). There was a Gogarene province in Iberia (Georgia) in the Caucasian Mountains.

Some Muslim scholars believed that Gog and Magog are the Mongols who in the past caused a lot of damage to Muslim Civilization in Central Asia. The Great Wall of China in the Arabic language is called 'the Wall of Al Magog'.

In Midrashic literature Gog is linked with Romulus, a legendary founder of ancient Rome. In Midrash Bereishis Rabban 76:5 Gog is "the 11th king of the 4th beast with the 10 horns" of Daniel chapter 7.

The Hebrew Bible (1Chronicles 5:4) mentions the name Gog as that of an ancestral figure from the tribe of Reuben, first born son of Israel.

There is also a Talmudic tradition that Gog will be a descendant of Esau (Edom), the archenemy of Israel, and his fighting forces will consist mainly of Japhethic nations in alliance with Hammitic countries.

Malbim, (1809-1879a.c.), the Russian Rabbi Meir Leibush, a preacher and Bible commentator, said that the identity of Gog will remain shrouded in mystery until the time he actually arrives.

The Land of Magog and People Associated with It

There are many opinions concerning the whereabouts of this Land of Magog and what people possess it. The majority of Bible scholars agree that the Land of Magog geographically represents the territory of Central Asia, including regions of Southern Russia with all its Islamic nations north of the Caucasus Mountains. In conjunction with the phrase of Ezekiel 38:3, "Behold, I am against thee, O Gog, prince of Rosh, Meshech and Tubal", this most certainly points to Russia. A wrong translation of the Hebrew word "rosh" also heavily contributed to the Russian identification. Instead of translating "rosh" as an adjective, meaning 'head' or 'chief', as it has been translated from Scripture on more than 400 occasions, the word 'Rosh' was mistranslated as a noun, indicating a place. Rosh sounds like Rossia, Rashu, Ros, Rus, Russia. Meshech and Tubal are too easily associated with the Russian capital Moscow and the biggest city of western Siberia—Tobolsk. After all of this, how is it possible that the Land of Magog could not be Russia? In this case, Biblical Gog will appear in Russia and will lead the massive military forces of Russia, all the—'stan' Muslim republics of Southern Russia; plus Iran, Ethiopia, Sudan, Libya; "Gomer with all his troops and house of Togarmah of the north quarters, and all his bands, many people with you" (Ezekiel 38:5-6).

'Many people with you' is understood here as all the lands surrounding Israel i.e. the Arab and Muslim nations. They will join the armies of Gog against Israel. **This is the so-called 'Russian Theory'.** It is the most popular one, and amongst its followers are well known theological writers such as Hal Lindsey, Dwight Pentecost, John Walvoord, Jack Van Impe, Pastor F.M. Riley, and, of course, Steven M. Collins (we will discuss his teachings later), and many more.

Other researchers strongly object to the 'Russian Theory' and come up with different explanations concerning the climactic events of the End Times. They say that 'Meshech' is not Moscow but 'Moshi', 'Moscocheni', 'Mushki', ancient tribes from the time of Ezekiel 27:13; that 'Tubal' is not Tobolsk but 'Tubalu', 'Thobelites', 'Tibareni', who dwelt in Central Asia and in the regions of the Black and Caspian Seas. The Land of Magog, according to this theory, is the modern day Muslim Republic of Turkey, Southern Russia with all the 'stan' countries and Northern Iran. Gomer, Gimarrai, are according to historian Josephus Flavius, 'Antiquities of the Jews', chapter 6:1, "those whom the Greeks now call Galatians, (Galls), but were then called Gomerites". The Scythians were called Magogites. In 700 b.c. they were expelled from the Southern steppes of Russia into what is today Turkey.

Togarmah, the third son of Gomer, dwelt in ancient Cappodocia, which is in modern Turkey, and was known by the names of Tegarma, Tagarma, Til-garimmu, and Takarama.

Meshech, Tubal, Gomer and Togarmah, with all their bands, are descendants of Japheth, and the place of their settlements is mainly in Turkey and the Southern countries of Russia: Turkmenistan, Uzbekistan, Azerbaijan, Kazakhstan, Kyrgyzstan, Tajikistan, and Pakistan-about 30 nations, united by Islam and by the Turkic languages. They will form a confederation to conquer and destroy Israel. It will also be a religious crusade in the spirit of Islamic Jihad for the sole purpose of proving that the Muslim religion of the god Allah and his messenger Mohammed is superior to the religion of the God of Israel and His prophet Moses.

Most of these people are Sunni Muslims and very radical Islamists. They hate the Jewish people, America and the Western democracies. Their goal is to unite the Central Asian nations and, ultimately, the entire World under the Muslim religion and establish a Global Caliphate with Shariah Laws. Given the latest political developments of Turkey in the international sphere, its ties with Syria and Iran, support of radical Islam and the terrorist activities of Hezbollah and Hamas against Israel, the impression is that the current leadership is pushing the country away from Ataturk's vision of a peaceful secular Republic. They are moving away from NATO and towards radical Islam. It would not be a surprise to see King Gog coming out of Turkey, the land of Magog, to lead that vast multitude of Islamic nations in attack against Israel. There are indications that the Russians with troops and advisers will be involved. Russia has been heavily committed to arming and training their Arab and Muslim client-states for many years, and anti-Semitism in Russia is on the rise. **This is the so called 'Caucasian Theory'.**

Close to this scenario is the **'Hashemite Kingdom Theory'**: the Islamic coalition of nations make up the lands occupied by Magog, Gomer, Togarmah, Meshech and Tubal. Turkey will attack Israel from the north; Iran—from the east; Libya—from the west; and Sudan—from the south.

The 'All Europe Theory': Gog and Magog represent here the Japhethic races identified with European nations. This is not a widely supported interpretation of the Gog and Magog Wars.

And the last one is called the 'Indo-European Theory' where Gog and Magog include an alliance of Japhethic, Muslim and Arab nations: Russia, Turkey, the nations of Central Asia, Southern Russia and the Black Sea area.

Out of all these theories, most attention should be given to the 'Russian' and the 'Caucasian' ones.

The 'Dry Bones' and 'Two Sticks' Prophecies

Mr. S. Collins interpreted Ezekiel 37:1-14 as a future resurrection of 'the whole house of Israel' which will occur at the end of one thousand years after the Messianic Age. He said that this is a separate prophecy, distinct from the previous or following ones, with its own subject matter, timing, and there is no textual indications that this prophecy is chronologically linked with the "Two Sticks" or the Wars of Gog.

Do we accept this interpretation of Ezekiel 37:1-14? No, we do not. And here is why. Strangely enough, we found admission of the author that the 'separate' prophecy of resurrection might be a "continuation of the prophecy which began in Ezekiel 36:16". This undoubtedly suggested to us that Ezekiel 36:16 is a prophecy of resurrection too. Let us take a close look at those verses. In the verses 16-23 God rebukes Israel for their wrongdoings and disobeying Him.

"I scattered them among the heathen, and they were dispersed through the countries: according to their way and according to their doing I judged them" (Verse 19).

God said that He will have pity on Israel and will take them out from the lands of their exile to the Promised Land, clean them with His spirit and give them a new heart. All of this God will do in order to 'sanctify My great name'.

"For I will take you from among the heathen and gather you out of all countries, and will bring you into your own land" (Verse 24). God is reassuring His people that they are not forgotten by Him, that the time will come when He will fulfill all the good Words He spoke in Scripture concerning His People Israel.

"Then I will sprinkle clean water upon you, and you shall be clean. A new heart also will I give you. And I will put My spirit within you, and cause you to walk in My statutes, and you shall keep My judgments, and do them" (Verses 20-28).

In the conclusion of chapter 36:28-38 the prophet Ezekiel continues to inform his readers that Israel will again become 'My people' and the Almighty will be 'their God' (Verse 28). Israel will repent of all their iniquities and discard their abominations (Verse 31). The Land of Israel will blossom in beauty and productivity. "And the desolate land shall be tilled, whereas **it lay desolate in the sight of all that passed by**. This land is become like the garden of Eden" (Verses 34, 35). God will multiply the people of Israel, and their life stock, and rebuild the waste cities.

"I the Lord have spoken it, and I will do it" (Verses 36-38).

How in the world could one interpreted Ezekiel 36:16-38 as a prophecy of physical resurrection and connect it with Ezekiel 37:1-14?!

Objectively speaking, these two prophecies are connected, very much so, but not as prophecies of resurrection in the real, physical sense, as the author tries to convince us. Both chapters have the same theme which is the revival and renewal of the whole house of Israel with 'a new heart and a new spirit'. It is also a renewal of the Land, a new bond between the Israelites and the Holy Land. Throughout his entire book Ezekiel taught and prophesied to the exiled House of Israel God's message of hope and love, encouraged their faith and comforted them. The Israelites were contaminated with sin and punished by God for their transgressions by dispersion to the lands of their enemies. Being in exile for long centuries and exposed to its harsh conditions of persecutions and unspeakable sufferings, they lost their Israelite identity; their faith in God's Covenant was utterly gone; the light of the Torah did not shined, and they became spiritually dead. That is why these people (in the metaphorical form of dry bones) are crying:

"Our bones are dry, and our hope is lost: we are cut off for our parts" (Ezekiel 37:11). They are cut off from God, Torah, the Land of Israel, Jerusalem, and from the Judaic faith. They have no spiritual strength, no physical ability to deliver themselves from their graves to which they were forcefully (by the sword) confined in exile. The Jewish people considered the lands of their exile as the lands of their captivity, as being like prisons, and graves. The restoration from the lands of their enemies was regarded as 'like from the death'.

It is interesting to note that from the beginning of the vision of Ezekiel the 'dry bones' are displayed in the open field, representing those Israelites (the Ten Tribes) for whom exile was not actual captivity (Ezekiel 37:1-2); whereas in Ezekiel 37:12-13 the 'dry bones' are placed in graves representing the actual physical captivity of the Jews in exile. Nevertheless, in both cases the 'dry bones' are a metaphoric expression for the spiritual national death of the whole House of Israel. The task of the prophet was to bring good news to his people who had been deprived of their country and committed to the graves of exile; to revive their hope and encourage their faith, to stir up their spirit of freedom and redemption; to show that the House of Israel is still God's people, that the God of Israel has not broken His Covenant with them, that He still loves them, and that the time will come when He will take proper care of them.

The Prophets did not speak of a Physical Resurrection of the Dead in a Real Sense

"Thus saith the Lord God: Behold, O My people, I will open your graves, and cause you to come up out of your graves, and bring you into the Land of Israel" (Ezekiel 37:12).

This is not a separate and distinct prophecy of real physical resurrection which supposedly occurs after a thousand years of the Messianic Age. The 'open graves' events, the restoration of the most hopeless sinners of the whole house of Israel, must happen prior to the Messianic Age and the Wars of Gog and Magog. The Spiritual death of the children of Israel will not last forever. No matter how harsh, hopeless and seemingly endless the exile was, no matter how much the bones be dried out, the spirit of God has the power to restore the hope and faith of His people and ultimately redeem them. Through the prophet Ezekiel, God's spirit will awaken the Tribes of Israel to acknowledge their God and their Divine Destiny in the World to come. By opening their graves God ensured that the time of the exile is over. He will take them from the valley of the shadow of death (exile) and remove the darkness from the eyes and hearts of His People. The Prophecy will be fulfilled. "The people that walked in darkness have seen a great light: they that dwell in the land of the shadow of death, upon them hath the light shined" (Isaiah 9:2).

It is time for the Israelites to get out of the lands of their enemies and establish their own politically independent State in the Holy Land. The first stage of redemption was successfully accomplished by the Jewish people in 1948. The Zionists, great patriots and heroes of the Jewish nation, were the ones who built the state of Israel and made a 2000 years long dream become a beautiful reality.

"Who hath heard such a thing? Who hath seen such a things? Shall the earth be made to bring forth in one day? Or shall a nation be born at once? For as soon as Zion travailed, she brought forth her children" (Isaiah 66:8).

Rabbi Yehudah in the Sanhedrin 92b confirmed exactly what we are saying. In his opinion, **the entire episode of the 'dry bones' is a parable, a metaphor. Ezekiel did not mean an actual physical resurrection of the dead to eternal life.**

Rambam in Moreh Nevuchim (Guide for the Perplexed) 2:46 believes that the 'open graves' in the prophecy of Ezekiel is not physical resurrection of the dead, but rather in line with other symbolic prophetic visions often used by Ezekiel throughout his book. Even he admitted that in the Messianic Time, if God wills, there might be some resurrections of the dead, those resurrections will be temporary; the resurrected people will possess all the characteristics of mortals: eat, drink, be visible in their physical bodies, be able to produce offspring, and eventually die, as any other men on earth, after a long and happy life during the years of the Messianic Age. Maimonides strongly differentiates between a temporal physical resurrection in the Messianic Time and an eternal spiritual resurrection in the End Time for the World-To-Come, and calls those who believe otherwise 'utterly foolish' and their theories 'follies'.

The 'dry bones' prophecy of Ezekiel is not real physical resurrection of the dead. This prophecy is a continuation of previous passages of different chapters speaking of the same theme—the spiritual awakening and restoration of Israel. This may be seen from many verses in Ezekiel. Just compare the following wordings.

The 'Dry Bones' verses of Ezekiel 37:1-14

"These bones are the whole house of Israel: behold, they say, our bones are dry, and our hope is lost: we are cut off for our parts. I will open your graves, and bring you, My people, into the land of Israel. I shall put My spirit in you. Then shall you know that I the Lord have spoken it and performed id" (Ezekiel 37:11-14).

Relevant Verses from other Chapters of Ezekiel

"And I will give them one heart, and I will put a new spirit within you" (Ezekiel 11:19).

"For I will take you from among the nations, and gather you out of all countries, and will bring you into your own land. Then will I sprinkle clean water upon you, and you shall be clean. A new heart also will I give you, and a new spirit will I put within you.

And you shall be My people, and I will be your God. Then the nations shall know that I the Lord. I the Lord have spoken it, and I will do it" (Ezekiel 36:24-28, 36).

The wordings and the purposes of these prophecies are amazingly the same. They contain the same prophetic Plan outlined by God for the people of Israel which include the rejection of sin, turning to God, reunification of all the House of Israel, ingathering in the Holy Land, and Final Redemption with the advent of the Messiah, son of David.

Even the symbolic, metaphorical language is the same. Just consider: "I will sprinkle clean water upon you, and you shall be clean. A new spirit will I put within you" (Ezekiel 36).

Nobody would understand these passages as if God gave a bath or a shower to His People in order to wash them because they were dirty, or transplanted by means of surgery 'a new heart' because of the physical failure of a human heart.

"I will give them an undivided heart. I will remove from them their heart of stone and give them a heart of flesh" (Ezekiel 11:19).

What is the meaning of people having an 'undivided heart'? Is it really possible for the nations to have one undivided human heart? Do we have to believe that the house of Israel have hearts made of stone?

"Behold, I, even I, will search My sheep and seek them out. I will feed them in a good pasture" (Ezekiel 34:11-14).

Not one student of the Bible takes these words literally as if God is speaking of real sheep that He is going to 'feed in a good pasture'. Without doubt, anyone would understand that 'sheep' here is a mere metaphor for the people of Israel. And 'feed in a good pasture' means spiritual restoration to the Laws of Moses, to the Torah, to rebuilt Temple and return to the God of Israel.

"I will open the graves. I will put My spirit in you. Then shall you know that I am the Lord" (Ezekiel 37).

Here is the same story. Why would we interpret 'open the graves' as a real physical resurrection of the dead if the Prophet had not meant literal resurrection at all? In the prophecies of Isaiah, concerning the life of Israelites in exile, the Prophet also uses metaphorical expressions such as "people walking in darkness," and "valley of the shadow of death" (Isaiah 9:2).

Very interesting in this respect are verses 14 and 19 of chapter 26, where Isaiah speaks of the resurrection of the dead in terms remarkably similar to Ezekiel 37:13:

"Your dead will live; their bodies will rise. You, who dwell in the dust, awake and shout for joy. For you dew is as the dew of the morning; the earth will give birth to her dead" (v.19).

Many think that this prophecy speaks of a real, physical resurrection of the dead. We think that it is not the case. We see it as the spiritual expression, with the help of allegory and metaphor, of the Biblical story of the Babylonian Captivity and Exile. Here are the same motives as in the 'Dry Bones' passage of Ezekiel 37:1-14. These include God's people rooted out of their Land, their Temple destroyed, their king, princes and priests killed, deprived of the freedom and privileges they had enjoyed as a nation. Now they are captives and heavily oppressed in the lands of their enemies, "dwelling in the dust", in poverty and neglect. The impression is that the Prophet Isaiah himself asks God to restore His people from the death of Captivity to the previous condition of a free and independent nation, to return them to the Holy Land and Jerusalem, to rebuild the Temple, to become again God's chosen nation, when they 'awake and sing' in joy and happiness. This is similar to the 'open graves' of Ezekiel 37:13. Once again we have to remind our readers that the dispersion, captivity and oppression of the Jewish people in the lands of their enemies and the very harsh conditions of Exile were taken by them as synonymous of being in 'graves', in prison; while deliverance from the lands of their enemies and restoration they evaluated 'as resurrection from the death', as coming out 'from the graves'. Verse 14 confirms our position that Isaiah is not talking of a literal resurrection of the dead:

"The dead will not live. They are deceased, they shall not rise. You have visited and destroyed them, and made all their memory to perish" (Isaiah 26:14).

Why such a contradiction where in v.19 'the dead will rise' and in v.14 'the dead will not rise'? The answer is found according to the context of chapter 16. The explanation lies in the fact that verse14 speaks of the enemies of the Jewish People, tyrants and oppressors, the wicked idol worshippers who should be destroyed utterly for what they have done to the righteous people of Israel. They deserved severe punishment from God and 'their dead should not rise'. In contrast, verse 19 pleads with God to deliver His faithful People from the long-continued sufferings of captivity and oppression, to bring them back to the Promised Land, and restore them to glory and to the liberty of worshipping the God of Israel. That is why, contrary to their foes, 'your dead will live'.

"Soon all your captives will be released! Imprisonment, starvation, and death will not be your fate" (Isaiah 51:14).

These reassuring words of the Prophet are in line with what he said in Chapter 26:19, "Awake and sing, your dead will rise", meaning that people of Israel will be delivered from captivity and restored to their previous position as a free nation. Exile and captivity were always considered by the Jewish People as 'like death and the abyss' (Mid. Ps. to 71:4).

Both prophets, Isaiah and Ezekiel, use the same poetical and allegorical methods in expressing their prophetical visions of the future liberation of their people, the end of captivity and restoration to the Land and God of Israel. This way they provide comfort to captives, to shore up their spirits and keep their hopes alive. The same sentiments may be found in the words of the Prophet Jeremiah: "I will put My Law in their inward parts, and write it in their hearts" (Jeremiah 31:33).

The similes of 'clean water', 'new heart', 'new spirit', 'heart of stone', 'write My Laws in their hearts', 'your dead will live', 'valley of the shadow of death', 'dry bones' and 'open graves' are perfectly in line with the metaphorical symbolism the Prophet Ezekiel uses throughout his entire book, according to the Great Religious Philosopher, Rambam!

When will these Prophecies be Fulfilled?

God will spiritually revive His people ('open graves') and bring the house of Israel to the Promised Land in the 'latter years', at the end of this Age, **at the dawn of the Messianic Time, before the wars of Gog and Magog.** In no way can one interpret fulfillment of this prophecy as the physical resurrection of the whole house of Israel at the end of the Messianic Age after one thousand years! The 'opening of the graves' means rather the End of the Exile and the beginning of Redemption. The Prophet Jeremiah speaks in the same spirit of the 'open graves' speaks the prophet Jeremiah: "For the Lord hath redeemed Jacob; at the same time will I be the God of all the families of Israel, and they shall be My People" (Jeremiah 31:1, 11).

To bring the whole house of Israel to the Holy Land after one thousand years of the Messianic Age, is simply absurd, because in Ezekiel 36:10 the prophet said: "I will multiply the great number of people upon you, (the Land of Israel), even the whole house of Israel and the cities will be inhabited and the waste ruins will be rebuilt," or "You (Gog) turn your hand upon the desolate places that are now inhabited, and upon the people that are gathered out of the nations" (Ezekiel 38:12).

The timing of these events cannot be after the Messianic Age because it is hard to imagine that the millennia of the Golden Age of Humanity would bring destruction and waste to the inhabitants of the Earth, and particularly to the Land of God's people Israel.

"They shall beat their swords into plowshares and their spears into pruning hooks; **nation will not lift sword against nation** and they will no longer study warfare. **They will neither harm nor destroy** on all My holy mountain, for the earth will be full of the knowledge of the Lord" (Isaiah 2:4; 11:6-9). The Universal 'Day of rest' and Peace is what the Messianic World all about!

Despite the position of Mr. S. Collins that the prophecies of Ezekiel 37-39 are not sequential and belong to three different Biblical 'ages' and are written in reverse time order, especially the 'Dry Bones' prophecy requiring an interval of one thousand years after the others, we cannot accept his reasoning because it is not supported by evidence from Scripture. Of course, if one takes the 'Dry Bones' as the prophecy of a future physical resurrection of the whole House of Israel which will occur one thousand years after the Messianic Age, and stick (wrongly!) to this position, then all above mentioned fantasies are possible. We have already shown that this is not the case.

The prophecy of the 'Dry Bones' is also directly connected in time sequence and subject matter with the following prophecy of the 'two sticks' described in Ezekiel 37:15-28. These two prophecies are speaking of the same events which are supposed to happen in the future with "the whole house of Israel" in the same time context of the 'latter years', just before or at the dawn of the millennial reign of the Messiah. The 'Dry Bones' episode will definitely precede the events of the 'Two Sticks'. Without the spiritual revival of 'the Dry Bones', there will be no reunification of Judah and Joseph of 'the Two Sticks'. Firstly, God will 'open graves' of the 'whole house of Israel' by means of 'a new heart and a new spirit' which in turn will help awaken them to their Israelite identity (the so called Ten 'Lost' Tribes of Israel). The 'opening of the graves' is a Divine Decree, issued by God Himself, and simply means the End of the Exile and the beginning of Redemption. Secondly, this spiritually reborn 'whole House of Israel' that rejects the sin and turns to God, will be ready for the 'Two Sticks' to join together. God will make them one Kingdom and one nation again,—a nation of priests, a light to the World. Still, it will not be the final Redemption of Israel but a preliminary one, a step or stage closer: The Final Redemption of the whole House of Israel will follow immediately the destruction of the armies of Gog and Magog and the end of the war (Ezekiel 39:22-29).

The Exact Timing of the Gog-Magog Wars

This is the question. Mr. S. Collins believes that the attack of Gog will happen "during the climatic years at the end of our current age before the Millennium/Messianic Age begins". According to him, "there can be no doubt about the time-setting for Ezekiel 38-39's prophecy. All that is needed is to accept God's Word at face value".

We respectfully disagree with these statements. The sequential time order of the prophetic events of Ezekiel 37-39 is directly connected with, and lies within, the same Biblical Age of the 'Latter Years', just at the dawn of the Messianic Age. Many preceding chapters in the book of Ezekiel lead and prepare the way for the 'opening graves' of the spiritual revival of the whole house of Israel whose 'dry bones' had lost hope and faith to survive the seemingly endless imprisonment of the Exile. And, as we already pointed out, this 'opening of the graves', directly leads, in time sequence and subject matter, to the following events of: Reconciliation, Reunification, the Advent of the Messiah son of Joseph and the beginning of the blessed Messianic Age with the Messiah, son of David.

This scope of events and, particularly its timing, also includes defeating the surrounding Arab and Muslim nations (Zechariah 12:6; Isaiah 11:13-14), restoration of the Holy Land to its Biblical borders, tremendous development of economy, commerce, agriculture and establishment of a safe and prosperous environment for all people of Israel.

And then, when all the conditions of Ezekiel 37:8, 11-12 are met, then and only then, the hordes of Gog and Magog will attack Israel!

Rambam (Maimonides), the greatest Sage of Rabbinical Law and Tradition, was of the opinion that "the plain meaning of the words of the prophets seems to indicate that the **war of Gog and Magog will take place at the beginning of the Messianic Era**" (Mishneh Torah, Hilkhos Melakhim 12:2)!

Very interesting in this regard is the story of the eleven Century a.c. Midrash Vayosha (Wa-Yosha or Wayosha) based on Exodus 14:30 and 15:18 and describing events of the Gog and Magog War:

"**And when the days of the Messiah arrive**, <u>Gog and Magog</u> will come up against the Lord of Israel, because they will hear that Israel is without a king and sits in safety. Instantly they will take with them the seventy-one nations and go up to Jerusalem, and they will say; "Pharaoh was a fool to command that the males [of the Israelites] be killed and to let the females live. Balaam was an idiot that he wanted to curse them and did not know that their God had blessed them. Haman was insane in that he wanted to kill them, and he did not know their God can save them. I shall not do as they did, but shall fight against their God first, and thereafter I shall slay them . . ."

What we see from this passage is that the armies of Gog and Magog will attack Israel at the beginning of the Messianic Era, 'when the days of the Messiah arrive', and that the invasion of the hordes of Gog will be directed primary against the God of Israel Himself ('I shall fight against their God first') and then against His People Israel.

But God's response to this is clear: "I have many messengers whom I can send into battle. But the war against Gog and Magog I shall wage Myself. Their destruction shall be complete" (Esther Rabbah 7:23.)

The Reunification of all the Tribes of Israel (Judah and Ephraim) described in Ezekiel 37:15-28 is not one momentous event. It will not happen at once, but rather in a few stages, gradually. The same way as it was when Israel and Judah were dispersed in ancient times, 741-721 b.c., 597 b.c., 586 b.c., 70 a.c., and135 a.c.

This is a very 'meaty' prophecy, as S. Collins calls it, and contains a lot of information. There is a solid Talmudic tradition that this period of time, preceding the coming of the Messiah will be that of 'Jacob's trouble' of Jeremiah 30:7. A number of Sages, as quoted in Sanhedrin 98b, prayed that they might be saved the terrible experience of great fear and pain, unparalleled distress of the nations, gloominess and darkness, bloody wars and destructions of these times.

"Alas! For that day is great, so that none like it; but Jacob shall be saved out of it" (Jeremiah 30:7).

Our Sages have taught that the fulfillment of the prophecies of Ezekiel's 'two sticks' will be a slow process which they compare to the breaking of the day, when the dark long night slowly gives way to the morning light. The redemption will be realized in stages. At the beginning not all the people of Judah and Ephraim will be reunited. Before the coming of the Messiah son of David, another Messiah, son of Joseph, will appear among the Ten Tribes of Israel. He will be a forerunner and representative of the Davidic Messiah (Succah 52b). It is his task to reunite the Israelite Tribes and bring them to the Promised Land. He will fight God's wars, secure Israelite independence in newly reestablished Biblical borders of Greater Israel, rebuild the Temple in Jerusalem, resume the sacrifices and cleanse Israel. However, Rabbinical tradition says that this Messiah is destined to be killed in battle (Zechariah 12:10-14), and then, after forty years, the Messiah son of David will arrive to complete the final stage of Redemption as Ezekiel described it in Chapter 37:21-28.

Detailed discussions on these matters are to be found mainly in Kabbalah literature such as the book of Zohar and in Midrashim (e.g. Pirkei Heichalos Rabbasi 39:1); Pirkei Mashiach (Beis HaMedrash, Part 3).

This information is also given by R. Saadiah Gaon in his Emunos VeDeos (Beliefs and Principles 8:2, 5) and Ramban (Nachmanides) in his commentary to Shir HaShirim (Song of Solomon 8:13).

Now let us return to the question: When will the attack of Gog begin? Listen to what Prophecy says:

"After many days thou shalt be visited: in the latter years thou shalt come into the land that is brought back from the sword, and is gathered out of many people, against the Mountains of Israel, which have been always waste; but it is brought forth out of the nations, and they shall dwell safety all of them" (Ezekiel 38:8).

The pivotal points here are:

291

1. They (Judah and Ephraim, commonly called 'Israel' after the Reunification) must live safely, in a secure environment, all of them;

2. The Mountains of Israel are positively, without any shed of doubt, identified as the land of Gog's attack;

3. The Israelites will have been brought back from the sword from the nations of their exile. Rashi explained that the Israelites will have returned from the exile into which they had been driven by the sword). The Jews, for instance, were rescued (some of them) from the 'sword' of the Nazi Holocaust during the WWII.

Point #1

Additional information given in the prophecy supplements this point:

"I will go up to the land of unwalled villages; I will go against them that are at rest, that dwell safely, all of them dwelling without walls, and having neither bars, nor gates." And more: "You turn thine hand upon the desolate places that are now inhabited, and upon the people that are gathered out of the nations, which have gotten cattle and goods, that dwell in the midst of the land" (Ezekiel 38:11-12).

Verses 8, 11 and 12 are self-explanatory. They do not need extra commentary. As S. Collins said, all we have to do is trust the Almighty and accept His Word at face value.

So, we learn that the People of Israel (Judah and Joseph) will be reunited, will have returned to the Promised Land (under the leadership of the Messiah son of Joseph) from their countries of exile, will have rebuilt the wasted cities, and will have made the desolate land blossom as the Garden of Eden. The fact that they will have cattle and goods, gold and silver means that they will have developed a very healthy economy and high class commerce; and on top of it, the Israelites will feel confident and secure. They will live in their Land without fear because all the surrounding aggressive enemies will have been defeated and expelled out of the Land and the territory of Biblical Israel that will be restored to its previous borders. Ezekiel speaks of the same events in Chapter 28:25-26:

"Thus saith the Lord God; when I shall have gathered the house of Israel from the nations, then they shall dwell safely therein, and shall build houses, and plant vineyards; yea, they shall dwell with confidence, when I have executed judgments upon all those that despise them round about them; and they shall know that I am the Lord their God."

There are striking similarities between these verses and the wordings of Ezekiel 38:8, 11-12. In both chapters the prophet speaks of the same matters. The Tribes of Israel will return from their exiles to the Promised Land ('open graves'), reunite ('two sticks'), and build a sound economy and commerce. Together they will 'execute God's Judgments' on their enemies round about them. And together they shall live safely and with confidence, all of them.

It will be a peaceful time. The Israelites will have no aggressive designs against any nation (Metzudos, Malbim). By the way, here is another point against Steven Collins who says that Gog's war in Ezekiel 38 and 39 is the same as that of Zechariah 12 and 14. In another written article, 'Jerusalem: The Burdensome Stone', Steven Collins even declared that the War of Zechariah 12 was fulfilled in the series of Arab-Israeli Wars of 1956, 1967 and 1973.

Our position is that war in Zechariah 12 is an event for the future, and it will finish earlier, much before the war(s) of Gog in Ezekiel 38 and 39 have started. The surrounding aggressive Arab nations will have been eliminated. That is why they are not mentioned in the Prophecy of Ezekiel as participants on either side in the war(s) of Gog! Absolutely separate and not parallel wars are being considered. One may possibly make parallels between the wars fought in Zechariah 12:6; Isaiah 11:13-14; 34:5, 8; Ezekiel 25-all; Jeremiah 48-all; 49:24, 26-27; Zephaniah 2:8-10 because they describe the same events—destruction of the surrounding aggressive Arab-Muslim nations by the combined forces of Judah and Ephraim.

If all the above descriptions do not tell us that the prophet Ezekiel is speaking of the Messianic Age, then what does? Some kind of peace treaty like the ongoing infamous Peace Process; the post Cold War disarmament agreements; or aliens from out of space that somehow establish a peaceful environment for the people of Israel? No, Mr. Collins, your explanation how the West won the 'Cold War' and disarmed itself cannot persuade anyone that because of it 'all the people of Israel dwelled safely'. No one geopolitical action of World Governments towards Israel could create such a peaceful situation as that recorded in Ezekiel 38:8, 11-12.

HERE ARE OUR CONCLUSIONS: The Reunited Tribes of Judah and Joseph will have been brought from the "sword" of the exile ("open graves" Ezekiel 37:1-14) under the leadership of a Commander-in-Chief the Messiah son of Joseph. They will join together with their brother Israelis, the present-day citizens of the State of Israel, the Jews (Isaiah 56:8), "The Lord God which gathered the outcast of Israel saith, yet will I gather others to him, beside those that are gathered unto him".

Then those Israelites together will attack and defeat all the surrounding enemy-nations, mostly of Semitic stock, whose names are listed in Psalms 83:6, 7, and 8:

"The tabernacles of Edom, and the Ishmaelites; of Moab, and the Hagarenes; Gebal and Ammon, and Amalek; the Philistines with the inhabitants of Tyre; Assur also is join with them."

The identity and the role of Assur in the future eschatological events will be a subject of our separate discussion later.

The Prophets are in Agreement

The beauty of Scripture is that any verse of a particular prophet in question can find an additional explanation and be supplemented with detailed commentary from other verses penned by different prophets elsewhere.

The prophesied events of the 'dry bones' and the 'two sticks' of Ezekiel 37 are also reflected in the prophecies of Isaiah 11, where the reconciliation and reunification of Judah and Ephraim are described from different perspectives. Both prophets speak of the same events at the end of our age. As a matter of fact, the prophet Isaiah reveals that after the Tribes of Judah and Ephraim make peace and reunite, together they will defeat all the surrounding Arab and Muslim enemy-nations and "there shall be an highway for the remnants of His people, like as it was to Israel in the day that he came up out of the land of Egypt" (Isaiah 11:16).

Here again we find confirmation for our understanding of the eschatological events of the Latter Days. After defeating their enemies, the Israelites of the Ten Tribes will immigrate 'en masse' and restore the Promised Land to its Biblical borders and divide it by lot for inheritance among the twelve Tribes. We are not going to repeat the story of how the Messianic Age started but the description in Isaiah 11:1-10 might satisfy any curious reader.

"And He shall assemble the outcast of Israel and gather together the dispersed of Judah from the four corners of the earth ("open the graves" of the exile). The envy also of Ephraim shall depart, and the enemies of Judah shall be cut off: Ephraim shall not envy Judah, and Judah shall not vex Ephraim" (Isaiah 11:12-13). This closely resembles the 'two sticks' of Ezekiel 37:22, "I will make them one nation in the land, on the mountains of Israel. There will be one king over all of them and they will never again be two nations or be divided into two kingdoms".

S. Collins rightfully noticed that no one Semitic nation had been mentioned by Ezekiel 38 and 39, but, it seems, he does not realize the reason for it. No wonder, he discusses only a few possibilities, mainly concerning on which side of the forces of Gog in the invasion the Arab nations will be. Well, God knows precisely the events of the End Times, and the answer exactly corresponds to His Divine Plan: The Arab nations, the ancient sworn enemies of Israel, will not be able to take any side in the wars of Gog and Magog because they will have been soundly defeated and expelled from the Holy Land. Their lands will have been repossessed by the combined Tribes of Judah and Ephraim under the brilliant leadership of Messiah son of Joseph. This will be before Gog attacks Israel.

"They shall devour all the people round about, on the right hand (west: the Philistines) and on the left hand" (east: Edom, Moab, Ammon and others) (Zechariah 12:6).

The same theme of the same story is recorded in another prophecy (Isaiah 11:14):

"They shall fly upon the shoulders of the Philistines toward the west; together they (Judah and Ephraim or "Israel") plunder people of the east: they shall lay their hand upon Edom and Moab; and the children of Ammon shall obey them".

In our view the wars of Zechariah 12:6 and Isaiah 11:13-14 are very much connected to Psalms 83:4-8 where Scripture describes the destruction of the same nations in the region surrounding Israel. The same tragic faith of these nations is expressed in the different prophecies of Isaiah 17:1; 34:5, 8; Obadiah 1:18; Ezekiel 25:12-13,15, 17; Jeremiah 48-all; 49:24, 26, 27; Zephaniah 2:8-11; Zechariah 9:5-6.

The prophesied events of Isaiah 11:12-14 would not be possible without the Divine Decree to end the Exile and the spiritual revival of the "open graves" and reunification of the Tribes of Israel of the "two sticks" prophecies of Ezekiel 37.

Final Conclusion

The armies of Gog and Magog will attack Israel right at the beginning of the Messianic Age! Other attempts to place this attack prior to the Messianic Age or after it, find no validity in Hebrew Scriptures.

We were pleasantly surprised to discover a confirmation of our position on this very subject from the writings of the founder of the Brit-Am organization, popular author and expert on the Movement of the Ten Tribes of Israel, Yair Davidiy from Jerusalem. He, basically, said that:

"Before the hordes of German, Slavic, and Asiatic people of Gog's alliance will come pouring down out of the north in an attempt to conquer and destroy Israel, the Twelve Tribes of Judah and Joseph will have already been reconciled and reunited, due to the combined actions of Messiah son of Joseph (head of the Ten Tribes) and Messiah son of David. Prior to the attack of Gog and Magog it appears that the land of Israel will have been restored to its Biblical borders from the Nile to the Euphrates and divided among the Tribes. The Ishmaelites (Arabs) and Edomites (parts of Europe) will already have been defeated and placated. All these events concern the End Times. The above explanation is based on Biblical and Rabbinical sources. The actual chronological order in reality may be different but this is the way it seems to us according to our system of analysis which seeks to encompass and reconcile all relevant sources."

The great Rambam confirms our final conclusion when he wrote in Mishneh Torah, Hilkhos Melakhim 12:2:

"The plain meaning of the words of the prophets seems to indicate that the war of Gog and Magog will take place at the beginning of the Messianic Era."

The Target of Gog's Attack

Since we established the fact that the hordes of Gog will attack Israel just at the beginning of the Messianic Age, let us deal with the proper determination of the geographical location of this attack. S. Collins insists that this attack will aim for the territories where the Ten Tribes of Israel are dwelling, mainly the USA (Manasseh), Great Britain (Ephraim), Canada, Australia and a good dozen of European countries of Israelite origin. And the reasons for this, according to the author, are threefold:

a) Gog's attack will take place in the 'latter years', prior to the Messianic Age, before the reunification of Judah and Ephraim and the advent of the Messiah;

b) The prophet Ezekiel did not mention the name of Judah in chapters 38 and 39, therefore the word 'Israel' here means the Ten Tribes of Israel;

c) The Mountains of Israel cannot be identified with the Land of Israel because they are not high enough to be called mountains and, besides, they have not always been wasted, as required by the prophecy.

It is true that the name 'Judah' was not mentioned in Ezekiel 38 and 39. It is also true that when God speaks of the Jewish People, He refers to them by the names of 'Judah', 'Daughters of Zion', 'House of Judah' or 'Jerusalem' (Zephaniah 2; Zechariah 12 and 14). The same applies when God speaks of the Ten Tribes of Israel, for it is sufficient enough to call them 'Ephraim', 'Manasseh', 'Joseph', or 'House of Israel', which automatically means Israel. Of course, there are a few exceptions in the Scripture, when the term 'Israel' sometimes might refer to 'Judah' only (Ezra 2:2, 59-70; 3:1; Ezekiel 3:5; 8:10-12; 14:1) or to both Judah and Israel (Ezekiel 38 and 39), depending on the context of the chapter.

We are also in agreement that Judah and Israel are not synonymous at this point of time. They are different nations, having different spiritual values, history, cultures, traditions and religions, speaking different languages, living in different countries on the four corners of the Globe. And they will be different entities until the time of their spiritual resurrection ('open graves'), reconciliation and reunification ('two sticks') and redemption (partial, by stages, not final yet) with the advent of the Messiah son of Joseph (forerunner and representative of the Messiah son of David, with an interval of forty years, according to Talmudic tradition).

We think that our theological differences lie down in a "little" misunderstanding of the fact whether the attack of Gog against Israel happened before the Messianic Age, as S. Collins maintains, or at the beginning of it, as we outline in our discussion.

Sure, if Gog would have initiated his attack before the advent of the Messiah, 'the graves' would not have been opened; there would not have been a reconciliation and reunification of 'the two sticks': Then it would have been justifiable to use the word 'Israel' as synonymous with the Ten Tribes of Israel in exile. "Clearly, the nations of modern 'Israel' (not 'Judah') are the primary targets of Gog's attack in the latter days," says the convinced author.

But this is not so. The word 'Israel' in Ezekiel 38 and 39 most obviously means the whole House of Israel, Judah and the Ten Tribes of Israel combined, **because they will already have been reunited before the attack of Gog,** as we have proven from Bible verses and other sources. This means that the Messiah, son of Joseph will have been revealed, the Messianic Age will have begun, and the united Tribes of Judah and Israel will have been restored to the Promised Land. It is only after all these things happened, that Gog will unexpectedly attack Israel.

The Mountains of Israel

Since Mr. S. Collins has assumed (wrongly!) that Gog's attack against Israel will have taken place before the millennia of the Messianic World, he has no choice but to use a Procrustean bed tactic to fit all relevant Scriptural information into the shape and form needed in order to satisfy his preconceived ideas. That is why his explanation that the Mountains of Israel, for example, are too law, and look like mere hills, and have not always been wasted, therefore, they cannot be identified with the Land of Israel, sounds like shallow argumentation that could not withstand any serious theological criticism.

"The 'mountains' in the hill country of Ephraim would be classified as mere 'foothills' in comparison with the Rocky Mountains of North America", he said.

But what about the other mountains in the restored Biblical Land of Israel? Let us consider say, the snow-capped mountains of the Golan

Heights with the highest point in the Mount Hermon massif at 2,224 meters, or Mount Meron in Upper Galilee at 1,208 meters?

Another 'proof' according to S. Collins, that these Mountains cannot possibly be identified with the Land of Israel is the fact that "they have most assuredly not been always waste," continues S. Collins. "However, one can fly over Rocky Mountains of North America and not see any sign of human habitation over much of its expanse, and they are much higher than the Mountains of Israel". Based on these two 'very important' reasons, he comes to the conclusion that "the prophet Ezekiel describes North America, the home of the Israelite tribe of Manasseh, not the Israeli nation and the Holy Land".

These so called proofs do not give a good impression of their seriousness and reliability when faced with the simple and plain truth of Scripture at its 'face value'. Let us see what the Prophets say.

"For thus hath the Lord said, the whole land shall be desolate" (Jeremiah 4:27).

"For I will lay the land most desolate, and the pomp of her strength shall cease; and the Mountains of Israel shall be desolate, that none shall pass through" (Ezekiel 33:28).

These plain words of the Prophets perfectly meet the necessary conditions for Gog's attack on Israel described as an attack "against the Mountains of Israel, which have been always waste" (Ezekiel 38:8).

The Mountains of Israel throughout the Bible are everywhere identified with the Land of Israel (Ezekiel 36:1, 8-12; 37:22; 38:8; 39:4). It is also recorded in Scripture and secular history that terms for the Land of Israel and the Mountains of Israel are synonymous and imply no difference in their intention. Here is another example of this:

"I will bring them out from the people, and gather them from the countries, and bring them to their own land of Israel, and feed them upon the Mountains of Israel by the rivers, and in all the inhabited places of the country" (Ezekiel 34:13).

How could be the Mountains of Israel be located in the countries of the Ten Tribes of Israel in exile (North America, Australia, South Africa or Europe), if God clearly and plainly says that all the Israelites will be taken from the countries of their exile and be ingathered in their own Land of Israel, which are the Mountains (or hills) of Israel?!

"They shall know that I am the Lord, their God, which caused them to be led into captivity among the heathen: but I have gathered them to their own land, and have left none of them anymore there"

After the exile of the Jewish People by the Romans in 135c.e, for almost 2000 years they indeed "had been desolate and a continual waste" (Ezekiel 38:8).

It is not by accident that the Land of Israel throughout the centuries did not become the home state for any one of the Empires who happened to conquer it. This Land had lain desolate continuously from the time of the Romans through occupation by Byzantine Christians, Arabs, and Turks to 1967, when it was wrested back from Jordan ('under sword'). Victorious Empires had never found the Holy Land hospitable. The Land has always rejected other peoples.

It seems that Land has a loyalty to the Israel People and mourns when they are not on it. God has kept the Promised Land in this way for His People Israel.

It takes a lot of imagination and guts to remove the 'Mountains of Israel' out of the Holy Land and place them elsewhere, transferring them to North America, Europe, Australia, or South Africa, as homelands of the Ten Tribes of Israel in exile. By doing this, S. Collins simply ignores the words of the prophets and does not take the plain meaning at its 'face value'.

"And thou shalt come against My people of Israel, as a cloud to cover the land; it shall be in a latter days, **and I will bring thee against My Land**" (Ezekiel 38:16).

'My Land' here does not mean America, Great Britain, Australia, Europe or any other territory where the Ten Tribes of Israel live in exile: it surely means the Holy Land, the home of the Twelve Tribes of Israel, as any student of the Bible knows.

There is another 'hint' in Ezekiel 38:12 saying that Gog will attack the people **"that dwell in the midst of the land."** All translators of the Scripture have understood that 'midst of the land' is the Land of Israel!

God said to Gog: "Thou shalt fall upon the mountains of Israel. I will give unto Gog a place there of graves in Israel, the valley of the passengers on the east of the sea; and they shall call it 'The valley of Hamon-gog'. And also the name of the city shall be Hamonah" (Ezekiel 39:5, 11, 16).

There are so many strong proofs here that the war and campaign of Gog and its tragic finale will take place on the 'Mountains of Israel', which is the Land of Israel. Mr. S. Collins makes no comment on any of these. Indeed, what country of the Ten Tribes in exile fits the descriptions of Ezekiel 38-39?

Meanwhile, in rabbinical tradition, the geographical places mentioned in Ezekiel 39:5, 11, 16 were well known to the Jewish People. Targum identifies the sea of Verse 11 as the Sea of Ginossar i.e. the Sea of Galilee (Radak). Ginossar was known as the Royal Gardens for its luscious produce and attracted many tourists, 'passengers' and 'travelers' (Bereishis Rabbah 98).

"I will give unto Gog a place there for graves in Israel, the valley of the passengers on the east of the sea" (Ezekiel 39:11). The valley of Hamon-gog will extend to the east of Jerusalem, along the Jordan to the lake of Kinneret and up to the city of Tiberias.

The prophet, in connection with Gog defeat and burial, speaks of the one 'field', one 'valley', one 'city', one 'Sea', one 'Land of Israel'. **Is it not obvious that Ezekiel 38 and 39 picture the Holy Land as the target of Gog's attack against Israel?!**

All of his arguments against our understanding are put forward in order to fit the author's theory that at the time of Gog attack the tribes of Israel will not have been united, the Messiah not revealed and the Messianic Age will not have been started. It is up to our readers to judge whether to believe in the technique and tactic of the 'Procrustean bed' of S. Collins or our own position based on the undeniable meaning of verses of the Bible, the Sages of the Talmud, and other Historical and rabbinical sources.

Why Gog will Attack Israel?

Really, why will all this multitude of nations go against Israel? Because all of them are evil and hate God's chosen People? Or, may be, there are some other reasons? Let us see what the Prophet says of Gog's intentions:

"I will plunder and loot and turn my hand against the resettled ruins and people gathered from the nations, rich in livestock and goods, living at the center of the land" (Ezekiel 38:12).

He will come to take a spoil, to take a prey—is this the reason for the attack of Gog! But what kind of spoil could they rob and loot from Israel? Ezekiel speaks of live stock (cattle), properties and goods. Of course, it includes gold and silver, the wealth and riches of the Israelite nation. In ancient times victorious enemies plundered the immense treasures of the Temple and the city of Jerusalem. In the same way, Nebuchadnezzar King of Babylon looted and plundered Egypt of her wealth (Ezekiel 29:19).

We have already pointed out that this prophecy is not speaking of the present-day Jewish state of Israel, but rather of the time, when the Messiah will be revealed, when Judah has already been reunited with the Ten Tribes of Israel. It will happen in the 'latter days', at the beginning of the Messianic Era. The riches and wealth of Ephraim's nations, primarily the USA, England, Europe and other countries of

Israelite origin will relocate together with the Israelite population to the Promised Land.

"Lift up your eyes roundabout and see; they all gather together, they come to you. Your sons will come from afar, and your daughters will be carried in the arms. Then you will see and be radiant, and your heart will thrill and rejoice; because the abundance of the sea will be turned to you, the wealth of the nations will come to you. A multitude of camels will cover you, the young camels of Midian and Ephah; all those from Sheba will come; they will bring gold and frankincense, and will bear good news of the praises of the Lord. And the ships of Tarshish will come first, to bring your sons from afar, their silver and their gold with them" (Isaiah 60:4-6, 9).

The Land of Israel will be free of all surrounding enemy nations as we have positively demonstrated in many places above. Israel will live in peace and safety. Gog could not have found a more favorable situation to attack Israel at its most vulnerable than this one:

"I will invade a land of unwalled villages; I will attack a peaceful and unsuspecting people, all of them living without walls and without gates and bars" (Ezekiel 38:11).

By this time the people of Israel have built the best economy and commerce in the World. The national talent of innovation in science and technology will bloom and open a new era of prosperity and happiness.

Their people will have the highest standard of living and live longer than anybody else. Most of the countries of Gog's alliance will not have such a prosperous situation as that which Israel shall enjoy. Their economies will be poor and on the verge of collapse. There will be an energy crisis, shortages of oil and gas, foods, minerals and other life essentials. And now we come closer to the real reason why Gog's armies will invade Israel.

LEVIATHAN

What is the Leviathan? It is a huge and terrible serpent, a sea monster of Near Eastern mythology. It is also the name given to a large natural gas field in the Mediterranean Sea, discovered by Israeli scientists in June 2010. It is located approximately 130 kilometers south-west of the port of Haifa off the cost of Israel, 1500 meters deep in waters. It is estimated that the Levantine basin contains 450 billion cubic meters of natural gas. The Leviathan portion is 253 billion cubic meters alongside with 4.2 billion barrels of oil. The prospects of this discovery are enormous. This 'gift from God' will tremendously change the life of the Israeli nation for the better, resembling the Biblical expression of Israel as 'land of milk and honey'. Israel plans to fully develop it and start production of fuel in full capacity by the year of 2014-2015. Israel will not be totally depend on coal and crude oil imports from foreign countries any more, and will have its own supplies of fuel oil which should be sustainable for more than two decades. The vast reservoir of natural gas should meet the needs of Israel for more than 100 years; some even predict that it will last for 200 years. It will provide Israel with some $300 billion over the life-span of the Leviathan field. The cost of energy will be significantly reduced. The environmental damage of generating electricity will decline substantially. Overnight Israel from fossil fuel importer will become potential exporter of natural gas.

Our readers might wonder what connection this story of the recent discovery of the Leviathan natural gas and oil fields has with the subject of this Chapter 'The Wars of Gog and Magog'? Well, we think there is a direct connection! Even though we mentioned before that the spoil and prey Gog will be going for in Israel, as described in Ezekiel 38:13, are gold and silver, livestock, goods and properties, this is not the most important treasure that Russia, China, Turkey and the rest of the alliance will be looking for. Everybody knows what a crucial role oil, gas and coal have played in our highly industrial age. But these sources of energy are limited and non-renewable. With the fast growing economies of China, India, Pakistan and the other previously undeveloped countries of Asia, South America and Africa, these resources have already reached their 'peak' production levels and have began to decline. The World desperately needs re-newable sources of clean and inexpensive energy which change the way of living on our planet. Can you imagine that the Sun produces enough energy in one second to power the World's current needs for a million years?! Until Humanity finds new sources of energy and revolutionizes live on Earth, we have to deal with what is available and make the best of it. We see how the most powerful countries in the world bend themselves over (often playing politics and betraying their friends and allies) to please Saudi Arabia and other oil producing countries in order to secure the oil flow to their countries. Quite often the Arab nations have threatened countries who support Israel with their 'oil weapon', and twice they made their threat a reality by reducing oil production and through crippling OPEC oil embargoes.

We see how Russia, one of the largest producers of fossil fuel, tries to politically control entire Europe, by at will closing or opening the gates of their pipe lines. If Israel builds natural gas pipes and starts to export it to the democracies of Europe with better prices and more reliable, friendlier service, it will have undermined Russia's interests and influence, which in turn will make them very furious and violent.

Russia is not the only country who will oppose the desire of Israel to develop cheap energy resources for their own needs, not even mentioning the profitable export of it to other countries. It has already drawn some enemies in the region. Lebanon, supported by the Islamic Republic of Iran, and pushed by the religious extremists of Hezbollah, declared that part of a newly discovered Leviathan natural gas field belongs to them and not to Israel. They warned the Israelis not to drill in their territorial waters; otherwise they will face serious consequences. Israel in reply threatened to use force if needed to protect their rights to the natural gas fields. Turkey, who controls the Turkish Republic of northern Cyprus, supports Lebanon and the Palestinians of Gaza in their claims to portions of the Leviathan gas fields. Egypt, Saudi

Arabia and Iran do not like the idea of Israel becoming self-sufficient in fossil fuel supply and exporting natural gas to other countries. The sudden interest of these countries in the potential hydrocarbon fuel resource wealth of the Mediterranean depth could ignite a new war in the region.

The possibility that the enemies of Israel round around will target the installations of the Leviathan fuel fields in the next Arab-Israel war(s) is real, and so is the potential of an ecological catastrophe in the region. A situation such as this may well trigger the War of Gog and Magog because the Leviathan fuel fields might become that important "spoil" Russia, China, Turkey and the rest will come to plunder from Israel. This is the kind of treasure Israel was abundantly blessed with by God Almighty in many instances in the Hebrew Bible (Genesis 49:25; Deuteronomy 33:13).

Many theologians have seen in these blessings hidden allegorical references to vast treasures deep underneath the Land of Israel. 'Milk and honey' of Deuteronomy 32:13 they interpret as 'Shemen Adama' or 'Shemen Avanim' in Hebrew which may be translated into English as 'earth oil' or 'stone oil'. The People of Israel will 'suck oil out of the flinty rock'. The expressions of the blessings as 'precious thing', 'chief things' of 'everlasting hills' and 'ancient mountains', 'blessings of the breasts and of the womb', 'living by the well', 'blessings of the deep that lie beneath', they explain, indicate that the prophecies speak of an immense wealth of oil and gas in the Promised Land. Compare Job 29:6 ". . . and the rock poured me out rivers of oil". The blessings of the Tribe of Asher, ". . . let him dip his foot in oil" (Deuteronomy 33:24), directly points to the geographical location of Asher on the shores of the Mediterranean Sea where the enormous reservoirs of hydrocarbon fossil fuel fields were recently discovered. There is a huge amount of oil in the forms of 'stone oil', 'earth oil' and 'rock oil' to be sucked out of the 'breasts' and 'womb', plus an "abundance of the seas and treasures hid in the sand" (Deuteronomy 33:19).

Those people who used to joke that Moses at the time of the Exodus from Egypt made a big mistake by turning left (to the Land of Israel) instead of right (to Saudi Arabia), choosing the only place in the Middle East with no oil, have been proven wrong by the prophetic Word of the Holy Bible and the real geological discoveries of the 'glory of the Deep' by Israeli's scientists.

Of course, there will be other motives for some countries to attack Israel as well. Iran with the Islamic camp, for instance, will be moved by anti-Semitic hatred and the goal to prove that the Muslim religion of the god Allah and his messenger Muhammad is superior to that of the Jewish Faith in the God of Israel and His prophet Moses. These are some of the reasons for the sudden attack of Gog on Israel. The main reason however for this attack is the Sovereign Lord Himself:

"This is what Almighty God says; Behold, I am against you, O Gog, the chief prince of Meshech and Tubal. I will turn you around and lead you on from the uttermost parts of the north against the Mountains of Israel" (Ezekiel 38:2; 39:1-2).

And, as the result of this war, when the armies of Gog will be destroyed and, ironically, find their burial place in the Land of Israel,

"From that day forward the house of Israel will know that I am the LORD their God" (Ezekiel 39:22).

The Gog and Magog War(S) and the Stages of Redemption

There is a dispute on the question as to how many wars will be fought by Gog in the end of our age. Some scholars believe that there will be two major wars, one is described by Ezekiel 38 and 39, and another war, which will be the final one, is described in Zechariah 14, when Gog actually breaks into Jerusalem and a half of the city will be captured by him. The most detailed and specific accounts of these wars are contained in the books of the prophets Ezekiel, Zechariah, Joel, and Daniel.

The Sages, and particularly Malbim (Rabbi Meir Leibush, 1808-1879), spoke of three separate wars which are supposed to be fought by Gog's armies in the latter years. According to Malbim, the prophecy of Ezekiel 38 and 39 speak of two separate wars because in chapter 39:1 Ezekiel is charged with a new prophecy. If S. Collins followed the reasoning of his observations, he would have come to the same conclusion as Malbim.

"Each prophecy of the book of Ezekiel is clearly marked by specific language so the reader can understand when each prophecy begins and ends," he wrote. Normally, this 'specific language' or 'distinctive wordings', used by the prophet look like: "Son of man . . . I will speak to you," or "The word of the Lord came to me, saying . . .", or "The hand of the Lord was upon me . . ."

These kinds of wordings are dividing marks between the previous prophecy and a new one. Chapter 38 of Ezekiel begins with "And the word of the Lord came to me saying, Thus says the Lord God" (Verses 1, 3). In the next chapter 39 the prophecy starts, "Son of man, prophesy against Gog and say . . ." (Verse1).

Mr. S. Collins gives us excellent guidance how to distinguish between old and new prophecies, but for some strange reason has not followed this pattern. Malbim knew the Ezekiel 'marker' and taught that such an introduction to chapter 39 means that the prophet speaks a different prophesy, in this case of a Second War of Gog. In addition, he points out, that Ezekiel 38 is not a new prophecy, predicting a Gog and Magog campaign against Israel in the latter years as 38:17 clearly indicates.

"Thus says the Lord God: Are you he of whom I have spoken in former days by My servants the prophets of Israel, who prophesied for years in those days that I would bring you against them".

The Talmud says this refers to the prophets Eldad and Medad who, according to the Targum of Jonathan, were brethren of Moses by his mother's side. They prophesied in ancient times about the wars of Gog and Magog, their armies, and of their destruction by the Messiah in the Messianic Times (Numbers 11:27). On the other hand, the subject of chapter 39, the Second War of Gog, will never have been foretold by anyone else. Another difference between the two wars is that in chapter

38 the earthquake which annihilates Gog's forces, comes on the very day that Gog sets foot upon Israel's soil, cf. Ezekiel 38:18,

"And it will come to pass at the same time, when Gog comes against the Land of Israel", says the Lord, "that My fury will show in My face. For in My jealousy and in the fire of My wrath I have spoken: Surely in that day there shall be a great earthquake in the Land of Israel".

In contrast, chapter 39 shows the prophet seeing Gog coming all the way to the mountains (hills) of Israel, a destination Gog could not have reached immediately. This explained by the Malbim. The third war, in his view, is described in the book of Zechariah 14, when Gog's armies will have surrounded Jerusalem, and half of the city will fall into his hands.

Other expositors believe that Ezekiel 39 describes the last war of Gog. This will result in the final eradication of evil on earth. How long will this war(s) last? Rabbi Akiva suggests it will continue for the duration of the twelve months (Eduy, ii: 10). Leviticus Rabbah, xix says the conflict will last for seven years, in accordance with Ezekiel 39:9.

Speaking of the stages of Redemption, this process will not be in a moment. Rather it will take time and be realized in stages. The very first stage, the beginning of the Redemption has already occurred. This was the immigration of the Jewish People to the Promised Land and establishment there of the Jewish State of Israel in 1948 right after WWII and the Holocaust. They have their own task to fulfill: to prepare the way for the rest of their brothers of the Ten Tribes who will be coming back and need accommodation in the Land of Israel.

'Come together' from the exile (Jeremiah 3:18) reminds us of Isaiah 11:14, when Judah will be reconciled and united with Joseph and 'together' they fly upon the shoulders of the Philistines toward the west; together they shall spoil them of the east.

What we see described here is another stage of Redemption (not yet the final one), when Judah and Joseph will have reconciled their differences and be reunited in the realization that they are all sons of their father Jacob, and, as brothers, have to begin to cooperate in their common affairs. At this stage, the Messiah, son of Joseph, will have been revealed. Under his leadership the combined forces of Judah and Joseph will defeat the surrounding enemy-nations and liberate and restore the Land of Israel to its Biblical borders from the Nile to the Euphrates. Exactly at this period of the beginning of the Messianic Age, the armies of Gog and Magog will attack peaceful Israel.

The same motifs written by different prophets are found in many prophecies through-out Scripture. For instance, in the book of Zechariah, "And I will strengthen the house of Judah, and will save the house of Joseph, and I will bring them again to place them; for I will have mercy upon them. I will give them a sign, and gather them; for I have redeemed them" (Zechariah 10:6, 8).

Regardless, as whether Ezekiel 38 and 39 describe one or two wars; the final result will be the same, the total destruction of the hordes of Gog and the Complete Redemption of the whole House of Israel.

Finally!

Why should we have to wait for the End-Time Salvation to come to Israel and then only after the War(s) of Gog and Magog? The answer is simple: That is how God Almighty has decided it is to be! This is His Word. This is His Divine Plan as recorded in the book of Ezekiel:

"So the house of Israel shall know that I am the Lord their God from that day and forward. Therefore thus saith the Lord God; now I will end the captivity of My people; I will have mercy upon the whole house of Israel, and will be jealous for My holy name.

Then shall they know that I am the Lord their God, which cause them to be led into captivity among the heathen: but I have gathered them into their own land, and I have left none of them anymore there" (Ezekiel 39:22, 25, 28).

It will be the Final Redemption after the destruction of Gog because from this day onward the whole house of Israel (at last!) will 'know' their Lord, the Almighty God of Israel. All Israelites will have been returned and settled on the Promised Land. With the Advent of the Messiah son of David the Final Redemption of the whole House of Israel and, then, Redemption of all the nations of the World will have been completed. Humanity will usher in a Golden Age of Peace,

Prosperity and Brotherhood, commonly known as the Messianic World. God's knowledge will descend on all people, and the nations will serve the God of Israel with one consent and in the spirit of God's Love.

"And the Lord shall be King over all the earth: in that day shall there be one Lord and His name one" (Zechariah 14:9).

The final stage of the people's drama and the triumph of God's Design is set: Humanity is ready to usher in a new perfected, beautiful and purely spiritual existence of the World-To-Come, the Olam Habah, the 'blessed seventh day' of Universal Sabbath and Rest, which will last forever.

CHAPTER XV:
WILL ALL ISRAEL RETURN TO
THE PROMISED LAND?

Will there be enough room for all of them?

This is the question that has received many controversial answers. Some scholars say that it will hardly be possible to accommodate a multi-hundred million people from the Ten Tribes of Israel in the 'tiny' territory of the ancient Promised Land. They accept the idea that many representatives of all Twelve Tribes will settle in the Biblical Land of Israel in their tribal allotments in the Messianic Era, but not all Israelites will return to the Land of their fathers. Is the ancient Biblical Land of Israel really that small? We do not think so. The expanded Land of Greater Israel from Nile to Euphrates has enough territory to settle all the Israelites together with the strangers among them! There is an opinion that the entire population of the world could be placed in the State of Texas, which consists of 268,820 square miles or 696,200 square kilometers. By comparison, the Biblical Land of Israel is not "tiny" at all. Its borders will include the Eastern part of Egypt, Sinai, Lebanon, Jordan, the Island of Cyprus, part of Saudi Arabia, Kuwait, Syria, and parts of Iraq and Turkey. It is estimated that the Promised Land is eight times the size of Texas. The population of all the children of Israel is much less than that of the whole world. It would be no problem to accommodate all Israelites on their Land. Especially, as the prophets say, all the Arab and Muslim enemy-nations surrounding

Israel will have been defeated and expelled out of the Land. Their lands will be repossessed by Israelites.

"Those who laid you waste depart from you. They that swallowed thee up shall be far away" (Isaiah 49:17, 19).

The Israelites will act according to God command:

"They shall devour all the people round about, on the right hand and on the left" (Zechariah 12:6). "Those who harass Judah shall be cut off" (Isaiah 11:12). "With Your hand You drove out the nations and planted our fathers. I will crash his foes before him and strike down his adversaries" (Psalm 44:2; 89:23).

What do the Critics Say?

The proponents of the opposite idea put forward a few Biblical verses trying to prove that it was divinely foreseen that a huge portion of the Israelite population will remain in the countries of their present dwellings. They do not realize or ignore the fact that the prophecies, they rely on, are all about the past. They have been fulfilled at other times. They do not directly connect to the prophecies of final reunification, ingathering and redemption on Mountains of Israel. Here are some examples:

"Thou shall spread abroad to the west, and to the east, and to the north, and to the south" (Genesis 28:14).

Similarly, God said of Joseph: "Joseph is a fruitful bough by a well; whose branches run over the wall" (Genesis 49:22).

These verses are quoted as confirmation of their theory that not all Israelites will be resettled in the Promised Land; plus Genesis 48:19 where it is said that Ephraim will be greater than Manasseh, and his seed shall become a multitude (Commonwealth) of nations, whereas Manasseh will become the single most powerful nation on the earth. The revisionist "scholars" maintain that these prophecies pertain to the future, and, therefore, a large chunk of the Israelite population will continue to live in their various countries abroad even in the time of the Messianic Era.

Another so called "proof", introduced by some theologians, that many Israelites will not return to the Promised Land and will continue to live in their "appointed places" outside the Land is found in verse 2 Samuel 7:10:

"I will appoint a place for My people Israel and will plant them, so that they may dwell in their own place and be disturbed no more. Evil nations will not oppress them as they have done in the past."

By adding a few key words such as 'new appointed place', Israel's 'future location', 'move no more', these scholars have argued that there is not enough space to accommodate the vast multitudes of the Twelve Tribes of Israel on the territory of the ancient Promised Land, therefore God appointed them 'new' places outside the borders of the Land of Israel, in the countries where the Ten Tribes in exile have been resident, so that they may live in the place of their own and 'move no more'.

This interpretation of the Prophecy is wrong. Words have been taken out of context with intention to change the meaning of the verse. If one were to continue to read the next verse 2 Samuel 7:11, it will have become clear that the previous verse is a continuation of the present one, (that is why verses are connected not with a period, but with a comma), and there is no such things as a "new place" and "new future location" for Israel. The intentions of the Prophet words are very different from this kind of understanding. The plain meaning of the Prophecy is that God was pleased with King David that he had in heart to build a house for Him. God therefore told David that He has it in His heart to make him a house and establish a place of his own.

". . . since the time I appointed Judges over My people Israel. And I will give rest from all your enemies. Also the Lord declares to you that He will make a house for you" (Verse 11).

The difference between verses 10 and 11 is that in the times of the Judges the Israelites were greatly afflicted and suffered from the hands of the evil nations around them; but, now, God declares, He will put an end of it. The land of Canaan will be entirely free of enemy-nations.

The Israelites will possess it for themselves, a place of their own. God promises them quietness, peace, prosperity and independence in the Kingdom of Israel under the leadership of Kings David and his son Solomon. That is all.

Another author wrote: "During the Millennium only a small percentage of Israelites actually return to Canaan". He derives this conclusion from the verse of Jeremiah 3:14 which says:

"I will take you one of a city, and two of a family, and I will bring you to Zion."

It is quite unclear how this verse contributes to the conviction that "not all Israelites will return to the Holy Land"? The wording of this verse does not indicate that above mentioned selection will have taken place among the Jewish or Israelite populations.

One of the best translators and commentators of the Bible, Rabbi David Kimchi (1160-1235, Portugal), explained this verse in this way: "Though there may be but one Jew in a city of the Gentiles, or two only in a nation ('family' in the Scripture connotes country or nation), the Lord will take them from thence." The authoritative translation of Kimchi finds its support by the context of the whole Chapter 3 of Jeremiah where the main subject is not selection but repentance:

"Return, faithless sons; I will cure your backsliding. I will restore you health and heal your wounds.—Yes, we will come to You, for You are the Lord, our God."

Jeremiah 3:14 is an additional proof confirming that all Israelites and Jews will return to the Promised Land when the appropriate time will arrive! (Amos 9:9; Ezekiel 36:10; 39:28).

Other 'scholars' refer to Zechariah 14:16 as a proof that the majority of Israelites will remain in their 'Appointed Places' throughout the Millennium and 'go year-by-year to pay homage to their Messiah'.

"And it shall come to pass that **everyone who is left of all the nations which came against Jerusalem shall go up from year to year to worship the King, the Lord of hosts, and to keep the Feast of Tabernacles**" (Zechariah 14:16).

They 'somehow' overlooked the fact that after the destruction of the Gog and Magog hordes, the nations who go year-by-year to Jerusalem to warship the Lord (not the Messiah!) are not the Israelite nations! These kinds of 'tricks' do not give a good impression about those who make such claims and nullify their argumentation. The Prophet specifically said he was referring to **"every one that is left of all the nations which came against Jerusalem."** In Ezekiel 38 and 39 and Zechariah 12 and 14 these events are clearly described in detail. Even the names of the nations in dispute are given (Ezekiel 38: 2, 5, 6)! They should have known that during the Wars of Gog and Magog in the time of the beginning of the Messianic Era, the Jews and Israelites will have been reunited under the leadership of the Messiah, son of Joseph, and be dwelling in their Ancient Land restored to its Biblical borders. They will live in the Promised Land in peace and security, all of them (Ezekiel 38:8, 11). The attack of Gog will have been against the united House of Israel.

What do the Prophets Say?

It would seem that the Prophet Isaiah also speaks of those heathen nations who in the future will come to Israel to beg for forgiveness and learn the ways of the Lord, God of Israel:

"The sons also of them that afflicted thee shall come bending unto thee; and all they that despised thee shall bow themselves down at the soles of thy feet; and they shall call thee, The city of the Lord, Zion, of the Holy One in Israel"(Isaiah 60:14).

It is very obvious that the nations mentioned in Zechariah 14:16 and Isaiah 60:14 are not those of Israelite origin and will have had nothing in common with them.

The simple and plain truth of above mentioned prophecies (except Zechariah 14:16 and Isaiah 60:14) is the fact that all of them have been precisely fulfilled in various times in the past! Yes, the Twelve Tribes of Israel and Judah were sent by God into exile in the four corners of the World (Genesis 28:14). Yes, the descendants of Joseph were world colonizing people (Genesis 49:22): Manasseh became the single most powerful nation of America, and Ephraim the very populous Commonwealth of Nations of Great Britain (Genesis 48:19). Yes, the Israelites had a place of their own and lived in peace and prosperity under the great King Solomon (2 Samuel 7:10-11). So what? Where do you see a single prophecy saying that not all Israel will have returned to the Holy Land in the days of Mashiah? On the contrary, after dispersion to the lands of their enemies, the Almighty on a quite a few occasions reassured His People that He will return them to the Holy Land at the appointed time, all the remnant of Israel.

"Behold, I am with you, and will keep you in all places wither you go, and will bring you again into this Land; for I will not leave you, until I have done that which I have spoken to you of" (Genesis 28:15).

There are dozens upon dozens of prophecies in the Hebrew Scripture that speak of the same theme of the ingathering of all the remnant of Israel into the God given Land.

"Behold, I will take the children of Israel from among the heathen, where they be gone, and will gather them on every side, and bring them into their own Land; and **I will make them one nation upon the Mountains of Israel**" (Ezekiel 37:21-22).

If these quoted verses of the Bible still do not satisfy some of our readers that all Twelve Tribes of Israel will return to the ancient Promised Land, the following verses definitely nail it:

"Then shall they know that I am the Lord their God, which caused them to be led into captivity among the heathen: but I have gathered them unto their own Land, **and have left none of them anymore there**" (Ezekiel 39:28).

What do the Sages Say?

Rabbi Shlomo Yitzchaki (1040-1105, France), better known by the acronym Rashi, the "father" of all commentaries, said that, according to Ezekiel 39:28, **No one will be left in the Exile!**

Another famous commentator R. Chaim Dov Rabinovitz (1909-2001, Lithuania), Daat Sofrim, said: "This is the most explicit promise concerning the ingathering of all the outcast of Israel."

"I will multiply people on you (Mountains of Israel), **all the house of Israel, all of it**" (Ezekiel 36:10).

People Make Plans, God Decides

It is just amazing how God repeatedly stresses the very point that not only the Ten Tribes of Israel alone will return to the Promised Land, but all the Twelve Tribes together, all of them will return! The Almighty knew precisely that there would be controversies about the Babylonian captivity's return and the last and Final Exodus. Make no mistake, said the Lord, I will gather all My people from their countries in exile, and will have left none of them anymore there. This is explicitly clear and understandable.

The next passage from Scripture perfectly illustrates what we just said:

"For on My holy mountain, on the high mountain of Israel," declares the Lord GOD, "there the **whole house of Israel, all of them** in the land, will serve Me" (Ezekiel 20:40).

Every word of God in Scripture has its own place, meaning and importance. If the Almighty did not want to say that all the House of Jacob will return to the Promised Land, He would have said so. Meanwhile, by using imperatively such words and expressions as "all the House of Israel", "all of them in the land", "I have left none of them anymore there", God has left no room for doubt and guessing that He will have gathered all the Twelve Tribes of His People to the Holy Land.

319

Here is one more example proving that God will gather all the people of Israel to the Promised Land, no matter how far they are and how difficult for them it may be to return:

"The Lord will return your captivity and have compassion upon thee, and will return and gather thee from all the people whither the Lord thy God hath scattered thee. If any of thine that are dispersed be in the uttermost parts of heaven, from thence will the Lord thy God will bring thee into the Land which thy fathers possessed, and thou shall possess it (Deuteronomy 30:3-5).

Again and again God emphasizes the fact that all His People will return, and He will have left none of them any more in the countries of exile.

In the initial stage of the process of Ingathering, it seems that there will not be enough room for all the newcomers: "This place is too small for us; give us more space to live in" (Isaiah 49:20; Zechariah 10:10).

God advises His People what to do: "Enlarge the place of your tent, stretch your tent curtains wide, do not hold back; lengthen your cords, strengthen your stakes" (Isaiah 54:2). In other words, go ahead, enlarge the curtains of your habitation, bring "the fist of My Judgments" on the enemy-nations roundabout and establish the boundaries of the Promised Land, according to My Word. Israel will have obeyed perfectly the directives of God and will restore the borders of the Holy Land from the Nile to the Euphrates. As the Lubavitch Rabbi, M.M. Schneerson, said, these Biblical "Occupied Territories" belong to Israel. There will be more than enough space for all the families of Israel together with the strangers living among them.

Regardless of how many nations and countries belonging to Israel exist in their places of exile and how many hundreds of millions they may number, after the defeat of Gog and Magog, the Messiah, son of David, will complete the process of the total ingathering of all the Children of Israel to the Holy Land. This will proceed as part of the final redemption of the whole House of Jacob, and they will know their God, all of them.

God will have left none of them anymore there. No one member of the remnant Israelite family will be left behind in the countries of their exile!

The Twelve Israelite Tribes will have become one People again, a Kingdom of Priests, a light to the World. Through this unified and redeemed nation of Israel all the Divine Blessings of the Bible will come to pass in this world. It will be their Divinely ordained task and destiny to teach and guide the nations to worship the one God of the Universe, the God of Israel, by demonstrating righteousness, holiness, kindness and God's love to all inhabitants of the earth in order to merit together the Messianic Era and life in the World-To-Come.

CHAPTER XVI:
THE MESSIAH,
AGE OF THE EARTH,
AFTERLIFE AND RESURRECTION,
THE MESSIANIC AGE AND
THE WORLD-TO-COME

The Messianic World—what exactly is it? When will it start and for how long will it continue or, will it last forever? Where it will take place: on heaven or on earth? Will it be a purely physical or a spiritual world? Will it be a combination of both? Is it the ultimate goal of Humanity or there is something else after it?

The World-to-Come—what exactly is it? Is it the same as the Messianic World or are they different? How and when will these two Worlds originate? If they are different, which one comes first: the Messianic World or the World-to-Come? For how long will each World last? And where will it be: on heaven or on earth? Is it a continuation of our World, as we know it, or will it be a completely different reality?

Afterlife and Resurrection—is there such a thing? Is there life after death? What do we know of it? When and where will the resurrection of the dead occur: during the years of the Messianic Era or in the time of the World-to-Come?

The Messiah—who will he be? When will he come? What will he come for and what is he supposed to do? Will he live forever or will he die at some point in his life as any other mortal? How many Messiahs will come? Do we know particulars of the advent of the Messiah?

State of Israel. Its friends and enemies. Prophetic future

The Age of the Earth—is the age of our planet 15 billion years 'old' as scientists estimate, or 'young' such as the 6 thousand years according to the Biblical account of Creation? Who we are to believe: the scientists or the Bible? Is there a contradiction between them on the age of the Earth and the Universe?

We have all heard and read of these questions. There are so many opinions on them that we are confused and not so sure to which version of the story to cleave to. Let us start from the beginning. We will try to explain these things as simply as possible by using the teachings of Judaism, Hebrew Scripture, the Rabbinical Authorities, Talmud, Midrash and other related sources.

The Messiah (Mashiach)

The belief in a Messiah and a Messianic era has been deeply rooted in traditional Judaism since ancient times. (Isaiah 2:2-4; 11:1-10; 60:14-21; Zechariah 8:23; 14:9; Micah 4:1-4; Ezekiel 37:21-28; Jeremiah 23:5-6; 30:9; 31:33-34; 33:14-17; Hosea 3:4-5). Any Jew who denies the coming of the Messiah, is called a 'heretic' (Sanhedrin 91a), the same way as if he denies the physical resurrection of the dead or Israel being chosen (Sanhedrin 99a).

The meaning of the word Messiah in Hebrew is "the anointed one", and pronounced as mashiah, moshiah, mashiach, or moshiach. Any Israelite King, High Priest or Prophet who was anointed with the special 'holy' oil prepared according to the directions of the Almighty (Exodus 30:22-32), was called "the anointed one". The Sages of the Talmud have said that in every generation of the nation of Israel there is a person possessing the potential characteristic to become the Mashiach.

"I have found David My servant and anointed him with my holy oil" (Psalm 89:21).

This is how the Scripture describes the anointing of the first King of Israel Saul son of Kish, of the tribe of Benjamin, by the Prophet Samuel:

"Then Samuel took a flask of oil and poured it over Saul's head. He kissed Saul and said, 'I am doing this because the Lord has appointed you to be the ruler over Israel, His special possession" (1 Samuel 10:1).

It is not necessary that the Messiah ought to come only from Israel. As we can see from the Bible, the non-Israelite, the Persian King Cyrus was called by God "anointed one" too:

"Thus said the Lord to His anointed, to Cyrus, whose right hand I have holden, to subdue nations before him; and I will lose the loins of kings, to open doors before him so that gates will not be shut" (Isaiah 45:1).

To be an "anointed one" means that this personality has established a define spiritual relationship with God and set apart by Him to accomplish a special divine mission. They were also protected by God.

"Do not touch My anointed ones, and do not hurt My prophets" (Psalms 105:15).

The Hebrew word 'mashiach' is often translated in English as 'Savior' or 'Redeemer' which is in contradiction with its plain meaning as 'Anointed'. It simply refers to the person chosen by God to be anointed with the specially prepared oil. The idea of an innocent human or divine or semi-divine being sacrificing himself in order to save humanity from the consequences of Adam's sin is purely Christian and has no foundation in Judaism.

Since any king of Israel, under certain circumstances, could be anointed with oil, he could be the potential Messiah. But the real Davidic Messiah of whom the Hebrew Scripture speaks and for whom the Jewish People have been waiting, will be called 'The Messiah'.

The Messiah will be chosen by God to usher humanity into the Messianic Era, where he will be the leader-King and rule over a redeemed and perfected World. He will be a man of flesh and blood, a mortal like all other people, from the house of King David, a direct descendent through King Solomon (2 Samuel 7:12-15; 1 Chronicles 17:11-14).

There is another opinion expressed in the Book of the Zohar that the Messiah will be descended from Solomon's brother Nathan, another son of David. But Nathan (it is well established fact) died childless. Then, how could it be possible for the Messiah to come from the childless Nathan? The Zohar finds an explanation. Actually, it says, Hephzibah, the wife of Nathan, will be the mother of the future Messiah. It is she 'who brings good tiding to Zion' (Isaiah 40:9).

After the death of Nathan, his brother Solomon, following the requirements of Jewish Laws, married his widow Hephzibah and restored the seed to his deceased brother. Although this first born boy was a result of the marriage between King Solomon and Hephzibah, widow of Nathan, by levirate marriage the child is consider as being a continuation of the deceased Nathan's line.

That is why the Zohar assumes that the Messiah will descend through the lineage of Nathan (Zohar 3:173b).

The Messiah will be a righteous man with a highly developed spiritual status, of great virtue and understanding of the World of God. The "spirit of the Lord" will be upon him, and he will have a "fear of God" (Isaiah 11:2). **The Messiah of the prophets is not a deity and is not a subject of worship.** He also must be a living personality of the same generation of the Messianic Age; not one who was dead and resurrected. Obviously, the King Messiah, after a very long and successful life will naturally die. (There is an opinion of R. Baḥya ben Joseph in his commentary to Genesis 11:11 which says: "The Messiah will not die").

In any event, the purpose of his coming, the task of the Redemption and perfection of this World will have been accomplished before his death. His accomplishments will include: Victorious wars which will be fought at the beginning of the Messianic Age; the reunification and ingathering of the Twelve Tribes into the Land of Israel which will have been re-established according to its Biblical borders; the rebuilding of the Temple and renewal of the sacrificial services; the turning of all people to worship the one God of Israel; abolishing wars forever and bringing Peace and Justice to the World. These achievements are needed for the Anointed to have been legally qualified by Scripture to be the real Messiah. His son will continue to lead the World (and his son's son, if needed) until the time of the end of the Messianic Era. The personality of the Messiah is not as important as the goals imposed on him to transform the reality of this physical world into the future Age of human refinement, harmony, and peace in the spirit of God, where all men and women will become holy and worship the one and the only Supreme God of the Universe—the God of Israel.

What will His Task be?

According to the Hebrew Bible, the Messiah, the future Messianic King of Israel and the spiritual leader of the World of the End Times has to accomplish a few monumental tasks:

—Reunite all the Tribes of Israel and bring all of them to the Promised Land and restore the Kingdom of David and his throne (Isaiah 11:12; 27:11; Ezekiel 37:21; 39:28);

—Restore the Holy Land to its Biblical borders and divide it as an inheritance among the Twelve Tribes (Numbers 34:13; Ezekiel 45:1);

—Defeat God's enemies and secure peace and safety in the Land of Israel (Zechariah 9:5-6; 12:6; 14:9-12; Isaiah 11:13-14; 17:1; 34:5, 8; 60:18; Obadiah 1:18; Ezekiel 25:12-17; Jeremiah 48 and 49; Zephaniah 2:8-11).

—Cleanse all Israelites of their abominations, teach them to learn and practice the Torah, make them again one nation of priests, a light to the world, and worship the God of Israel (Deuteronomy 7:6-8; 14:2; 30:8, 10; Jeremiah 31:32; Ezekiel 11:19-20; Exodus 19:5-6; Zechariah 8:23);

—Rebuild the Holy Temple and reinstate sacrificial services (Micah 4:1-2; Isaiah 2:2-3; 56:6-7; 60:7; Malachi 3:4; Zechariah 14:20-21); There are two traditions regarding the building of the third Temple. The first one is that the Temple will be built supernaturally by God and 'descend from heaven' and will last forever, "Thou shalt bring them in, and plant them in the mountain of thine inheritance, in the place, O LORD, which thou hast made for thee to dwell in, in the Sanctuary, O LORD, which thy hands have established" (Exodus 15:17). The second tradition is that the Temple will be built by the Messiah by natural human ways with the help of Almighty, of course. Actually, there is a dispute among the rabbis whether the Temple will be built before the coming of the Messiah or after it. Most sages have agreed that the Temple will be constructed before the revealing of the Messiah. Maimonides also supports this version from the prophecy of Malachi 3:1 in his famous letter to Yemen: "For suddenly the master whom you are seeking will come to his sanctuary;"

—Abolish wars. Establish Universal Peace and Justice. Lead and teach the nations "the ways of the Lord". "For out of Zion shall go forth Torah and the word of the Lord from Jerusalem" (Micah 4:2-4; Hosea 2:20; Isaiah 32:16-18; Jeremiah 33:9; Psalms 86:9);

—Bring the Universal knowledge of God to all inhabitants of the earth that all nations will know and worship one God of Israel (Zephaniah 3:9; Zechariah 14:9; Isaiah 45:23; 66:23; Jeremiah 31:33; Ezekiel 38:23; Psalms 86:9);

—Lead the people of the Messianic Era to regeneration to the state of righteousness and holiness and prepare all the nations to usher in wonderful, spiritual, and everlasting World-to-Come, the final destination for the mankind.

Note: According to Maimonides, the Messiah does not have to perform signs, wonders or miracles.

If any anointed King of Israel should do everything listed above, we would surely be able to say: This man is the Messiah!

Messianic—Imposters. How to Recognize the True and Genuine Messiah?

Jewish history has known many false messiah-imposters. Among the most notable claimants are:

—**Simon of Peraea** (circa 4 b.c.), a former slave of Herod the Great who rebelled and was killed by the Romans.

—Jesus of Nazareth (circa 6 b.c-30 a.c.), a religious teacher and reformer, crucified by the Romans.

—Simon bar Kokhba (circa 135 a.c.), a great military leader of the revolt and devoted religious patriot of the Jewish nation. Killed by the Romans in the Second Jewish-Roman War.

The Talmudic story of R. Akiva tells how this great spiritual leader and teacher of Israel announced Bar Kokhba to be the Jewish Messiah. After the failure and death of Bar Kokhba, R. Akiva acknowledged his huge mistake, on which account the Sages condemned any guessing about manmade predictions of the time of the arriving of the Messiah.

"He who announces the Messianic time based on his own calculation forfeits his own share in the future" (R. Jose, in Derek Erez Rabbah xi).

—Sabbatai Tzvi (1626-1676 a.c.), a Sephardic Rabbi and Kabbalist from the Turkish Ottoman Empire, founder of the Messianic Sabbatean movement. This movement indeed engulfed all Jewish communities around the world. In preparation for the Great Exodus to the Promised Land, Jews began to sell their houses and other properties. They were excited by the thought of a coming imminent redemption, dancing and singing with overwhelming joy. Synagogue posted the initials of Sabbatai on its walls, and new prayers for him were introduced, like this one: "Bless our Lord and King, the holy and righteous Sabbatai Tzvi, the Messiah of the God of Jacob".

At the age of forty he was forced to convert to Islam. He mysteriously died a few years later in isolation in a small town in Montenegro on September 17, 1676 a.c., which was the day of Yom Kippur.

—Menachem Mendel Schneerson (1902-1994 a.c.), the seventh Lubavitch Rebbe. Actually, this righteous Rebbe never claimed that he is the Messiah. During his lifetime many of his followers had considered him to be the Jewish Messiah. After his death, the religious leaders of the Chabad-Lubavitch messianic movement officially proclaimed R. Schneerson as the Messiah sent by God and they have continued to await his resurrection from the dead to resume his Messianic duties. This belief is strong reminiscent of Christian theologian doctrine about the Second coming (return) of the Messiah and has been unanimously rejected by the Sages and Rabbinical literature for almost 2,000 years.

How may people recognize if the Messiah is a true and genuine one, send by God? By his life and deeds! This answer, actually, belongs to the Great Rambam (Rabbi Moses ben Maimon, Maimonides, Talmudist, Halachist, physician, philosopher 1135-1204 a.c.). That is what he wrote in his main work Mishneh Torah, a 14 volumes compendium of Jewish Law, in the section Hilkhot Melakhim, chapters 11 and 12.

"The anointed king is destined to stand up and restore the Davidic Kingdom to its antiquity, to the first sovereignty. He will build the Temple in Jerusalem and gather the strayed ones of Israel together. All Laws will return in his days as they were before: Sacrificial offerings will be offered and the Sabbatical Years and Jubilees kept, according to all precepts that are mentioned in the Torah. Whoever does not believe in him, or whoever does not wait for his coming, not only does he deny the other prophets, but also the Torah and Moses our teacher."

"And if a king shall arise from the House of David, and occupied with the commandments like his father David, according to the written and oral Torah, and he will impel all of Israel to follow it and to strengthen breaches in its observance, and will fight Hashem's [God's] wars, this one is to be treated as if he were the anointed one. If he succeeds and builds a Holy Temple in its proper place and gathers the dispersed ones of Israel together, this is indeed the anointed one for certain, and he will mend the entire world to worship the Lord together, as it is stated: "For then I shall turn for the nations a clear tongue, to call all in the Name of the Lord and to worship Him with one shoulder (Zephaniah 3:9)."

What happen if 'an anointed one' dies before he fulfils all the tasks entrusted to him by the Almighty? Maimonides gives an answer on this too, from the same source:

"But if he did not succeed to this degree, or if he was killed, it becomes known that he is not the one of whom the Torah had promised us, and he is indeed like all proper and wholesome kings of the House of David who died. The Holy One, Blessed Be He, only set him up to try the public by him, thus: Some of the wise men will stumble in clarifying these words, and in elucidating and interpreting when the time of the end will be, for it is not yet the designated time" (Daniel 11:35)."

Yes, it is a serious matter to rightfully recognize the legitimate Messiah. Even one of the most learned Rabbis of all times, the greatest authority of the Jewish Law and Tradition, 'Head of all Sages', the founder of Rabbinical Judaism, Rabbi Akiva (circa 50-135 a.c.), even such a renowned man, made a mistake, 'stumbled', when he acknowledged Bar Kochba, the heroic leader of the Jewish revolt against the Romans, a brave general and true believer in God, who was killed in battle, as the King Messiah (Jerusalem Talmud, Ta'anit 4:8).

The Messiah Son of Joseph

The story of the Messiah son of David is not complete without mentioning another important figure in Jewish Messianic Thought, the Messiah son of Joseph. If the name and the actions of the first Messiah have many references throughout the Tanakh, especially in the section of the Prophets, the name of the second Messiah has not been mentioned in the Jewish Bible whatsoever. We learn about him in the sources of rabbinical apocalyptic literature, from around 250 a.c. in Succah 52 a, b, where three statements are given. We are told, by authority of R. Dosa, this Messiah's name and the fate which he is to meet, namely, willingly undergo suffering for the sake of the nation (Isaiah 53) and to fall in battle in the Gog and Magog War. Later on, more details were established in Kabbalistic eschatology such as the books of the Zohar and "Kol Ha Tor" by followers of Eliyahu of Vilna and in Midrashim (e.g. Pirkei Heichalos Rabbasi 39:1; Pirkei Mashiach, Beis HaMedrash, part 3). Some related information has also been given by R. Saadiah Gaon in his Emunos VeDeos (Beliefs and Principles 8:2, 5) and Ramban (Nachmanides) in his commentary on Shir HaShirim (Song of Solomon 8:13).

According to these sources, the Messiah ben Joseph will appear among the 'Lost' Ten Tribes of Israel in Exile (Malbim, 1809-1879 a.c.) and will be the forerunner and the representative of the Messiah son of David. He will undertake the task to reconcile and reunite all the Israelites Tribe and bring them home to the Promised Land. He will fight God's wars, victoriously apply 'the fist of God's judgment' against the surrounding enemy-nations (listed in Psalms 83:6-8) and secure the Israelite independence in the newly reestablished according to Biblical borders, Land of Greater Israel. He will rebuild the Temple in Jerusalem, resume the sacrificial services and cleanse the Israelites. However, rabbinical tradition says that this Messiah is destined to be killed in battle: "They shall look unto him whom they have pierced and mourn for him" (Zechariah 12: 10-14; Succah, 52a). Then, after forty years, the Messiah son of David will arrive to complete the final stage of Redemption as the Prophet Ezekiel described it in Chapter 37:21-28. Other Rabbinical sources say that there is a 45 day period following the death of Messiah ben Joseph, before the appearance of Messiah ben David, it is during this period Elijah, the forerunner of the Messiah, makes his appearance.

God will avenge the death of Messiah son of Joseph by 'destroying all the nations that attack Jerusalem' (Zechariah 12:9).

Some Sages taught that the Messiah ben Joseph, being a perfectly righteous man, a divinely appointed King, will undergo torture and suffer a painful death for the sin of Israel in a manner of sacrificial death described in Isaiah, chapter 53. He voluntarily and gladly takes upon himself this mission for the sake of saving Israel. As it is written in Pesikta Rabbati, 'The Holy One, blessed be He, made an agreement with him. He said: Those whose sins are stored up with you will bring you into an iron yoke and make you like this calf whose eyes are dimmed with pain. They will force your spirit into a yoke, and because of their sins your *tongue will cleave* to your jaws (Ps. 22:15-16). Are you willing for this? He replied in His presence: Lord of the Worlds, with gladness of soul and rejoicing of heart I take it upon me, on the condition that not one will perish from Israel'.

Will the Messiah Son of David Resurrect the Messiah Son of Joseph?

There is also an opinion that at the time of his appearance, the Davidic Messiah will resurrect the Messiah son of Joseph. We are over-cautious about this. Since the power over life and death is a prerogative of God Almighty, who alone holds the key of resurrection of the dead, and the Messiah son of David is a human, not a deity; he would not be able to have such a power of the resurrection of the dead (Talmud, Ta'an 2a; Sanhedrin 113a).

There is strong belief in the Torah in resurrection after death.

"There is no god besides Me. I put to death and I bring to life" (Deuteronomy 32:39).

"The Lord brings death and makes alive" (1 Samuel 2:6).

"Multitudes who sleep in the dust of the earth will awake" (Daniel 12:2).

The same opinion was expressed by Rambam, who considered that the descriptions of the prophet Isaiah 11:6-7 were the pure metaphors and symbols. The physical World will remain as it is. The Messiah must not perform miracles such as resurrection for him to be believed. There might be some physical resurrections of the dead by the Will of God in the Messianic Time, but these resurrected saints will not live forever, and they eventually will die at some point in time after a long and happy life. They still will have possessed the common physical characteristics: "eat, drink, copulate, beget, and die after a very long life, like the lives of those who will live in the Days of Messiah." This was his comment on the physical resurrection prophesied by Daniel 12:2,

13. Maimonides differentiates temporal bodily resurrections in the Messianic Age (also in some cases he describes them as metaphorical, a symbol, or allegory, Ezekiel 37:1-14; Isaiah 26:19) from the Universal spiritual resurrection of the souls of the people with 'immaterial perfected intellect' to immortality in the Universal World-To-Come. Maimonides called those who believed in physical resurrection in the World-to-Come on Earth as 'utter fools' and their belief as 'folly' ('The Guide for the Perplexed' and 'The Treatise on Resurrection').

The Messiah son of Joseph will be resurrected at the end of the Messianic Era, after 1000 years of the seventh day of the Universal Sabbath, when the WORLD will remain 'fallow' (mushmat) and desolate (haruv) in a state of rest and peace, a time of completeness of the 'work' performed in the previous 6000 years of 'This World' (Olam Hazeh). There is another opinion that the Messiah, son of Joseph, being a righteous man of God, will not have to be a part of the spiritual universal resurrection. His immortal soul, as the souls of all righteous people, shall already merit the life in the World-to-Come: Such souls will be taken to a special temporal place in Heaven, a World of Souls, where they will be purified and charged with the Divine knowledge how to see God 'face to face' and obtain His likeness and holiness. It is of interest to mention here that all Divine knowledge shall be imparted and the spiritual growth of the Souls accomplished through studying the Torah, which will finally and completely be understood only in the spiritual World of souls. The universal resurrection will include only those multitudes that have not repented and not accepted the God of Israel and, therefore, not merited life in the World-to-Come: They will face the Final Judgment. After the Final Judgment, glorious bodies will rise to immortality and reunite with their souls, and the new perfected highly spiritual World-to-Come (Olam Habah) will begin forever. Other scholars say that all the souls will be taken to the Realm of souls, regardless as to whether they belong to the righteous or the sinners, and will be there for one thousand years, preparing for the universal resurrection.

The Messianic Era ('the days of the Mashiach') is definitely not a part of the World-to-Come, because it is a continuation of this historical and physical World, a transitional stage to the next World, which may continue for 40, 70 years ('those generations'), 365 years (as the days of the solar year), and/or 400 years (Sanhedrin 99a). Meanwhile, the World-to-Come is a purely spiritual new realm which is not compatible with physical existence, the final Divine Kingdom of God. As Rambam said in his 13 articles of faith, "I believe with perfect faith that the dead will be brought back to life when God wills it to happen". God created World-to-Come as a fulfillment of the Divine Plan and an ultimate destination for spiritually regenerated Humanity (Genesis 2:3).

When will the Messiah Come?

Classical Jewish sources say that the Messianic Age is a part of "This World' which is supposed to last for 6000 years, according to the six days theory of Creation. The dead line for the Messiah to arrive is the year 6000. There are many versions of the timing of his coming. Some say that the Messiah can come before the dead line, even today, if all people were to repent and turn to God. It depends on us. God is ready when we are. The other scholars believe that the Almighty set aside a special day for the coming of the Messiah when a certain number of saints and martyrs will have lived or the number of human souls sent from Heaven will have reached a fixed number of created souls on earth. That date is known only to God and will remain a Mystery to people until the actual day of His revealing. Others say that the conduct of mankind will determine the time of his coming: The Messiah will come in either (a) a generation that is totally evil and self destructive, at the time when he is most needed cf. the teaching of Rabbi Elazar, that the messianic age will begin in a generation with the power to destroy itself (Song of Songs Rabbah 2:29); or (b) in a time of total repentance, when the World is good and deserves his appearance (Isaiah 59:20). In the Midrash Nistarot Rav Shimon ben Yohai points out that 'If they are not pure, the Messiah ben Ephraim will come; and if they are pure, the Messiah ben David will come'. This is referring to the fact that the task of the Messiah ben Joseph is to correct the impurity of Israel, and make them repent and become righteous.

"It is inconceivable that the Redemption shall come about while we are still steeped in the sins for the sake of which God exiled us," said Saadiah Gaon (Egypt-Babylon, 882-942 A.C.) in his Book of Beliefs and Opinions (Kitab).

The Babylonian Talmud, Sanhedrin 97b says: "If the Israelites repent, they will be redeemed. If not, the Holy One, blessed be He, will rise up a king whose decrees will be even more severe than those of Haman and then they will repent and be redeemed."

There are many opinions of the rabbis about the particulars and conditions of the coming of the Messiah recorded in the Babylonian Talmud, Sanhedrin 97a.

R. Nehorai said: "In the generation when Messiah comes, young men will insult the old, and old men will stand before the young [to give them honor]; daughters will rise up against their mothers and daughters-in-law against their mothers-in-law. The people shall be dog-faced, and a son will not be abashed in his father's presence".

It has been taught, R. Nehemiah said: "in the generation of Messiah's coming impudence will increase, esteem be perverted, the vine yields its fruit, yet shall wine be dear, and the Kingdom will be converted to heresy with none to rebuke them".

This supports R. Isaac, who said: "The son of David will not come until the whole world is converted to the belief of the heretics".

Others say: "The son of David will not come until denunciators are in abundance".

The rabbis also elaborated on the way the Messiah will appear. R. Alexandri said: "R. Y'hoshua'a ben Levi explained: 'If they will be righteous (Israelites), the Messiah will come on the clouds of heaven (Daniel 7:13); if they will not be righteous, he will come as a poor man riding upon an ass (Zechariah 9:9; Babylonian Talmud, Sanhedrim 98a).

The Almighty has openly explained to His People that the arrival of the Messiah depends on them. "If you are worthy, I will hasten it; if not, it will come in its own time."

In the Babylonian Talmud, Sanhedrin 98b it is mentioned that R. Hillel said "there will not be a Messiah for Israel, since they have already enjoyed him during the reign of Hezekiah" (King of Judea, 716-697 b.c.). Rav Yosef said: "May Rabbi Hillel's Master forgive him. Hezekiah lived during the First Temple while Zechariah prophesied during the Second Temple".

It is not that R. Hillel rejected future redemption and the Messianic World; what he said is:—There will be no human individual messenger-Messiah sent by God for people redemption. God will Himself initiate the redemption process and the Messianic World without a human messenger, when the appointed time arrives and when people will be ready, 'ripe' for it.

As King David said, 'Redemption will come today, if you hearken to His voice'. The Sages of the Talmud strongly warned those who try to predict the exact time of the advent of the Messiah, because errors in calculation of such predictions could lead to grave consequences and damage faith in the Messiah and in Judaism itself. This was the case of the Jewish Revolt against the Romans (132-135 a.c.), when the greatest religious authority, head of the all Sages, Rabbi Akiva, together with the Sages of Yavneh and Sanhedrin mistakenly acknowledged Bar Kokhba, the wrong men, brutal tyrannical leader of the Revolt, as the Jewish Messiah.

It is taught that **"He who announces the Messianic time based on calculation forfeits his own share in the future"** (R. Jose, in Derek Erez Rabbah xi.)

"May the bones of those who calculate the end rot", for they say: "Since the time has arrived and he has not come, he will never come" (Sanhedrin 97b).

Rambam, in his twelfth article of faith, expressed it this way: "I believe with a full heart in the coming of the Messiah, and even though he may tarry I will still wait for him." Indeed, the Messiah is approaching; we can almost hear his footsteps.

THIS WORLD AND THE MESSIANIC ERA

This World, 'Olam Hazeh' in Hebrew, will last for 6000 years since Creation and will end in the year 2240 of Common Era. From the Creation to the beginning of the Christian era is 3,760 years, according to the Jewish calendar. Today's year 2012 a.c. corresponds to the Hebrew year of 5772. There are left 228 years to complete 6000 years of existence of This World then the Messianic Age will come and last for another 1000 years (from year 6000 to year 7000 Hebrew calendar). All of these are the teachings of Scripture, the Talmud, the Midrash and the Kabbalistic book the Zohar (Talmud Rosh Hashana 31a; Sanhedrin 97a; Zohar 1:117a; Zohar Vayera 119a).

The concept that this World (Olam Hazeh) will last 6000 years and the Messianic Era is for 1000 years comes from the Scripture:

"For six days the Lord made the heavens and the earth, the sea, and all that in them, but He rested on the seventh day. Therefore the Lord blessed the Sabbath day and made it holy" (Exodus 20:11).

"On the seventh day God had finished His work of creation, so he rested from all His work. And God blessed the seventh day and made it holy" (Genesis 2:2-3).

"Six eons for going in and coming out, for war and peace. The seventh eon is entirely Shabbat and rest for life everlasting"
(Midrash, Pirke De Rabbi Elieazer).

According to Talmudic tradition, each of the six days of Creation corresponds to one thousand years (eon), therefore This World (Olam Hazeh) was designed by the Almighty to last for 6000 years. The seventh day of the week which God made holy is the Universal Day of Rest, the Sabbath, and will last for another 1000 years, designated as the millennium of the Messianic Era. There is another Talmudic opinion that this seventh day of Creation, blessed and set apart by God is a new afterlife in the World-to-Come (Olam Haba), a higher level of spiritual being, which is separate and different in time and space from the Messianic World.

"For a thousand years in Thy sight are but as yesterday when it is past, and as a watch in the night" (Psalms 90:4; Sanhedrin 97a).

"A thousand years in Your eyes are like a day that passes. For six thousand years the world will exist" (Talmud, Rosh Hashana 31a).

R. Abaye did not agree with R. Kattina who said that the World will be desolate for one thousand years out of seven days of the existence of this World, as it is said: "And the Lord alone shall be exalted in that day" (Isaiah 2:11); in R. Abaye opinion, this World (after six thousand years of Creation), will be desolate for two thousand years, as it is written: "After two days will he revive us: in the third day, he will raise us up, and we shall live in his sight" (Hosea 6:2).

The Tanna debe Eliyyahu teaches: "The world is to exist six thousand years. In the first two thousand there was desolation (without the Torah); two thousand years the Torah flourished; and the next two thousand years is the Messianic era".

Belief in the Messianic Age has contributed to many religions and been accepted by multitudes of people around the world. Many think of the Messianic Era as if it will be God's Heavenly Kingdom on earth or the World-to-Come, the ultimate destination of mankind and the highest peak of its existence and spiritual development. Some scholars believe that the Messianic World is something different and separate in time and space from This World (Olam Hazeh) and rather connect it to the future World-to-Come (Olam Haba). Others say that the Messianic Age is a part of This World, only much improved on the spiritual level when people "will neither harm nor destroy on all My holy mountain, for the earth will be full of the knowledge of the Lord as the waters cover the sea" (Isaiah 11:9).

If we follow the theory of the six days of Creation and one day of Sabbath, it is commonly recognized that This World will exist for 6000 years after which will come the millennium of the Messianic World.

All together This World plus the Messianic Age will last for 7000 years. The 'Golden Age' of humanity, according to this theory, will last only 1000 years. Is that all? What is next? Have we indeed reached the height of our potential and fulfilled the Almighty's Plan for our future in His Divine Kingdom? Not so!

Before we proceed with the answer to these questions, we would like to briefly describe what the Messianic World is all about. The understanding that the Messianic World is a part of This World in which we are all living, means that people will have continued to live on planet Earth in the same way as they have been living for the past 6000 years, from the physical point of view. The physical laws of the Universe will not change. People will still eat and drink; there will be death and birth. But the quality and longevity of life will tremendously improve. People will live much longer and happier lives. Progress in scientific knowledge will be unprecedented. All diseases will be curable and eventually will disappear. Pain and sufferings will be eradicated. People will not labor for a living anymore because food, goods and clothing will be in abundance. No more wars, aggressiveness of the nations, or any kind of oppression. No crimes, no sins.

"They will beat their swords into plowshares and their spears into pruning hooks. Nation will not take up sword against nation, nor will they train for war anymore. The wolf will live with the lamb, the leopard will lie down with the goat, the calf and the lion and the yearling together; and a little child will lead them" (Isaiah 2:4; 11:6).

Rambam (Maimonides) interprets the prophet's description of the Messianic World of peace and tranquility as a highly poetical and symbolical form commonly used in ancient writings in describing a 'golden age'. Ramban (Nachmanides) understands Isaiah wordings as a literal description of miraculous events and criticizes Maimonides for his allegorical approach and minimizing supernatural miracles, especially in the time of the Jewish Messiah. As our reader, probably, figured out, we support the position of Maimonides in these matters (Isaiah 11:6-8; 26:14, 19; Ezekiel 37:1-14). Maimonides rejects all corporeal references, miracles and other manifestations of physicality to the World-To-Come as simple metaphors, symbols, and allegories. In all his writings concerning this matter, Maimonides stresses that the World-To-Come is a domain of spiritual souls, and it is a final destination for humanity and the ultimate purpose of Creation.

All the nations of the World will worship one God—Creator of the Universe, the Almighty God of Israel. People will live in harmony and happiness.

"No longer will a man teach his neighbor, and every man his brother, saying, "Know the Lord", because they will all know Me, from the least of them to the greatest", said the Lord. "For I will forgive their iniquity, and their sin I remember no more" (Jeremiah31:34).

"For the earth shall be filled with the knowledge of the Lord" (Isaiah 11:9).

As we fully acknowledged in Chapter XVII, all the above conditions have been achieved thanks to the heroic effort of the Israelites and the resurrected saints. In the Messianic Era Israel will have fulfilled its Divine mission as a nation of priests, a light to the World. God has made them to be a Covenant and a Light for Gentiles. They will have brought God's Glory and Redemption to the ends of the earth (Isaiah 42:6; 43:21; 49:6).

This is how Rambam describes the Messianic Age in his Mishneh Torah:

"And at that time there will be no hunger or war, no jealousy or rivalry. For the good will be plentiful, and all delicacies available as dust. The entire occupation of the world will be only to know God."

Now, since we learn the general characteristics of the Messianic World, and we assume that it is a part or continuation of This World as we know it, we will try to answer whether it is the seventh day of the Universal Millennial Rest spoken of in Scripture or not. There are two points of significant importance here:

1). If the Messianic Era is a part of This World which is supposed to last for 6000 years all together, it means that the Messianic World is incorporated in these 6000 years, (as of to-day, it is left 228 years), and it is unknown precisely what portion of these 228 years belongs to the Messianic Age;

2). If the Messianic Era is not a part of This World but something separate and different, designated as the "Seventh day" Sabbath which is supposed to last for one thousand years, it means that another 1000 years are needed on top of the 6000 years of existence of This World which brings us to 7000 years. If the Messiah will not come on time, who knows, how many years the World has still to wait until his actual coming? These calculations so far are certainly in line with the theory of the 'Seven days' of the Biblical Creation week.

Has it not become more confusing? Well, slowly but surely we are moving ahead with hope to clarify all these matters.

If we assume that the idea of the Biblical Sabbath, the seventh day of Creation, the Universal rest for life everlasting, is a Millennium of the Messianic Age, as many have insisted, what is the World-to-Come then, where and when should we place it in the Torah's Creation week theory?

THE WORLD-TO-COME

There are some other opinions, based on the Kabbalistic work, the Zohar, and on the Talmud, connected with the World-to-Come (Olam Habah). They are saying that This World (Olam Hazeh) has to last for 6000 years, including the years of the Messianic Age. Eventually, This World will come to an end, when people "with immaterial intellect" will have perfected themselves by studying the Torah and performing the Mitzvoth of good deeds, the way God desires it. So how many years do they attribute to the Messianic World? Precisely 2000 years, no less, no more! The counting goes like this: from the creation of Adam to Abraham is 2000 years without the Torah; from Abraham to the Christian Era is another 2000 years with the Torah; and the final 2000 years are supposed to be the Messianic Age. As of today, the

Messiah, son of David, has not arrived and the Messianic World has not started.

The Hebrew 6000 years of This World will expire in the year 2240 of the Common Era. Today, as we mentioned above, is the year 2012 which corresponds to 5772 Hebrew year from the Creation, so there are left 228 years to complete six millennia of the six days of the Creation week. Does this mean that the Messianic World will last only as long as what is left from 6000 years—228 years or less? No, they say, the Messianic World has to last for 2000 years, no matter what it takes! In this scenario, the span life of This World will obviously over-reach the designated 6000 years given for its existence by 2000 plus years. We do not know for certain when the final redemption and the Messianic Era will come. Even if it seems that we live in the Biblical "End Times", nobody knows how long it will take before the advent of the Messiah. These calculations of 8000 plus years for the duration of This World, which include the Messianic Era, also do not correspond to the 'six days' Creation theory which consists of exactly 6000 years for the duration of This World.

So, we have, basically, two opinions:

I: Many Rabbis have understood the Messianic World as the 1000 years of the seventh day of the Creation set apart from This World by the Lord as the Sabbath, a Universal Day of rest and peace, sanctified as a Holy Day (1000 years). It would seem, they have identified the Messianic World with the World-to-Come (Olam Haba) and understood the Messianic Era as a culmination of the historical process, the ultimate design of Almighty for humanity. Their calculation of 6000 years for This World and 1000 years for the Messianic Age, the Holy Sabbath, is consistent, on first sight, with the Seven Days theory of Creation.

II: Other Sages have included the Messianic Era in 6000 years of This World, made these two Words inseparable, with the only difference being that the Messianic World will be a better place to live where all people will have become righteous and holy, ready and deserving to usher in a future everlasting purely spiritual World-to-Come. They say that the Messianic World should have lasted exactly for 2000 years. According to their calculation, the six days (6000 years) of This World will become at least eight days (8000 years) plus unknown numbers of years of expectation for the coming of the Messiah. This, certainly, does not fit the theory of the seven days of Creation. Does it really require 2000 years to complete the Messianic World? With widespread knowledge of the Lord? With Universal Peace, Justice, Prosperity and the Love of God and His Torah?

And what will happen with the seventh day of Creation, the day of Universal rest and peace, the Sabbath, sanctified by the Almighty as a holy day? Does it correspond with the Millennia of the Messianic World? No, it does not!

Before we continue the story of the 'Seventh Day of Creation', let us take a little step back and shed some light on the question: How old is the Universe and the planet Earth we are living on?

HOW OLD IS THE EARTH?

There are too many opinions on this. Classical Jewish sources, the Talmud, the Midrash, and the Kabbalistic book, the Zohar, support the literal Bible version of six days Creation and one day of the holy Sabbath. That is why the Hebrew calendar starts at the day of Creation of Adam and Eve. Today it is configured with year 5772 as equivalent to the year 2012 of the Common Era. According to Judaism, each day of Creation corresponds to one thousand of 'earthy years' culminating in 6000 years as the life span for the existence of this World. The seventh day of Creation was designated as a universal 'day of rest' and peace, a time of completeness of the work performed in the previous six millennia, which will culminate in another 1,000 years of the Sabbatical Day. In other words, to put it simply, the World, people and all other species living on earth now, are no older than 6,000 years.

"The World will exist for 6,000 years, and in the 7,000th year, it will be destroyed" (Talmud, Sanhedrin 97a). Many rabbis teach that the Universe is 5772 years old. This chronology is the basic teaching among most of Orthodox Jews today.

This is what the literal interpretation of the Bible holds.

Rambam taught that the Genesis account might be understood and interpreted as being an allegory, a parable, not to be taken literally. In his opinion, the story of Creation is very mystical in nature and symbolical in its spiritual concepts; with a lot of hidden knowledge and secret meanings. To translate it literally, means to translate it wrongly. **"I will open my mouth in parables; I will utter hidden things, things from of old"** (Psalm 78:2).

What does science say on this matter? Of course, scientists have disagreed with the Biblical seven days Creation theory and have maintained that the Earth and the Universe are much, much older than 6,000 years. All over the Continents of our planet and on the Moon scientists have found pre-historic rocks and meteorites which radioactive dating gives dates well exceeding 3.5 billion years. The oldest rocks were found in Northwestern Canada near Grate Slave Lake—4.03 billion years. Various methods of radioactive dating (uranium-argon, potassium-thorium, racemization and thermaluminescence) have been applied to analyze these rocks, and the results were consistent with insignificant differences within a few percent. These geological findings indicate that planet Earth has existed for billions of years before the Biblical account of man's recorded history.

Paleontologists have discovered plentiful remains of pre-historic mammoths and dinosaurs with a wide range of their being dated from 65-220 millions years to 10,000-50,000 thousand years.

Basically, scientists say that the Earth is 4.5 billion years old, and the age of the Universe they estimate at between 13-15 billion years.

How is one to reconcile such a huge differences between the Biblical account (6,000 years) and the estimation of the scientists (15 billions)?

There are a few explanations for this. First of all, the Bible never specified when the Universe and the Earth were created. There is no affirmative statement in the Hebrew Scripture how old the Earth is. The Biblical account of Creation does not actually contradict the scientific conclusion of the age of the Universe and the Earth. These differences become obvious only when the proponents of religious fundamentalism argue for veracity of the literal Biblical account of Creation and say things that the Bible actually does not say. On the other hand, some scholars have discovered in verses Genesis 1:1, 2 proofs that the Earth and the Universe could have been created 15 billion years or so ago as scientists have insisted. In addition to the age, the Bible indicates that there was the 'beginning' of all things—the Creation of heavens and earth (Genesis 1:1). In scientific language this beginning is called the 'Big Bang' theory. Even the great Albert Einstein for fifteen years refused to accept that the Universe had a beginning.

The Gap Theory

When did it begin? They named this version "The Gap Theory" which means that between the beginning of creation of the Earth and the Universe mentioned in Genesis 1:1 and the beginning of the six days of Creation of Genesis 1:3-31 (two 'beginnings'!) is a huge time-gap of 15 billion years. This very remote and unknown period of antiquity is hidden in the depth of eternal ages. According to their explanation, the first day of Creation started in Genesis 1:3-5, "And God said "Let there be light". God saw that the light was good, and He separated the light from the darkness. And God called the light Day, and the darkness he called Night. And the evening and the morning were the first day."

This account of the first day of Creation clearly points to the fact that the Earth had already been created and had been in existence, possibly, for billions of years. The original creation of heaven and earth was the actual beginning of all things. The second and the third days of Creation, when God separated the waters and made a dry firmament which He named 'earth', and the gathered waters He called 'seas' (Genesis 1:6-13), do not speak of the creation of a new Earth. These creation actions are also indicative that the Earth was in existence: "And the earth was without form, and void; and darkness was on the face of the deep. And the Spirit of God moved on the face of the waters" (Genesis 1:2). The first verse of Genesis 1:1 gives us a satisfying and useful account of the beginning of the Earth and Heaven.

Some people, in defense of the literal Biblical story of Creation, criticize those who stick with the 'Gap Theory' and advocate a billions of years old Earth, saying that during the six days of Creation God Himself planted geological and paleontological evidences of an 'old' Earth to deceive and confuse unbelievers. This explanation sounds like an anecdote, but nevertheless it has few a followers. To downplay the 'Gap Theory' they come up with the declaration of Exodus 20:11, "In six days the Lord made heaven and earth, the sea, and all that is in them." In the same context they use verses Job 40:15-24 describing the awful creature 'behemoth' whose bones are 'like bars of iron'; 'he move his tail like a cedar'; 'and he drinks up a river'. By referring to this evidence, the proponents of 'Young Earth' say that the 'strange' animals like the behemoths, mammoths, and all kind of dinosaurs were created together with Adam and Eve and, therefore, the Age of the Earth is no more than 6000 years. According to our understanding, on which account we are providing a full and detailed explanation, the six days of Creation, (with one day set apart as the Sabbath), recorded in the Genesis, is not the primeval Creation of the new Earth and the Universe. It is rather the re-creation of the planet Earth and everything on it after the Earth became destroyed: 'formless and empty, dark, cold desert, covered with deep waters' (Genesis 1:1-2). The actual initial Creation of the Earth, mentioned in Genesis1:1, could have happened billions years prior to the Biblical six days Creation and the appearance of Adam and Eve. And, of course, all those 'strange' gigantic creatures were in existence at that time.

Incidentally, the enormously large 'behemoth' of Job 40:15-24, in the opinion of scientists, was not a pre-historic creature of billions of years ago. A few fossil remains of these previously unknown 'behemoth' animals were found a few years ago in Baluchistan, a province of Iran.

They have been extinct for a long time. Their size was astonishing: 26 feet in full height, 30 feet in length, weighing 20 tons, which might be comparable to the weight of three elephants. These huge mammals, named the 'Beasts of Baluchistan', in reality possessed the physical characteristics of Job 40 and matched in particular verses such his height being tall 'like a cedar' (verse 17); 'his bones are like bars of iron' (verse 18); or 'drawing up the Jordan into his mouth' (verse 23). The fact that these animals were in existence in the same time as Humans, does not serve as a proof of a 'Young' Earth. It does confirm the validity of the Biblical account of the six days Creation, which, in fact, was a Re-construction and Re-creation of a planet Earth that had previously existed and was later destroyed.

Other people questioned verse 3 in Genesis 1:3, "Let there be light" as an impossible reality because the sun and moon, the light-givers, were created later, on the fourth day of Creation. For determination of the mornings and evenings, days and nights, there should have been sun-sets and sun-rises and light from the moon and the stars. This is exactly what God did on the fourth day of Creation!

"God made two great lights—the larger one to govern the day, and the smaller one to govern the night. He also made the stars. God set them in the expanse of the sky to give light on the earth, to govern the day and the night, and to separate light from darkness. And God saw that it was good. There was evening and there was morning, a fourth day" (Genesis 1:16-19).

Defenders of the Biblical account of Creation answer this with the categorical statement: 'God does not need the sun and the moon to separate light from the darkness because God is the source of all light!'

Their opponents argue that the sun and moon were created in the beginning when the Universe and Earth were originally created because Job 38:7 and Isaiah 45:18 clearly speak of that God being pleased with the results of His created Works. The angels, sons of God, and myriads of created spiritual beings praise the Almighty for a magnificent World. The 'star wars', as we note below, or another kind of catastrophe of a huge magnitude must have brought the Earth to a state of chaos, lifelessness, darkness and flood as we find in Genesis 1:2. The Earth's atmosphere became dark, thick, so heavily polluted that the light of the sun, moon and the stars could not penetrate it. In the time of reconstruction and recreation (the Earth of Genesis 1:2), God first cleaned the atmosphere and caused the sun, moon and the stars to show light again, bringing days and nights, mornings and evenings. By establishing order in the atmosphere and separating light from darkness, He brought forth (renewed) all kind of life on the planet Earth once more.

There are a few legitimate questions raised on Genesis 1:2 verse, "And the earth was without form, and void; and darkness was on the face of the deep. And the Spirit of God moved on the face of the waters."

It is known that everything God created is good. In the beginning, when He created the Earth, it was so beautiful, perfect and glorious that all heavenly Angels, the sons of God, the multitude of spiritual created beings, who were in existence before the creation of Heaven and Earth, when they beheld the primeval earth, joined together in a magnificent chorus to sing a song of praise, joyfully celebrating completion of the new World—the Earth. God asked Job:

"Whereupon are the foundations thereof fastened? Or who laid the corner stone thereof; when the morning stars sang together and all the sons of God shouted for joy (Job 38:6-7)?

The entire holy Heavenly host, comparable to the morning stars for their light and glory, honored God for a creation of a new magnificent World, for His goodness, wisdom and power. This also serves as a proof that the Universe had already been created, and that the earth is one of the last of the worlds which have been called into being. God created the Earth not to be formless, lifeless, dark and chaotic ('tohu'), to be a vast dead desert covered with the deep waters, as Genesis 1:2 described it. God formed the Earth to be inhabited. Scripture shows that God designed the Earth 'not in vain', but to be beautiful and to be inhabited with a variety of life forms; with a suitable atmosphere, water and air (Isaiah 45:18).

What had happened to the first perfectly created Earth and its inhabitants to make it a cold, empty, dark, dead desert flooded by deep waters? And for how long beforehand had this transformation taken place? We cannot answer these questions with certainty. Some theologians have come up with the theory that it was due to Lucifer (the Satan) having rebelled with his angels against God and His Angels. In this cataclysmic 'Star Wars' many Worlds of the Universe were destroyed or damaged. Those heavenly spiritual beings are very powerful! One of the consequences of this heavenly drama was the defeat of Lucifer and his army, and the changes that occurred on planet Earth, as described in Genesis 1:2. That is why, as a result of the course of these gigantic catastrophic events of heavenly warfare, the Earth was transformed from Genesis 1:1 to Genesis 1:2.

Biblical scholars and scientists have said that life on Earth has experienced several periods (cycles) of mass extinction and rebirth. According to the 'Gap Theory', many billions years have passed between verse 1 and verse 2 of Genesis 1 when God might have created and destroyed (renewed) the Earth and life on it on a few (multiple?) occasions. Actually, the fact that we are now in the seventh Sabbatical cycle, point out that the Worlds were destroyed and renewed six times. One of these 'fresh' periods is aptly described in the Bible, Noah's Flood (Genesis 6-9); the other is called 'Lucifer's Flood', which allegedly occurred deep back in the far-distant catastrophic past.

The Worlds were Created, Destroyed, and Renew again

The Sages teach that **there were created Worlds that existed before ours and these were eventually destroyed and renewed again.** Beside the stories of prehistoric mammoths and dinosaurs, there were the Centaurs of Greek mythology, part human and part horse; Sphinxes of Egypt, mystical creatures with the body of a lion and a human head; the water-nymph mermaids, the Serpent who could speak to humans of Genesis 3:1—All these could well indicate a variety of human-like species previously created and destroyed by God. The Rabbis and earlier generations of Kabbalists explain that there were human pre-Adamic civilizations in existence on earth that God had created, destroyed and renewed on a few occasions. The veracity of the existence of these pre-Adamic Worlds has not been denied in rabbinical literature, Torah and Talmud. Many kinds of human fossils have been found in our Planet dated thousands and even millions years prior to the creation of Adam and Eve. These races of human-like beings had been exterminated or 'wiped out' at various times in the past. They were spiritless creatures, with whom God was not pleased. Adam and Eve were created in the form, likeness and image of God, having an immortal spiritual soul, the essence of God Almighty. This is the difference! At the time of Recreation and Renewal, God was very pleased with the Work of His hands and He blessed Adam and Eve (Genesis 1:28, 31).

Another story, closely related to our discussion here, is a strange narrative mentioned in Genesis 6:4, "There were giants (Nephilim) in the earth in those days; and also after that, when the sons of God came in unto the daughters of men, and they bare children to them, the same become mighty men which were of old, men of renown". More confirmations of Nephilim can be found in Numbers 13:33-34; Ezekiel 32:27; the Book of Jubilees 7:21-25. There was another 'relative' of Nephilim known from Greek mythology by the name Cyclopes. These were giant, one-eyed in the center of the forehead monstrous humanoid creatures, 'arrogant, lawless men-eater beings', well described by the Greek author Homer in his poem 'Odyssey.'

Who were those Nephilim, sons of God? Were they from the old prehistoric ages, pre-Adamite human-like creatures? Well, they could have been. Normally, the Bible depicts the 'sons of God' as created heavenly being, Angels, who are also called God's messengers, guiders and protectors of human beings and avengers of God's justice. They are purely spiritual beings, incorporeal; they do not possess human abilities to eat, to drink, to have sex or to die. How could they, then, have married the daughters of men and begot from them children (Genesis 6:2, 4)?

On the other hand, there is the view that these 'sons of God' were fallen angels who had disobeyed and rebelled against the Lord. They irrevocably rejected the Creator and freely chose evil. Consequently, they were punished by being banished from Heaven to Earth. It is possible that they were stripped of some Divine attributes (immortality and holiness, for instance) and were 'rewarded' with human physicality enabling them to live and die among people and produce offspring. Their children, Nephilim, were the giants, the evil monsters of iniquity who **"became mighty men which were of old, men of renown"**. As a matter of fact, it was because of their evil and sinful way of life that God had decided to annihilate the human race, "And it repented the LORD that he had made man on the earth, and it grieved him at his heart. I will destroy man whom I have created from the face of the earth" (Genesis 6:6-7).

We are extremely lucky that there was one righteous man among all people, Noah, for whose sake God spared humanity from total annihilation (Genesis 6:8).

There is another explanation of the identity of the 'sons of God' as being human, formerly righteous descendants of Seth who had rebelled against God and intermarried with the daughters of the evil Cain, and the Nephilim who were the offspring of their union.

Also, there is some evidences and opinions that the North Pole use to be in the place of the South Pole and vice versa. The Sun not always has risen from the East and set down on the West, there was a time when the Sun had risen from the West and set down in the East and the magnetic poles were completely reversed.

"What was God occupied with, before He created out World"? Asks a very famous Midrash. The answer goes like this: **"God was busy building and destroying other Worlds"** (Genesis, Rabbah 3:7).

Rav Abahu's opinion of 'worlds being created and destroyed' is that this process continued until God was satisfied with His newly created World.

Rabbi Pinchas said: "This is R. Abahu's reason: "And God saw everything He had, and, behold, it was very good" (Genesis1:31). "This pleases Me, but those did not please Me" (Midtash Rabbah, Genesis III: 7).

There is a Talmudic tradition that the Torah was in existence 2000 years before the beginning of the six days of creation, and God used it as a blueprint in creating our World. Our World will be destroyed too, and will be replaced by a new one, the World-to-Come, Olam Haba. This new World definitely will please God because it is the ultimate Good that He can offer to Mankind. That is why the Almighty designed and blessed the purely spiritual World-to-Come (Genesis 2:3).

The Age of the World is 14,340,500.000 years

Now we would like to end our discussion with the same question we started it, 'How old is the Earth?

There were two outstanding Jewish Rabbis, Kabbalists, who lived approximately1.200 years apart and amazingly had each independently come to the same conclusion about the age of the Earth which they estimated as being 15, 340, 500.000 years.

Rabbi Nehunya ben Ha-Kanah, Tanna of the first century, in his book 'Sefer HaTemunah', ('Book of the Figure', i.e. shape of the Hebrew letters), expressed a, quite unpopular in his time, opinion that the age of the Earth can be calculated as analogous to seven Sabbatical cycles of 7,000 years, as one day in God' sight is a thousand years. The Sabbatical cycle is followed by a Jubilee (every 50th year). 7,000 years is one Sabbatical cycle, so the Universe must have existed for seven Sabbatical cycles (parallel to the Jubilee), giving in total 49,000 years. Human civilizations, according to his view, will thus also rise and fall seven times during this period. This is the so-called Shmita Theory which became known as the Shitat Sefer Ha-Temunah. There are different opinions regarding which Sabbatical cycle we are currently in: some say we are in the sixth cycle (42,000) years, others say we are in the seventh cycle (42,000+5,772=47,772). As of today, 1,228 years are left to complete the seventh Sabbatical cycle, the last one of the Jubilee.

Rabbi Isaac of Acco, a 13th century Kabbalist, in his works *Otzar haHaim*, "Treasury of Life", agreed with the earliest teachings of R.

Nehunya ben Ha-Kanah. In his opinion, the Sabbatical cycles existed before Adam was created; therefore those years should be calculated in 'divine years', not as 'human years'. The Bible and Talmud say that one year in the eyes of the Lord is a thousand years for people on Earth (Psalm 90:4). Since the earthly year consists of 365.25 days, one 'divine year' would be 365,250 'earthly' years long. To calculate one Sabbatical cycle of 7,000 years, we must multiply it by 365,250 years which gives us 2,556,750,000 'earthly' years. Because we have completed the sixth Sabbatical cycle, it means that age of the Earth, before the 'freshly' originated seven days of Creation recorded in the Bible (Genesis 1:3-31), and the appearance of Adam and Eve, would have been 2,556,750,000 x 6 = 15,340,500,000 'earthly' years old. From the creation of Adam and Eve, in the opinion of R. Isaac and the other proponents of 'old' Earth, the calculation of the last, seventh Sabbatical cycle, must be measured in 'human', not 'divine' years. And the main reason for this is the fact that Adam, contrary to the other human races, created before him, was created in the shape and image of his Creator, who gave him an immortal soul, which is an essential part of God Almighty. At the end of Creation God blessed Adam and Eve. Everything He had created was good and pleased Him (Genesis 1:28, 31).

In no way does the Biblical account of Creation, properly understood in the light of the first two chapters of Genesis, contradict evolutionary theory and scientific findings. On the contrary, both views complement each other. There is no contradiction between science ('Big Bang') and the Biblical account (Creation) concerning the age of the Universe and planet Earth.

The Seventh Day of Creation

We are convinced that the Messianic Era is an integral part and continuation of this physical World. But we are not sure for how long it will last: A few hundred years, exactly 1000 or 2000 years, or something in between, we do not know. One thing is for certain; the

Messianic World is limited in time and space and will not last forever! It is a transitional, temporally period of time, a preparation for a better, beautiful and never ending spiritual World-to-Come, which truly will last forever.

The seventh day of the Creation week is not the 1000 years of the Messianic Era! It is not an era of history incorporated in This World. It is something different. It is another World of pure spirituality not compatible with the physical World as we know it. It is a crown of the Creation, the blessed eternal "Sabbath" for sake of which the whole World was created. Maimonides praised and highly esteemed this spiritual World:

"The final goal is the attaining of the World-to-Come, and it is to it that all our effort must be directed."

In the Messianic Time the people will try to get better and develop their spirituality on the highest level possible in the physical world in preparation to merit life in the World-to-Come. There will be no place of physicality in the World-to-Come; it is a purely spiritual existence, the fulfillment of God's Divine attributes and His essence, the ultimate purpose of God Creation, when the people be 'in likeness of God' and be able to see Him 'face to face', and that will last forever.

"The World-To-Come will have neither eating or drinking" (Berashot 17a).

The Rabbis of the Talmud have given some information about the seventh millennium of the Universal Sabbath, the day of rest and completeness of the 'work' performed in the previous 6000 years of This World.

Rabbi Katina said in the Talmud, Sanhedrin 97a:

"Six thousand years the World will exist and one thousand, (the seventh), it shall be desolate (haruv). Just as the seventh year is the Shmita year, so too does the World have one thousand years out of seven that are fallow (mushmat), as it is written, "And the Lord alone shall be exalted in that day" (Isaiah 2:11).

"The seventh eon is entirely Shabbat and rest for live everlasting" (The Midrash in Pirke De-Rabbi Eliezer).

"Happy are those who will be left alive at the end of the sixth millennium to enter the Shabbat, which is the seventh millennium; for that is a day set apart for the Holy One on which to effect the union of new souls with old souls in the World" (Zohar, Vayera 119a).

Our understanding is that after the expiration of the Heavenly determined years for the existence of the Messianic Age as an integral part of This World and the complete achievement of the goals of the Plan of the Almighty for Mankind, This World (Olam Hazeh) together with the Messianic World will cease to exist and become dormant for 1000 years. Judaism firmly believes that Humanity is capable of transforming itself with the help of Israel, a redeemed nation of Priests and a Light to the World. Humanity may be uplifted in holiness and the righteousness of God's Torah and be enabled to merit life in the highly spiritual World-to-Come. **This is what we call the 1000 years of the Seventh Day of Creation.** There will be no life left on planet Earth. It will be a Sabbatical Year of complete rest and peace. As Rabbi Katina said, "the seventh year is the Shmita year, so too does the world have 1000 years out of seven that are hallow (mushmat) and desolate (haruv), as it is written, "And the Lord alone shall be exalted in that day" (Isaiah 2:11).

Ramban says that "the sixth millennium will see the advent of the Messiah and the seventh millennium will be the Shabbat of the World-to-Come, wherein the righteous of all nations will be resurrected and rejoice." He also interpreted the verse, "And God blessed the seventh day and sanctified it" (Genesis 2:3) as a reference to His blessing of the World-to-Come at the beginning of the seventh Millennium (Ramban, Shaar HaGemul, ch.58).

THE AFTERLIFE. LIFE AFTER DEATH

Is there such a thing? Apparently yes, there is. Judaism firmly believes in an afterlife, in bodily resurrection and reincarnation (transmigration of the soul), although it is stated in the Talmud that 'no eye has seen' these things (Sanhedrin 99a). "I believe in the resurrection of the dead", written in the Thirteen Principles of Rambam (Maimonides). The concept of death as an end of human existence does not correlate with the understanding of God's attributes as an All-powerful, Good, a Merciful and Just Creator of the Universe. No wonder that believe in an afterlife has been accepted by most major civilizations and their religions.

"Those who are born are destined to die, and those who died are destine to live" (Ethics of the Fathers, 4:22).

For some strange reason the Torah does not speak of an afterlife and the World-to-Come. Nobody can give a clear explanation for this. There is an opinion that the answer to this lies in the fact that the Torah wants people to be concerned with their lives in this time, here and now, and deal with this World, Olam Hazeh, leaving discussion of the next World, Olam Habah, to the later prophets and Sages of the Talmud. People could not live with the idea that death is the end of men's life: no more dreams, love, hopes, and no future—a complete cessation of human existence. God definitely created man for better than this. And, indeed, we have found many references in the Hebrew Scripture where God has revealed to us that death is not the end but the beginning of something new, unseen and glorious, full of joy and incredible happiness; a Heavenly place of dwelling in the presence of God Almighty, when everybody, who merit to be there, will see God 'face to face'. This place is called the World-To-Come. It will be an invisible, highly spiritual existence, when nothing will be impossible, because people will be 'like God' having His image and His Divine attributes of all-Power and Holiness. This is the time when the ultimate Heavenly Justice, that mankind has lodged for, will finally transpire. The righteous and the sinners will be given their rewards according to their lives, deeds and faithfulness to God Almighty. Without an afterlife in this future World-to-Come there would be no justice done and all evil in this World would go unpunished.

"I, the LORD, will punish the world for its evil and the wicked for their sin. I will crush the arrogance of the proud and humble the pride of the mighty" (Isaiah 13:11).

How will the resurrection of the dead take place? A universal resurrection of bodies involved involve all the people who ever lived on this planet, beginning with Adam and Eve, the first humans created by God who died thousands of years ago. All that have remained from these people, literally, is now dust of the earth. In the Prophet Ezekiel's description of the Valley of Dry Bones, all what remained of the dead was the dry bones. And what about those dead who were cremated into ashes or those who died in the depth of the seas and oceans? In the Hebrew Bible there are two or three instances of resurrection of the dead: 1 Kings 17: 21-24; 2 Kings 4: 32-35; 13: 21. In all these cases the deceased had 'freshly' died in the interval of few hours (the young son of the widow and the baby boy of the reach women) or one or two days (e.g. the one who was buried in the sepulcher of Elisha). The boy of the widow "became ill. He grew worse and worse, and finally stopped breathing" (1 Kings 17:17). The occasion of death of another child was: "He said to his father, "My head, my head!" His father told a servant, "Carry him to his mother. "The boy sat on her laps until noon, and then he died" (2 Kings 4:19-20).

The methods of restoration to life of these two boys were quite similar. The Prophet Elijah took the boy from the mother's hands, brought him to his room, and laid him upon his own bed. Then he prayed to Lord: "O Lord my God, let this child's soul come into him again. And Lord heard the voice of Elijah; and the soul of the child return into him again, and he revived" (1 Kings 17:19-22).

In the second restoration of the dead body of the child brought to life by the Prophet Elisha who "found the dead child laid upon his bed. He went in therefore, and shut the door, and prayed unto the Lord. After he lied upon the child, and put his mouth upon his mouth, and his eyes upon his eyes, and his hands upon his hands. And the flesh of the child waxed warm, and the child sneezed seven times, and the child opened his eyes" (2 Kings 4:32-34).

The Prophet Elijah in his restoration of the dead body relied totally relied on God who heard his prayer and returned the dead boy to life.

In the second case it seems that the prayer of the Prophet Elisha alone was not enough to bring the boy back to live and he had to perform a special reanimation technique to resuscitate the child.

However, their bodies had not been in the grave for a long time (actually, they had not even been buried) and had had no chance to decay. One cannot compare the temporal physical restoration to life of these personalities, who eventually sooner or later would die as all other human mortals, with a universal spiritual resurrection of those 'who sleep in the dust of the earth' and will awaken for everlasting life in the World-To-Come. Flesh and blood cannot inherit the future Divine Kingdom of God. That is why Maimonides calls those who believe in a general physical resurrection as part of the purely spiritual World-To-Come 'utter fools' and their beliefs are 'follies'.

There are too many controversies in Scripture on the subject of a resurrection of the dead. Ecclesiastes draws a pessimistic picture: "All go into one place; all are of the dust, and all turn to dust again. For the living know that they shall die: but the dead know not anything. Vanity of vanities said the Preacher; all is vanity" (Ecclesiastes 3:20; 9:5; 12:8).

"If a man die, shall he live again?" asked Job. A few chapters later in his book Job answered the posited question: "For I know that my Redeemer lives and at the end shall stand upon the dust; and after my skin is destroy, this [I know], that in my flesh I shall see God" (Job 14:14; 19:26).

Many scholars, in order to prove the physical resurrection of the dead, refer to Daniel 12:2," Multitudes who sleep in the dust of the earth will awake: some to everlasting life, others to shame and everlasting contempt". The prophet is speaking of a universal resurrection which is supposes to occur in the 'End Days'. He says that some of those resurrected will awake 'to everlasting life'. This means immortality. Meanwhile, according to the great Rambam (Maimonides), whose views on resurrection and immortality we strongly support, says that a physical resurrection of the dead, if God wills, may happen, especially in the time of the Messianic Era, but any such resurrection will be temporal and the resurrected people will definitely later die again. "They will be restored to life with all human characteristics: drink, eat, copulate, beget and die after a very long life, like the lives of those who will live in the Days of the Messiah", wrote Maimonides.

We think that Daniel 12:2 is more applicable to a spiritual universal resurrection of the dead, whose names 'shall be found written in the Book'. The timing of this universal resurrection is not in the Messianic Era, when a partial temporary resurrection of the saints might take place. The spiritual resurrection for life everlasting cannot be compatible with a physical Messianic World, which will be an essential part of this World. It is rather a future glorious purely spiritual Kingdom of God, where there is no place for physicality. The World-To-Come will be the recipient of all those multitudes who awake from death to immortality and are reunited with their purified souls. Their newly incorruptible resurrected glorious bodies will be spiritual habitats and beautiful garments for perfected souls. It is of those righteous who merit the life in the World-To-Come, says the Prophet: "Those who are wise will shine like the brightness of the heavens, and those who lead many to righteousness, like the stars forever and ever" (Daniel 12:3).

There are more references to a physical resurrection of the dead in Scripture: Isaiah 26:14, 19; Ezekiel 37: 1-14; Hosea 13:14 and others). In our opinion, these verses are not referring to a real physical resurrection of dead bodies. According to the Sages of the Talmud, these descriptions are parables, metaphors, and symbolic allegorical prophetic visions used by the prophets throughout the Scripture (R. Yehudah, Sanhedrin 92b; R. Maimonides in Moreh Nevuchim, Guide for the perplexed, 2:46).

More on this subject may be found in Chapter XIV of this book.

It is the will of God to bring His heavenly everlasting Kingdom on Earth.

"He will swallow up death forever. I will ransom them from the power of the grave; I will redeem them from death. Where, O death, are your plagues? Where, O grave is your destruction?" (Isaiah 25:8; Hosea 13:14). Death will be utterly defeated by God.

All these references to the resurrection of the dead in the End Time have nothing to do with the former physical bodies of blood and flesh. They pertain to a glorious spiritual restoration of completely transformed bodies (like the angels) to immortality in a purely spiritual Kingdom of God in the World-To-Come.

The Skepticism of Few

Some authors have tried to deny the existence of a God-given spiritual immortal soul to man by saying that there is nothing spiritual in the description of how God blew air with oxygen into the man lungs through his nostrils, 'the breath of life', and the man began to live. In the same way, they suggest, life was given to the animal world, so do the animals also have immortal souls? Men and animals, they continue, do possess souls, but these souls are material, not spiritual, and souls are mortal the same way as men are: When man breathes, he is a 'living soul'. When man stops breathing, he becomes dead, and so does his soul. With the cessation of the vital organs and brain, the physical body and its soul are pronounced dead. That the soul dies together with the body, they say, finds its confirmation in Scripture: "The soul who sins shall die" (Ezekiel 18:4). It is not an immortal soul that humans possess but rather a human spirit which is mortal and dies when the body of a man dies. The immortality of the soul is not the doctrine of the Bible but rather the ancient teachings of the Egyptians, Babylonians, and Greeks. It is also supported by the philosophies of Plato, Aristotle, Virgil, and Origen.

If a man is in possession of an immortal soul and if death of the body releases this soul, they argue, then there would be no need for resurrection of the body to immortal life. His immortal soul would continue living for ever since it has all the necessary spiritual capabilities for independent survival i.e. consciousness, hearing, seeing, and invisibility—all spiritual gifts from the Creator. If the soul was in heaven enjoying immortality with God, what need would there be for a resurrection of the dead?

Instead of an immortal soul, explain these theologians, man has a 'spirit essence', 'the spiritual element' in him planted by God. According to their teaching, this 'spiritual essence' joins with the physical brain of man and forms the human mind which enhances the ability of man to think, learn and make free-will decisions. When man dies, this 'spiritual element' in man becomes a 'spiritual recording' and 'mold' enabling the preservation of the 'memory, knowledge, character and outward appearance' of the dead man. Obviously, with the death of a person this 'recording spirit' returns to God and gets 'filed away' until the resurrection of the individual and his return to consciousness.

Their teaching does not reflect the Scriptural passages that God created man in His own image. The animals, by comparison, were not created in the image of God. Their lives are simplified by innate instincts, and they never are able to ask 'Who am I? What am I living for?' Meanwhile, the creation of man was different:

"So God created man in His own image, in the image of God He created man" (Genesis 1:27).

The Divine Attributes of God

To underline the importance of how man was created, it is repeated twice that "God created man in His own image"! This means that man was created in the form and likeness of the Almighty. We do not perceive God as having a human form and shape with a face, arms and legs, although this kind of primitive imagery is still appropriate for older and uneducated believers in many countries.

"Precious is the human being, who was created in the image of God" (Tractate Abot 3:14).

God is not corporeal. He has no beginning and no end, no form and no shape. Neither time nor space limits Him. God is eternal, without beginning and end, above time. He is the most Spiritual of all essences; infinitely Benevolent, Beneficent: the cause of all beings, the upholder of all things; Omnipotent, Omnipresent, Holy, Good,

Loving and Merciful. These are the attributes of God Almighty. These are the meanings of His "shape, form and likeness" to which the Torah referred when describing how God created man!

"And the Lord God formed the man from the dust of the ground and breathed to his nostrils the breath of life, and the man become the living being" (Genesis 2:7).

All humanity, regardless of color and race, Jews and Gentiles, equally has possesses the attributes of a Divine soul because all of them were created in the image of God. All of them inherited the 'breath of God into his nostrils at the moment of Creation' (Genesis 2:7).

"Beloved is man, for he was created in God's image; and the fact that God made it known that man was created in His image is indicative of an even greater love. As the verse states (Genesis 9:6), "In the image of God, man was created" (Mishnah, Pirkei Avot 3:14).

The Bible commentators say that God blows the breath of life from within Himself. The "breath of life" is an essential part of God, His great spiritual likeness, His Soul of Life. Every man has within himself a little bit of God's Divine spirit, a likeliness of the Creator. And because God is Eternity, how is it possible for man, having an immortal Divine Soul within him, to die? God has foretold mankind that the death is not his ultimate destination that he is a carrier of a Divine soul, an essence of the Almighty, and as such, man is entitled to immortality in the everlasting wonderful World-To-Come, the ultimate destination for a spiritually regenerated Mankind. "The dust returns to the ground it came from, and the spirit returns to God who gave it" (Ecclesiastes 12:7).

The Day of Judgment, Gehinnom, and Gan Eden

The emphasis on the spiritual afterlife here is so strong and sure and the Goodness and Care of our Creator towards the man is so visible that we should better embrace His Plan of a future highly spiritual immortality and do everything possible in our power to merit life in the World-To-Come. Not all souls will deserve to enter this glorious World. Those who love the God of Israel and live by His Torah, the righteous of all nations, their immortal and spiritually purified souls have already merited the privilege to see God 'face to face'. For those who do not deserve it, there will be a general resurrection and Day of Judgment. In Jewish eschatology the Resurrection of the Dead and the Last Judgment at the end of the Messianic Era goes together: "God summons the soul from heaven and couples it again on earth with the body to bring man to judgment" (Sanhedrin 91b.). On the Day of the 'Great Judgment' angels and men alike will be judged, and books opened in which the deeds of men are recorded for life or for death; books in which all sins are written down, and the treasures of righteousness for the righteous will be open in this day (Syriac Apoc. Baruch, xxiv. 1). "All the secret thoughts of men will then be brought to light."

Those souls which neglected the Torah, the haters and evildoers, will go to a place of punishment called Gehenna, where they will be purified. They will then be allowed to move on to Gan Eden, which is also called the 'Garden of Righteousness' (Enoch, XXXII. 3), the Heavenly place of the perfected righteous souls "clothed with garments of light and eternal life, and eat of the tree of life in the presence of the Almighty". The time of the judgment of the sinful soul in Gehenna is limited to twelve months. However, the soul might avoid this period by repenting at the Gate of Gehenna, be purified and admitted to Gan Eden without punishment. Besides, there are differences of opinion as to who will merit life in the World-to-Come and who not. The Talmud speaks of particular 'mitzvah' which will guarantee a person a place in the World-to-Come and particular deeds that will prevent a sinner from entering into it. In Mishnah Sanhedrin 10:2-3, for example, it states that the 'generation of the Flood' and the men of 'Sodom', because of the severity of their sins, will not deserve life in Olam Haba. Among those who will not merit resurrection and a place in the future World, are three kings of Israel: Jeroboam, Ahab and Manasseh; the spies of Numbers 13:3; the Sadducees because they did not believe in the resurrection of the dead; and even so-called 'generation of the Dispersion' spoken of in Genesis 11:8. On a few occasions theologians have confused the 'Dispersion' at the tower of the Babel with the later Dispersion of the Northern Kingdom of Israel by the Assyrians: Based on the Talmudic opinion of the Mishnah Sanhedrin 10:3 they have understood that the 'Lost' Ten Tribes will never return and will not merit life in the World-to-Come. It is still questionable, whether or not the generation of the Babylonian Dispersion, which includes all the children of Noah (Shem, Ham and Japheth) after the Flood, will deserve a place in the future World on account of their rebellion against God. Who, then, will inherit this spiritual heavenly Kingdom?

There is another opinion of some scholars who have a different perspective on these matters. They say that all the dead souls, the evil and the righteous, go to the same place called Sheol. This is not in Heaven but somewhere underneath the earth. The souls will be in Sheol until the Universal Resurrection and the Judgment Day at the End of Time.

The 'heavenly' Kingdom mentioned here does not imply that the place of the World-to-Come will be in heaven. It is the will of God to bring Heaven on Earth. That is why the Bible says, "Behold, I will create new heavens and a new earth. The former things will not be remembered, nor will they come to mind" (Isaiah 65:17). The God of the Universe will come down to Earth to meet His transformed and renewed creation, and will remain forever with us in His wonderful spiritual Kingdom.

In another place the Mishnah says that belief in the resurrection is an essential part of Judaism: "**All Israel have a portion in the world to come,** for it is written: 'Thy people are all righteous; they shall inherit the land forever, the branch of my planting, the work of my hands, that I may be glorified.' But the following have no portion therein: one who maintains that the resurrection is not a biblical doctrine, the Torah was not divinely revealed and a heretic" (Mishnah Sanhedrin 10:1, Talmud Sanhedrin 90a.).

Some Rabbis (e.g. Rabbi Eliezer), contrary to Rabbi Akiva, believed that all people will be resurrected, the righteous and the wick, and will be given an opportunity to face judgment at the time of the resurrection; for some will awake to everlasting life, others to 'shame and everlasting contempt' (Daniel 12:2). Rabbi Nehemiah said that the generation of the Dispersion and those of Sodom and Gomorrah will have no opportunity to stand in judgment. Rabbi Akiva's opinion was even more severe: He includes in this category not only the 'Lost' Ten Tribes of Israel (Deuteronomy 28:29), but also the congregation of Korach (Numbers 16: 1-2, 32) in the time of their rebellion against Moses and Aaron; and the generation of the Israelites who died out in the desert (Numbers 32:13) before Joshua conquered Canaan. They are all denied the right of resurrection and from being part of the World-to-Come. For their sin was the worst—a lack of faith in God. On these accounts R. Akiva had many opponents among the Sages, including his own disciples, who disagreed with him and took the side of R. Eliezer: Rabbi Shimon ben Manasya, Rabbi Yehudah the Prince, Rabbi Simeon ben Judah of Acco, and Rabbi Nahmanides. The Talmud itself in Sanhedrin 110b views the opinion of Rabbi Akiva without favor: "Rabbi Akiva abandoned his usual spirit of kindness and generosity" (Rabbah b. Bar Hanna in R. Johanan's name).

Rabbi Eliezer ben Hyrcanus, (c.40-120), was the most prominent teacher of Israel, one of the Tannaim of the first and second Centuries and is the sixth most frequently mentioned Sage in the Mishnah and Talmud and he is called "Rabbi Eliezer the Great." He could not agree with Rabbi Akiva, his former disciple, on almost any of the points of Resurrection, Judgment and World-to-Come regarding groups of people and individuals who will not, according to R. Akiva, merit resurrection, judgment and life in the future Kingdom of God.

"Concerning them, said R. Eliezer in Mishnah, Tractate Sanhedrin 11:5, "The Lord kills and resurrects, brings down to Sheol and brings up again" (1 Samuel 2:6).

According to the opinions of these rabbis, the Ten Tribes will be restored along with the rest of the Jewish People when the Mashiach comes (Sanhedrin 110b), and together they will merit life not only in the Messianic World, but in God's spiritual Kingdom as well.

The third opinion is that only the righteous that had known the Torah and lived by its laws, who died and were buried in the Land of Israel, will be resurrected and inherit the Kingdom of God. For those righteous Israelites who died and were buried in the Diaspora, at the time of resurrection God will make underground passages for them to come back to the Holy Land. Similar to this opinion is the view held by some scholars that the souls of those righteous do not need resurrected bodies because they will have already received a body of glory and light; in a manner of Enoch and Elijah, they will go straight to God. Only the wicked evildoers will go to Sheol, the place of Judgment.

Since we mentioned the Prophet Elijah, there are a few accounts in the Talmud explaining how he was taken to heaven and the way he will return. Some sages, who did not believe in a physical, bodily life in God's Heavenly Kingdom, say that the body of Elijah, while ascending to heaven in a whirlwind of fiery chariot, was consumed by the fire and only his soul returned to the Creator. When the appointed time comes, which is shortly before the imminent revelation of the Messiah, God will recreate for Elijah a new spiritual body and reunite his soul with his glorious immortal body and send him back to earth. He will be the first man ever resurrected from the dead at this particular time.

On the other hand, there are sages, who say that Elijah was taken to heaven alive in his physical body and soul together, in the same manner as a few people before him: Enoch (Genesis 5:24); Serach, the daughter of Asher (Midrash Yalkut Shimoni, Ezekiel 367) and even Moses. Reish Lakish in Moed Katan 26a says that Elijah is still alive and his soul did not leave his body. Accordingly, Elijah the prophet will be sent back to earth before the coming of the 'great and dreadful day of the Lord' to 'turn the hearts of the fathers to the children, and the hearts of the children to their fathers' and make peace between Israel and the nations of the world (Malachi 4:5-6). This view is well accepted among some scholars (see Kuzari 1:115).

There is a controversy among the rabbis about Gan Eden (paradise). Some say that it is a part of the Messianic World where "God will establish peace for the nations and they will sit at ease and eat in Gan Eden" (Exodus Rabbah 15:7). This is definitely not the afterlife future purely spiritual World we are talking about.

On the other hand, there is the description of Rabbi Yohanah ben Zakkai just before he died: "There are two roads before me, one leading to Gan Eden and the other to Gehenna, (Gehinnom which is the synonym for Purgatory), and I do not know by which I shall be taken" (Berakhot 28b). This story surely relates to an afterlife and a realm of souls in the World-to-Come. We may say the same of the rabbinical text in Berachot 17a: "In the World to Come there is no eating, or drinking nor procreation or commerce, nor jealousy, or enmity, or rivalry—but the righteous sit with crowns on their head and enjoy the radiance of the Divine Presence."

In Rabbinical Literature there are plenty of controversies on the subject of the World-to-Come, whether it is a physical or purely spiritual reality. Sometimes the Messianic Age after the advent of the Messiah is described as the Paradise for the resurrected saints and considered as the 'End of Time'; or the place of afterlife for the immortal souls after their bodies die. It is also not specified when those souls go to the World of souls: immediately after death or at some point in the future. There are some stories in Midrash saying that after the body dies, its soul spends three days trying to get back into the body. Another Midrash says that the soul during the seven days of mourning goes back and forth between its 'sepulchral abode' and its former home. It is still not clear who exactly will be resurrected and who will not, when and how it will happen, and what exactly will take place.

Confusion remains about the question whether the soul can exist without the body or does it requires the general resurrection of the dead, as has been written often in Scripture, to reunite new spiritual bodies with their immortal souls?

A very interesting view, that tantalizes our thoughts on the World-to-Come, is found in the Talmudic statement,

"The sages have taught us that we human beings cannot appreciate the joys of the future age. The World to come is the one waiting for man after this world. But there is no basis for the assumption that the World to Come will only begin after the destruction of this world. What it does imply is that when the righteous leave this world, they ascend on high . . ." (Tanhuma, Vayikra 8).

This passage confirms the belief that all the righteous souls who died way back in past ages of human history ever since the first death, were taken into the World of Souls and have since enjoyed life in paradise which is called the 'Garden of Eden'.

There are beliefs that many who committed grievous sins (wicked people like Haman, Antiochus IV, Nero, Stalin or Hitler) will be cut off eternally. Their souls will be utterly destroyed, cease to exist, and will not have a part in the World-To-Come. Others think that in Gehenna any sinful soul may be cleansed and repent and after twelve months be allowed to go to Gan Eden.

"You will have to account and give a reckoning in the Olam Haba before the supreme King of Kings, the Holy Blessed One," says the Mishnah, Avot 4:29.

It is here, in This World, that people have to deserve and prepare themselves for God's blessed Heavenly Kingdom by studying the Torah and doing the Mitzvoth and good deeds. It is only because of sin that there is a division between heaven and earth, spirit and flesh. With the complete eradication of sin, this division will cease to exist. The heavenly and spiritual will completely prevail over earthly and bodily realities. There is an opinion that no matter how smart or great a genius one may be and how hard he might study, it is impossible in This World to fully fulfill the required degree of learning and understanding of the Torah. Only in the World-to-Come will a perfect knowledge of the Divine Torah be attained. Only in a spiritual reality, freed from the physical limitations of the body and all material substance, may the soul perfect its divine knowledge of God and His immortal Torah. Of course, in the future world, the Torah will be changed in a way that there will be no physical mitzvoth in it but only spiritual ones and these are eternal.

The Rabbis of the Talmud say that better one hour in repentance and good deeds in This World than all life in the World-to-Come. And, from another hand, better one hour of tranquility of spirit in the World-to-Come than all life in This World. One hour in the World-to-Come contains more pleasure in it than all the pleasures of This World. The righteous of all nations definitely will be part of this glorious World.

Another facet taught on resurrection and the afterlife is the mystical belief in, and idea of, Gilgul, Reincarnation of the souls. This metaphysical theology is not widely accepted in classical Judaism. It is not mentioned in the Hebrew Bible and not discussed in rabbinical literature of Talmud and Mishnah; nor is it mentioned in Maimonides' thirteen Principals of Faith, but it is a universally accepted belief of Hasidic Judaism. It finds its roots in the mysticism of Kabbalistic books. Many Sages supported the idea of reincarnation (Nahmanides, Isaac Luria, Baal Shem Tov and Vilna Gaon). On the other hand, many well known Rabbis have equally rejected it (Maimonides, Saadia Gaon, David Kimchi, Joseph Albo).

When the blessed seventh Millennium, the Sabbath, arrives, this World (Olam Hazeh) will pass away, being destroyed; then the souls will be taken to a special place in Heaven called "Realm of Souls" or "World of Souls", known as Gan Aden Elyon in Hebrew (Upper Garden of Eden). They shall be there for 1000 years to be purified and charged with the Heavenly Knowledge how to see God 'face to face' and obtain His 'holiness' and 'likeliness'. They shall prepare themselves for the Universal Resurrection of the rest of the dead and for the Final Judgment and life in the World-to-Come (Olam Haba), which is not limited in time and space and will last forever. This is a purely spiritual World, the Purpose of all Creation, a Final Majestic destination for Humanity, the completeness of the Divine Master Plan of God Almighty. Such is the position taken by our Great Sage Maimonides.

The other Great Sage, Nachmanides, disagrees with him, particularly on the matter of Resurrection. The essence of this disagreement is, according to Nachmanides, that the World-To-Come is not purely spiritual reality of righteous souls, but rather a mixture of resurrected eternal physical bodies with their souls, when Divine Perfection will be attained when the material body and the spiritual soul come together and are enable to live in Harmony and Godliness forever in the World-To-Come.

CHAPTER XVII:
ISREAL. PROPHETIC FUTURE

What is Next?

"We cannot start analyzing God's passages about Israel's prophetic future without dealing with the soon coming wars of Gog and Magog prophesied by Ezekiel 38 and 39 and Zechariah 12 and 14 (siege of Jerusalem), because the future fate of Israel totally depends on the outcome of these wars." This was written before we completed Chapter XIV which dealt with the Wars of Gog and Magog.

So, what is next? The House of Judah, the Jewish People, will finally have reunited with their brothers and sisters of Joseph, the Ten Tribes of Israel. They will become again one nation called Israel. All the enemies of Israel, the hordes of Gog and Magog, including the arch-enemy Edom, will have been soundly defeated. Evil will have been eradicated from the face of the earth. The Messiah, son of David, will be the only King for all Israelites. They will never again be divided into separate kingdoms nor be different nations. Never again will they be uprooted from the Holy Land (Ezekiel 37:22; Amos 9:15). The God of Israel will cleanse them from all their idols and vile images, detestable things and rebellion. Israel will truly repent of all their sins, "And they will be My People and I will be their God" (Ezekiel 37:23).

The Land of Israel will have been already restored to its Biblical borders from the Nile to the Euphrates and divided by lot for inheritance amongst the Twelve Tribes (Ezekiel 47:13-14). "The land of Israel will in time to come be divided between thirteen tribes" (Baba Bathra 1224).

The Third Holy Temple will have been built, the priests will have begun their services and the Glory of God of Israel will have come into the House: "Son of man, I will dwell in the midst of the children of Israel forever" (Ezekiel 43:7). The highest Rabbinical Court, the Sanhedrin, will be restored alongside subsidiary Rabbinical Courts in the Holy Land. All of God's Laws, as they were in the past, will be reinstated and observed by all Israelites. All the nations of the world with their kings and rulers will listen and obey the Messiah, son of David.

"All kings shall bow down before him: all nations shall serve him" (Psalm 72:11).

The wars, aggressiveness, jealousy and enmity of the nations will cease to exist. There will be no criminals, no sin. Physical pain and sickness will have become sad memories of the past. Food, clothing, and a variety of free services will be abundant and accessible to everyone. People will live long and have happy lives. An Era of Peace and Justice that was awaited for so long by all nations will arrive. The World will usher in a Golden Age of Humanity, the blessed Messianic World.

A Nation of Priests, a Light to the World

That is what God calls the nation of Israel. That is why He chose them from among other people. Israel is God's treasure, His special possession. They have a task to perform, a Divine mission to accomplish:

"For you are people holy to the Lord your God. For the Lord your God has chosen you out of all people on the face of the earth to be His People, His treasured possession" (Deuteronomy 7:6).

"You only have I chosen of all the families of the earth" (Amos 3:2).

"The Lord did not set His love upon you, nor choose you, because you were more in number than any people; for you were the fewest of all people: but because thou art a holy people unto the Lord thy God and the Lord loved you" (Deuteronomy 7:7-8).

Make no mistake, God speaks here of the real nation of the whole Twelve Tribes of Israel, the sons of Jacob; not of Judah alone, not of Christian 'spiritual Israel', nor the nation of Muslims, nor any other nations who try to replace real Israel by themselves. God states it clear, **'Israel has been chosen out of all people on the face of the earth!'** And there was a reason for God to choose Israel!

The best way to explain Israel having been chosen and their Divine mission is given in Scripture by the Prophet Isaiah:

"I have formed Israel for Myself that they will declare Me before the whole world. I will make you to be a covenant for the people and the light for Gentiles, that you will bring My salvation to the ends of the earth. And the Gentiles shall come to thy light, and the kings to the brightness of thy rising" (Isaiah 42:6; 43:21; 49:6).

The Time Has Not Yet Arrived!

Many Bible scholars and theologians have written on the subject of Israel being chosen, a 'nation of the priests', a 'light to the World'. Numerous books, articles, and valuable research papers have been produced on this subject. We are going to add a few modest thoughts to this matter. First of all, we would like to ask a few questions: Has Israel fulfilled its Divine mission? Has she become 'a Covenant for the people and Light for Gentiles?' Have they brought God's Salvation to the ends of the earth?'

The answer on the posed questions is, NO! Why is this so? Because the time has not arrived yet for Israel to do what the Almighty has designated them to do. At the present time the Israelites of the Ten Tribes in exile cannot truly even be called 'Israelites' in the correct, religious sense because of their lives and faiths. They may rather be categorized as Gentiles consciously not knowing of their Israelite origin. They have mingled with godless foreigners, making themselves as worthless as a half-baked cake (Hosea 7:8).

"Like a woman unfaithful to her husband, so you have been unfaithful to me, O house of Israel," declares the LORD (Jeremiah 3:20); "They have dealt treacherously against the LORD, bearing children that are not His. Now their false religion will devour them along with their wealth (Hosea 5:7); "Like Adam, they have broken the covenant—they were unfaithful to Me there" (Hosea 6:7).

How could they be today a nation of the Priests and bring the glory of the God of Israel to the ends of the earth? Definitely, not as being Christians. But, no matter what, hundreds of millions of the 'Israelites' from the Ten Tribes will acknowledge their Israelite identity! They will turn to the God of their fathers and His Divine Torah. The Almighty will acknowledge and accept them.

"In the place where it was said to them, "You are not My people", it will be said "You are the sons of the living God" (Hosea 1:10).

"Sing for joy, O heavens, for the LORD has done this; shout aloud, O earth beneath. Burst into song, you mountains, you forests and all your trees, for the LORD has redeemed Jacob, he will display His glory in Israel" (Isaiah 44:23).

All of this will happen in the 'latter days', in the End Times, at the dawn of the Messianic Era, and will be possible with the help of the Jewish nation, the keepers of the Law; (Yalkut Shimeoni, Song of Solomon 905 on Jeremiah 3:18; "For Torah will go forth from Zion, and the word of the Lord from Jerusalem" (Isaiah 2:3; Micah 4:2); the Prophet Elijah (Malachi 4:5-6) who 'will turn the hearts of the fathers to their children, and the hearts of the children to their fathers'; and the advent of the Messiah, the King of Israel.

"And in that day shall the deaf hear the words of the book, and the eyes of the blind shall see out of obscurity, and out of darkness" (Isaiah 29:18).

God Himself in many instances in Scripture has reassured us that the 'lost' Ten Tribes will definitely repent and return to Him and to the Promised Land.

"I have surely heard Ephraim's moaning: 'You disciplined me like an unruly calf, and I have been disciplined. Restore me, and I will return, because you are the LORD my God. Is not Ephraim my dear son, the child in whom I delight? For since I spoke against him, I do earnestly remember him still: therefore My heart is troubled for him; I will surely have mercy upon him", says the LORD. "How long will you wander, O unfaithful daughter? Return, O Virgin Israel, return to your cities" (Jeremiah 31:18-22).

Our Sages have warned those skeptics and unbelievers that the future imminent Return and God's Redemption of all the Tribes of Israel are well described in the Hebrew Bible as the Will of God. Whosoever does not accept this plain Biblical Truth is guilty of denying the Sacred Word of the Almighty.

For a more detailed description of how it will happen, we refer you go back to Chapter VI 'Judah and Israel' (the Ten Tribes).

A Few Necessary Conditions that have to be Met

If one carefully reads the Scriptural passages concerning Israel's obligations towards making a Covenant with the Gentile nations and bringing God's Salvation to the whole World, it should be obvious that all the acts or prophetical charges of God on the part of Israel (the Ten Tribes) are to be applicable in the future. When exactly in the future? The prophecies have existed for more than twenty seven hundred years. Is it that still not enough time has passed for them to have been fulfilled? No, there has not! For these prophecies to be fulfilled, a few necessary preconditions have to be met.

1. Up until today, there has been no Biblical Israel in the Holy Land. Despite the fact that in 1948 the State named 'Israel' was established, it does not represent the Ten Tribes of Israel in exile. The populations of this state are Jewish People from the Tribes of Judah, Benjamin and most of Levy who historically were descendants of the citizens of the state called 'Judaea'.

According to Scriptures and the Sages (Nahmanides, "The Book of Redemption" (Sefer Ha Geulah), the Ten Tribes are the real Biblical Israel (as distinct from Judah), which may also be identified by the names of Ephraim, Manasseh or Joseph (Genesis 48:5, 16; Jeremiah31:9; Hosea 11:8). Jews and Israelites are not synonymous terms. Throughout Scripture God has made a careful differentiation between these nations. The prophets also speak of them as two separate entities. For the sake of historical continuity, many authors and scholars erroneously have called Abraham, Isaac, Jacob, and their descendants by the name 'Jews'. This is not correct historically or scripturally. The ancient Hebrews or Israelites could not be called Jews because the origin of this name came much later with the birth of the fourth son of Jacob named Judah. Even Jacob could not be called a Jew because his God given name was Israel. Only the descendants of Judah and those joined to him from the Tribes of Benjamin and most of Levy, citizens of the former state of Judaea, are those who rightfully may be called the Jewish People (Jeremiah 32:12; Esther 2:5).

To simplify our understanding of the terms 'Judah' and 'Israel', let us apply geography. The USA, for instance, represents the Ten Tribes of Israel; the State of Florida represents Judah. All citizens of Florida are Americans, or in the other words, all Jews are Israelites. But all Americans cannot be called citizens of the State of Florida. Similarly, not all Israelites are Jews!

Since the separation of the United Kingdom of Israel circa 930 B.C.E, Judah and Israel have become different nations, living in all corners of the globe; having different cultures, traditions, languages and religions. Their differences and even enmities are well recorded in Scripture (Isaiah 9:21; 11:13; 1 Kings 14:30; Zechariah 11:14) and, undoubtedly, this kind of relationship between different countries of Israel's origin has still existed in our days. The Twelve Tribes will become one nation again after reconciliation and reunification under the leadership of the King of Israel, their Messiah son of David (Ezekiel 37:22).

2. The other necessary conditions for Israel to accomplish their Divine mission are the advent of the Messiah and the beginning of the Messianic Age. As evidence shows, Israel in the past has not accomplished its God-given mission. The same can be said of modern

times. Why? Because, since the separation of the United Kingdom, the nations of Israel have been 'lost' (1 Kings 12:19). The World and History have been relating to the nation of Judah, the Jewish People who are part of Israel, as though they were all of Israel though most of Israel are the 'Lost' Ten Tribes. At this point of time, Judah and Israel are not synonymous nations: Israelites are not Jews; and the Jewish People are not Israelites. Why in the world should the Ten Tribes of Israel be called 'Jews', if they are not direct descendents of Judah, Benjamin and most of Levy? All three Tribes are known as the modern day Jews. On top of this, the Israelites in exile have not only forgotten their ancestral identity, but their way of life, faith and religion has nothing to do with the God of Israel, His Divine Torah, and Judaism?! This is the simple truth of the Bible! **Nowhere in the Bible does God say that Israel is Judah and Judah is Israel. He has always spoken of them as two separate entities.** More details on the subject of Judah and Israel can be found in Chapter VI of this book.

To accomplish their unique mission successfully, the Houses of Judah and Israel must be reunited; the Messiah son of David must be revealed; the Messianic World must be started; Israel, as a nation, must be redeemed by the Almighty.

First these numerous Biblical prophecies of reunion and the Messianic Age must come to pass, and Israel become one nation as it was in the time of Moses when God formed the Israelite nation and gave them His immortal Torah on Mount Sinai. Only then will Israel reach the heights of God's Wisdom and Perfection, overcome the limitations of the physical world, be redeemed and become a nation of Priests, a Light to the World, and a Salvation for the Gentiles.

The reunification of the whole House of Jacob is a very important stage in the fulfillment of Israel's mission. God gave this mission to Israel, to the Twelve Tribes, not only to Judah (Isaiah 42:6; 43:1, 3-4, 21; 44:1; 49:3, 6; Jeremiah 31:1, 9-11).

"At the same time, saith the LORD, will I be the God of all the families of Israel, and they shall be My People" (Jeremiah 31:1).

Why do we think that to become a nation of Priests, Light to the Gentiles, who will bring God's Salvation to the World, Israel will need the time and environment of the Messianic Era? The answer is simple—the Final Reunification and Redemption of the whole House of Israel is directly connected with the advent of the Messiah and the beginning of the long anticipated Messianic Age (Ezekiel 37:22; Isaiah 11:12; Jeremiah 30:22). **Only in the time of the Messianic Era the house of Israel will, finally, know their Lord, God of Israel (Ezekiel 39:22, 28-29);** "And those who go astray in spirit will come to understanding, and those who murmur will accept instruction" (Isaiah 29:24).

A Paradise on Earth

The Messianic Age will eventually bring Peace, Justice and material prosperity to the people of the World. Thanks to innovations and tremendous technological progress, people will not have to work as hard as before to earn the necessities of everyday life. Food, clothing and all kinds of services and pleasures will be in abundance and free. Sin, at last, will be eradicated from the face of the earth. Life in this sinless society will look like a miracle, although the laws of the nature of the surrounding physical world will remain the same. The nations will still be divided by geographical borders. Each country will have their governments, (some say there will be a World Government under the leadership of the Messiah), flags, national hymns, cultures, traditions, languages, religions and, of course, many gods and idols. Only in this kind of environment of peace and prosperity might all Israel be fully preoccupied with the study of Torah and attain knowledge of God and perform the Mitzvoth (commandments) and good deeds.

"**At this stage, when it becomes possible to observe the Torah and its *mitzvoth* in their totality, the era of the Messiah *will* have actually begun**" *(Maimonides, Laws of Kings and Wars 11:4)*.

By doing this, the Israelites will grow spiritually to overcome the imperfections of physicality and uplift themselves to a higher level of holiness, righteousness, and Godliness. They will understand and consciously accept God's mission to go to the Gentiles and 'teach them the way of God' and 'bring the glory of God to the ends of the Earth'. The Israelites will listen to God's Command "Be holy because I, the Lord your God, am holy" (Leviticus 19:2) and through obedience and love for their Creator they will become the holy nation.

The Amazement of the Nations. Jacob's Trouble. Victory and Redemption

The people of the World with great curiosity and astonishment will observe the geopolitical changes under the leadership of the Messiah. Before his arrival, they will have noticed that the countries of Israelite origin in exile, the Ten Tribes of Israel together with the Jewish People will have cardinally changed their way of life, have totally repented and turned to their God. When the Messiah appears among them, he will re-affirm both Judah and Israel with complete faith in the God of Israel and His Heavenly Torah. They will be perfectly ready for the 'two sticks' of Ezekiel 37. The first thing the Messiah will do—will be to reunite all the twelve Tribes of Jacob and bring them home to the Promised Land. The amazement of the Gentiles will increase even more, when they see how the strong united armies of Israel under their Commander-in-Chief, the Messiah, will have destroyed all the surrounding aggressive enemies from Arab and Muslim nations. He will have restored the Holy Land to its Biblical borders from the river Nile to the river Euphrates. This territory will include the eastern part of Egypt, Sinai, Lebanon, Jordan, Syria, the island of Cyprus, Kuwait, parts of Saudi Arabia, part of Iraq and part of Turkey. All this Land will be divided by lot for an inheritance among the Tribes of Israel. The Israelites will enjoy prosperity, peace and happiness in their studies of the holy Torah and worship the God of Israel.

Not everything will be going nice and easy for the Israelites, especially in the period prior to the coming of their Messiah and the beginning of the Messianic Age. The Rabbis of the Talmud prayed that they would be spared the terrible experience of the tribulation of the 'dark days' which were to precede the coming of the Messiah. It was the time of Jacob's trouble, the pain of the pre-Messianic period, an unparallel period in all Human history of distress, hatreds of the nations and bloody persecutions; a Great Day of unspeakable and intensive sufferings for the House of Israel; a time of trouble, such as has never been since there was a nation even to that same time. Thanks to God, He will shorten those days and save Israel out of it! The People of Israel will be delivered, every one that shall be found written in the Book of Life (Jeremiah 30:7; Daniel 12:1).

The culmination of Jacob's problems will be at the beginning of the Messianic Era. There will be an attack by Gog and Magog on the peaceful and defenseless People of Israel who will just recently have been gathered from the lands of their enemies where they had been in exile. Many evil nations of the World will join in this war not only for the purpose of annihilating God's chosen People and taking plunder, loot and spoil, but also to challenge God Almighty Himself.

"Now also many nations are gathered against thee, that say, let her be defiled, and let our eye look upon Zion. But they know not the thoughts of the LORD, neither understand they his counsel: for he shall gather them as the sheaves into the floor" (Micah 4:11-12).

"Why do the nations conspire and the people plot in vain? The kings of the earth take their stand and the rulers gather together against the LORD and against his Anointed One. The One enthroned in heaven laughs; the Lord scoffs at them (Psalms 2:1-2, 4).

The Lord will not just laugh and scoff at them, but will destroy them:

"My wrath will be roused in anger, My fury will boil over, and in My zeal and fiery wrath I will consume them". Instead of the victory and great spoil, the hordes of Gog, ironically, will find their graves in the Land of Israel (Ezekiel 38:18-18; 39:11). It will be the last war in human history.

Everything is Possible when you are Walking with God

At that time, the nations of the World will understand that Israel was punished by the Almighty and sent into exile to the lands of their enemies due to their iniquity, for their unfaithfulness to their God. **The purpose of those unprecedented sufferings will have been to purify the nation and make them repent and return to their Creator again.** The nations of the World will also know that God will have compassion and mercy on all the House of Israel; He will return the captivity of Jacob, Redeem and restore them to the Promised Land (Ezekiel 39:23-25). Our Merciful and Just God will say to the house of Israel, 'You are My People'; and Israel will gladly and joyfully respond, 'You are our God!' (Hosea 2:23). God will also let the nations know that anyone who harms Israel harms 'My most precious possession'. The Prophet Zechariah put it this way, "For whoever touches Israel, touches the apple of His eye" (Zechariah 2:8).

The World will marvel looking at the nation of Israel. What will have happened to this nation in front of their eyes in a short interval of time, the transformation that this nation will have experienced, will be beyond comprehension. Their faith in the God of Israel, reunification of the Tribes, arrival of their Messiah, victories in wars, establishing the Biblical Land of Israel, rebuilding the Holy Temple and ushering in the Messianic World,—all of this would have sounded as fantastical fairy-tales and unheard-of miracles, if the nations had not have seen and witnessed all of it themselves. No matter where the Israelites go, no matter what they do,—their God is with them. He helps and defends them in wars. He leads and protects them in everyday life to prosperity and happiness. He transformed them spiritually and redeemed them. Everything is possible and achievable for Israelites when they walk with their God and are faithful to Him and His Laws. The Israelites will look forward to conquering the last boundary of God's future, to merit life in the wonderful World-to-Come, the ultimate destination for Humanity, the conclusion of the Heavenly Plan of God Almighty for mankind.

The Divine Task and Destiny of Israel

But what about the Divine Task of Israel? Were they not supposed to become a nation of Priests and lead the rest of the World in righteousness and holiness to God's redemption? Were they not charged by the Almighty to enlighten the nations in order to bring all of them to the one and only God of the Universe, the God of Israel? Do not the Israelites have a moral obligation to spiritually transform the rest of the World to attain Torah requirements and earn together the right to, and place in, the future paradise in the World-to-Come?

Yes, yes, and yes! All of this is the task of Israel, her Divine mission. That is why Israel was chosen for by the Almighty! It is their monumental responsibility and obligation to proclaim the Glory of the Lord to the ends of the Earth, "For then will I restore to the people a pure language, that they may all call upon the name of the LORD, to serve him with one consent" (Zephaniah 3:9). As preparation to assuming the spiritual leadership of the World, Israel must be uplifted to the Torah's level of holiness and righteousness and become an example to the nations. The Messiah son of David, together with the brilliant Sages will help the Israelites to accomplish this through studying the Torah, obeying God's Commandments and doing the Mitzvahs of good deeds. Israel will become one people, a united holy nation in their worship of God Almighty and righteous in their obedience of His Holy Laws. It is at this time, when their spiritual growth allows them to control the physical needs of the body, when their spirituality will completely prevail over their physicality, then the old Jewish principal 'Love your neighbor as yourself' (Hillel, Akiva) will be possible to be upheld in life. The soul freed of the chains of the body sees and feels the Divine beauty of other souls like-unto-themselves around them not only among Israelites, but also amidst the souls of other people, who will have reached a similar status of spiritual development.

For their devotion, love and righteous conduct in helping the nations to reach the moral and spiritual standards required for inheritance of the future World, God will be pleased and will bless them.

"And their seed shall be known among the Gentiles, and their offspring among the people; all that see them shall acknowledge them, that they are the seed which the Lord has blessed" (Isaiah 61:9).

"And you shall be to Me a kingdom of priests, and a holy nation" (Exodus 19:6).

"Then all the nations will call you blessed, for yours will be a delightful land," says the LORD Almighty (Malachi 3:12).

Yes, the nations indeed will acknowledge Israel as a chosen People of God, as His special treasure, as a nation of priests and a light to the World. They will see the holiness and righteousness of this nation when the Israelites will literally go out to the World to bring to the inhabitants of the earth, their former enemies and bloody prosecutors, the love and knowledge of Almighty God and His future Kingdom.

"And it shall come to pass in the last days, that the mountain of the LORD'S house shall be established in the top of the mountains, and shall be exalted above the hills; and all nations shall flow unto it" (Isaiah 2:2).

For right faith and true religion the heathen nations will turn to Israelites, who will teach the World that they are all the children of God, His sons and daughters, created in His own image, carriers of His Divine attributes and His immortal soul.

"I said, 'You are "gods"; you are all sons of the Most High" (Psalm 82:6).

They will let all the nations know that there is only one God of the Universe, the Almighty God of Israel and there is none beside Him.

"There is no other God—there never has been, and there never will be. I, even I, am the Lord; and beside Me there is no Savior. From eternity to eternity I am God. I am the Lord, your Holy One, the Creator of Israel, your King" (Isaiah 43:10, 11, 15).

The people of the World will learn that this World is a temporal place for Humanity; that this World eventually will be destroyed by God; that the people are destine to return to their permanent home, granted by God, "Behold, I will create new heavens and a new earth. The former things will not be remembered, nor will they come to mind" (Isaiah 65:17). The God of Heaven will descend on a new earth to be with a spiritually transformed creation forever in the wonderful World-to-Come, where resurrected people will be in the likeness of God and see Him face to face in His highly spiritual Kingdom surrounded by the everlasting Shekhina—The Divine Glory of Almighty God.

In the Messianic Era the Israelites under the leadership of their King, the Messiah son of David, will become 'a Covenant for the Gentiles', and bring God's salvation to the World.

"This is what the LORD Almighty says: "In those days ten men from all languages and nations will take firm hold of one Jew by the hem of his robe and say, "Let us go with you, because we have heard that God is with you." (Zechariah 8:23).

'Ten men' in this verse symbolically means all the nations of the World who will eagerly seek to learn and share the religious privileges of Israelites. They will come from all the ends of the earth. They will fall to their knees in front of the Israelites, disgraced and humiliated all together, and in their supplication proclaim, "Surely God is in thee; and there is none else beside the God of Israel" (Isaiah 45:14-16)!

The Prophet Isaiah 60:14 speaks on the same theme,

"The sons of your oppressors will come bowing before you; all who despise you will bow down at your feet and will call you the City of the LORD, Zion of the Holy One of Israel".

For the nation of Israel it is not the honor and the praise of the people of the World they will have been striving for. In their zeal and love for God they will voluntarily chose the hardship of the missionary pattern to go to the nations and bring them back to God. It will be their sacred duty, the way of the teaching of the Divine Torah, the direct task of the Almighty:

"I will make you to be a Covenant to the people and a Light for the Gentiles, that you will bring My Salvation to the ends of the earth" (Isaiah 49:6).

It is not an exaggeration to say that Israel and their King the Messiah son of David will save the ungodly World.

"They will neither harm nor destroy on all My holy mountain, for the earth will be full of the knowledge of the LORD as the waters cover the sea" (Isaiah 11:9).

Through their acts of righteousness and holiness the Israelites will transform the World from being violently sinful and idolatrous to reaching the highest level of spirituality and belief in the one God of Israel. They will worship and serve the Creator with 'purified lips and hearts', unanimously, with 'one consent' (Zephaniah 3:9).

"And many people shall go and say, Come, and let us go up to the mountain of the LORD, to the house of the God of Jacob; and he will teach us of his ways, and we will walk in his paths: for out of Zion shall go forth the law, and the word of the LORD from Jerusalem" (Isaiah2:3).

Israel will accomplish their Divine mission successfully! God says of Israel:

"I will bless those who bless you and whoever curses you I will curse; **and all peoples on earth will be blessed through you**." (Genesis 12:31). This ancient prophecy will find its complete fulfillment only in the Messianic Time! Because of the Israelites and through them, the Almighty will bless all the people of the Earth.

To succeed in this grandiose transformation of Humanity that enables them to merit life in the World-to-Come, the Israelites in all their actions will have followed the Wisdom of God Almighty and His Anointed One, the Mashiach son of David.

"Let us hear the conclusion of the whole matter: Fear God, and keep his commandments: for this is the whole duty of man. For God will bring every deed into judgment, including every hidden thing, whether it is good or evil" (Ecclesiastes 12:13-14).

All the above Scriptural passages will have been fulfilled only in the time period of the 'latter years', the 'end of days', the 'end time', all of which unwaveringly points to the Messianic Era.

At the end of the Messianic Age, when the Israelites have brought Heavenly knowledge and God's redemption to all the inhabitants of the earth, 'from sea to sea', and most people of the World will have become holy and righteous, ready and meriting to usher in the wonderful, highly spiritual, everlasting World-to-Come, for which sake everything was created, the uttermost Goodness that God Almighty will have been prepared for Humanity, – The Divine Mission of Israel on the planet Earth will have been successfully accomplished.

Alexander Zephyr